Historical
Research in Crit

Volume 18 Issue 2
2010

CONTENTS

BRILL

Historical Materialism 18 (2010) 3–34

historical materialism
research in critical marxist theory
brill.nl/hima

Historicising the International: Modes of Foreign Relations and Political Economy

Kees van der Pijl
University of Sussex
K.Van-Der-Pijl@sussex.ac.uk

Abstract

This paper is based on the Isaac and Tamara Deutscher Memorial-Prize Lecture given at SOAS in London, on 27 November 2009. It claims that Marxism remains built around a critique of political economy ('economics') but lacks a parallel critique of international relations (IR). IR naturalises the organisation of inter-state relations along lines comparable to the naturalisation of the capitalist economy by economics. The paper argues that the disciplinary organisation of Western academia is part of the class-discipline in society at large. It was triggered by the abstraction of economics from the field of the broader social sciences. IR, in turn, was codified in the slipstream of Woodrow Wilson's response to the Russian Revolution that followed on from the US-intervention in World-War I. The discipline was built around a founding myth of global liberalism and national self-determination. It served, among other things, to disqualify the claims of the theory of imperialism on disciplinary grounds, and its initial connections with Western hegemony, capital, and the national-security state remain in place today. Distinguishing modes of foreign relations, and specifying the occupation of space, protection, and exchange for tribal and empire/nomad foreign relations, as well as sovereign equality and global governance, on the other hand make it possible to understand the rise and continuing hegemony of the West in its own right, rather than as a superstructure of the transnationalisation of capital.

Keywords

Modes of foreign relations, academic disciplines, economics, international relations

The project, of which *Nomads, Empires, States*[1] comprises the first volume, aims to develop a critique of the academic discipline of international relations (IR), complementing Marx's critique of political economy. I see the lack of

1. Text based on the Isaac and Tamara Deutscher Memorial-Prize Lecture held at SOAS in London, 27 November 2009. I thank the jury and those attending for their encouragement. In writing this text, I have profited from discussions with Alex Colás, Samuel Knafo, Ben Selwyn and Benno Teschke. Alex Anievas and Gonzalo Pozo-Martin as editors of *Historical Materialism* helped me with detailed critical comments.

DOI: 10.1163/156920610X512426

such a critique as a huge and debilitating gap in the historical-materialist legacy. It fatally compromised the ability of the Russian Revolution to realise a multi-national democracy and move beyond an embattled state-socialism, and it continues to undermine the hegemonic potential of socialist thought.

The critique of political economy was intended to de-naturalise the capitalist economy, present it as an historical form, and demonstrate how its naturalisation as 'economics' had come about. However, just as people in the reproduction of their own lives involuntarily enter into a definite pattern of relations of production,[2] they also enter into *foreign relations* – relations between communities occupying separate spaces and considering each other as outsiders. Modern IR does not acknowledge the prenational and transnational forms of foreign relations that run through inter-state relations, and, instead, naturalises the relations among nation-states (which, in practically all cases, are, of course, not 'national' to begin with) in terms of a security-dilemma. In parallel, and in apparent contradiction to it, there is a discourse referring to an 'international community', which goes back to the very origins of the discipline.

The starting point of any critique of social practices must be that they arise in the exploitation and transformation, or *socialisation*, of the human relationship to nature. The common foundation of every aspect of social relations resides in that metabolism, just as all historical activity, in its infinite complexity, is internally connected because of it. This is not a matter of economic causation, not even 'in the final instance'. Humanity engages in the process of socialisation as distinct communities, the groups in which it emerges from nature. The transition from animal species to historical humanity relies on a myth of descent from another time; a cosmogony that is universal, even if each community has a separate story of how it got here from eternity.[3]

Alienation, then, is inherent in the 'involuntary' way in which humans enter into social relations – both in the productive sphere and in relations of ethno-cultural difference. Through the lens of alienation, different communities are perceived as foreign, a condition lifted out of history and naturalised. Once modern states assume the sole right of handling foreign relations on the basis of their territorial sovereignty, 'international relations', understood as relations among states that are nominally equal, come to be viewed as the normal state of affairs. The academic discipline of IR is built around this presumed

2. Marx and Engels 1956–71a, pp. 8–9.

3. The role of magic and ritual, myth and religion in foreign relations is the topic of the second volume of the *Modes of Foreign Relations* project, *The Foreign Encounter in Myth and Religion* (Van der Pijl 2010).

normality, just as economics takes the operation of a capitalist economy as its sole reference.

I will first give an overview of how IR was established as part of a broader academic division of labour, before outlining the central claims of a historical-materialist critique of the discipline. Why IR has all along rested on a premise of the universality of Western values will concern us in the final section.

The academic division of labour against historical materialism

The academic division of labour itself has proved a crucial mutation in Western intellectual life. By setting the parameters of legitimate speculation about society for the cadre trained in higher education, it is a key transmission-belt by which the dominant order of society is being reproduced.[4] Obeying the strictures of the disciplinary division of labour is a precondition for the hegemony of the liberal order; to be a 'Marxist' *within the confines* of one of the squares of the disciplinary grid means little if the broader context is left unaddressed.

The emergence of the 'disciplines' through which a more comprehensive, class-discipline is maintained (ever more so as the middle-class cadre, whose allegiance to Western pre-eminence and the capitalist economy is primary ideological, grows in number) was itself a response to the rise of the labour-movement, Marxism, and the spectre of socialist revolution. The founding of a separate economics represents the first and crucial rupture with the philosophically-grounded Western intellectual tradition. Yet the classical political economists devoting their attention to this area still 'were polymaths who wrote on economics, politics, civil society, language, morals and philosophy', and their theoretical endeavours were '*pre-disciplinary*'.[5]

By the mid-nineteenth century, the growth of accumulated knowledge made it increasingly impossible for a single person to master it in its totality within the space of a single lifetime. This coincided with the emergence, in response to class-struggles in the centres of capitalist production, of an approach to political economy that was apologetic, justifying capitalist market-discipline and private property against the growing resistance to its dislocations and degradations. John Stuart Mill was an important figure in this movement. Marx called the strand of thought represented by Mill, 'vulgar economy, which deals with appearances only'.[6]

4. Van der Pijl 1998, Chapter 5.
5. Jessop and Sum 2001, p. 90.
6. Quoted in Dobb 1972, p. 44 (footnote).

Even the classical political economy of Smith and Ricardo had, by then, become suspect. It had, after all, been their quest to discover the inner workings of the economy that allowed Marx to develop his critique of capitalism. Declaring this investigative focus out-of-bounds was at the heart of what became the marginalist revolution of the 1870s. It built on Mill's idea that a capitalist is not a functionary of capital, in an exploitative social relation with labour, but a *rational subject* who simply puts his assets (which happen to be capital in the sense of investment-funds) to the best possible use, just as a worker would with labour-power. Changes in the class-structure of late nineteenth-century capitalist society, notably the growth of a class of inactive, 'rentier' savers-investors branching off from the classical owner-manager capitalist, contributed to creating the support-base for this theoretical repositioning.

The solution to the dilemma's of scholarly limitations thus was found in a disciplinary turn which happened to satisfy the concerns of those whose wealth and well-being was dependent upon capital; more specifically, the rentier-element in the bourgeoisie. The marginal-productivity theory of income-distribution replacing the original labour-theory of value (which articulated the bourgeois case for wealth as the product of work, as against feudal inheritance), assuaged the sensibilities of this class. It simultaneously gave the academic practitioners a more detached, 'scientific', and 'expert' social profile.[7] Indeed, from the marginalist perspective, given that everybody is rewarded in direct proportion to what they contribute, 'there was no possibility of exploitation and no economic grounds for conflict'.[8]

The political nature of this reformulation, which remains in operation to the present day as neoclassical micro-economics, was never in doubt. Echoing earlier concerns expressed by Mill, Stanley Jevons warned in the 1870s that 'erroneous and practically mischievous' ideas about political economy were gaining ground and 'becoming popular among the lower orders'. Hence, in his view, the term 'political economy' should be replaced by 'economics'.[9] By removing the adjective 'political', the idea that economic processes could be subject to social preferences and state intervention was thus sidelined. Classical value-theory, claimed Jevons's American colleague Frank Fetter, had come 'under pressure of radical propaganda'.[10] According to Eugen Böhm-Bawerk, author of *Karl Marx and the Close of his System* of 1896, Adam Smith had still

7. Bukharin 1972.
8. Perry 2009, p. 95.
9. Quoted in Meek 1972, pp. 88 (footnote), 90 (footnote).
10. Quoted in Ross 1991, p. 177.

treated political economy in a spirit of neutrality, but his followers had failed to insulate themselves from class-conflict.[11]

When actual class-conflict mounted in the 1880s, many scholars who had previously adopted historical or institutionalist, even Marxist positions, converted to marginalist economics. In this way, they turned into organic intellectuals of ascendant rentier-capital. John Bates Clark, who had earlier signalled an interest in socialism, was prominent in this shift in the United States. 'The desire to legitimate the capitalist market in the face of radical challenge was the major element in Clark's thinking', writes Dorothy Ross.[12] Clark's concern to declare the world of the new economics a natural rather than a historical (let alone, political) phenomenon, is evident from his 1891 claim that '[w]hat a social class gets is, *under natural law*, what it contributes to the general output of industry.'[13]

Thus, economists, united in their assumptions about the subjective valuations of 'economic man', by a large majority moved into the role of apologists for the order that maintained them. Within academia, from which the remaining Marxists were removed in due course, only institutionalists in the tradition that runs from Thorstein Veblen to Karl Polanyi, maintained a measure of distance, by relying on anthropological insights to analyse the economy.[14]

Recasting political economy as economics triggered a general movement towards the disciplinary re-organisation of Western academia. The immediate counterpart of the separation of a distinct, axiomatic economics (the axiom being that every subject is a self-interested, utility-maximising participant in the great game of the market-economy), was sociology. If economics crystallised as an organic perspective of the rentier-class, shaping its response to working-class demands and socialism, sociology evolved to serve the needs of the managerial cadre.

For obvious reasons, the managers had less use for fixed conceptions such as the self-interested individual, so congenial to the rentier world-view. Their concern was for the empirical working class which was, or might yet pass, under the influence of Marxism. To try and control their labour-forces and the proletariat at large, managers both in the factories and in city-councils and governments rejected deductive axiomatics and adopted an empirical attitude to the working class. Thus sociology (positivist or hermeneutic) became what Göran Therborn calls 'an investigative instead of a dogmatic guardian of the

11. Quoted in Dobb 1972, p. 44 (footnote).
12. Ross 1991, p. 118.
13. Quoted in Hunt and Schwartz 1972, p. 16, emphasis added.
14. See Van der Pijl 2009, Chapter 5.

ideological community' on which social cohesion is premised.[15] This was no less directed against socialist ideas. 'The common polemical target of the thinkers of the Classical period was Marxism.... Classical Sociology was the great achievement of the middle class of Western Europe ... when in general, the middle class was increasingly threatened by the rise of Marxist Socialism'.[16]

In the same conjuncture, anthropology mutated from a concern of gentleman-amateurs into an academic training ground for colonial administrators; psychology emerged to deal with the mental mutations occurring as a result of the downscaling of family-size in an urbanising mass-society. Political science branched off to control that mass-society through electoral engineering and party-organisation, whilst IR, as we shall see below, emerged as the specialisation concerned with maintaining Western liberal pre-eminence against revolutionary aspirations, be they social or national.

In all cases, disciplinary segregation was instrumental in neutralising dissent or resistance encountered in each separate domain, and with it, socialism and historical materialism. Training the future-managerial cadre into so many 'disciplinary' languages, each with their own provincial hierarchies of authority, does not merely serve to narrow their understanding of the world in its fundamental unity. It equally eclipses any awareness of their own role and replaces it by the facile arrogance of technocracy.

Yet, as Peter Bratsis points out, '[a] social compulsion must be understood in its totality, as a product of a totality of practices not limited by the typical academic boundaries and departmental subfields'. The organisation into separate academic disciplines accordingly has

> much less to do with the requisites of intellectual production than ... with Taylorizing academic labour and standardising curricula so as to increase the 'efficiency' of higher education and decrease the power of faculty by making them much more interchangeable.[17]

This phenomenon is not confined to the social sciences either. James Lovelock, author of the Gaia-hypothesis in geophysics, argues that the late discovery of global warming was the result of the fact that 'science ... was handicapped in the last two centuries by its division into many different disciplines, each

15. Therborn 1976, pp. 224–5.
16. A. Gouldner, quoted in Seidman 1983, p. ix.
17. Bratsis 2006, p. 113 and footnote.

limited to seeing only a tiny facet of the planet, and there was no coherent vision of the Earth'.[18]

The emergence of the IR-discipline

The connection between international relations as a separate, Anglo-American academic discipline and the rise of the United States to the position of primacy within the English-speaking liberal heartland in the global-political economy, must be traced to Woodrow Wilson's intervention in World-War I. Dedicated IR-courses had been introduced at Columbia and a few other US-universities from 1914. But, at the time, the understanding of the relationships between the world-market and world-politics, between colonialism and war, was entirely dominated by the phenomenon of imperialism. Dramatised by the World-War and the Russian Revolution in its closing stages, imperialism was the dominant frame of reference in which these epoch-making events made sense, to academics and the lay public alike. In the understanding of world-affairs, global political economy came as naturally as biology to the study of plants and animals; IR would change precisely that.

Wilson was a lone scholar among US-politicians, and early on adopted the positivist idea that politics must be based on scientific insight. Certainly, he gave it an American, pragmatist inflection that was even more resistant to any axiomatic, fixed rules or conceptions. 'Will you never learn from this fact,' Wilson asked in a lecture just before his first presidential election victory in 1912, 'that you do not make governments by theories? You accommodate theories to the circumstances. Theories are generalizations from the facts. The facts do not spring out of theories ... but the facts break in and ignore theories.'[19]

This would not have earned him in a place in the annals of philosophy, but it did certainly inspire a flexible response to the Russian Revolution. This in turn stamped the new discipline of IR with the enduring imprint of its initial association with Western intelligence and policy-planning. Let me briefly recapitulate how this connection came about.

Wilson's self-imposed task when he travelled to the Versailles peace-conference was to neutralise the spread of Bolshevism.[20] To this end, mobilising national sentiments against Russia and the other dissolving empires extending across Central Europe appeared the most pressing task – given that all currents

18. Lovelock 2007, p. 6.
19. Quoted in Sklar 1970, p. 52.
20. Mayer 1967.

of the revolutionary movement had developed their own theses on national self-determination. Were the Bolsheviks able to enlist national aspirations for the socialist cause, the route to Germany – via Hungary and Austria – lay open. Revolutionary ferment was rife in all of these countries, and nationality-issues were at the heart of it. Dealing with the threat of revolution involved insight into the possibilities and limits of the territorial re-organisation of Europe (although the more mundane distribution of American food-aid was equally important, and often decisive).

The Congress of Vienna that had settled European affairs after the fall of Napoleon, provided a blue-print for Versailles. From the Vienna-negotiations onwards, Britain had taken the lead, intuitively rather than intellectually, in instrumentalising aspirations for national independence to suit its interests. When Latin America broke away from Spain, this policy had already matured to the point where the British foreign secretary, Canning, made his famous comment that 'Spanish America is free, and if we do not mismanage our affairs sadly, she is English'.[21] At Versailles, however, Britain had to allow the United States to guide the process in the wider interests of the liberal West. In addition, the emerging insight that social cohesion is premised on some sort of ideological community shaped the Wilsonian response to socialism.

The Congress of Vienna had reshuffled territories by simply counting heads, and thus arrived at solutions acceptable to the various European rulers. But, with entire peoples in open revolt, and national self-determination a key demand, counting heads was no longer an option at Versailles. 'A Statistical Committee of the sort that had rendered such useful services at the Congress of Vienna could not instantly have provided the political intelligence required for lasting decisions.'[22] Wilson therefore relied on a qualitatively different sort of committee, nicknamed the 'Inquiry', an intelligence-cum-academic operation which had been assembled from American universities and other institutions to serve as a think-tank backing up the president's political proposals.[23] Its creation had been suggested by Felix Frankfurter, one of the bright young assistants of Secretary of War Newton Baker and a future Supreme-Court Justice. Colonel House, Wilson's chief of staff, appointed his own brother-in-law as head of the eventual 126 academics assembled to provide the president with information on the secret treaties, war-goals, and ethno-political issues a peace-arrangement would have to address. Wilson himself then proposed another young assistant of Secretary Baker's, Walter

21. Quoted in Gallagher and Robinson 1967, p. 241.

22. Mayer 1967, p. 372.

23. Smith 2004, Part II. Benno Teschke pointed me to this important book when I was finishing this paper.

Lippmann, to be added as secretary. Other important members were the director of the American Geographical Society, Isaiah Bowman, and Columbia University historian James T. Shotwell.[24]

When the Bolsheviks, having seized power in Russia, sent out a series of appeals to the rest of the world to rise up in revolution in early December 1917, House summoned Lippmann 'to get the Inquiry busy on preparing a policy proposal for the president'.[25] Working closely with US-intelligence, the Inquiry also relied on information provided by the National Geographic Society, the Carnegie Institution and Endowment for International Peace, as well as the General Rubber Company, Standard Oil of New York and the American Tobacco Company. This sums up the field of forces within which the discipline of IR took shape and still continues to operate.

Through Carnegie, the connection was made with Atlantic capital-circuits linking Britain to the United States. J.P. Morgan had reorganised Andrew Carnegie's iron- and steel-assets into US Steel, the biggest industrial corporation of its day. With half a billion dollars paid to him by Morgan, a fortune by any standard, Carnegie, who had emigrated to the US as a boy, created the philanthropic empire that is still active today. It was officially dedicated to world-peace but, more specifically, to 'the propagation and dissemination of knowledge and understanding among the peoples of the United States and the British Dominions and colonies'.[26] The Carnegie Endowment for International Peace connected the Inquiry with the budding discipline of IR. In addition, via Lippmann, a channel of communication was created between the internationalists in Wilson's entourage and the Rhodes-Milner group, the forward-looking fraction in the British imperial ruling class, and trustees of Cecil Rhodes who, like Carnegie, believed in the civilising mission of the English-speaking peoples.[27]

On the margins of the Versailles-negotiations, Shotwell, Lippmann, and Thomas Lamont, a banker of the J.P. Morgan firm, worked out the project for an Institute of International Affairs with Lionel Curtis, secretary of the Round Table, one of the fronts for the Rhodes-Milner Group, and Alfred Zimmern, one of its members. The Institute failed to materialise in its original, transatlantic format when the mood in the United States turned away from Wilson's universalism; a Council on Foreign Relations in the US and Royal Institute for International Affairs (Chatham House) in Britain were established

24. O'Toole 1991, pp. 301–3; Hofstadter 1955, p. 155.
25. O'Toole 1991, p. 306.
26. Quoted in Nielsen 1985, p. 136.
27. Quigley 1981.

separately in the end.[28] Zimmern in 1919 became the first chair of IR in Britain, created at the University of Wales at Aberystwyth.

Complementing the separation of economics from the broader political economy and polymathic social science, the newly-established IR-discipline worked to sideline the problematic of imperialism. Not by refuting it, as Joseph Schumpeter had still attempted in 1919,[29] but by declaring it out of bounds – as it confounds the disciplinary boundaries of 'Economics' on the one hand and 'International Politics' on the other. Here, the inner connection between Wilson's intervention, the crystallisation of a new academic discipline with a narrow focus, and the discipline of the ruling class of the English-speaking West, is pertinent. This connection imprinted on the new discipline what Klaus-Gerd Giesen calls, a 'moralistic founding myth', a particular ethics that ascribes to all peoples of the world the innate right to the 'pursuit of happiness' as formulated in the American Declaration of Independence.[30] The liberalism that animated the Anglophone heartland, in this myth found its expression as far as IR is concerned. The doctrine of its universal validity, the observance of which is today entrusted to a supposed 'international community', has its origin here.

As I will argue below, the antinomy with a supposed realism, which denies that such a thing as the international community can exist, surfaced soon after. But mainstream-IR retains the birthmark stamped on it by the Wilson-intervention. The selective promotion of the right to national statehood (these days eclipsed by 'human rights', understood primarily as individual rights against the state), and the playing-off of separate 'national' claimants for power against each other under the theorem of the balance of power (both critical elements in the panoply of Western hegemony) became the pillars of the discipline. The intelligence-aspect, the role of the large foundations spun off from the top corporations, and the imbrication with ruling-class circles of the Anglophone heartland, all remain in place.

As to the foundations, in addition to the Carnegie-network, the Rockefeller and Ford Foundations emerged as key sponsors of 'International Studies'. This comprised both IR proper and 'Comparative Politics', the sister-discipline investigating other societies by the standards of the liberal ideal realised in the English-speaking West. As with sociology, discovering the optimum-format of the ideological community for these societies began by investigating the working class. The Ford Foundation in 1952 launched a mammoth research-project, entitled 'Labor Problems in Economic Development', to back up US

28. Shoup and Minter 1977, p. 16.
29. Schumpeter 1951.
30. Giesen 1992, p. 14.

foreign policy in the nation-building domain. The Universities of Chicago and Princeton were selected as the chief centres for the research, and internationally-oriented political scientists such as Walter Galenson, Reinhard Bendix, Bert Hoselitz, and Seymour Martin Lipset made their names through this programme.[31]

The intelligence-connection of IR was reproduced after World-War II as well. When the CIA was created in 1947 out of the wartime Office of Strategic Services, centralising the flow of information from the IR-discipline was one of its major tasks. In 1965, the President of the International Studies Association, John Gange, recalled that the OSS 'was like a big university faculty in many respects – sometimes, staff meetings were just like faculty meetings'.[32] Prominent figures within IR, such as Max Millikan, Klaus Knorr, Robert Bowie, Philip E. Mosely (then director of studies of the Council on Foreign Relations), Hamilton Fish Armstrong (editor of its quarterly, *Foreign Affairs*), along with various historians and Soviet specialists, worked through the 1950s and 60s for the then-head of the CIA, Allen Dulles. Nation-building expert and Asia-specialist Lucian W. Pye of MIT joined this élite-body, known as the 'Princeton Consultants', later in the 1960s. The director of the Carnegie Institution, Caryl P. Haskins, and Harold F. Linder, assistant secretary of state and chair of the Export-Import Bank, completed what was almost a remake of the Inquiry of Wilson's days.[33]

The Vietnam-War was the high-tide of IR's involvement in US-imperialism, and to a considerable extent worked to streamline it as a 'behavioural' science.[34] In 1966, Admiral William Raborn, director of the CIA, prided himself on the intense traffic between academe and the agency, whilst the State Department (which runs its own intelligence-agency, the Bureau of Intelligence and Research) had connections with universities that were even more extensive. Deputy Under Secretary of State William J. Crockett in that year boasted of having on file more than 5,000 current IR research-projects being conducted at US-universities, and of receiving some 200 unpublished scholarly papers each month.[35] In 1967, it became public that the executive director and the treasurer of the American Political Science Association, Evron M. Kirkpatrick and Max Kampelman, were also president and vice-president, respectively, of a CIA-funded organisation called Operations and Policy Research, Inc.[36]

31. Carew 1987, p. 196; Van der Pijl 1996, pp. 309–11.
32. Quoted in Windmiller 1968, p. 120.
33. Cavanagh 1980, p. 2.
34. Chomsky 1969.
35. Quoted in Windmiller 1968, p. 121.
36. Windmiller 1968, p. 122.

Certainly, the link between the national-security state and the American IR- and comparative-politics professions seemed to meet its nemesis in 1976, when the Senate Select Committee on Intelligence chaired by Senator Frank Church reported that academics collaborating with the CIA 'are located in over 100 American colleges, universities and related institutes'.[37] At this point, the US seemed to veer back towards a Wilsonian, forward-looking perspective, of which the Carter-administration and its human-rights policy would be the epitome. The debacle of the Vietnam-adventure also discredited the 'behaviourists' who had served as expert-advisers, and the IR-discipline shifted its focus to themes like 'liberal internationalism' and 'interdependence'.

The Wilsonian turn of the Carter-years was prepared to a considerable extent in the Trilateral Commission, another contemporary remake of the Inquiry. The IR-discipline (like economics) was embedded in it along with the major foundations, big business, and (less prominently) the national-security state. As Stephen Gill points out, left- or (far) right-wing thinkers were not part of the Trilateral Commission network. They are what the Trilateral Commission qualifies as 'value-oriented' intellectuals, whose views are largely irrelevant to the 'Commission's major discourses, which are liberal and functionalist'.[38] The Trilateral Commission-type of intellectual is policy-oriented, well-connected to the key centres of national policy-planning, and associated with élite-universities. The late Samuel Huntington, Zbigniew Brzezinski, Henry Kissinger, Joseph Nye, Henry Owen, Richard Gardner, C. Fred Bergsten, Graham Allison and Karl Kaiser have been among the IR-scholars typically active in the Trilateral Commission.

> These theorists consistently emphasise the necessity of international coordination of policy, under conditions of concentric circles of participation, with the United States at the core, and other Trilateral and developing countries involved in decision-making according to functional criteria.[39]

The link with the national-security state was never suspended. When President Carter commissioned an outside review of the CIA in 1979 to set things right, one of the three consultants was IR-scholar Klaus Knorr, himself also a CIA-consultant.[40] Carter's CIA-Director, Admiral Stansfield Turner, appointed Robert Bowie of Harvard to head a Foreign Assessment Centre, and Turner's successor in the Reagan-administration, William Casey, further stepped up

37. Ege 1984, p. 4.
38. Gill 1990, p. 159.
39. Gill 1990, p. 161; for the list of Trilateral-Commission reports, see Gill 1990, Appendix 4, pp. 238–9.
40. Cavanagh 1980, p. 7.

the collaboration with universities. Two hundred and fifty universities and colleges had Pentagon-contracts in 1980–1, with MIT and Johns Hopkins accounting for half of them.[41]

In November 1984, the *New York Times* reported that Rutgers University IR-scholars Richard Mansbach and Harvey Lee Waterman had been admonished by their school-officials for not observing the rule that students' papers should not be fed into a CIA-funded research-project without their knowledge.[42] Mansbach and his team at the time worked on the European Non-State Actors Project (ENSAP) and, in that capacity, solicited European colleagues to identify finished work or work-in-progress dealing with forces affecting attitudes towards the Atlantic alliance – this being the period of widespread protest against the 1979 NATO missile-decision and the new Cold War launched by the Reagan administration.[43] I met Mansbach at a conference on interdependence and conflict in the Netherlands in 1986, in which he commented with mild disapproval on the conservative turn to IR-neorealism in the Reagan-years.[44] But this, of course, only added to the readiness of his European interlocutors to engage.

Clearly, the limits of a discipline which in the 1980s reaffirmed its focus on interstate-diplomacy and US-unilateralism, are bound to surface as the nation-building exercise draws the United States and Britain deeper into involvement with premodern societies. As they find themselves ill-prepared to deal with the challenges facing them in societies where tribal and clan-, religious and other prenational practices of dealing with foreign presence persist, the power-apparatus mobilising academics for the enterprise, must necessarily step over disciplinary boundaries. In 2004, the CIA launched a $4 million pilot-project to place trainees in UK anthropology-departments under the Pat Roberts Intelligence Scholars' Programme (PRISP), funding students on the condition that they sign up for intelligence-work after their degree and take military-intelligence summer-courses.[45] In Iraq and Afghanistan, the US Army operates Human Terrain Systems (HTS), a programme operational for a number of years and expanded in 2007. Subcontracted to BAE Systems, the HTS programme relies on anthropologists embedded with troops at the brigade- and division-levels to assist in interpreting popular responses to military actions.[46]

41. Hulnick 1987, p. 44.
42. Quoted in Ege 1984, p. 6.
43. Ege 1984, p. 2.
44. Mansbach 1989, pp. 220–39.
45. Baty 2005.
46. Beeman 2008.

The need to transcend disciplinary limits obviously cannot solely be a concern of the CIA and the US Army. This takes me to the modes of foreign-relations project.

Modes of foreign relations – points of departure in Marx

The historical-materialist legacy, as noted already, is incomplete in many respects, including the domain claimed by IR. More particularly, it suffers from an 'economistic' distortion. Economism, or economic reductionism, is a bourgeois way of looking at society. It is a perspective that arose in the context of the formation of the modern bourgeoisie, which owes its existence to the market-economy and entrepreneurialism. Hence, the assumption that all social forms – and all progress – depend on the economy, came naturally to it. The modernising state-classes outside the English-speaking heartland of bourgeois class-formation, in their attempt to emulate the path taken by the North-Atlantic pioneers, in effect took the same view. In Russia, Gramsci wrote, 'Marx's *Capital* was more the book of the bourgeoisie than of the proletariat. It stood as the critical demonstration of how events should follow a predetermined course: how in Russia a bourgeoisie had to develop, and a capitalist era had to open, with the setting up of a Western-type civilization.'[47]

Certainly, one can debate to what extent the use of the term 'superstructure' by Marx did not invite the idea of a space of reflective diffraction arising from an economic basis which alone accounts for substantive change; just as the materialistic, economistic reduction of the concept of production to (manual) 'work' as the determining aspect of the metabolism with nature may have been influenced by the association with the labour-movement. But Marx's transcendence of materialism, and the historicising *critique* of political economy, are what define his method.[48] It is on this basis that analysing patterned social relations, as coming about involuntarily in every aspect of human existence, can be developed. The result is an evolving, multi-dimensional process in which each set of relations becomes a structural constraint through which others develop in turn. It is perhaps best pictured as a double-helix, in which the impulse for change emerges from a particular set of practices and wraps itself around the others as they progress in combination. The ideological aspect of each merges into a comprehensive cultural sphere in the process, in the way the commodity-fetishism that turns a Nike-shoe into

47. Gramsci 1977, p. 34.
48. Pannekoek 1938, p. 25.

an object of desire whilst occluding the conditions of its production is compounded by the foreignness of the actual producers at the East-Asian end of the product-chain.[49]

The Althusserian imagery of levels, with the economy determining which level determines the others, by contrast leads to a proliferation of disciplinary departures, losing the common anchorage in the exploitation of nature that energises each aspect of historical-human existence.[50] But the powers a community acquires in the process of exploiting nature (in the classic nomenclature, the 'productive forces'), enable it not only to reduce the time necessary to reproduce its social existence, thus determining the speed of social change in production. They also allow it to extend itself in space, shaping the modalities of the encounter with others, including exogamy, conquest and integration, and thus modifying, through foreign relations, the space occupied under one particular mode of existence. The concept of 'modes' then allows us to recognise the structural constraint generated in the process in which a new level of exploitation and socialisation of nature is attained. As André Drainville writes, 'thinking from modes will encourage us to reflect on what is being born of present circumstances that may later set limits to political possibilities'.[51]

That the Marxist legacy can be developed beyond the notion of modes of production so as to account for foreign relations (other than as a superstructure of the economic basis) has certainly been recognised. Giovanni Arrighi concludes from the correspondence between Marx and Engels that had the latter found the time, 'he might have been able to demonstrate the rightness of his and Marx's views concerning the connection between the productive forces and social relations, but *only if he redefined the productive forces to include the production of protection*.'[52] There are indeed important openings in Engels. In the *Anti-Dühring*, he argues that 'Power is determined by the economic condition, which provides [a community] with *the means* to equip and maintain its instruments'. Characteristically, however, he traces these means to

49. Merk 2004.

50. Althusser 1977.

51. Drainville 2004, p. 12. At the Deutscher-Lecture, I was asked if my modes of foreign relations would not open up an endless number of other modes too. The answer is yes, because the number of aspects of human existence that systematically congeal into patterns at a given level of exploitation of nature is indeed endless. However, the aspect of, say, gender-relations, does not determine production and foreign relations to the same extent that these determine gender-relations. What I challenge is not determination as such, but a reductionist determination by the economy.

52. Arrighi 2007, p. 265, emphasis added.

'the appropriation of alien products of labour and alien labour power'.[53] On the other hand, in a separate fragment on 'power-theory', Engels writes that men mobilised for war, as human material, *change* along with other productive forces.[54] This was later taken up by Bukharin in his *Economics of the Transition Period* when he writes that states wage war by

> disposing of the live force of peoples on the battlefield just as they utilise it in the factories and mines. . . . In production relations men are arranged according to a specific hierarchical scale, corresponding to class groupings; in the same way this social hierarchy is apparent in the state apparatus itself and particularly, in the army.[55]

For the elements of an analysis of foreign relations, however, we may also turn to the sketches for *Capital* (the *Grundrisse*) and the *Ethnographic Notebooks* in which Marx summarised his readings of Lewis Morgan and others (and which, in turn, formed the basis of Engels's *The Origins of the Family, Private Property and the State*). Andrew Linklater was among the first to recognise that there is a potential in the Marxist legacy for beginning to analyse foreign relations in historical-materialist terms, but that one would then also have to move *beyond* the existing corpus of Marxist writing.[56]

As noted above, the exploitation and socialisation of nature necessarily have their origin in separate communities. There is no way in which we can imagine that historical self-consciousness (which initially is entirely mythical, shrouded in cosmogonic concepts that gave humans the ability to become aware of themselves as collective subjects)[57] can be a species-characteristic. On the contrary, what is left behind in the transition from instinct-governed species to historical humanity is precisely this – it is the distinct kin-community which discovers itself as a unit. In the encounter with other units, it further develops this initial awareness. In Marx's words, 'The only barrier which the community can encounter in relating to the natural conditions of production – the earth – is *another community*, which already claims it as its own inorganic body.'[58] Hence the community must occupy, however fleetingly and precariously, a space which it claims for itself and which the other community/-ies must acknowledge. This act is 'the great communal labour which is required . . . to occupy the objective conditions of being there

53. Marx and Engels 1956–71b, pp. 586, 588, emphasis added.
54. Marx and Engels 1956–71b, p. 155.
55. Bukharin 1976, p. 63; cf. Kaldor 1982, p. 268.
56. Linklater 1990.
57. Van Binsbergen 2005.
58. Marx 1973, p. 491.

alive'.[59] Note that 'being there alive' is the common denominator of both productive organisation, and the occupation of space (with its implication of encountering others).

This is a point of departure that cannot be considered a mere preliminary to the later theories of imperialism. These have often, mistakenly, been understood as adding the chapter on the world-market to the unfinished project of *Capital*, in the sense in which Hilferding's *Finance Capital* was praised by Kautsky as adding the 'fourth volume' to Marx's three. The classical-Marxist theories, however, are all, without exception, examples of the economistic turn after Marx. As John Milios and Dimitris Sotiropoulos explain, these theories, each in their own way, tend to 'reduc[e] imperialism to "rule of monopolies", downgrad[ing] imperialist policy to a simple reflection of the economic base.'[60] Trotsky's theory of combined and uneven development, which has recently been revived to deal with the phenomenon of 'the international', likewise remains anchored in an economic reductionism. The very notion of 'backwardness' is only acceptable and meaningful as an economic category, and once the component of permanent revolution (which, for Trotsky, provided the foundational rationale) is removed, what remains is a de-subjectified sociology of catch-up industrialisation for which we do not need Marxism.[61]

The idea of occupying space in itself is not new. It has been theorised by Henri Lefebvre as the *production* of space. However, by reducing it again to modes of production, this results in a view from which the idea of a community encountering others has entirely disappeared and a succession of curiously empty spaces remains.[62] David Harvey, warning against a notion of space as 'a mere reflection of the processes of accumulation and class reproduction', instead proposes to look at it in terms of 'the production of spatial configurations [which] can then be treated as an "active moment" within the overall temporal dynamic of accumulation and social reproduction'.[63] But reducing the foreign encounter to an aspect of the capitalist mode of production also reduces the potential of understanding the comprehensive process of social change. Its 'active moment' has a logic of its own which contributes to the culture of communities, societies, and the emerging global society in its own right. Changing conceptions of difference and foreignness relate to production only

59. Marx 1973, p. 474.
60. Milios and Sotiropoulos 2009, p. 31.
61. See Löwy 1981; Rosenberg 2006; Şenalp 2008.
62. Lefebvre 1978, pp. 283–90.
63. Harvey 2006, p. 374.

by their common anchorage in the exploitation of nature, and by the accumulated control of the mental and material environment thus achieved.

The particular relations among communities occupying separate spaces and considering each other as outsiders arises in the process of the emergence of historical humanity itself. The intuitive appreciation that such a separate dimension of social existence was operative, inspired a long line of Marxist writing on national self-determination. But the mainly tactical political arguments that Marx and Engels developed on this issue, elaborated in various directions by Otto Bauer, Lenin and Stalin, never remotely reach the theoretical sophistication of the critique of political economy, and in no way can be related to Marx's initial notes cited above.

To fall back on geopolitics, another route enjoying a certain revival today, can never be a way forward for Marxism either. It is a reactionary approach, the antecedents of which go back to mediaeval concepts of the value of the soil as the key political-economic asset, and it was at the heart of Nazi-thinking on foreign relations.[64] To develop Marx's analysis of the role of occupying space, Russian and Soviet ethnography (we should properly refer to it as anthropology, as it was much more comprehensive and ambitious than the mere recording of habits, but, in Soviet times, the term was contentious) offers a more promising route, albeit with its own limitations.[65]

Russian ethnography

The precursor of the Russian ethnographic tradition, S.M. Shirokogorov, was considered an émigré in the USSR because he chose to stay in Manchuria after the Bolshevik Revolution. (Whether he encountered other scholars active on the Inner-Asian Frontier in the same period, such as Pierre Teilhard de Chardin, Aurel Stein or Owen Lattimore, remains to be investigated.) It is to Shirokogorov that later work by Yulian Bromley, Lev Gumilev (son of the murdered poet Gumilev and Anna Akhmatova) and other Soviet ethnographers must be traced.

Community-formation on the fault-line between nature and history, *ethnogenesis*, is, from this perspective, the result of the adaptation to and socialisation of the natural environment. Occupying a space for 'being there alive' does not usually mean demarcating a territory – communities originally were migratory, and occupying space could, for instance, consist of exploiting

64. Teschke 2003, pp. 65–7; Teschke 2001; Van der Pijl 1996, pp. 154–62.

65. The Indian Marxist and long-time editor of the Calcutta-published *The Marxist Review*, Ajit Roy, pointed me to this strand of literature. See also Shanin 1986 and Kuznetsov 2006.

a river-estuary for trade. Such choices, in turn, determine the course of a community's development, shaping its outlook including its mythology and the language in which it is expressed. But the geographical conditions in which a community finds itself is only one of the determinants of its profile as an *ethnos*, which Soviet ethnographers typically define as 'an aggregate of people which recognises itself as such, distinguishing itself from other similar communities'.[66]

Shirokogorov already distinguished between three determining conditions shaping the process of ethnogenesis:

> Conditions beyond the control of man, which may be called *primary milieu*; conditions created by man, which are essentially a product of culture, or *secondary milieu*; and conditions which are formed by other ethnical units in the midst of which the unit is living, called here *tertiary*, or *interethnical, milieu*.[67]

Hence, foreign relations are constituted from the outset by communities encountering each other in the process of their adaptation to their environment, and, in doing so, they enter into complex relationships with their surroundings, including a particular cultural infrastructure arising from those relationships, and with each other – all at once. There is no biology involved here, except that once kin-groups have established stable networks for procuring spouses from others (and, in doing so, established the exogamous clan/endogamous tribal structure), they tend to intermarry within their (larger) communities. As a rule of thumb, this occurs at a rate of around 90 per cent and to that extent, 'the boundaries of endogamy form a sort of genetic barrier for the ethnos concerned'.[68] By then, *ethno-transformation*, another concept in the Soviet-ethnography-tradition, has begun to make ethno-cultural difference more complex and diffuse. Traits inherited from natural adaptation and early ethnogenesis become subject to social synthesis, just as ethnogenetic mythology is transformed into epic mythology and religion. Thus, in the Greek myth of Jason, the fact that the Argonauts accompanying him on his Black-Sea expedition supposedly included Heracles and other heroes not from Thessaly, with Orpheus signing for the music on board, was meant to weave together various local myths into a pan-Hellenic epic.[69]

Once a community has taken shape in the process of ethnogenesis, Shirokogorov writes, it 'transmits its experience of adaptation to the local

66. Bromley et al. 1982, pp. 9–10.
67. Shirokogorov 1970, p. 15.
68. Bromley 1974, p. 65.
69. Van der Pijl 2010, p. 112.

conditions through tradition, and its physical adaptation through the complex mechanism of inheritance; accumulating, in this way, the work of previous generations'.[70] At no point can we assume that a community or society can be understood as having developed in isolation from either the natural context or from others – these are constitutive of every ethno-political entity and are reproduced by its manifold social relations, including foreign relations. 'Ethno-cultural differences, which lie at the basis of interethnic relations ... are the result of asynchronous adaptation of various groups to the natural, anthropogenic, technogenic, and civilisational conditions of mankind's development in time-space'.[71]

Certainly, there are strong economistic accents to be found in the work of both the Soviet writers and, for instance, Ber Borochov, the Marxist Zionist, who was thinking along comparable lines.[72] Gumilev even makes a point of emphasising his economism in order to defend himself against the accusation of geographical determinism when he writes that 'the historical fate of a people [*ethnos*], being the result of their economic activity, is not determined by, but is linked with, the dynamic condition of the landscape they occupy'.[73] After the demise of the USSR, Gumilev even drifted off into the realm of 'Eurasian', Russian-nationalist discourse.[74]

We may, however, retain that the relations into which communities and societies enter involuntarily, and which crystallise into definite modes, begin with ethnogenesis, in which the productive forces are generated by which both relations of production and foreign relations are then made possible. Again, as Marx puts it in the *Grundrisse* (retaining the reference to the mode of production),

> The original unity between a particular form of community (clan) and the corresponding property in nature, or relation to the objective conditions of production as a natural being, as an objective being of the individual mediated by the commune ... has its living reality in a specific mode of production itself, a mode which appears both as a relation between the individuals, and as their specific active relation to inorganic nature, a specific mode of working (which is always family labour, often communal labour). *The community itself appears as the first great force of production.*[75]

70. Shirokogorov 1970, p. 12.
71. Masanov 2002, p. 9.
72. Borochov 1972, p. 137.
73. Gumilev 1987, p. 26.
74. Evrazia 2006.
75. Marx 1973, p. 495, emphasis added.

'Being there alive' is the condition of which the community now becomes conscious; its subjectivity then is put to the set of tasks implied by the precariousness of that condition. This is what ethnogenesis refers to – the mobilisation of a community by itself through socialising its own and surrounding nature, into a source of power placed at its own disposal. Those leading this mobilisation, acting as mediators with the world outside of the community including the spiritual world, take up their positions in this process.[76] Relations of ethno-cultural difference are then mythically accounted for by pseudo-speciation, the denial of other communities' humanity.[77] The designation of foreigners as subhuman, as dogs or apes, bereft of divine protection, or even as demons themselves ('evil'), is a phenomenon that is still with us. But it can be traced to the earliest mythologies dealing with foreign relations. The strange sound and unintelligibility of a foreign language ('Barbarian', 'Tartar', 'Hottentot'), or the destiny of strangers to be enslaved ('Slav', 'Serb', or Indian *dasa*), all have left the traces of early pseudo-speciation in contemporary terms.

The contradiction between community and humanity

The ubiquity of pseudo-speciation in foreign relations should not be read as pointing to a 'state of nature' characterised by perennial animosity and war, as assumed in the realist tradition of international studies that goes back to Hobbes and was revamped in the 1930s. Like relations of production, foreign relations develop within a contradiction. Just as humanity develops by the quest to overcome the limitations imposed by its natural state, and, in so doing, mobilises the productive forces within a set of relations that serve it for a definite period before they become fetters on further development, foreign relations develop within the contradiction between the separate community/society and the unity of the humanity.

Contradiction here should be properly understood as mediated by consciousness. As Samuel Knafo writes, contradictions 'do not exist in the world but only in the way subjects invest the world with meaning'.[78] Pseudo-speciation, in that sense, was an early (and persistent) way out of the perception of human groups which were ethno-culturally different but yet were obviously human – the readiness to mate being the surest sign of this side of mutual perception. Even today, when many habits are becoming universal, their

76. Al-Khafaji 2004, pp. 145–6.
77. Tiger 1970, p. 213.
78. Knafo 2002, p. 153.

'meaning' in most cases remains culturally specific. The common humanity that arises from the natural substratum of the species, but which is contradicted, through the lenses of those occupying separate spaces and considering others as outsiders, remains operative too. The eagerness for exchange, mixed with uncertainty about the other's intentions, can be traced back to the original group lacking sufficient mates and other means of reproduction.

That such a thing as a contradiction (or at least, an antinomy) between common humanity and separate community exists, has been recognised widely. The debates on 'communitarianism' versus 'cosmopolitanism'[79] are testimony to it, and, from Herbert Spencer onward, the idea that society in its historical development moves from war to trade has been a recurrent theme in historical sociology. From the historical-materialist perspective, however, contradiction refers to the specific structure of a given level of socialisation of internal and external nature and a range of modes of social relations. This structure is dynamic, because from its perception as contradictory, follows human action to overcome it; this action, in turn, brings out the limits of the possible inherent in the prevailing social relations.

We can now appreciate that Marx, in the *Grundrisse*, identifies the two contradictory aspects of the occupation of space. One, *protection*: the community's effort 'to protect and perpetuate the occupation';[80] and, second, *exchange*. Although Marx does not introduce the concept in this connection, exchange is equally vital to 'being there alive' – it primarily concerns, for the primitive group, the procurement of spouses for which the group itself is too small, and which will allow it to expand. Exchange appears first 'in the connection of the different communities with one another, not in the relations between the different members of a single community',[81] because, *within* the community, the forms of appropriation that are implied in the notion of exchange, cannot develop towards equal exchange, with its attendant notions and practices of compensation and obligation, beginning with dowry and bride-price. Here we may also think of Lévi-Strauss's theory that what distinguishes historical humanity from the animal world is the regulation of incest.[82]

The contradiction between separate community and common humanity that governs foreign relations, and which defines a community's tasks in the field of protection whilst simultaneously requiring it to regulate the exchanges with others, thus sets the limits within which these relations develop. Given a

79. Manokha 2008, pp. 43–6.
80. Marx 1973, p. 474.
81. Marx 1973, p. 103.
82. Lévi-Strauss 1962.

certain level of development of the socialisation of nature, definite modes crystallise, combining particular forms of occupying space, protection and exchange. These modes arise, as do the modes of production which account for the temporal aspect of community-development and in a certain simultaneity with them, in a historical sequence, but they are not discrete stages. Each progressively more-developed mode (that is, resting on a more advanced level of socialisation of nature) envelopes, 'over-determines', prior ones without entirely obliterating them; just as the spatial reach of a given society also brings different modes of production into a single grid. The idea of a culture as the repository in which the successive instances of occupying space and organising production, are sedimented then allows us to understand their persistence in the collective subconscious and the possibility of incomplete mutation or actual regression.

Let me briefly sum up, at the risk of over-schematising, the modes I have distinguished in *Nomads, Empires, States*. In the tribal mode, space is occupied on account of totemic ancestry, which alone authorises legitimate presence. From body-paint in New Guinea to the festive colours of contemporary football-fans, this is how, in the tribal pattern, mutual foreignness is manifested and recognised. Protection is likewise, in the first instance, ritual, whilst exchange, as noted, primarily concerns exogamy. Rules of intermarriage are at the heart of how communities deal with each other in the tribal mode, hence the highly emotional issue of attitudes to women that characterise it.

With the emergence of land-empires based on agriculture, the sedentary societies created by conquest or otherwise migration of a new ruling group inevitably face tribal groups on their frontiers. Whilst the empire considers its sovereign occupation of space to be boundless, the nomadic communities on its perimeter have a mobile concept of occupying space, which also is typically non-territorial. In Marx's phrase, 'Among nomadic pastoral tribes ... the earth appears like other natural conditions, in its elemental limitlessness, e.g. in the Asiatic steppes and the high plateau'.[83] Sea-nomads too have been an important historical force in this connection. Toynbee observes that there is no difference in terms of motive forces

> between those explosive movements of population which impel Norsemen or Minoans or Crusaders to take to their ships and to break like tidal waves upon the coasts of Europe or the Levant, and those other movements which impel Imoshagh or Arabs or Scyths or Turks or Mongols to swing out of their annual

83. Marx 1973, p. 491.

> orbit on the steppe and to break, with equal violence and equal suddenness, upon the settled lands of Egypt or Iraq or Russia or India or China.[84]

Foreign communities granted legitimate presence in the empire, often as members of a commercial diaspora resident in its urban centres, typically have enjoyed the particular hospitality that is imperial incorporation. The Ottoman *millet*-system would be a late example of it. Both cities hosting incorporated foreign communities, and the external frontier, are zones of exchange (exchange being usually dressed-up as tribute to the empire, but reversible, in that powerful nomadic formations may require the empire paying tribute to them).

The frontier is also a zone of intense interaction because, in the empire/nomad-mode of foreign relations, protection is typically organised by recruiting nomadic auxiliaries in the service of the empire. That these auxiliaries, upon receiving the keys of the empire, have often used them to take over the empire altogether, can be illustrated with regard to all the great land-empires – from China to Rome, Persia to Russia. I give examples in *Nomads, Empires, States* on the basis of the classic writers on this theme such as Lattimore.[85]

Imperial universalism versus sovereign equality

Let me turn now to the supposed antinomy within IR between an idealism built around the 'moralistic founding myth' of an international community observing conformity of all states with its basis-rules, and realism.

The 'West', in terms of modes of foreign relations, emerged as a specific synthesis between imperial aspirations inherited from the Roman past (and Church), and the dynamic impulse instilled by Norman warriors. These were Viking marauders assigned their own frontier-sectors on the perimeter of the empire of Western Christianity. England was at the centre of the intersecting influences, both Viking raids and settlement, and the 1066 Norman conquest. In the encounter between the new Norman king and earlier settlers, equally of Nordic-Germanic origin, a unique compromise was reached in that the monarch had to acknowledge the rights of the Anglo-Saxon inhabitants, 'English birthright'. The king's limited rule was embodied in the institution of the Anglo-Saxon Lord Chancellor, the 'Keeper of the King's Conscience', who acted as his confessor.

84. Toynbee 1935, pp. 7–8.
85. See also Turchin 2009. I owe this reference to Alex Anievas.

When the Tudor king Henry VIII broke with Rome in 1534, he also invested himself with imperial (religious and worldly) supremacy, symbolised in the closed crown.[86] In doing so, he overstepped the boundary laid down in the 1066 compromise, and his Roman-Catholic Lord-Chancellor, Thomas More, ended up on the scaffold. As Eugen Rosenstock-Huessy has argued, Anglophone history henceforth has been the history of the restoration of 'English birthright' against the encroaching monarchy or state.[87] The 'Glorious Revolution' of 1688, for which Locke's *Two Treatises on Government* provide the justification, in that sense was a *restoration* of liberty. In the same way, the American secession from the British Empire resulted from a reassertion of birthright against the overstepping of the bounds of legitimate authority by the king. It was not, by any means, a 'national' event, but a liberal revolt set in the wider, transatlantic Anglophone society.[88]

The basis in birthright of one's membership in a community in the English-speaking West never fully became attached to the single state as in postrevolutionary France. It expressed itself in an allegiance to the wider, transnational space in which this right was recognised.[89] When Wilson recognised (no doubt selectively, with an eye to isolating the Bolshevik Revolution) the right to national self-determination in Central and Eastern Europe, it was part of a projection of an international community in which such rights can be universally upheld against illegitimate authority – in this case, the empires holding the nations captive. The 'nations', in turn, were ideological communities in which, ideally, governing classes sharing the liberalism of the West held power.

The rise of the West, then, from this perspective is not a matter of capitalist expansion. The capitalist mode of production only came of age in the context of a pre-existing, transnational, 'Lockean' heartland. Capital only in this context obtained the free space required for its circulation, a space elsewhere confiscated by sovereign states not (yet) subject to the constitutional compromise the English conquerors had to grant the Anglo-Saxon and Danish locals in 1066 and which was reproduced as modern liberalism in the Glorious Revolution and the American secession. It was this juridical separation of a self-regulating sphere from the prerogatives of the monarchy that allowed (through successive struggles enforcing it) the establishment of an 'offshore', transnational space distinct from the territorial jurisdictions of the separate states. This separation, in turn, made it possible for the English-speaking West,

86. Armitage 2000, p. 34.
87. Rosenstock-Huessy 1993, p. 267 and passim.
88. Kaufmann 1999, p. 443.
89. Stewart 1995, p. 66.

first led by Britain and then, by the mid-twentieth century, by the United States, to become the pivot of global capitalist development.[90]

When the British Isles were engulfed in the civil war that would ultimately end with the crucial Glorious Revolution, the Treaties of Westphalia instead consolidated the exclusive sovereignties emerging from the wars of religion on the continent.[91] These sovereign entities henceforth have sought to uphold their territorial jurisdiction against the universalistic aspirations of the Anglophone West. The states of the Lockean heartland, in turn, have sought to impose their preferred world-order by propagating what we now call the international community, or 'global governance'.

Each of the two principles involved here, Westphalian sovereign equality and the global governance espoused by the liberal West, can be understood as referring to a particular mode of foreign relations. So, in addition to the tribal and empire/nomad-modes, the sovereign-equality and global-governance modes should be recognised as historically-specific combinations of a level of development of the socialisation of nature, and a pattern of foreign relations – a particular way of occupying space and organising protection and exchange. However, it is a reminder of the status of such modes that, in historical practice, they are operative only in combination, and hence present the confusing array of 'an entire series of phenomena of fractioning of classes, dissolution of classes, fusion of classes..., specific categories, etc.'[92]

Thus the imperialism of the turn of the twentieth century, and the hegemony of the financier, overseas-adventurer and military, against the backdrop of chauvinism and racism, can be broken down in terms of different modes. Empire/nomad-relations with the subjected peoples, sovereign equality between rival European formations, but also, the quasi-imperial global governance in the relations between the English-speaking West and the rest of the world. The initial understanding of these modes in terms of the ways of occupying space, as well as organising protection and exchange, then allows us to reconstruct the real complexity of imperialism on these different axes. Complemented by an analysis of the equally-complex combination of modes of production, which rest on a common basis in terms of the development of the productive forces, this gives us a more comprehensive understanding of imperialism than seeing it as the mere superstructure of a particular stage in capitalist development, 'the highest', 'the last', or otherwise.

In the historical confrontations between of the English-speaking West and the strongest states rising from the world of sovereign equality laid down by

90. Palan 2003.

91. Teschke 2003.

92. Poulantzas 1971, p. 72.

the Westphalian Treaties, and which I call *contender-states*, the two IR-perspectives associated with each, also confronted each other – idealism and realism. Wilson's idea of 'Making the World Safe for Democracy' and the work of the Inquiry which laid the foundations for the transatlantic integration of this idealist perspective, left little doubt about the priority of the universalistic point of departure. However, the prospect of a new round of contender-state challenges taking shape in the aftermath of Versailles, led a number of academics in the IR-discipline as it crystallised in that period, to proclaim themselves as critics of the explicit liberal universalism espoused by the American president.

When these realist critics had to seek refuge in the United States from the anti-Semitic and anti-Marxist politics of the Nazis, IR-icons like Hans Morgenthau, Arnold Wolfers and others brought with them a tradition of anti-liberal thought that can be traced to Friedrich Nietzsche, Max Weber, and Carl Schmitt, Hitler's crown-jurist. The idea that *reality is irrational*, which, in various ways, runs through the thinking of these authors, resonated in the theses of the IR-realists. In 1929, in his doctoral dissertation on international justice, Morgenthau already expounded upon the 'irrational tension' among states, which resulted from the gap between the prevailing juridical situation and the real relations of force.[93] Here, we see how realism articulates the singular, individualising way out of the contradiction between community and common humanity, reproducing it by emphasising inter-national foreignness.

Ultimately, the work of the intellectual refugees from Nazi-Europe was incorporated into the Anglo-American academic infrastructure with its particular funding-structures, linked to the national-security state and transnational capital. Realism became an option that could be rolled out when the needs of the West required it – as in the Reagan-years, when, as we saw above, (neo-)realism resurfaced again. Equally, it served to explain the behaviour of contenders resisting the West, and the mechanism of the balance of power by which they could be played off against each other.

However, the idea of an antinomy between idealism and realism at the core of the IR-discipline (never mind the labels by which it has been reproduced to account for contemporary forms of each), is profoundly ideological. Not unlike the mystifications of micro-economics which have been exposed in the capital-controversy by Joan Robinson and others,[94] IR rests on a central ideological fiction. In the case of IR, this can be traced to the contradiction

93. Quoted in Giesen 1992, p. 56.
94. Robinson 1972.

between separate community and common humanity, which, in the epoch in which the discipline was established, was in the process of being transcended by a quasi-imperial global governance projected by Wilson. Through this process (which no doubt was itself subject to a conjuncture of favourable and unfavourable phases), the West lays down the rules for a world-order modelled on its own liberal constitution, refusing to recognise any legitimate sovereign equality that would contest this order. Hence, as Rob Walker writes, '[i]f it is necessary to identify a tradition of international relations theory,'

> [t]hen the most appropriate candidate is not 'realism' but 'idealism'. For what is systematically obscured by the reifying claims about political realism as a tradition is that realism has been constituted historically through the negation and displacement of a prior understanding of political life understood in the context of universalist aspirations. ... The tradition of political realism as we have come to know it is unthinkable without the priority ascribed to universalist claims within political theory.[95]

Marxists have analysed the rise of the West primarily in terms of the transnationalisation of capital. But the hegemony of the transnational ruling class and the Western way of life, which have their basis in the English-speaking heartland, also rests on the projection of its particular political forms as a precondition of membership of the 'international community'. The nation-state, paradoxically, has been key among these preconditions. The critique of the IR-discipline in its naturalising of this complex of foreign relations is the task which I have set myself in the project the Deutscher-Prize jury has judged so generously.

References

Al-Khafaji, Isam 2004, *Tormented Births: Passages to Modernity in Europe and the Middle East*, London: I.B. Tauris.

Althusser, Louis 1977 [1965], *Pour Marx*, Paris: Maspero.

Armitage, David 2000, *The Ideological Origins of the British Empire*, Cambridge: Cambridge University Press.

Arrighi, Giovanni 2007, *Adam Smith in Beijing: Lineages of the Twenty-First Century*, London: Verso.

Baty, Phil 2005, 'CIA Outrages UK Academic by Planting Spies in Classroom', *Times Higher Education*, 3 June, available at: <http://www.timeshighereducation.co.uk/story.asp?storyCode=196432&sectioncode=26>, accessed 22 April 2010.

95. Walker 1993, p. 42.

Beeman, William O. 2008, 'Les Etats-Unis vont-ils gagner la guerre en Irak? L'anthropologie, armée des militaires', *Le Monde Diplomatique*, March, available at: <http://www.monde-diplomatique.fr/2008/03/BEEMAN/15713>, accessed 22 April 2010.

Borochov, Ber 1972 [1937; written between 1905 and 1916], *Nationalism and the Class Struggle: a Marxian Approach to the Jewish Problem*, Westport: Greenwood Press.

Bratsis, Peter 2006, *Everyday Life and the State*, Boulder: Paradigm.

Bromley, Yulian V. 1974 [1971], 'The Term Ethnos and its Definition', in *Soviet Ethnology and Anthropology Today*, edited by Yulian Bromley, The Hague: Mouton.

Bromley, Julian V. and others working at the Institute of Ethnography of the USSR Academy of Sciences 1982 [1977], *Present-Day Ethnic Processes in the USSR*, translated by Campbell Creighton, Josef Shapiro and Sheena Wakefield, Moscow: Progress.

Bukharin, Nikolai 1972 [1927], *Economic Theory of the Leisure Class*, New York: Monthly Review Press.

—— 1976 [1919–20], *Économique de la période de transition: Théorie générale des processus de transformation*, translated by E. Zarzycka-Berard and J.-M. Brohm, Paris: Études et Documentation Internationales.

Carew, Anthony 1987, *Labour under the Marshall Plan: The Politics of Productivity and the Marketing of Management Science*, Manchester: Manchester University Press.

Cavanagh, John 1980, 'Dulles Papers Reveal CIA Consulting Network', *Forerunner*, 29 April, available at: <www.cia-on-campus.org/princeton.edu/consult.html>, accessed 11 February 2010.

Chomsky, Noam 1969 [1967], *American Power and the New Mandarins*, Harmondsworth: Penguin.

Dobb, Maurice 1972 [1940], 'The Trend of Modern Economics', in Hunt and Schwartz (eds.) 1972.

Drainville, André C. 2004, *Contesting Globalization: Space and Place in the World Economy*, London: Routledge.

Ege, Konrad 1984, 'Rutgers University: Intelligence Goes to College', *CounterSpy*, June–August: 42–4, available at: <www.cia-on-campus.org/rutgers.edu/ege.html>, accessed 1 February 2010.

Evrazia 2006, 'The Work of L.N. Gumilev as a Development of the Eurasist Thinking', at: <http://www.evrazia.org/modules.php?name=Newsandfile=articleandsid=86>, accessed 22 June 2006.

Gallagher, J. and R. Robinson 1967 [1953], 'The Imperialism of Free Trade', in *European Political History, 1815–1870: Aspects of Liberalism*, edited by E.C. Black, New York: Harper and Row.

Giesen, Klaus-Gerd 1992, *L'éthique des relations internationales. Les théories anglo-américaines contemporaines*, Bruxelles: Bruylant.

Gill, Stephen 1990, *American Hegemony and the Trilateral Commission*, Cambridge: Cambridge University Press.

Gramsci, Antonio 1977, *Selections from Political Writings 1910–1920*, translated and edited by Q. Hoare, New York: International Publishers.

Gumilev, L.N. 1987 [1970], *Searches for an Imaginary Kingdom: the Legend of the Kingdom of Prester John*, translated by R.E.F. Smith, Cambridge: Cambridge University Press.

Harvey, David 2006 [1982], *The Limits to Capital*, revised edition, London: Verso.

Hofstadter, Richard 1955, *The Age of Reform: From Bryan to F.D.R.*, New York: Vintage.

Hulnick, Arthur S. 1987, 'CIA's Relations with Academia: Symbiosis Not Psychosis', *International Journal of Intelligence and Counterintelligence*, 1, 4: 41–50.

Hunt, E.K. and Jesse G. Schwartz (eds.) 1972, *A Critique of Economic Theory*, Harmondsworth: Penguin.

Jessop, Bob and Ngai-Ling Sum 2001, 'Pre-Disciplinary and Post-Disciplinary Perspectives', *New Political Economy*, 6, 1: 89–101.

Kaldor, Mary 1982, 'Warfare and Capitalism', in *Exterminism and Cold War*, edited by *New Left Review*, London: Verso.

Kaufmann, Eric 1999, 'American Exceptionalism Reconsidered: Anglo-Saxon Ethnogenesis in the "Universal" Nation, 1776–1850', *Journal of American Studies*, 33, 3: 437–57.

Knafo, Samuel 2002, 'The Fetishizing Subject in Marx's *Capital*', *Capital & Class*, 76: 145–75.

Kuznetsov, Anatoly M. 2006, 'The Theory of Ethnos by S.M. Shirokogorov', *Ethnographicheskor Obozrenie* [2006, issue 3; manuscript translated by Ekaterina Korotayeva for the author].

Lefebvre, Henri 1978, *De l'Etat*, Volume 4: *Les contradictions de l'Etat moderne*, Paris: 10/18.

Lévi-Strauss, Claude 1962, *La pensée sauvage*, Paris: Plon.

Linklater, Andrew 1990, *Beyond Realism and Marxism: Critical Theory and International Relations*, Basingstoke: Macmillan.

Lovelock, James 2007, *The Revenge of Gaia*, Harmondsworth: Penguin.

Löwy, Michael 1981, *The Politics of Combined and Uneven Development: The Theory of Permanent Revolution*, London: Verso.

Manokha, Ivan 2008, *The Political Economy of Human Rights Enforcement*, Basingstoke: Palgrave Macmillan.

Mansbach, Richard W. 1989, 'The Realists Ride Again: Counterrevolution in International Relations', in *Interdependence and Conflict in World Politics*, edited by J.N. Rosenau and H. Tromp, Aldershot: Avebury.

Marx, Karl 1973 [1857–8], *Grundrisse: Foundations of the Critique of Political Economy (Rough Draft)*, Foreword and translation by M. Nicolaus, Harmondsworth: Pelican.

Marx, Karl and Friedrich Engels 1956–71a, *Marx-Engels-Werke* Volume 13, Berlin: Dietz Verlag.

—— 1956–71b, *Marx-Engels-Werke* Volume 20, Berlin: Dietz Verlag.

Masanov, Nurbulat 2002, 'Perceptions of Ethnic and All-National Identity in Kazakhstan', in *The Nationalities Question in Post-Soviet Kazakhstan*, Chiba: Institute of Developing Economies, available at: <http://www.ide.go.jp/English/Publish/Download/Mes/51.html>, accessed 21 April 2010 [Chapter 1 of a collaborative volume by Andrei Chebotarev, Erlan Karin, Nurbulat Masanov and Natsuko Oka].

Mayer, Arno J. 1967, *Politics and Diplomacy of Peacemaking: Containment and Counterrevolution at Versailles 1918–1919*, New York: Alfred J. Knopf.

Meek, Ronald 1972 [1956], 'The Marginal Revolution and its Aftermath', in Hunt and Schwartz (eds.) 1972.

Merk, Jeroen 2004, 'Regulating the Global Athletic Footwear Industry: The Collective Worker in the Product Chain', in *Global Regulation: Managing Crises After the Imperial Turn*, edited by K. van der Pijl, L. Assassi and D. Wigan, Basingstoke: Palgrave Macmillan.

Milios, John and Dimitris P. Sotiropoulos 2009, *Rethinking Imperialism: A Study of Capitalist Rule*, Basingstoke: Palgrave Macmillan.

Nielsen, Waldemar A. 1985, *The Golden Donors: A New Anatomy of the Great Foundations*, New York: Dutton.

O'Toole, G.J.A. 1991, *Honorable Treachery: A History of U.S. Intelligence, Espionage, and Covert Action from the American Revolution to the CIA*, New York: Atlantic Monthly Press.

Palan, Ronen 2003, *The Offshore World: Sovereign Markets, Virtual Places, and Nomad Millionaires*, Ithaca: Cornell University Press.

Pannekoek, Anton 1938, *Lenin als filosoof*, Amsterdam: De Vlam.

Perry, James 2009, *Goodwill Hunting: Accounting and the Global Regulation of Economic Ideas*, doctoral dissertation, Amsterdam: Vrije Universiteit.

Poulantzas, Nicos 1971, *Pouvoir politique et classes sociales*, Volume 1, Paris: Maspero.

Quigley, Carroll 1981 [1949], *The Anglo-American Establishment: from Rhodes to Cliveden*, New York: Books in Focus.
Robinson, Joan 1972, 'The Second Crisis of Economic Theory', *The American Economic Review*, 62, 1/2: 1–10.
Rosenberg, Justin 2006, 'Why Is there No International Historical Sociology?', *European Journal of International Relations*, 12, 3: 307–40.
Rosenstock-Huessy, Eugen 1993 [1938], *Out of Revolution: Autobiography of Western Man*, Providence: Berg.
Ross, Dorothy 1991, *The Origins of American Social Science*, Cambridge: Cambridge University Press.
Schumpeter, Joseph A. 1951 [1919], 'The Sociology of Imperialisms', in *Imperialism and Social Classes*, New York: Kelley.
Seidman, Steven 1983, *Liberalism and the Origins of European Social Theory*, Berkeley: University of California Press.
Şenalp, Örsan 2008, 'Nomads, Empires, States: Modes of Foreign Relations and Political Economy', *International Journal of Contemporary Sociology*, 45, 2: 131–5.
Shanin, Teodor 1986, 'Soviet Theories of Ethnicity: The Case of a Missing Term', *New Left Review*, I, 158: 113–22.
Shirokogorov, S.M. 1970 [1931], *Ethnological and Linguistical Aspects of the Ural-Altaic Hypothesis*, Oosterhout: Anthropological Publications [reprint from Volume 6 of the *Tshing Hua Journal*, Beijing; transcribed by Shirokogoroff].
Shoup, L.H. and W. Minter 1977, *Imperial Brain Trust: The Council on Foreign Relations and United States Foreign Policy*, New York: Monthly Review Press.
Sklar, M.J. 1970 [1960], 'Woodrow Wilson and the Political Economy of Modern United States Liberalism', in *For a New America*, edited by J. Weinstein and D.W. Eakins, New York: Vintage.
Smith, Neil 2004, *American Empire: Roosevelt's Geographer and the Prelude to Globalization*, Berkeley: University of California Press.
Stewart, Angus 1995, 'Two Conceptions of Citizenship', *British Journal of Sociology*, 46, 1: 63–78.
Teschke, Benno 2001, 'Geopolitik', in *Historisch-Kritisches Wörterbuch des Marxismus* Volume 5, edited by W.F. Haug, Hamburg: Argument Verlag. [Translated in Historical Materialism, 14, 1, 2006: 327–35.]
—— 2003, *The Myth of 1648: Class, Geopolitics and the Making of Modern International Relations*, London: Verso.
Therborn, Göran 1976, *Science, Class and Society: On the Formation of Sociology and Historical Materialism*, London: NLB.
Tiger, Lionel 1970, *Men in Groups*, New York: Vintage.
Toynbee, A.J. 1935 [1934], *A Study of History*, Volume 3, second edition, Oxford: Oxford University Press/London: Humphrey Milford, for the Royal Institute of International Affairs.
Turchin, Peter 2009, 'A Theory for Formation of Large Empires', *Journal of Global History*, 4: 191–217.
Van Binsbergen, Wim 2005, 'Mythological Archaeology: Situating Sub-Saharan African Cosmogonic Myths within Long-Range Intercontinental Perspective'. Revised version of a paper for the seventh ESCA Harvard-Kyoto Roundtable on 'Ethnogenesis of South and Central Asia', Kyoto, 6–8 June 2005, available at: <www.shikanda.net/ancient_models/kyoto%20as%20published%202006%20EDIT2.pdf>, accessed 11 March 2009.
Van der Pijl, Kees 1996 [1993], *Vordenker der Weltpolitik Einführung in die internationale Politik aus ideengeschichtlicher Perspektive*, revised edition, translated by W. Linsewksi, Opladen: Leske and Budrich.

—— 1998, *Transnational Classes and International Relations*, London: Routledge.
—— 2007, *Modes of Foreign Relations and Political Economy*, Volume 1: *Nomads, Empires, States*, London: Pluto.
—— 2009, *A Survey of Global Political Economy*, Version 2.1, available at: <http://www.sussex.ac.uk/ir/1-4-7-1.html>.
—— 2010, *Modes of Foreign Relations and Political Economy*, Volume 2: *The Foreign Encounter in Myth and Religion*, London: Pluto.
Walker, R.B.J. 1993, *Inside/Outside: International Relations as Political Theory*, Cambridge: Cambridge University Press.
Windmiller, Marshall 1968, 'The New American Mandarins', in *The Dissenting Academy*, edited by Theodore Roszak, New York: Vintage.

BRILL
Historical Materialism 18 (2010) 35–76

historical materialism
research in critical marxist theory
brill.nl/hima

Khaleeji-Capital: Class-Formation and Regional Integration in the Middle-East Gulf*

Adam Hanieh
Zayed University, Dubai
ahanieh@gmail.com

Abstract

The countries of the Gulf Cooperation Council (Bahrain, Kuwait, Oman, Qatar, Saudi Arabia and the United Arab Emirates) are most typically understood from the perspective of their position as the world's key oil- and gas-producing states. This essay explores the largely-overlooked processes of class-formation in the GCC, and argues that very profound tendencies of capital-internationalisation are occurring alongside Gulf regional integration. The circuits of capital are increasingly cast at the pan-Gulf scale, and a capitalist class – described as *khaleeji-capital* – is emerging around the accumulation-opportunities presented within the new regional space. The formation of *khaleeji*-capital represents the development of a class increasingly aligned with the interests of imperialism and has important ramifications for understanding the region's political economy.

Keywords

Middle East, Gulf Cooperation Council, class-formation, regional integration, internationalisation, political economy.

1. Introduction

Ongoing imperialist intervention in the Middle East has made the Gulf-region an important thematic focus within broader political-economy debates. Over the two decades stretching from the end of the Iran-Iraq War (1980–8) to the invasion and occupation of Iraq (from 2003 up until the present day), competing arguments have been advanced to explain the nature of imperialism in the region. Numerous theorists have variously emphasised the region's importance as a source of oil and super-profits in the context of

* The author would like to thank Greg Albo, Sam Gindin, Ananya Mukherjee-Reed, David McNally, Alfredo Saad-Filho, Sabah Al-Nasseri, Anna Zalik, Gilbert Achcar, Rafeef Ziadah, the *Historical Materialism* editorial board and two anonymous reviewers for valuable comments and criticisms of the arguments made in this essay.

DOI: 10.1163/156920610X512435

declining reserves, its role in ensuring US-hegemony vis-à-vis other powers, and the 'system-supporting' function that US-intervention plays within the region.[1]

But, while the literature on imperialism and political economy provides essential insights into an understanding of the Gulf states' location in global hierarchies, it has tended to conceptualise the Gulf solely through the lens of oil, and ignore the important processes of class- and state-formation that are occurring internally within the region. This lacuna is particularly evident in the literature on the countries of the Gulf Cooperation Council – Bahrain, Kuwait, Oman, Qatar, Saudi Arabia and the United Arab Emirates. For these countries, oil is assumed as the 'prize' (either as a scarce commodity, source of profits or element of control vis-à-vis other powers). The Gulf is thereby reduced analytically – and some theorists make this analogy explicit – to a 'giant oil-field', rather than a region with its own history, struggles and social relations.

Indicative of this weakness is the absence of any radical analysis of the political economy of the GCC regional-integration project.[2] The GCC was formed in 1981 yet – almost three decades later – there has been no sustained historical-materialist treatment of regional integration in the Gulf. This is a major gap in our theorisation of imperialism in the region. The GCC-economy has become a major component of the world-market – indeed, its 2007 GDP was around the same as that of Australia.[3] GCC-capital dominates many other economies of the Middle East and is a very significant determinant of accumulation-patterns in neighbouring regions such as Africa, the Indian subcontinent and Asia. The way that capital-accumulation has proceeded in the GCC has acted to reinforce overall US-power in the region, and has simultaneously become an important element in the overall functioning of the global political economy. It is not possible to understand the Middle East today without placing the changing political economy of the GCC-states at the core of our analysis.

The dominant academic approach to the GCC argues that security-concerns were the primary impetus behind its formation.[4] According to these

1. See, for example, Klare 2002; Bellamy-Foster 2003, Harvey 2003; Callinicos 2005; Bromley 2005; Stokes 2007.

2. This is not meant as a criticism of the stimulating work on different aspects of individual GCC-countries (see, for example, Crystal 1995; Chaudry 1997; Said-Zahlan 1998; Vassiliev 1998; Champion 2003; Niblock 2006; Vitalis 2007). Most of this work, however, focuses on the social and institutional histories of individual countries rather than the political economy of the region as a whole.

3. The Institute of International Finance 2007, p. 3.

4. See Nakleh 1986; Walt 1987; Braun 1988; Ramazani 1988; Peterson 1988; Kechichian 1990.

perspectives, the growth of left-wing and Arab-nationalist movements from the 1950s to the 1970s presented the Gulf-régimes with numerous external and internal threats. These threats, compounded by the 1979 Iranian Revolution and the subsequent Iran-Iraq War, pushed the Gulf-states to make common cause to protect their teetering monarchies. Uprisings and armed attacks by underground-organisations in Oman (the Dhofar-rebellion), Saudi Arabia (1979), Bahrain (1981) and Kuwait (1983) confirmed the belief of the six GCC member-countries that 'if they did not hang together, they would hang separately'.[5] Spurred on by these threats, the Gulf-régimes embarked on the unification-process.

In contrast to the 'security-thesis', this essay argues that the real significance of the GCC goes far beyond pragmatic calculations of national security. Two decades of regulatory changes have precipitated a re-scaling of institutional power across the Gulf-region, with economic integration promising a common currency and full monetary union (originally scheduled for 2010 but now delayed in the wake of the current economic crisis). New forms of capital-accumulation are occurring in the Gulf concomitant with this institutional realignment. An examination of each of the GCC-circuits of capital reveals the formation of large capital-groups that dominate the respective economies of the new regional bloc. Although historically based within specific GCC-states, these groups now conceive their field of accumulation as extending across the Gulf as a whole. They constitute what is described below as *khaleeji*-capital, an internationalising, pan-GCC capitalist class, which – in some cases – has begun to interpenetrate across the borders of the Gulf-states.

The growth of *khaleeji*-capital is mapped below through an analysis of internationalisation in the GCC's productive, commodity- and financial-circuits. The tendency of capital to internationalise should not be understood, as Christian Palloix has emphasised, as simply the cross-border expansion of money or firms.[6] Rather, capital is a social relation, and it is this social relation that undergoes self-expansion through internationalisation.[7] As different circuits of capital interlock across national borders, the production and realisation of value is increasingly conceptualised at the international

5. Ramazani 1988, p. 11.

6. Cf. Palloix 1977, p. 5: 'The multinational firm only designates the forms which the self-expansion of social capital assumes. We cannot focus too long on these forms which are always subject to change in response to the requirements of self-expansion. The issue of the multinational firm is thus nothing but the ideological expression of other issues which are more substantial: the internationalisation of capital, the international modes of accumulation of capital, and the class struggle on an international scale'.

7. Palloix 1975, p. 74.

scale.[8] The challenge is to map the new social relations that form around these intermeshed circuits of capital and, moreover, to understand the ways in which they are reflected in institutional realignments.

The internationalisation of capital, and the consequent development of a pan-GCC-capitalism, does not mean that the individual Gulf-state has lessened in importance. Accumulation is always territorialised – specific to a particular place and time – and the institutional arrangements that coalesce within a given territory serve to manage, legitimate and uphold the particular set of social relations necessary for this accumulation to occur. As integration deepens, the state-apparatus is compelled to comply with the conditions set by the new regional scale. Internationalisation means, therefore, that the nation-state becomes more – not less – important to this territorialisation of economic and political power.[9]

This methodological focus on the circuits of capital runs against standard interpretations of the Gulf-countries that emphasise the 'rentier-state' and its control over the distribution of oil-rent. Oil-revenues are clearly essential to understanding capitalism in the Gulf, but the rentier-state approach tends to essentialise the Gulf-state – separating it from the typical class-relations of capitalism, the tendencies of accumulation, and their determination within a hierarchically-striated world-market. We need to be wary of what Marx called 'commodity fetishism' – an attempt to explain patterns of social development through a commodity rather than understanding the significance given to that commodity by the social relations within which it is embedded and thereby given meaning.[10] For this reason, an understanding of the Gulf-region should not be framed by oil as such, but rather through the wider motion and tendencies of capital-accumulation that confer a particular significance to oil as a commodity. One of the main aims of this essay is to strongly affirm the relevance of this historical-materialist framework for understanding Gulf-capitalism.

We begin below with an outline of Gulf class-formation, developed through an analysis of value-flows between and within the interlocking circuits of capital of the Gulf-region. These flows give rise to a process of capitalist class-formation and are marked by a particular configuration of

8. Palloix 1977, p. 20.

9. This point is theoretically developed by a variety of authors. See, for example, Murray 1971; Panitch 1994; Albo 2004.

10. Although vastly different in context, this methodological argument is inspired by a similar critique made by David McNally of the main institutionalist school of Canadian political economy, the 'staples approach' (McNally 1981). The staples-approach interpreted the phases of development of Canadian capitalism through the lens of various 'staple'-products such as furs, timber and other natural resources.

labour that is unique to the Gulf-states. The second section examines how a new territorialisation of institutional power brought about by the regulatory changes of the GCC has underpinned the internationalisation of these circuits within the GCC-space. This process of internationalisation of the Gulf-circuits of capital reflects the development of *khaleeji*-capital. The conclusion draws out how this perspective can help in understanding the implications of the current economic crisis on the Gulf, and the ramifications of this process of class-formation for left political forces in the Middle East.

2. Gulf class-formation

A key feature of capitalism is the continuing expansion of the scale and scope of commodity-production. The number and variety of commodities in both the machinery and consumer-goods sectors tends to undergo frequent qualitative leaps as new goods are developed, productive capacity increases, and phases of technological innovation are generalised throughout industry.[11] This expansion of commodity-production is not only indicated by the increasing quantity of goods, but also develops through the transformation of sectors that were previously supplied by natural materials and have now become manufactured commodities. Since the Second World-War, vast new fields of production have opened up based upon this commodification of natural materials through human-made technologies, including the production of plastics, nylons, artificial fertilisers and other synthetic goods.

As both the scale and scope of production increases globally, there is an accelerating demand for the basic inputs of production – energy and raw materials – described by Marx as 'circulating constant capital'. Oil and gas are the key elements of this circulating constant capital because, in addition to their role as an energy-source, they formed the basic feedstocks for the emerging petrochemical and transport-industries in the postwar-era.[12] This

11. Marx 1990, pp. 784–5.

12. The development of petrochemicals began in the 1930s, when a rapid proliferation of synthetic commodities such as plastics, synthetic fibres, fertilisers and detergents replaced materials such as natural rubber, cotton and soaps. Up until the end of the Second World-War, Germany was the most advanced manufacturing centre of these products, utilising coal-derivatives as the raw material in production. At the end of the War, the centre of gravity of the world-chemical industry shifted towards the US under the domination of large chemical companies such as Dow, Union Carbide and Standard Oil. These companies benefited from the technological advances made by the German chemical industry and, like their German counterparts, were intimately linked to military industry. A key feature of the postwar-industry that distinguished US-companies from their German competitors, however, was the use of petroleum and natural gas, rather than coal, as the feedstock used in the manufacture of synthetic

has had key implications for the Gulf-region – while some of the growing postwar demand for oil and gas was initially supplied by increased production in North America and Europe, it was the expansion of production in the Gulf that became central to underpinning world-consumption. Oil-concessions in the Gulf-region had been granted to various US-, British and French companies from 1923 onwards, but it was not until 1931 that the first oil was discovered in Bahrain. Full-scale production began immediately after the War in Saudi Arabia, Kuwait, Qatar and Bahrain, and, by the early 1960s, in the UAE and Oman. By 1969, the Middle East had surpassed North America and Europe as the world's major oil-provider, a position consolidated throughout the 1970s.

The prominence of the Gulf as the key source of circulating constant capital for an expanding global capitalism meant that US-control of the postwar-international system increasingly came to rest upon domination of this region.[13] This process was reinforced by the move away from coal (which Europe had in abundance) to that of oil as the energy-source underpinning postwar-capitalism.[14] Furthermore, the development of US hegemony was underpinned by a military expansion that literally ran on oil.[15] The Gulf-region, as the central production-zone of hydrocarbons in the world-market, was thus of growing significance to global productive circuits as well as the maintenance of US-power. Of particular importance to this process was Saudi Arabia, which successive postwar US-administrations fought hard to bring under their sphere of influence.[16]

---

commodities. This shift was made possible by technological developments in petroleum-cracking that enabled the utilisation of more reactive hydrocarbons and significantly cheapened the cost of production. Indeed, the nomenclature 'petrochemical industry', which began to be commonly used in the late 1930s and early 1940s, signified the shift in feedstocks facilitated by this new technology (see Spitz 1988; Chapman 1991; and Giannetti and Romei 2007 for detailed histories).

13. Bromley 1991 describes this process thoroughly. For a broader analysis of the evolution of US-power in the postwar-period, see Panitch and Gindin 2004.

14. See Painter 1984 for a discussion of Europe's transition from coal to oil in the postwar-period, and the role played by the Marshall Plan in ensuring US dominance of oil-imports. Painter also notes that oil was considered 'politically more reliable' as many coal-miners belonged to Communist-led unions (p. 361). Many thanks to Sam Gindin for alerting me to this reference.

15. The Second World-War marked a shift to oil as the key energy-source on which military power was based. The US-output of gasoline for military use at the end of the War was about eighteen times greater than at the beginning, and that of aviation-gasoline about eighty times greater. Allied forces consciously targeted German, Italian and Japanese oil-supplies and this was a major factor in the eventual collapse of the latter's military machines (Baldwin 1959, pp. 10–11).

16. See Vassiliev 1998 and Vitalis 2007 for two deeply engaging histories of this process.

As the Middle East's significance to US-power was increasing, however, anticolonial struggles were gaining ground across the globe. The success of the anticolonial movements led to a wave of Third-World nationalisation of natural resources and other productive capabilities, including that of oil. In turn, growing industrialisation of the Third World acted to reinforce the importance of oil to the system. By 1976, over twenty oil-producers – accounting for 74 per cent of international production – had nationalised their production at the global level (excluding the Soviet-bloc countries). In the Gulf-region, the struggles of the 1960s and 1970s were partially reflected through (a very qualified) political independence, the end of direct colonial control and increasing state-control of oil-revenues.[17] By 1980, international oil-companies owned less than a third of the crude oil outside of the United States.[18]

The contemporary processes of accumulation underpinning capitalist class-formation in the Gulf-region date essentially from these shifts in the 1970s.[19] Although the US retained essential control of the Gulf-region, the form that this took shifted from that which had existed under British colonialism. Instead of direct colonial rule, US foreign policy evolved through the Truman, Nixon and Carter doctrines towards a reliance on 'friendly régimes', US-bases and the stationing of military equipment and personnel throughout the Gulf-region.[20] The political independence that Gulf-states gained through this process, in particular the greater control over oil-production, enabled the redirection of state-revenues to an emerging capitalist class rather than solely to those foreign companies protected by colonial rule.[21]

17. In the Middle East, this wave of nationalisation included Iraq, Algeria, and Libya in 1971 and Kuwait in 1975. A key turning point occurred in 1979 with the overthrow of the US-backed Shah of Iran. The Iranian Revolution struck a severe blow to US-control of oil in the region, with US-exports and investments in Iran banned after the Revolution.

18. Kobrin 1985.

19. Merchant-classes had formed during earlier periods of development but were largely stunted with the arrival of colonialism. Kazim 2000 provides a good overview of merchant class-formation and the impact of colonialism in the southern Gulf-countries (historic Oman). See Crystal 1995 for Kuwait and Qatar; Chaudry 1997 and Vasilliev 1998 for Saudi Arabia.

20. See Stork 1975 and 1980 for a discussion of evolving US foreign policy in the Gulf and Marschall 2003 for the impact of the Iranian Revolution on the Gulf-states.

21. This notion of 'political independence' is not meant to imply that the Gulf-states are markedly independent from US foreign policy. Rather, the control that Gulf-states gained over upstream production of oil (see below) was a partial outcome of the anticolonial struggles occurring at a global level and which were reflected in the region. At the same time, the Gulf-states were reincorporated into a new configuration of US-power of which the formation of the GCC was a key element.

Although state-structures continued to closely parallel those established under colonialism – hereditary monarchies based upon a ruling tribal group[22] – this redirection of state-revenues marks the beginning of contemporary class-formation in the Gulf. Most significantly, domestic accumulation began to occur within family-based groups that were allied (and often related by blood or marriage) to the ruling monarch.[23] The family-based companies that were the initial recipients of state-largesse were to develop into massive conglomerates with economic activities stretching across all moments of the circuits of capital: production, the sale of commodities and financial accumulation. As is to be expected, these activities were buttressed by – and inter-penetrated with – accumulation-structures of state- and large foreign capital. These groups [*majmoua'*], strikingly similar in their historical evolution, are now predominant across all six GCC-economies.

In order to understand how this process of class-formation has materialised over the last few decades, it is necessary to situate each of the Gulf-circuits of capital within the broader motion of the global economy. An examination of accumulation-patterns in each of these circuits reveals the flows of value that have underpinned the development of the GCC capitalist class.

2.1. *The Gulf productive-circuit*

The character of the GCC productive circuit has been shaped by its role as the key supplier of circulating constant capital in the global economy. The production of hydrocarbons forms the core of this circuit and the massive flows of value that enter the Gulf-region have facilitated the development of other extended and interlocked circuits linked to this industry.[24] It is around these circuits that the accumulation-processes underpinning the development

22. Aqil Kazim notes that – contrary to popular conception – the idea of a hereditary ruler was not necessarily present in precolonial Gulf tribal relations. Tribes organised themselves through a council, in which they elected a leader [*za'im*] on the basis of his qualities of generosity, responsibility, and ability to balance the different interests of the tribes. The hereditary transfer of leadership was largely an invention of the British, imposed as a means of seeking reliable indigenous allies as the Gulf-region was divided into artificial nation-states (Kazim 2000, p. 152).

23. The distinction between state and private capital is often blurred within the GCC-states. In most cases, ruling families have significant private investments that are closely related to their control over the state. This distinction is important, however, in relation to the motives driving foreign-investment choices. Overseas-investment by state-owned funds (such as sovereign wealth-funds) can often be shaped by geopolitical considerations rather than those of profit.

24. It is beyond the scope of this paper to discuss how these value-flows are formed in the context of the appropriation of ground-rent in the world-market. Interested readers are referred to Mandel 1975; Fine 1979; Bina 1989.

of capitalist social relations have occurred. Capital-flows from the sale of crude oil and natural gas continue to constitute the bulk of the Gulf-states' GDP, exports and government-revenues (see Table 1).

Table 1: Oil in the GCC

	GDP (billion US$)	Population	GDP per capita ($ '000)	Oil-production (million barrels per day)	Oil as a percentage of state revenue	Oil as percentage of exports	Oil and gas as percentage of GDP	Manufacturing as percentage of GDP
Saudi Arabia	376.8	25.3	14.9	9.4	89.4%	89.4%	48%	11%
UAE	188.8	4.5	42.1	2.4 (mostly Abu Dhabi)	69.4%	47.7%	35.7%	12.6%
Kuwait	114.8	3.4	33.7	2.50	94.4%	95%	52.9%	7.2%
Bahrain	16.7	0.8	21.9	0.2	76%	78%	25.2%	13.0%
Qatar	63.6	0.9	67.7	0.8	67.1%	89%	61.9%	7.2%
Oman	39.0	2.7	14.4	0.74	64%	67%	48.4%	10.4%

Source: *The Institute for International Finance* 2007, p. 3; various central-bank reports 2006. GDP, population and GDP per capita figures are for 2007, other figures are for 2006 except Qatar, the figures for which are for 2004.

Private-sector Gulf-capitalists have generally not been directly involved in the upstream-sector of the oil-industry (the exploration and extraction of crude oil). Prior to the 1970s, upstream-production was essentially controlled by foreign multinationals that paid royalties and other rents to the ruling monarch. As the Gulf-states gained more control over these revenues, state-owned oil-companies took over this sector and have (in most cases) dominated it since that time. State-control became most complete in Saudi Arabia and Kuwait, where a direct role for foreign companies in extraction and exploration was virtually eliminated. In the other Gulf-countries, foreign oil-multinationals continued to play a role (albeit weakened) in the production of crude oil.[25]

25. In Saudi Arabia, upstream-production is controlled by the state-owned Saudi Aramco, which has been the largest oil-company in the world for eighteen years. In Kuwait, the state-run Kuwait Oil Company (KOC) is responsible for the upstream-sector and the constitution mandates that foreign companies may not control the country's oil-resources. In the UAE, each of the Emirates has its own state-owned company but there is considerable foreign investment through the subsidiaries of these companies. For example, in Abu Dhabi, the Abu Dhabi Company for Onshore Oil Operations (ADCO) is 40 per cent owned by foreign multinationals and 60 per cent by the state-owned Abu Dhabi National Oil Company (ADNOC). ADCO

Excluded from upstream-production, accumulation-opportunities for private capital occurred around other industries that were derivative to the extraction of crude oil. Initially, the most important of these were contracts granted to local companies by governments and foreign multinationals in the fields of construction, maintenance, transport and related support-activities in the oil-sector. Virtually all of the large domestic Gulf capital-groups are characterised by their initial involvement in these types of activities, ranging from building accommodation for desert oil-exploration, supplying food and transportation, the manufacture of pipes and other basic infrastructure-requirements, and provision of security. In this manner, revenues from the upstream hydrocarbon-sector were redirected into the private accumulation of domestic Gulf-capital – laying the ground for its future expansion.[26]

The weight of crude oil and gas in the productive circuit has shaped the character of other productive activities interlocked with this basic hydrocarbon-production. Most specifically, access to large and relatively cheap energy-sources in the Gulf-states has promoted the development of those industries – such as aluminium, steel and cement – that are highly dependent on the cost of electricity.[27] In the case of aluminium, for example, energy represents around 30 per cent of production-costs – leading one analyst

generates more than half of Abu Dhabi's oil-production and is the largest crude-oil producer in the southern Gulf (United Arab Emirates Yearbook 2006, p. 127). In Qatar, foreign companies accounted for one-third of Qatar's oil-production capacity in 2007 (Oil and Gas Directory 2007, p. 305). In Oman, more than 90 per cent of oil-exploration and production in Oman takes place through Petroleum Development Oman (PDO), which is a joint-venture between the government (60 per cent), Royal Dutch Shell (34 per cent), Total (4 per cent) and Partex (2 per cent). In Bahrain, onshore oil-production is controlled by the state-owned Bahrain Petroleum Company (Bapco) while exploration-concessions have been awarded to foreign investors in offshore-areas.

26. One illustration of this is the massive Saudi conglomerate, the Dallah Al Baraka Group. Al Baraka won many of the early contracts in Saudi Arabia for the construction of aircraft-hangars and spare parts used within the oil-industry. It manufactured steel-wire, pipes and other cables for the industry and was also involved in the provision of food, maintenance and operation-services at airports, military bases and hospitals. Through these state-contracts, Al Baraka developed into one of the largest Saudi groups, owning a network of banks across the Middle East, one of the largest media-conglomerates in the Middle East (the Arab Media Corporation), an advertising company and the largest juice-manufacturer in the Middle East.

27. It should be noted that the generation of power has itself become a major source of value-accumulation for foreign internationalised capital as well as domestic capital-groups. Since the 1990s and the deepening of neoliberalism in the Gulf, energy-production has moved quickly towards privatisation in every GCC-state except Kuwait. More than twenty private power-projects have been launched since the region's first in Abu Dhabi in 1998. The cost of future projects is estimated at more than US$100 billion, making the GCC one of the most important private power-markets in the world (*APS Review Downstream Trends* 2007).

to note that its export 'is often equated with exporting electricity'.[28] Much of the global aluminium-industry has begun to relocate to the GCC-region, which now holds the world's largest aluminium-plant and is predicted to produce around 20 per cent of the world's aluminium-output by 2020, with a cost of production $200 per metric tonne cheaper than its nearest rivals, the countries of the former Soviet Union.[29]

The expansion of aluminium, cement and other similarly energy-intensive industries forms a major source of accumulation for large Gulf-capitalists and has occurred through interlocking joint-ventures between these domestic capital-groups and state- and foreign capital.[30] In addition to exports, these materials (and their refined products) feed back into the local productive circuit in two major ways. First, as elements of circulating constant capital, they enter into the production of various commodities for sale on the market, such as apartments and commercial buildings. Second, these raw materials are central to the production of fixed constant capital such as infrastructure, power-plants and refineries.

The scale of both these forms of construction in the Gulf is massive. According to HSBC, the value of Middle-East projects reached US$1 trillion in 2006, making it the world's largest project-finance market and claiming one-third of global project-financing.[31] Most of this financing went to real-estate construction ($525 billion), followed by oil and gas ($228 billion), petrochemical ($100 billion), power and water ($70 billion) and industry ($44 billion).[32] By November 2008, the value of GCC-projects had almost

28. *Middle East Economic Digest* 2009e, p. 4; Ford 2006, p. 50.

29. *Platts* 2007.

30. In the cement-industry, energy constitutes around 30–40 per cent of total production-costs (HSBC 2005, p. 19). For this reason, and because of the vast construction-needs of the GCC (see below), there has been a very rapid expansion of the Gulf cement- and ceramics-industries (the world's largest ceramics-plant is to be found in the UAE-emirate of Ras Al Khaimeh). Although there are around 30 cement-producers in the entire GCC, major control is extremely concentrated in a handful of companies that are owned by the large capital-groups in each GCC-state.

31. *Middle East Economic Digest* 2006. A striking example of the scale of this is the Qatargas II project, the world's largest LNG project and third-largest project-financing in history (behind the Channel Tunnel and a Taiwanese high-speed rail-financing). According to the law-firm that represented Qatar Petroleum (QP) and Exxon in the negotiations for the financing, it took forty-eight commercial banks, one Export Credit Agency, six Islamic banks and one ExxonMobil Lender to finance the project (see White and Case 2004).

32. *Middle East Economic Digest* 2006, figures for 2006. This bias towards construction and the oil- and gas-sectors can also be seen at the country-level. In Kuwait, for example, 95 per cent of the country's US$235 billion in planned mega-projects (projects worth more than $1 billion) were in these two sectors, with construction alone accounting for 72 per cent of overall value in 2008, see *Middle East Economic Digest* 2009a, p. 10.

doubled, reaching US$1.9 trillion and equivalent to 170 per cent of the 2008 Gulf GDP. Saudi Arabia and the UAE accounted for almost 70 per cent of total project-value.[33]

The growth of the GCC project-market is reflected in FDI-flows into the region. Although representing a small proportion of total global FDI-inflows, the GCC was the fastest-growing region for FDI in the world over the last decade.[34] In 2007, the GCC attracted over 61 per cent of all FDI-inflows into the entire West-Asia region, around double that attracted by its nearest rival, Turkey.[35] The importance of the region's expanding project-market was graphically symbolised by the decision of Halliburton in 2007 to move its headquarters from the US to the UAE in order to improve its chances in the region.

Along with foreign capital, large domestic Gulf-groups have been the primary beneficiaries of the construction-work accompanying these industrial and commercial projects. Utilising those companies established in the early stages of the oil-industry, Gulf-conglomerates have rapidly expanded their construction-, engineering and contracting work to build private apartments, shopping malls, bridges, roads, power-plants and petrochemical refineries.[36] According to the *Middle East Economic Digest*, of the top 50 contractors active in the GCC during 2007, 31 were from the GCC itself (eleven from Saudi Arabia, nine from the UAE, five from Kuwait, three from Qatar, two from Oman and one from Bahrain).[37] These figures confirm the centrality of construction-related activities to the accumulation of domestic capitalist classes.

In more recent years, these accumulation-patterns have begun to shift following an expansion of the downstream-sector of the Gulf hydrocarbon-industry (for example, production of petrochemicals, plastics, fertilisers and so forth). Historically, the downstream-sector has been dominated by foreign multinationals that purchased crude oil (or gas) from the Gulf-states and

33. The Institute of International Finance 2008, p. 1.

34. Dun and Bradstreet 2008, p. 3.

35. United Nations Conference on Trade and Development 2007, p. 54.

36. This construction-activity is generally structured through tiered levels of subcontracting. A development-company, usually controlled by a Gulf capital-group, owns the overall project and often benefits from access to cheap or free land granted to it by the ruler. In many cases, particularly for complex projects, the architectural design and engineering will be contracted to a foreign company. The owner will contract another large company to construct the project. In turn, this company will sub-contract unskilled labour to smaller companies in order to complete the work. While there are thousands of small-scale construction-companies, a few large companies dominate building activities for the major real-estate projects.

37. *Middle East Economic Digest* 2007.

then located their downstream-activities in an advanced capitalist country where they produced gasoline or more complex petrochemicals. Neoliberal reforms and global trends in the petrochemical industry have seen an increasing relocation of this sector to the Gulf to take advantage of the cheaper feedstocks of raw material and energy. In 2005, investments in the GCC-petrochemical sector totalled US $29 billion, and accounted for approximately 60 per cent of the region's manufacturing-sector investments. Saudi Arabia dominates this industry and accounts for 76 per cent of total regional petrochemical production, followed by Qatar with 11 per cent. It is estimated that the share of the global petrochemical industry of Saudi Arabia alone will increase from 7 per cent in 2005 to 13 per cent by 2010.[38]

Large Gulf capital-groups have been inserted as a junior partner in these petrochemical projects alongside foreign and state-capital. In this manner, they profit from both the production of petrochemicals and the construction- and engineering work involved in the development of these multi-billion-dollar facilities. The institutional mechanism through which this has taken place is usually a state-owned industrial company, closely affiliated with the national oil-company, that underwrites project-development using state-revenues and other financing to invest in a joint-venture with foreign multinationals and domestic capital.[39]

These different branches of productive activities related to the hydrocarbon-sector – construction, maintenance- and service-work; energy-intensive manufacturing industries; construction and infrastructure-development; and downstream-petrochemicals – form the major routes of capital-accumulation for domestic capital within the Gulf productive circuit. Non-hydrocarbon sectors of the productive circuit, such as the production of consumer commodity-goods and so forth, are relatively underdeveloped. This creates a particular dependency on foreign imports, which has formed another key mechanism of accumulation for the Gulf capitalist class.

38. Global Investment House 2007a, p. 37.

39. The pre-eminent example of this process is the Saudi Basic Industries Corporation (SABIC), founded in 1976 when the Saudi-Arabian government decided to capture the natural gas associated with the production of crude oil and use it to make chemicals, polymers, fertilisers and metals. SABIC has 14 affiliates and petrochemical joint-ventures in which its ownership-share ranges from 30–70 per cent. Its partners in these companies include prominent private-sector Gulf-capitalists as well as large foreign capital. Moreover, SABIC is the most profitable publicly-listed non-oil company in the Middle East, but its shares can only be held by GCC-investors. This represents another mechanism through which value is re-distributed through the Saudi stock-market to regional domestic capital-groups. See Global Investment House 2007a.

2.2. *The Gulf commodity-circuit*

As with all countries within the world-market, the Gulf-states present a potential location for the realisation of value. For advanced capitalism, the Gulf plays a particularly significant role in this respect due to the character of the productive circuit noted above. The large amounts of available liquidity, rapid industrialisation, and the expansion of infrastructure and petrochemical-related activities mean that the size of the region's markets is significant relative to other areas outside of the advanced-capitalist core.

The value of US-exports to the GCC-states has historically exceeded those of other advanced-capitalist countries although this advantage has narrowed since the late 1990s. When trade is examined at the bloc-level, however, EU and Asian exports to the Gulf-states widely surpass those of the US. One consequence of this competition has been a proliferation of Free-Trade Agreements (FTAs) with the Gulf, as part of a broader attempt by the advanced-capitalist states to strengthen their regional influence.[40]

In this context, class-formation around the Gulf commodity-circuit is characterised by the role of local capital as import-agents and distributors for large foreign commodity-capital. This characteristic is reinforced by the bias within the Gulf productive circuit towards hydrocarbons and energy-intensive industries, which weights the Gulf commodity-circuit towards a reliance on the advanced-capitalist countries for the external provision of basic consumer-goods. As Gulf-states gained independence in the 1970s, laws were passed that required foreign importers to partner with a local company as their agent and distributor.

Many of the same large Gulf capital-groups involved in the construction- and service-related activities noted above held these agency-rights. Most of these groups historically acted as import-agents for foreign producers in sectors such as automobiles, electrical items, food and beverages, and household consumer-goods. In many cases, a group's agency and franchise-

40. The US announced in mid-2003 a plan to achieve a Middle-East Free-Trade Area (MEFTA) from North Africa to the Gulf by 2013. The US-strategy has been to negotiate individually with 'friendly' countries in the region using a graduated six-step process eventually leading to a fully-fledged free-trade agreement (FTA) between the US and the country in question. FTAs have been signed between the US and Bahrain (2004), Oman (2006) and negotiations have begun with the UAE. Kuwait and Qatar have also expressed interest in obtaining an FTA with the US (Katzman 2006, p. 28). FTA-negotiations are ongoing between the GCC and China, Australia, New Zealand, Iran, Turkey, Pakistan, India and Singapore. The EU signed an Economic Cooperation-Agreement with the GCC in 1988 which opened the way to negotiations for a bilateral FTA that began in 1990. If the negotiations are successful, the European Union-Gulf Cooperation Council FTA would represent the first ever FTA between two regional blocs.

rights encompassed a variety of different commodities and sectors. In this manner, domestic capital captured a portion of the surplus-value realised through the sale of foreign goods.[41]

As the commodity-circuit expanded, many of these same groups came to own the retail-venues in which imported goods were sold. Of particular recent significance is the expansion of large supermarket- and hypermarket-chains that sell a wide range of commodities such as food-items, clothing, gold and electronic appliances within a single store. In Saudi Arabia and the UAE, the value of hypermarket-sales constitutes 50 per cent and 70 per cent respectively of total retail-sales and makes up the fastest-growing retail-sector in both countries.[42] Large capital-groups, particularly those originating from Saudi Arabia and the UAE, dominate ownership of these retail-chains. In some cases, these groups operate franchises for foreign retail-giants such as Geant and Carrefour, with their rights extending across all GCC-countries.[43] In other cases, large retail-chains are fully-owned by Gulf-based capital, once again with a predomination of UAE and Saudi conglomerates.[44] The

41. The UAE-based Al Gurg Group provides a good example. The group was founded in 1960 and remains controlled by the Gurg family. The group holds agency-rights for over 200 international brands from the consumer- and retail-sector (for example, Benetton, Unilever, ID Design, 3M, Better Life, Electrolux, Samsung, Fisher and Paykel), tobacco (Benson and Hedges, British American Tobacco, Dunhill, Lucky Strike, Rothmans, Silk Cut, Viceroy) and industrial goods (Dulux, Siemens, ICI, Leigh Paints, Osram). As well as this involvement in the commodity-circuit, companies owned by the group manufacture basic explosives, iron-castings, chemicals, concrete-products, ceramics, copper-pipes and items used in the oil industry. Gurg is also the largest private shareholder in the National Bank of Fujairah, one of the biggest banks in the UAE. In addition to these economic activities, the chairperson of the Group, Easa Saleh Al Gurg, is the UAE-Ambassador to the Republic of Ireland.

42. *Business Monitor International* 2007a, p. 50; *Business Monitor International* 2007b, p. 49.

43. Geant is the fifth-largest retail-chain in the world. In the GCC, it operates in Saudi Arabia, Bahrain, the UAE and Kuwait. The French-owned Carrefour is the second-largest retail-group in the world with GCC-stores located in the UAE (first opened in 1995), Saudi Arabia (first opened in 2004), Qatar and Oman. Geant is operated by the UAE-based Ghurair Group in Bahrain, UAE and Kuwait, and by the Saudi-based Fawaz Al Hoikar Group in Saudi Arabia. Carrefour is operated by the UAE-based Majd Al Futtaim Group across the GCC.

44. These groups include: the UAE-based Emke Group, which operates 51 supermarkets and hypermarkets in the UAE, Qatar, Oman, Bahrain and Kuwait, with plans to open in Saudi Arabia (Ditcham 2007) – it is the largest retailer in the UAE, and the twelfth-largest retailer in the Middle East and Africa with US$1.07 billion in sales for 2006; the massive Saudi conglomerate Savola, which owns the Aziza Panda and Hyperpanda hypermarkets. Savola is the largest food-retailer in Saudi Arabia and the thirteenth-largest retailer in Africa and the Middle East with sales of US$1.06 billion for 2006. Although Savola has historically been focused on the Saudi-Arabian market, in 2005 it announced an expansion to the rest of the GCC with plans to open ten Hyperpanda stores across the Gulf (Thomson 2006, p. 49); and the Al Maya Group which operates supermarkets in the UAE, Bahrain, Kuwait, Oman and Qatar.

concentration of this ownership is very high. In Saudi Arabia, for example, the top five retailers are predicted to control just under 40 per cent of all retail-sales in the country by 2012.[45]

The circuit of commodity-capital can be further extended to include another location of value-realisation: malls and shopping centres. This retail-capital realises a portion of the total commodity surplus-value through the rent it charges for bringing together a large number of retailers in one space. The expansion of this form of commodity-capital is a very noticeable feature of recent Gulf-development – GCC-malls generate around US$30 billion in sales annually, and in 2006 represented around 84 per cent of the Middle East's Gross Leasable Area (GLA), a measure of total shopping space.[46] The UAE dominates this retail-trade with the second-largest number of recreational shoppers in the world (people who shop for 'something to do' or 'entertainment-purposes'), and a tourism-industry largely structured around the country's attraction as a shopping destination.[47] Indeed, in 2007, the UAE ranked twenty-eighth in the list of top thirty merchandise-importers globally.

The development of malls is an important part of the formation of the Gulf capitalist class around the commodity-circuit. Many of these malls are owned by the same large capital-groups that are active in the earlier moments of the commodity-circuit (that is, as agents and distributors of foreign imports, or as owners of supermarkets and hypermarkets).[48] These groups tend to

45. Heins 2007.

46. Rahman 2006.

47. *Colliers International* 2007, p. 4. The city of Dubai alone makes up 23 per cent of total retail-sales in the GCC, and by end 2008, three of the ten largest malls in the world were located in Dubai. Most of the large shopping malls are anchored by a hypermarket- or supermarket-chain, and then filled with international franchises and entertainment-facilities. Examples of these 'entertainment'-attractions include an Olympic-size skating rink and the world's largest aquarium in the Dubai Mall, a dinosaur theme-park in the Mall of Arabia, and the world's largest indoor ski-slope at the Mall of the Emirates.

48. The Saudi-based Fawaz Hokair Group provides an excellent illustration of these patterns. Hokair began in 1989 with two menswear-stores and has expanded into one of the largest Saudi retail-capital groups. The group owns franchise- and agency-rights for around 60 international commodities concentrated in clothing (including the brands Accessorize, Adams Kids, Aldo, Ann Harvey, La Senza, Le Chateau, Marks and Spencer, Massimo Dutti, Sports City, Vero Moda and Zara) and food (including Booster Juice, Cinnabon, London Dairy, and Seattle's Best Coffee). A central component of the Hokair Group's accumulation is the Geant Hypermarket chain (the fifth-largest in the world), which it operates across Saudi Arabia. Geant acts as an anchor-store for large Hokair-owned malls, of which there are six in Saudi Arabia, housing over 900 stores between them. In addition to these activities centred on the commodity-circuit, Hokair is also involved in luxury hotels, finance, construction, healthcare and telecommunications, and distributes the Chinese-made car, the Chery.

originate from Saudi Arabia and the UAE, and generally own malls in more than one GCC-country.

One final important element of the commodity-circuit – which lies far outside everyday retail-goods – is GCC-purchase of military hardware from the advanced-capitalist countries. The GCC is one of the most important markets in the world for weapons. From 1999 to 2006, Saudi Arabia was the largest arms-recipient of all countries outside of the advanced-capitalist core, with military imports valued at $45.8 billion. The UAE ranked fourth with total deliveries worth over US$10 billion.[49] During this period, the US provided 24 per cent of Saudi deliveries (worth US$4.4 billion), 75 per cent for Bahrain (US$300 million), 67 per cent for Oman (US$600 million), 82 per cent for Kuwait (US$900 million) and 9 per cent of UAE deliveries (US$600 million).[50] Suppliers from the UK, France, Germany and Italy provided most of the remaining arms to the GCC. These levels of imports are set to increase further, with Saudi Arabia's military expenditures predicted to remain at the 2008 level of $36 billion over the next five years – the highest of any country in the Middle East.[51]

As with other components of the commodity-circuit, the military trade also provides an opportunity for individuals in the GCC to capture part of the import-value. This practice is known as 'commission-harvesting', and involves Western military corporations recruiting well-connected Gulf-representatives as their go-between for the sale of military hardware. Huge amounts of money are involved in these contracts, particularly in the case of Saudi Arabia where middle-men are reported to have received up to 30 per cent of the value of contracts.[52]

2.3. *The Gulf finance-circuit*

As the current economic crisis confirms, a key characteristic of neoliberal capitalism has been the qualitative increase in financialisation-processes and the growing expansion of debt-based consumption at a global scale. The significance of financial-flows to contemporary capitalism underpins a further aspect to the integration of the Gulf-region into the global circuits of

49. Grimmett 2007, p. 67.
50. Grimmett 2007, p. 66.
51. Bekker 2009, p. 10.
52. For a detailed discussion of commission-harvesting in Saudi Arabia see Champion 2003. One controversial example of this is the Al Yamamah arms-sales between Saudi Arabia and BAE Systems. The ongoing deal has been worth over £43 billion and is Britain's largest-ever export-agreement. The results of ongoing investigations into corruption around Al Yamamah have yet to be publicly released by the British government.

accumulation. The Gulf's position as a major supplier of oil – particularly following the price-rises of the 1970s – led to significant capital-flows into the region.[53] While some of these flows entered the productive and commodity-circuits of the Gulf, a large proportion was re-directed back to the financial circuits of the advanced-capitalist core. These flows, or petrodollars, were a central feature of the wave of internationalisation of global finance that occurred during the 1970s. Gulf-funds were particularly important to the development of the Eurodollar-market – a critical institutional component to the initial phase of neoliberal restructuring in the advanced-capitalist world – as well as the dominance of the US-dollar in the post-1971 period.[54]

The relationship between the financial circuits of the Gulf and the advanced-capitalist markets has tightened from the late 1990s concurrent with the most recent expansion of debt-driven growth at a global scale. The 1999–2008 oil-price rise precipitated a new flow of petrodollars from the Gulf, which acted as a critical prop to US financial power. More than any other oil-exporting country or region, Gulf financial-flows helped the US sustain its current-account deficit through the early 2000s. Indeed, in 2006, these were equivalent to about 25 per cent of the US current-account deficit.[55] The Institute of International Finance estimates that US equities, debt and other assets accounted for around 57 per cent of total foreign purchases by investors from the Gulf-region from 2002 to 2006.[56] Gulf capital-flows have thus been very important to the maintenance of US-power and the overall financialisation of advanced capitalism – the functioning of the world-system has become ever more reliant upon the ways in which the Gulf financial-circuit is integrated with global flows.

Class-formation around the Gulf financial circuit has been subjected to a strong impact due to this location within the overall development of the global financial circuit. The importance of the Gulf financial circuit to the making of the global economy and US-power far exceeds its role in satisfying domestic financial needs. Consequently, the financial circuit occupies a disproportionate weight within the overall circuit of capital – relative to the productive and commodity-circuits – and is very significant to the formation of the leading sections of the domestic capitalist class.

53. See Wilson 1983 and 1987 for some of the early history of banking in the Gulf.

54. See Sherbiny 1985, Gibson 1989, Gowan 1999 and Spiro 1999 for a discussion of the formation of Euromarkets and the role of petrodollars in the development of US financial power.

55. The Institute of International Finance 2007, p. 9.

56. The Institute of International Finance 2007, p. 10. See also Setser and Ziemba 2006, Lubin 2007 and Tolui 2007 for various calculations of petrodollar-flows.

Banking assets are extremely concentrated at the national scale. In Bahrain, the top three banks control 80 per cent of total banking assets. In Oman, the proportion is 79 per cent, in Qatar 75 per cent, in Kuwait 64 per cent, in Saudi Arabia 55 per cent, and in the UAE 51 per cent.[57] Moreover, some markets are dominated by single banks. In both Qatar and Oman, the largest bank controls around 50 per cent of banking-sector assets. In Kuwait and the UAE, the figure is around 25 per cent.

Many of the same large GCC-groups that control the productive and commodity-circuits are heavily invested in the financial circuit – represented on the boards of the large banks and holding significant shareholdings in them, alongside state-capital.[58] Ownership of the top Gulf-banks has tended to remain dominated by capital of the same national origin. A significant exception to this lack of cross-border ownership, however, is found in the case of Bahrain. Around two-thirds of the capital of Bahraini banks is owned by groups from other GCC-countries. This is because of Bahrain's specific development as an offshore-banking zone with a low regulatory and taxation-environment.[59] Similar centres in other countries are emerging as GCC regional integration deepens.[60]

A second important branch of the finance-circuit consists of a range of new financial bodies that act to pool regional capital through investments and asset-management funds. Of particular significance is the proliferation of private-equity funds throughout the GCC. These private-equity funds

57. Calculated from information listed at *GN Financial Review* 2009, pp. 22–3. Figures cover commercial banks that are active locally, not international banks or those in the offshore-sector.

58. With the exception of the Saudi market and two Omani banks, foreign financial capital is not heavily involved in the direct ownership of GCC-banks. This should not be taken to mean, however, that foreign banks have not penetrated the GCC financial circuit. This penetration has taken place through the opening of foreign bank-branches in GCC states and activities in offshore-markets that hold few restrictions on foreign activities such as Bahrain and the Dubai International Financial Centre (see below).

59. In 1975, the Bahraini government introduced regulations similar to the Cayman Islands and Singapore to allow banks to operate 'offshore-banking units' (OBUs) on the island. Offshore-banks were exempt from all corporate taxes and were only required to pay a small fee to set up on the island. This process coincided with the beginning of restrictions on foreign banks in Saudi Arabia. Bahrain's location as an offshore-banking centre permitted foreign banks to provide financing and financial advice for most industrial projects in Saudi Arabia, despite their lack of a direct, independent presence in the country (Economic and Social Commission for Western Asia 2001, p. 29). The development of the finance-industry in Bahrain has promoted the internationalisation of Gulf-capital by acting to deepen the inter-penetration of capital within the finance-circuit (see below).

60. The Dubai International Financial Centre (DIFC), which operates an offshore-structure resembling that of Bahrain, has licenced 482 institutions since it opened in 2005. Qatar and Saudi Arabia are also looking at establishing similar zones.

typically pursue financial activities such as the purchases of equity and bonds, as well as investments in international markets. They also directly purchase companies with the intention of obtaining a controlling (or major) interest in the target-company, which is often then sold after restructuring.[61]

There has been a very rapid and recent growth in the size of GCC private equity. According to the Gulf Venture Capital Association (GVCA), a regional industry-network of private equity and venture-capital firms, nearly 90 per cent (US$16.5 billion) of the total PE raised in the Middle-East and North-Africa (MENA) region from 1997 to 2006 (US$18 billion) was raised in the 2005 period.[62] The total MENA PE fund-size in 2001 was US$78 million. By 2006, the value exceeded US$14 billion with four funds reaching a value of US$1 billion for that year.[63] Between 2004 and 2007, the average investment per fund increased from US$10 million to US$103 million.[64]

The rapid growth in private equity is one indication of the increasing size of fixed capital required for profitable investment in the productive process. A range of large industrial projects – particularly those in the downstream petroleum-sector – require massive amounts of capital increasingly beyond the capabilities of governments, single capitalists or a group of capitalists of one national origin. This process is accelerated by the rapid wave of privatisation that occurred across the Middle East consequent to the implementation of neoliberalism. The purchase of privatised telecoms, banks, and oil- and gas-assets requires huge outlays that reinforce a pooling of available capital across national boundaries.[65]

---

61. The company is often restructured through a range of measures typical to neoliberalism (such as sharp cuts in staff, selling-off of assets, and debt-refinancing) or by splitting it up into profitable sections such as real estate. In doing so, they will often take on debt from international banks. Once restructuring is complete, the companies are then offered for sale (typically through a stock-market IPO).

62. Gulf Venture Capital Association 2006, p. 15.

63. Global Investment House 2006, p. 8.

64. Solh 2008, p. 7.

65. One of the large Gulf PE firms, Global Investment House, made precisely this argument in its July 2007 strategic report on private equity in the Middle East: 'It is expected that the privatization pipeline in the MENA region to reach [sic] US$900bn with approximately 147 privatization transactions either announced or planned in the next ten years. Such infrastructure assets include roads, airports, bridges, public transit systems, seaports, power stations, power lines, gas pipelines, and communications networks. Private equity funds plays the role in filling in the gap of financing as the burden becomes increasingly large for the governments to tolerate on a stand alone basis, in addition the added value that private equity plays in this industry [sic]. It is argued that private equity ensures effective corporate governance, provides financial engineering, growth capital, a clear strategic vision, creates incentives for efficiency, amongst others' (*Global Investment House* 2007b, p. 15).

Gulf private-equity companies have complex institutional forms that may involve a variety of holding companies, offshore-banking units, and shell-companies. Characteristically, the largest of these companies will have multiple headquarters across the globe with a strong presence in several Gulf-markets. In some cases, they integrate Gulf-capital with other foreign internationalised capital. As is shown below, private equity is a key vehicle for the internationalisation and regional integration of capital-groups from different GCC-states within single ownership-structures.

2.4. *Formation of the Gulf working classes*

The process of capitalist class-formation in the Gulf has been accompanied by its dialectical opposite: the development of the Gulf working classes. The specificity of this process is particularly important to highlight as it holds important ramifications for any political assessment of the Gulf-region as well as broader implications for neighbouring countries. Moreover, a proper conception of this class-structure is necessary in order to understand the impact of the current economic crisis on the Gulf.

Most of the work in the GCC is carried out by migrant-labour. The majority of the variable capital that it receives in exchange for its labour-power returns to its home-country in the form of remittances. No other region or country of the world has a working class that is so peculiarly formed – characterised by its temporary, unstable nature and total lack of citizenship-rights. The severe exploitation of these workers has been widely discussed by human-rights organisations, journalists, and in the academic literature.

It is important, however, to go beyond the simple moral outrage against exploitation that typifies much of this analysis and understand why this system has evolved in the way that it has. This is not an accidental class-structure that results from a lack of regulation or the shortcomings of Gulf rulers, but a direct consequence of the Gulf's ascension as a core-zone within the global economy. The centrality of the Gulf to the making of both global capitalism and US-power means that the working classes of the Gulf (and, by extension, the broader Middle East) present an immanent threat to capital-accumulation at a global scale. Any attempt by labour within the Gulf to wrest control of the value it produces would profoundly impact the stability of capitalism at a global scale (and the position of domestic Gulf-capital as a layer that has adhered onto global power-structures). As a consequence of this potential threat, GCC-states moved towards the systemic reliance on temporary, migrant-workers as a particularly effective mechanism of social control (and this is the key difference between the GCC-states and neighbouring Iraq and Iran).[66]

As the fascinating work of Robert Vitalis has shown in the case of Saudi Arabia, Gulf labour-markets in the oil-sector were not initially structured in this manner. Within the kingdom, US oil-companies established a system of extreme racial division in which Saudi and other Arab workers were subject to discrimination reminiscent of South-African apartheid. This model was directly inspired by US frontier mining towns, and provoked a range of worker-demonstrations and illegal strikes from Saudi employees. This resistance faced very severe repression by the Saudi monarchy, supported – as Vitalis convincingly demonstrates – by the US-government and oil-companies. This was the only period of Saudi history in which left-wing and worker-organisations gained any significant traction within the country.

With the transition to national-based oil-companies and the increasing control of the Gulf-states over their economies, this class-structure began to change. Citizens of the Gulf-states were placed in high-ranking public-sector and management-positions and migrant-labour was imported to constitute the majority of the working class. This was an ideal means of social control, as it neutralised any potential threat to régime-stability. With no working-class continuity – and no possibility of gaining citizenship – most migrant-workers were simply concerned with earning remittances for their families back home. The possibility of sustained social movements based on the working class, or the growth of genuine left culture that can organise for radical change, is extremely difficult in such a situation.[67] As we shall see below in examining the Gulf's response to the global financial crisis, labour in the Gulf can be simply threatened with deportation at the slightest evidence of discontent or crisis.

Table 2 demonstrates the remarkable extent to which the GCC depends on this labour. The migrant-population ranges from 24 per cent (Oman) to 78 per cent (Qatar) of the entire population, a proportion that has generally increased over the last decade. Most of these migrants are young males (ranging between 70 to 80 per cent), although female migrant-labour is heavily concentrated in some sectors such as domestic and retail-work.

66. This argument is developed further in Hanieh 2010.

67. Of course there are partial exceptions to this observation, particularly in those Gulf-countries where the historical pattern of class-formation tended to occur along lines that reflected religious divisions. In the case of Bahrain, for example, the Shia majority were generally proletarianised while control of the state remained in Sunni hands. Although migrant-labour became highly significant to the Bahraini economy, limited trade-union activity is present and can be traced to Shia-based worker-activism. In the case of Oman, leftist movements during the 1960s and 1970s were related to guerrilla-organisations based in the Dhofar-region.

Table 2: Migrant-population in the GCC

Country	Migrant-worker population	Migrant-worker population as percentage of total population		Proportion of migrant-worker population female	Migrant-workers as percentage of total labour-force	Migrant-workers as percentage of public-sector workforce	Migrant-workers as percentage of private-sector workforce
Year	**2005**	**1995**	**2005**	**2005**	**2005**	**2001**	**Various**
Saudi Arabia	6,360,730	24.7	25.9	30.1	50.2	11.2	95 (2004)
Kuwait	1,668,991	58.7	62.1	31.0	80.3	24	78 (2005)
UAE	3,211,749	70.5	71.4	27.8	91.3	55.5	98 (2004)
Bahrain	295,461	37.5	40.7	30.9	58.8	9.3	79
Qatar	636,751	77.2	78.3	25.8	85.9	33.9	83
Oman	627,571	26.3	24.4	20.9	79	21.9	N.A.

Source: http://esa.un.org/migration; Shamsi 2006, pp. 61, 63; Shah 2006, p. 6.

Within the labour-force, the migrant-proportion is even more highly concentrated than the general population, making up 50 per cent of the Saudi labour-force and 91 per cent of the UAE's. Furthermore, this labour is heavily biased towards the private sector. In both the UAE and Saudi Arabia, migrant-workers constitute close to 100 per cent of the private-sector workforce.[68]

There has been a dramatic shift in the geographical origins of these workers over the last two decades. Initially, this system depended upon Arab labour such as Palestinian, Lebanese, Egyptian and Yemeni workers. During the 1970s and 1980s, however, many of these workers became sympathetic with Arab-nationalist, leftist and Nasserist movements and began to challenge the régimes and their perceived ties with US-imperialism.[69] In response, the system of control was altered during the 1990s – capitalising on the Palestine Liberation Organisation's support for Iraq during the first Gulf War – to shift the migrant-labour source countries away from the Arab world towards the Indian sub-continent. It is estimated that around 2 million Arab workers and

68. It should be noted that these figures are likely to underestimate the number of temporary migrant-workers throughout the GCC. If the numbers of workers who are living and working illegally are included, this figure would rise considerably. Saudi Arabia, for example, deports around 700,000 'illegal' workers on an annual basis, more than ten per cent of the total number officially recorded as present in the country (Shah 2006, p. 6). In 2003, around 100,000 non-status workers left the UAE voluntarily as part of one of the regular amnesty-programmes offered by the government (Shah 2006, p. 6).

69. Kapiszewski 2001; Kapiszewski 2004.

their dependents lost employment in the GCC at this time.[70] By 2002, the Arab proportion of migrant-workers in the GCC had fallen to 25–9 per cent, compared with 72 per cent in 1975.[71]

Most of the migrant-workforce in the GCC is now of South-Asian origin. In turn, the GCC constitutes the major global zone of employment for many countries in Asia. In 2003, 97 per cent of Pakistanis working oversees were employed in the GCC. For Bangladesh and Sri Lanka, the figure exceeds 80 per cent. In 2004, Saudi Arabia alone was the source of 39 per cent of total global worker-remittances received by Bangladesh.[72]

These South-Asian workers, and the smaller numbers of Arab workers who remain in the GCC, form the overwhelming majority of the labour-force in key value-producing sectors of the economy: manufacturing, agriculture and construction. In the mining and quarrying sector, they form a smaller proportion, but this sector is also the least labour-intensive of all industrial activities. Furthermore, in regard to the types of work performed within these sectors, migrant-labour is concentrated in low-paid, manual activities, whereas domestic national labour predominates in managerial and higher-level administrative positions.

3. *Khaleeji*-capital and Gulf regional integration

The foregoing description of the three circuits of capital illustrates the major routes of accumulation around which the process of class-formation has occurred within the GCC. In each Gulf-country, large capital-groups – historically allied to the state and ruling families – have coalesced around these flows and risen to dominate the economies of the Gulf.

The influence of these groups has been strengthened through the process of economic integration inaugurated by the 1981 establishment of the GCC. In particular, integration has underpinned the internationalisation of the Gulf circuits of capital and thereby consolidated the increasingly pan-Gulf nature of capitalist accumulation.

Key to understanding this process of internationalisation is the re-territorialisation of economic and political power that has occurred as part of the formation of the GCC. A range of economic agreements signed between the member-states of the GCC have reconfigured the regulatory, co-ordinating and legitimating functions of individual member-states, in

70. Fergany 2001, p. 4.
71. Kapiszewski 2004, p. 123.
72. Figures from Bangladesh Bank, cited in Shah 2006, p. 23.

addition to forming new supra-national institutions that discipline and structure the array of possible policy-choices by state-actors. Economic decision-making and the institutions that govern it are thus increasingly developed at the regional level. In this manner, the Gulf operates as a single economic space, with its circuits of capital recast at a pan-Gulf scale. As noted above, however, this should not be taken to mean that the Gulf-state has been bypassed or has become in any way irrelevant. In fact – compelled to operate within these pan-Gulf circuits – the Gulf-state is the primary actor responsible for sustaining the internationalisation of accumulation within its territory.

The 2001 Economic Agreement between the States of the Cooperation Council (EASCC) was a landmark-point in this process. Its embrace of neoliberalism is clear from the preamble, where 'enhancing market mechanisms and fostering the role of the private sector' is explicitly laid out as a central goal of the agreement. The EASCC also links the achievement of 'advanced stages of economic integration ... lead[ing] to a Common Market and an Economic and Monetary Union among Member States' as a specific response to 'recent global economic developments'. Deepening integration is partly conceived as a defensive response to these shifts in the global economy, in order to enable GCC-capitalists to 'strengthen their negotiating position and competitive capacity in international markets'.[73]

The significance of the EASCC lies in its conscious embrace of the institutional restructuring necessary to reshape the relationship between the national and regional scales. By deepening the regional nature of accumulation, the EASCC hindered individual member-states from controlling the movement of capital and goods within the intra-GCC space, and forced them to comply with policies established at the regional scale. These institutional shifts are demonstrated by a raft of new policies initiated by – and immediately following – the ratification of the EASCC.[74]

Article One, for example, called for the establishment of a customs-union that ensured national treatment throughout the GCC for any good produced by a member-state. The Customs Union became a reality in 2003 with the adoption of the 'Common Customs Law for the Arab States of the Gulf (GCC States)'. This law removed certificate-of-origin requirements for all domestically-produced goods in the GCC. Previously, an elaborate procedure

73. All citations of the EASCC from Gulf Cooperation Council Secretariat-General 2001.

74. It should be emphasised that many of the EASCC articles discussed below are not necessarily fully-implemented by member-states and may be subject to intra-GCC disputes. This account, however, confirms the general trajectory of policy and is a strong indication of where regional integration in the Gulf is heading.

was required to prove a minimum 40 per cent domestic content and goods had to go through a customs-inspection at each internal border.[75]

Article Two of the EASCC established a common external tariff for the entire GCC-region. This single rate was eventually set at 5 per cent and meant that some states were forced to vastly reduce the costs placed on foreign importers to the region (in 1999 the simple mean tariff was 12.6 per cent in Saudi Arabia, compared with 4.8 per cent in Oman).[76] The regulations of the customs-union and the common external tariff meant that clearance of all goods would take place at the point of entry into the GCC and goods could then move freely across intra-GCC borders (apart from health- and quarantine-inspections). Furthermore, Article Three of the EASCC called for a common market that would permit GCC citizens to move freely across member-states and work without discrimination in all professions. This also meant standardised treatment in tax, pensions and social services, and the ability for citizens to own real estate in other Gulf-states.

Articles Four, Five and Six of the EASCC extended the integration-process to the financial-circuit by committing member-states to fully integrating capital-markets, harmonising all financial laws and regulations, and removing any discriminatory ownership-provisions for shares and other investments in the GCC. In general, although some individual company-restrictions remained, GCC-investors could freely own shares in any listed company across the region. Requirements for majority national ownership of strategic industrial and financial companies were dropped completely or replaced with majority GCC-provisions.[77]

The most important feature of the EASCC was an agreement to establish a monetary union and single currency by 2010. A 2001 meeting of the GCC's Supreme Council in Muscat, Oman followed this up with an explicit call for currency-unification and the adoption of economic criteria to bring member-states closer to the formation of a monetary union.[78] A timetable was established for this goal: by 2002 all national currencies would be pegged to the US-dollar (fulfilled in 2003);[79] by the end of 2005, a series of convergence-criteria would

75. Sturm and Siegfried 2005, p. 28.

76. With the exception of higher tariff-rates that existed for tobacco- and alcohol-products.

77. Sturm and Siegfried 2005, p. 31.

78. An earlier 1982 agreement raised the possibility of a monetary union but no concrete steps were taken in this regard. In December 2000, the GCC Committee of Monetary Agencies and Central Bank Governors, and member-states' ministers of finance were mandated by the GCC Supreme Council to devise a working plan and a timetable for a single currency, which they presented to the 2001 Muscat Summit.

79. Except for Kuwait that has pegged to a basket of currencies heavily weighted to the US-dollar.

be established that member-states would strive to reach by 2010; and, in January 2010, a single currency would be introduced. In 2009, this ambitious plan was forced to give way to the reality of ongoing rivalry between member-states over the location of the proposed GCC Central Bank. Saudi Arabia eventually won the location over the protests of the UAE, leading the latter to withdraw from the proposed monetary union. Despite this conflict, the formation of a monetary union is continuing (albeit at a slower pace) and it is clear that the GCC is increasingly becoming what its General Secretary, Abdul Rahman Al Attiyah, has described as 'one economic entity'.[80]

3.1. *Internationalisation and* khaleeji-*capital*

All of these measures have significantly strengthened the internationalisation-tendencies of Gulf capital. It is important to emphasise that this process of internationalisation should not be understood as delineating a 'thing' (for example, quantities of money or investment-flows) but, rather, is meant to convey the way in which the circuits of capital are themselves elaborated at the regional scale. Internationalisation expresses the way in which the production and realisation of value is increasingly conceived at the international scale, rather than through a nationally-bound perspective.[81] In this sense, it is the set of social relations expressed by these regionally-articulated circuits that is undergoing internationalisation through the regional space. These tendencies of internationalisation are exemplified through the inter-penetration (or, alternatively, the cross-border centralisation and concentration) of Gulf capital-groups within each of the Gulf-circuits.

In one of the most important sectors of the Gulf productive circuit – the Saudi petrochemical industry – evidence of internationalisation is extensive. Large volumes of capital-flows from neighbouring GCC-states have entered into joint-ventures with Saudi capital, with these joint-ventures carrying out one-third of the largest Saudi petrochemical projects in 2006 (7 out of 21 projects). While these projects tended to be smaller than those carried out exclusively by Saudi state-capital and international capital, they still constituted around 20 per cent of the total value produced in the Saudi petrochemical sector.[82] Moreover, seven out of the top nine non-state Saudi petrochemical companies have significant levels of ownership from other Gulf-states that range between 8–40 per cent. It is important to emphasise

80. Almezel and Bibbo 2007. We should remember that the adoption of the euro began with the 1992 Maastricht Treaty and, by 2009, only 16 out of 27 European-Union member-states were part of the euro-zone.

81. Palloix 1977.

82. Saudi Arabian General Investment Authority 2007, p. 49.

that this inter-penetration of Gulf-capital in the Saudi productive circuit has mostly taken place through hierarchical joint-ventures, in which one or more Saudi conglomerates dominate ownership and other large GCC capital-groups are inserted as junior partners.[83]

As noted above, another major branch of the productive circuit in the Gulf is the construction-industry. Over the last few years, the UAE has been the major centre of investment in this sector, with construction-contracts valued at just under US$230 billion over the 2005–8 period (compared to US$33 billion in Saudi Arabia).[84] Once again, this sector shows significant evidence of internationalisation, with much of the construction in the UAE carried out by companies from elsewhere in the Gulf. With the collapse of the UAE-market (in particular Dubai), Gulf construction-companies are placing their hopes on the Saudi market as their next major accumulation-zone (see below).

In the case of the Gulf commodity-circuit, the centralisation and concentration of retail-ownership across national borders indicated earlier is one confirmation of internationalisation. Ownership- and agency-rights for the largest supermarkets, hypermarkets and malls are concentrated in the hands of UAE and Saudi conglomerates, and operate across all GCC-states.[85] As a result, the Gulf-region is increasingly viewed by Gulf commodity-capital as a single market rather than an agglomeration of separate national markets.

Moreover, further pressure to deepen this integration comes from foreign capital, which seeks ever-larger and unified markets as the main supplier of imports. This provides a strong tendency towards the internationalisation of the commodity-circuit through the Gulf-region, in which each GCC member-state operates in a regionally-articulated fashion within a unified commodity-circuit. Striking evidence of this is shown by the entrepôt-roles played by the UAE and Saudi Arabia vis-à-vis international imports.[86] Exports

83. Hydrocarbon-related projects elsewhere in the Gulf also hold significant cross-border ownership. The UAE-based Dana Gas project, for example, is the largest private gas-project in the Middle East. Ownership is divided between major capital-groups in Saudi Arabia, Kuwait, UAE and Oman.

84. *Middle East Economic Digest* 2009a, p. 21. This figure refers to the value of construction, and not to the entire value of projects (i.e. including design, engineering etc.). A recent estimate calculates around 1,300 projects in the UAE, worth over $1 trillion – half of which have been suspended in the recent crisis (*Arabian Business* 2009, p. 40).

85. This should not be interpreted to mean that the commodity-chain is exclusively controlled by UAE or Saudi capital. Kuwait's Americana Group, for example, is the largest fast-food operator in the Middle East and runs the KFC, Pizza Hut and Hardees franchises across the Gulf-region.

86. In 2007, for example, 80 per cent of the UK's exports to the GCC-region went through the UAE and Saudi Arabia, compared to 7 per cent each for Qatar and Kuwait and 3 per cent

from advanced-capitalist countries enter the region through these two countries, and are then re-exported to the rest of the Gulf. By 2004–5, Saudi Arabia and the UAE were supplying Bahrain, Qatar and Oman with between 25–45 per cent of their total imports in each of the key sectors of food, manufactured goods, chemical products, and machinery and equipment. The UAE or Saudi Arabia ranked as one of the top five exporters to Kuwait, Bahrain, Qatar and Oman for every sector except for machinery and transport-equipment.[87] For Oman, the UAE was the top source of imports in every sector except for machinery and transport (in which it ranked second). These trends were made possible as a result of the establishment of a customs-union and free-trade area across the Gulf (see above), and provide striking substantiation of how the UAE and Saudi Arabia act as 'gateway'-markets to a commodity-circuit increasingly conceived at a pan-GCC scale.

The Gulf finance-circuit demonstrates the most developed tendencies towards internationalisation. In the banking sector, a particular role is played by Bahrain as the geographical space through which the internationalisation of banking capital takes place (as noted above, over two-thirds of Bahraini banking assets are owned by other GCC capital-groups). Cross-border expansion of the financial circuit has further increased since the eighteenth GCC-summit in Kuwait (1997) where an agreement was reached to allow all GCC-banks to open branches in member-countries.[88]

The clearest expression of internationalisation in the finance-circuit, however, is found in the development of financial forms such as private equity, which interlock the large capital-groups from across the GCC within single ownership-structures. These integrated ownership-structures then re-invest through all moments of the GCC-circuits. One of the largest private-equity groups in the Middle East, Abraaj Capital, provides a textbook-example of this cross-GCC integrated finance-capital.[89] The company was started by Arif Naqvi, who was a vice-president with the Saudi-based Olayan-group. Key Gulf business-groups investing in Abraaj and represented on the board of directors include al Turki (Saudi Arabia), Qassimi (UAE), Kanoo (Bahrain), NBK Group (Qatar), Nowais (UAE) and al Jaber (UAE). The geographical spread of these component-groups indicates that ownership of

---

each for Bahrain and Oman (*Gulf Daily News* 2007). Other advanced-capitalist states show similar export-patterns to the Gulf-region.

87. Calculated by the author from the UN Comtrade Database. Figures are for 2005, Kuwait figures based on the latest available from 2001.

88. The decision took several years to implement, but in 2004 Kuwait amended its Banking Law (1968) to become the final country in the GCC to open up its market to other GCC-banks.

89. Information on Abraaj is taken from the Abraaj website: <http://www.abraaj.com>.

Abraaj is widely distributed across different capital-groups throughout the GCC-region. In addition to these private GCC capital-groups, management and ownership of Abraaj also involves state-bodies such as the Public Institution for Social Security (Kuwait) and the General Retirement and Pension Authority (Qatar).

Abraaj established the first Middle-East buyout fund in 2003 with commitments of $116 million. The fund purchased strategic stakes in some of the largest companies in the Middle East: Amwal (the leading investment-banking firm in Qatar), Spinneys (the largest supermarket-chain in the Middle East), JorAmco (an aircraft-maintenance company privatised by the Jordanian government) and maktoob.com (the leading Arabic internet-portal). Abraaj has launched several more funds since that time, and now has over US$4 billion in assets under management. In September 2006, Abraaj purchased 10.7 per cent of Jordan National Bank (JNB) and became the largest shareholder (25 per cent) of EFG-Hermes, one of the largest investment-banks in Egypt and the number one securities-broker on the Cairo and Alexandria Stock-Exchange.[90]

These tendencies of internationalisation within the productive, commodity- and finance-circuits are indicative of a shift in the social relations that have developed around processes of accumulation in the Gulf-region. The increasing manner in which these circuits are conceived and articulate at a regional scale, reflects the emergence of a pan-Gulf capitalist class, *khaleeji*-capital.[91] *Khaleeji*-capital consists of those large Gulf-conglomerates that tend to operate within these internationalising circuits. These groups conceive their field of accumulation from the regional perspective, rather than that of the Gulf-state from which they originate, and also display a tendency to inter-penetrate with neighbouring capital-groups.

As analysis of each of the circuits has suggested, *khaleeji*-capital is structured around a Saudi-Emirati axis, with other Gulf capital-groups congealing as subordinate partners within interlocking hierarchical structures of

90. Another example of regionally-integrated finance-capital is Investcorp, formed in 1982 with around $13 billion in managed assets. The company prides itself on its 'flat corporate structure' (<http://www.investcorp.com>) with management distributed between three offices in Bahrain, London and New York. The company itself is a limited-liability company incorporated in Luxembourg, which is wholly-owned by Investcorp Holdings Limited (IHL), incorporated in the Cayman Islands. IHL is owned by Investcorp Bank, which is incorporated in Bahrain. In turn, Investcorp Bank is majority-owned by Ownership Holdings Limited (OHL), which is also incorporated in the Cayman Islands. The top of this ownership-structure leads finally to SIPCO Limited (Cayman Islands), which holds majority-ownership of OHL and is controlled by around 150 strategic shareholders from across the Gulf.

91. From the Arabic word, *khaleej* meaning 'Gulf'. *Khaleeji* conveys more than just a geographical connotation but also a sense of a unique pan-Gulf identity.

accumulation. The formation of these hierarchies occurs through the internationalisation of each moment of the circuit of capital, with this process taking a particular geographical and institutional form within each circuit. A leading GCC private-equity fund clearly expresses the outlook of *khaleeji*-capital:

> We look at the whole GCC, we believe that there is a customs union, a monetary union almost with a very close peg to the dollar, there is a cultural union and anything that sells in Saudi Arabia would sell in Dubai. So for us, we don't look at these markets as being separate entities we look at them as being one.[92]

The internationalisation-tendencies underpinning the development of *khaleeji*-capital have significant regional implications beyond the Gulf. There has been an extremely rapid increase in intra-Middle East FDI-flows over the past few years, with the bulk of this investment coming from the Gulf. From 2002 to 2006, FDI originating from GCC-countries was equivalent to a remarkable 13 per cent of the rest of the Middle East and North Africa's GDP.[93] Four Gulf-countries, Bahrain, Saudi Arabia, Kuwait and the UAE accounted for 79 per cent of all outward intra-Middle East FDI in 2007.[94]

These flows presage the increasing dominance of the Middle East as a whole by *khaleeji*-capital. According to the Central Bank of Egypt, the share of GCC-capital in Egypt's FDI rose from 4.5 per cent in 2005 to over 25 per cent in 2007. The Jordanian stock-exchange is heavily dependent upon GCC-investors – although they make up less than 1% of all shareholders they hold approximately 20% of market-capitalisation.[95] Nineteen out of the 20 largest Arab banks by capital-size were from the Gulf by 2005 and 29 per cent of Middle East and North Africa (MENA) mobile-phone subscriptions are controlled by just three Gulf-companies operating across a total of 26 countries.[96] These figures show that the tendency of internationalisation at the core of *khaleeji*-capital is a key element of the broader regional political economy.

3.2. Khaleeji-*capital and the financial crisis*

An understanding of *khaleeji*-capital provides a useful framework in which to assess the impact of the global financial crisis on the Gulf-region. While there has certainly been a slow-down in economic activity and

92. Growth Gate Capital, quoted in Dun and Bradsheet 2008, p. 8.
93. The Institute of International Finance 2008, p. 8.
94. Arab Investment and Export Credit Guarantee Corporation 2007, p. 22.
95. Calculated by author from annual data from the Amman Stock Exchange.
96. Timewell 2006.

accumulation-possibilities across the GCC, the response of the leading capital-groups is to further embrace the deepening internationalisation-tendencies of the Gulf-circuits. Furthermore, the structure of class-formation that has formed around these circuits has ensured that the crisis is displaced onto the migrant working classes rather than the tiny layer of citizenry in the Gulf. In other words, the crisis actually appears to be strengthening and consolidating the development of *khaleeji*-capital.

It is certainly true that the global drop in demand for hydrocarbons – reflected in a plunge in the price of oil of over 64 per cent from the peak of $147.27 in July 2008 – has meant that revenues to Gulf-states have fallen considerably. Many of the high-profile 'megaprojects' in the region have been cancelled or postponed, banks have been put under severe pressure as asset-prices fall, and several high-profile investment-firms have defaulted on their loans as a result of over-leverage. The flows of value to the Gulf capitalist classes described above have been curtailed, reflected in the 57 per cent decline in GCC equity-markets in the year to March 2009.

Dubai, one of the key centres of accumulation in the Gulf, has been worst hit. According to the US-company Jones Lang LaSalle, more than half of the real-estate projects planned for completion in Dubai by 2012 have been put on hold or cancelled.[97] This is having a knock-on effect – in the power-, electricity- and water-sectors, for example, several major projects have been postponed. By some estimates, property-prices in Dubai have dropped by as much as 70 per cent and commercial rents by 60 per cent.[98] The collapsing Dubai-bubble had government-departments predicting a staggering 20 per cent drop in population as employment-levels plummeted and workers were repatriated.[99] This would further reinforce plunge in consumption – having thereby an impact on sales in the region's malls and hypermarkets, many of which are highly leveraged.

Dubai is perhaps the most extreme example but other Gulf-states have also felt the effects of the crisis. In Saudi Arabia, for example, 54 major projects have been put on hold, including the construction of the massive King Abdullah Economic City – a US$27 billion investment that was planned to house two million people by the time of its completion in 2016. In Kuwait, a US$17.4 billion petrochemical joint-venture with Dow Chemical has been cancelled and real-estate sales dropped by 60 per cent in January 2009,

97. *Middle East Economic Digest* 2009c, p. 30.

98. *Khaleej Times* 2009.

99. According to the *Middle East Economic Digest*, the Dubai Roads and Transports Authority is revising its spending plans to take into account an anticipated one-fifth drop in population-levels over the next year (*Middle East Economic Digest* 2009d, p. 19).

according to leaked government-data.[100] There have also been some large, high-profile financial casualties. In mid-2009, two of the region's largest private conglomerates (and examples of *khaleeji*-capital), the Saudi-based holding companies Saad Group and Al Gosaibi Group, announced they would need to restructure US$10bn worth of debts. The news sent panic through neighbouring Gulf-countries due to the extensive cross-border investments of these two companies.

This slow-down in economic activity, however, has generally not meant a weakening of *khaleeji*-capital. Instead, it appears that the worst impacts of the crisis are being displaced onto the hundreds of thousands of migrant-workers across the Gulf. As projects are postponed or cancelled, workers are simply being repatriated to their home countries without compensation. The Indian consulate in Dubai, for example, reports that UAE construction-companies are block-booking entire planes in order to remove workers from the country.[101] The Minister for Overseas Indian Affairs, Vayalar Ravi, told the Indian parliament on 8 July 2009 that up to 150,000 Indian workers from the Gulf-countries have probably returned to the country due to the global economic slowdown. The number of Bangladeshi workers in GCC-countries has declined by 58 per cent from January 2008–May 2009, largely as a result of the virtually complete cessation of hiring in Saudi Arabia and Kuwait. The massive drop in employment is reflected in figures for air-travel from Bangladesh to the Gulf – with industry-spokespeople claiming a drop from 26,000 travellers per week in 2007 to 12,000 in mid-2009.[102]

Official remittance-figures are beginning to indicate the possibilities of a very severe social crisis emerging in the countries of South Asia due to the drop in labour-flows to the Gulf.[103] In Sri Lanka, for example, net remittance-inflows declined 3.8 per cent in the year to March 2009, posting the fifth consecutive month of decline (and on the heels of an 18 per cent decline in February). This should be compared with over 22 per cent annual growth-rate for the third quarter of 2008 period.[104] It is estimated that around 20 per cent

100. *Arabian Business* 2009, p. 13.

101. *Arabian Business* 2009, p. 30.

102. *The Financial Express* 2009.

103. We should add the proviso here that remittance-figures need to be treated with great caution. Much of these flows do not show up in official figures because they happen through informal channels rather than licenced money-exchanges or the banking system. Furthermore, with the onset of a severe crisis it is not unexpected to see a temporary rise in remittance-flows as long-term migrant-workers repatriate significant levels of accumulated savings in preparation for a return home. Finally, much of the geographical specificity of remittance-data can be misleading as it is common to route-remittances through correspondent-banks in the US, which thus appears to be a larger source of remittance-flows than it actually is.

104. World Bank 2009, p. 136.

of Sri Lanka's population is dependent on remittance-flows and 60 per cent of these flows come from the Middle-East region.[105] In the Philippines, remittance-income during the first quarter of 2009 compared to the same period in 2008 dropped 53 per cent for Kuwait, 10 per cent for Bahrain, and 2 per cent for the UAE.[106] In Bangladesh, remittances from the country's most important labour-destination, Saudi Arabia, dropped by 6 per cent from January to June 2009.

Concurrently with this displacement of crisis, there is a clear trend towards the centralisation and concentration of capital, most specifically within the finance-circuit. The local financial press and prominent government-spokespeople have urged banks and financial companies to merge in order to maintain adequate capitalisation. This is particularly the case in the UAE, where commercial banks were reliant upon high levels of external borrowing to finance real-estate and other projects.[107] Indeed, early 2009 saw the formation of the region's largest bank – Emirates National Bank of Dubai – born from the merger of Emirates Bank International and the National Bank of Dubai. Consolidation is also happening in other GCC-markets through share-swaps that merge conventional banks with those that offer Islamic banking.[108]

Centralisation and concentration is also occurring across Gulf-borders. In August 2008, Qatar National Bank – Qatar's largest bank with 47 per cent of the country's total bank-assets – acquired a 24 per cent stake in the Commercial Bank of Dubai, one of the ten largest banks in the UAE. The Commercial Bank of Qatar has also recently acquired the UAE-based United Arab Bank. These trends of internationalisation in the finance-circuit look set to continue under the pressure of the crisis.[109]

105. Central Bank of Sri Lanka, Annual Report 2008, Special Statistical Appendix, table 82.

106. Figures from the Central Bank of the Philippines, <http://www.bsp.gov.ph/>.

107. The Institute of International Finance estimates that international banks were providing between 20 and 50 per cent of the Gulf region's project-financing. Reliance on these loans was particularly evident in Dubai and Qatar (*Institute of International Finance* 2008, p. 8).

108. For example, Bahrain's BBK looks likely to merge with Shamil Bank and, in Kuwait, the National Bank of Kuwait recently gained central-bank approval to acquire 40 per cent of Boubyan Bank in order to gain access to the latter's Islamic banking capacities (Chawdry 2009, p. 46).

109. A manager of the Bahrain Islamic Bank has predicted the market would soon see: '... the emergence of the first true cross-GCC banking brand. This hasn't happened yet because there is still a mindset that banks are national assets, a thought process which takes time or an extraordinary environment (such as the present global financial crisis) to change.' Chawdry 2009, p. 47.

The deepening of internationalisation-tendencies is also seen in the productive circuit. Despite the cancellation or postponement of around half of the planned 'mega-projects' in the Gulf, the size of the project-market for the next five years is still very significant at an estimated US$1 trillion (about the equivalent of the combined GDP of GCC-economies in 2008).[110] With the weakening of the UAE construction-market (in particular Dubai), Gulf construction-companies are placing their hopes on Saudi Arabia as their next major accumulation-zone. The Saudi construction-market has now eclipsed the UAE as the core project-base in the GCC.[111] Indeed, leading UAE-based construction-companies have formed joint-ventures in Saudi Arabia to capitalise on the expected upturn in project-financing in the Saudi kingdom.[112] While arguably optimistic, this cross-border response to the economic crisis is indicative of the way in which accumulation in the productive circuit is conceived by the leading capital-groups from the perspective of the regional scale.

4. Conclusion: political implications

In the final analysis, the development of *khaleeji*-capital reflects the increasingly significant position and weight of the Gulf-region within the broader global capitalist economy. This process of class-formation has been underpinned by the development of the GCC and its re-territorialisation of economic and political power. The GCC regional integration-project has acted to facilitate the internationalisation of the Gulf-circuits and represents the development of a zone of accumulation interlaced with advanced capitalism.

The development of *khaleeji*-capital within these global hierarchies explains the conscious attempts to atomise and fracture potential regional rivals such

110. The Institute of International Finance 2008, p. 13.

111. In 2005, the UAE's construction-contracts were worth over 10 times that of Saudi Arabia ($28.7 billion compared to $2.4 billion). By the first three months of 2009, Saudi construction-contracts were worth $15.7 billion compared to the UAE's $4.1 billion. (*Middle East Economic Digest* 2009a, p. 21).

112. The CEO of Arabtec, one of the largest construction companies in the UAE, noted recently, 'We're making the necessary arrangements to mobilise for our first project in Saudi Arabia immediately... we haven't laid any labour off here in the UAE. They may go home as projects draw to a close, but we will redeploy thousands to Saudi Arabia ... [Saudi Arabia's construction market] can compensate for a drop in works in the UAE' (quoted in *Property Weekly* 2009, p. 6). Arabtec has formed a joint-venture with the Saudi Binladin Group and hopes to generate over US$1 billion from projects in Saudi Arabia over the next three years, *Middle East Economic Digest* 2009b, p. 20.

as Iraq and Iran. The critical difference between Iraq, Iran and the GCC-countries lies in the nature of their productive circuits. Iraq and Iran both depend upon domestic working classes for the production of hydrocarbons and other productive activities (regardless of the nature of their governing régimes). In contrast, the Gulf-countries' overwhelming reliance upon migrant-labour means that the potential threat presented by the working classes to régime-stability is much more remote. Class-formation in the Gulf has evolved in such a manner that it protects both the interests of a tiny layer of Gulf-capitalism (based on the broader social layer of citizenry in the Gulf) and the global hierarchies that it has been so central in constituting. The political cleavages in the Gulf-countries have come from inter-élite discord (such as between different branches of the ruling family, the conflict between religious *Ulama* and the monarchy) or Islamist movements based upon the petite bourgeoisie. As the response to the global financial crisis confirms, it is difficult to imagine that régime-stability would be threatened by migrant-labour open to deportation at the slightest evidence of discontent. This system of control has been further consolidated by the shifting of migrant labour-flows away from Arab countries towards the Indian sub-continent. In this sense, the formation of *khaleeji*-capital is directly dependent upon the subordination and exploitation of temporary migrant-workers from outside the Middle East.

This has important ramifications for left political strategy in these countries. In contrast to common academic arguments, the GCC is neither a neutral project of Arab unity nor a defensive response by jittery Gulf-monarchies to threats from neighbouring countries such as Iran. As a constituting force in the hierarchies of the world-economy, the Gulf-circuits of capital are tightly integrated with value-flows at the global level. They have thereby become central to the stability of global capitalism – underpinning the dominance of US-capitalism within the overall system – and will be essential to the re-configuration of capitalist power in the wake of the financial crisis. The formation of *khaleeji*-capital signifies, therefore, an internationalising Gulf-class whose outlook is deeply implicated in the future fortunes of the world-market. It will be key to the form that imperialism's domination of the Middle-East region takes in the future – including the rise of any potential challenger to US-power.

Khaleeji-capital is enriched through its specific position within this process. This class draws its profits from the very deep exploitation of non-citizen labour and its own regional and international export of capital. The nature of this accumulation and the régimes that support it are counterposed to the interests of the vast majority in the region and, for that reason, depend upon extensive foreign political and military protection (it is in this sense that the GCC can be thought of as a 'security'-agreement). As a reconfiguration of state-structures, the GCC aims to strengthen the position of this class-information against the general interests of the region's popular classes.

The development of *khaleeji*-capital also has profound implications beyond the Gulf-region. Precisely because of the internationalisation-tendencies that underlie the development of *khaleeji*-capital, all Arab social formations are being penetrated by these capital-groups. Some sense of this has been noted above, but more in-depth empirical investigations of the configuration of capitalist classes in places such as Jordan, Syria, Egypt and the West Bank/Gaza Strip is needed. This implies a reinterpretation of the nature of prominent capitalists throughout the region who are not generally considered part of 'the Gulf' (e.g. the Hariri Group of Lebanon or the Masri Group of Jordan/Palestine) but whose primary base of accumulation nevertheless takes place in the countries of the GCC. These groups should perhaps be considered as part of *khaleeji*-capital rather than viewed as 'Lebanese', 'Egyptian', 'Palestinian' and so forth.

Further afield, the internationalisation of *khaleeji*-capital has involved considerable capital-outflows to other areas of the world. GCC-countries accounted for 94 per cent of the entire West-Asia region's FDI outflows in 2007 (around US$41 billion).[113] This process has deepened alongside the financial crisis, as Gulf-investors have taken advantage of their accumulated surpluses and dropping asset prices. While much of these flows continue to go to the US and other advanced-capitalist markets, the Institute of International Finance estimates that over 20 per cent of Gulf capital-outflows went to the Middle East, North Africa and Asia in the 2002–6 period.[114] These flows require further investigation and a reassessment of the Gulf's position in the region – *khaleeji*-capital, for example, has been a major beneficiary of the US-occupation of Iraq and the investment-opportunities now opening up in that country.[115] Gulf-purchases of prime agricultural land across Latin America, Africa and Asia has provoked anger as food-exports are earmarked for the Gulf while domestic farmers lose their land and hunger remains rampant.[116]

---

113. United Nations Conference on Trade and Development 2007, p. 55.

114. The Institute of International Finance 2007, p. 10.

115. Gulf oil- and gas-companies have been awarded access to hydrocarbon-resources in Northern Iraq, a consortium of Qatari and Kuwaiti capital control three of Iraq's mobile-phone operating licences, and the Saudi giant SABIC is closely examining petrochemical projects in the country (Smith 2009, p. 46). The Iraqi banking system is also dominated by *khaleeji*-capital.

116. Blanche 2009, p. 10.

The GCC is thus principally a project of class-formation that has ever-more closely tied a section of the Arab world to the US-led reconfiguration of the region. This is not to deny the saliency of inter-capitalist competition between the Gulf and foreign capital – reflected, for example, by the ongoing disputes in Kuwait over opening up the country's upstream oil-production to foreign investment – but to emphasise that this conflict takes place within a structure aligned with the overall interests of imperialism. Analytical clarity on the nature of the Gulf has political conclusions: the enrichment and growth of *khaleeji*-capital occurs precisely because the majority of the region remains oppressed and impoverished. To a very considerable extent, the future shape of global capitalism will depend on how this struggle plays out.

References

Albo, Gregory 2004, 'The Old and New Economics of Imperialism', in Leys and Panitch (eds.) 2004.

Almezel, M. and B. Bibbo 2007, 'GCC Enters New Market Era', *Gulf News*, 5 December.

APS Review Downstream Trends 2007, 'Kuwait – Energy Crisis', 22/28 May.

Arab Investment and Export Credit Guarantee Corporation 2007, 'Investment Climate in the Arab Countries – Executive Summary', available at: <http://www.iaigc.net/>.

Arabian Business 2009, 'News in Numbers', 10, 10: 13.

Baldwin, Hanson 1959, 'Oil Strategy in World War II', in *American Petroleum Institute Quarterly – Centennial Issue*, Washington DC.: American Petroleum Institute, available at: <http://www.oil150.com/essays/2007/08/oil-strategy-in-world-war-ii>.

Bekker, Vita 2009, 'Defense Spending Set to Hit $100bn by 2014', *The National*, 26 August: 10.

Bellamy-Foster, John 2003, 'The New Age of Imperialism', *Monthly Review*, 55, available at: <http://www.monthlyreview.org/0703jbf.htm>.

Bina, Cyrus 1989, 'Some Controversies in the Development of Rent Theory: The Nature of Oil Rent', *Capital and Class*, 39: 82–112.

Blanche, Ed 2009, 'Give Us this Day Our Daily Bread', *The Middle East*, February: 6–10.

Braun, Ursula 1988, 'The Gulf Cooperation Council's Security Role', in *The Arab Gulf and the Arab World*, edited by B. Pridham, London: Croom Helm.

Bromley, Simon 1991, *American Hegemony and World Oil*, Cambridge: Polity Press.

—— 2005, 'The United States and the Control of World Oil', *Government and Opposition*, 40, 2: 225–55.

Business Monitor International 2007a, 'Industry News – Bahrain to Launch First Offshore Round in May', 3 May.

Business Monitor International 2007b, 'Saudi Arabia Business Forecast Report; 2007 2nd Quarter'.

Callinicos, Alex 2005, 'Iraq: Fulcrum of World Politics', *Third World Quarterly*, 26, 4/5: 593–608.

Central Bank of Sri Lanka, *Annual Report 2008*, Special Statistical Appendix, at: <http://www.cbsl.gov.lk/pics_n_docs/10_pub/_docs/efr/annual_report/ar2008e/15.ar08_spe_appe_tables_e.pdf>.

Champion, Daryl 2003, *The Paradoxical Kingdom: Saudi Arabia and the Momentum of Reform*, New York: Columbia University Press.

Chapman, Keith 1991, *The International Petrochemical Industry: Evolution and Location*, Oxford: Blackwell.
Chaudry, Kiren 1997, *The Price of Wealth: Economies and Institutions in the Middle East*, New York: Cornell University Press.
Chawdry, Rohit 2009, 'GCC: The Banks Urge to Merge', *The Middle East*, February: 45–8.
Colliers International 2007, 'Dubai Real Estate Overview', at <http://www.dubaicityguide.com/realestate/images/Dubai%20Overview%20Q4%202007.pdf>.
Crystal, Jill 1995, *Oil and Politics in the Gulf: Rulers and Merchants in Kuwait and Qatar*, Cambridge: Cambridge University Press.
Ditcham, R. 2007, 'LuLu to Enter India with Mall in Kerala', *Gulf News*, 27 June.
Dun and Bradstreet 2008, 'UAE Private Equity Report', *Industry Perspectives*, Dubai.
Emirates Industrial Bank 2006, 'Expansion of the UAE Aluminium Industry', *Journal of the Emirates Industrial Bank*, 21, 6.
Economic and Social Commission for Western Asia 2001, *Economic Diversification in the Oil-Producing Countries: The Case of the Gulf Cooperation Council Economies*, New York: United Nations.
Fergany, Nader 2001, *Aspects of Labor Migration and Unemployment in the Arab Region*, Giza: Almishkat Center for Research.
Fine, Ben 1979, 'On Marx's Theory of Agricultural Rent', *Economy and Society*, 8, 3: 241–78.
Ford, Neil 2006, 'Marubeni Powers up in the Gulf', *The Middle East*, 1 December.
Fund Strategy 2006, 'Recycling Petrodollars Boosts Global Markets, Says Morgan Stanley', 11 December, available at: <http://www.fundstrategy.co.uk/news/recycling-petrodollars-boosts-global-markets-says-morgan-stanley/133846.article>.
Giannetti, Renato and Valentina Romei 2007, 'The Chemical Industry After World War II: A Quantitative Assessment', in *The Global Chemical Industry in the Age of the Petrochemical Revolution*, edited by Louis Galambos, Takashi Hikino and Vera Zamagni, Cambridge: Cambridge University Press.
Gibson, Heather 1989, *The Eurocurrency Markets, Domestic Financial Policy and the International Instability*, London: Macmillan.
Global Investment House 2006, 'The Rise of Private Equity', July, Kuwait: Global Investment House.
—— 2007a, 'Saudi Arabia Economic & Strategic Outlook: Building Cities to House Economic Growth', February, Kuwait: Global Investment House.
—— 2007b, 'Private Equity – Luring Regional and International Investors Alike', July, Kuwait: Global Investment House.
GN Financial Review 2009, 'GCC Banks', February.
Gowan, Peter 1999, *The Global Gamble: Washington's Faustian Bid for World Dominance*, London: Verso.
Grimmett, R. F. 2007, 'Conventional Arms Transfers to Developing Nations 1999–2006', at: <http://www.sipri.org/research/armaments/transfers/transparency/Other_sources2/CRS/CRS_DevNat_1999-06>.
Gulf Cooperation Council Secretariat-General 2001, 'The Economic Agreement Between the GCC States', at: <http://library.gcc-sg.org/English/Books/econagree2004.htm>.
Gulf Daily News 2007, "UK Exports to UAE Reach £3.6bn", July 15.
Gulf Venture Capital Association 2006, 'Annual Report: Private Equity and Venture Capital in the Middle East', UAE: GVCA.
Harvey, David 2003, *The New Imperialism*, Oxford: Oxford University Press.
Hanieh, Adam 2010, 'Temporary Migrant Labour and the Spatial Structuring of Class in the Gulf Cooperation Council', *Spectrum: Journal of Global Studies*, 1, 3.
Heins, Oliver 2007, 'A Race for Opportunities: Top 30 Grocery Retailers in Africa and the Middle East', *Planet Retail*, 201: 27–32 (June 28).

HSBC 2005, 'Cement Industry in the GCC', *Industry Research*, January, Dubai: HSBC.

Kapiszewski, Andrzej 2001, *National and Expatriates. Population and Labour Dilemmas of the GCC States*, Reading: Ithaca Press.

—— 2004, 'Arab Labour Migration to the GCC States', in *Arab Migration in a Globalized World*, Geneva: International Organization for Migration.

—— 2006, 'Arab vs. Asian Migrant Workers in the GCC Countries', report prepared for the *United Nations Expert Group Meeting on International Migration and Development in the Arab Region*, Beirut: Department of Economic and Social Affairs of the United Nations Secretariat, 15–17 May.

Katzman, Kenneth 2006, *The Persian Gulf States: Issues for U.S. Policy*, Washington DC.: Congressional Research Service, The Library of Congress.

Kazim, Aqil 2000, *The United Arab Emirates AD 600 to the Present: A Socio-Discursive Transformation in the Arabian Gulf*, Dubai: Gulf Book Centre.

Kechichian, Joseph 1990, 'The Gulf Cooperation Council and the Gulf War', in *The Persian Gulf War: Lessons for Strategy, Law and Diplomacy*, edited by Christopher C. Joyner, New York: Greenwood Press.

Khaleej Times 2009, 'Dubai Property Prices Plunge Up to 70pc', 30 March.

Klare, Michael 2002, *Resource Wars: The New Landscape of Global Conflict*, New York: Owl Books.

Kobrin, Stephen 1985, 'Diffusion as an Explanation of Oil Nationalization: Or the Domino Effect Rides Again', *The Journal of Conflict Resolution*, 29, 1: 3–32.

Leys, Colin and Leo Panitch (eds.) 2004, *Socialist Register 2004: The New Imperial Challenge*, London: Merlin.

Lubin, David 2007, 'Petrodollars, Emerging Markets and Vulnerability', *Economic and Market Analysis*, 19 March, London: Citigroup.

Mandel, Ernest 1975, *Late Capitalism*, London: Verso.

Marschall, Christin 2003, *Iran's Persian Gulf Policy: From Khomeini to Khatami*, London: Routledge.

Marx, Karl 1990 [1867], *Capital*, Volume 1, Harmondsworth: Penguin.

McNally, David 1981, 'Staples Theory as Commodity Fetishism: Marx, Innis and Canadian Political Economy', *Studies in Political Economy*, 6: 35–64.

Middle East Economic Digest 2006, 'The $1 Trillion Project Market', 21 April.

—— 2007, 'Taking a Turn at the Top', *MEED Projects Contractor Survey*, 15 June.

—— 2009a, '2009 Political Turmoil Threatens Megaprojects', 20–6 March.

—— 2009b, 'Contractors Focus on Saudi Arabia', 20–6 March.

—— 2009c, 'Downturn Eases Supply Shortage', 20–6 March.

—— 2009d, 'Dubai Reviews Plans as Population Falls', 20–6 March.

—— 2009e, 'Building an Industry: Aluminium's Place at the Heart of the GCC Economy', 12–18 June.

Mohieldin, Mahmoud 2008,'Neighborly Investments', *Finance and Development*, 45, 4, available at: <http://www.imf.org/external/pubs/ft/fandd/2008/12/pdf/mohieldin.pdf>.

Murray, Robin 1971, 'The Internationalization of Capital and the Nation State', *New Left Review*, I, 67: 84–109.

Nakhleh, Emile 1986, *The Gulf Cooperation. Council: Policies, Problems and Prospects*, New York: Praeger.

Niblock, Tim 2006, *Saudi Arabia: Power, Legitimacy and Survival*, London: Routledge.

Oil and Gas Directory 2007, Dubai: Dar Al Fajr Group.

Painter, David 1984, 'Oil and the Marshall Plan', *Business History Review*, 58: 359–83.

Palloix, Christian 1975, 'The Internationalisation of Capital and the Circuit of Social Capital', in *International Firms and Modern Imperialism: Selected Readings*, edited by H. Radice, Hammondsworth: Penguin.

—— 1977, 'Conceptualizing the Internationalization of Capital', *Review of Radical Political Economics*, 9: 17–28.

Panitch, Leo 1994, 'Globalization and the State', in *Socialist Register 1994: Between Globalism and Nationalism*, edited by L. Panitch and R. Miliband, London: Merlin.

Panitch, Leo and Sam Gindin 2004, 'Global Capitalism and American Empire', in Leys and Panitch (eds.) 2004.

Peterson, Erik 1988, *The Gulf Cooperation Council: Search for Unity in a Dynamic Region*, Boulder: Westview Press.

Platts 2007, 'GCC Set to Claim 10% Share of World's Aluminium Output by 2010', *Platts Commodity News*, 16 May.

Rahman, Saifur 2006, 'Dubai Represents 23% of Gulf's Retail Sector', *Gulf News*, 18 April.

Ramazani, Rouhollah 1988, *The Gulf Cooperation Council: Records and Analysis*, Charlottesville: University of Virginia.

Roach, Stephen 2005, 'The Case of the Missing Petro-Dollars', at: <http://www.morganstanley.com/views/gef/archive/2005/20051128-Mon.html>.

Said-Zahlan, Rosemarie 1998, *The Making of the Modern Gulf States*, Reading: Garnet Publishing.

Saudi Arabian General Investment Authority 2007, Annual Report, SAGIA.

Setser, Brad and Rachel Ziemba 2006, 'Petrodollar Watch: October 2006', Roubini Global Economics, available at: <http://www.rgemonitor.com>.

Shah, M. 2006, 'Restrictive Labour Immigration Policies in the Oil-Rich Gulf: Effectiveness and Implications for Sending Asian Countries', paper presented to the United Nations Expert Group Meeting on Social and Economic Implications of Changing Population Age Structure, Mexico City, 31 August–2 September 2005.

Shamsi, Mohammed 2006, *Ta'qiym siyassay al hijra f'il dawla majlis attawan alkhaleeji* [*Evaluation of Labour Policies in the GCC*], report prepared for the United Nations Expert Group Meeting on International Migration and Development in the Arab Region, Beirut: Department of Economic and Social Affairs of the United Nations Secretariat, 5 May.

Sherbiny, Naiem 1985, *Oil and the Internationalisation of Arab Banks*, Oxford: Oxford Institute for Energy Studies.

Smith, Pamela 2009, 'Iraq Woos Big Oil Players... On its Own Terms', *The Middle East*, March: 44–6.

Solh, Karim 2008a, 'The Emergence of Regional and Global Investment Leaders out of Abu Dhabi', paper presented on behalf of Gulf Capital to the Abu Dhabi Economic Forum 2008, Emirates Palace, Abu Dhabi, 3–4 February 2008.

—— 2008b, 'Making International PE Models Work in the Middle East', paper presented on behalf of Gulf Capital to the Middle East Private Equity Conference, Park Hyatt, Dubai, 15–16 January.

Spiro, David 1999, *The Hidden Hand of American Hegemony Petrodollar Recycling and International Markets*, Ithaca: Cornell University Press.

Spitz, Peter 1988, *Petrochemicals: The Rise of an Industry*, New York: John Wiley.

Stokes, Doug 2007, 'Blood for Oil? Global Capital, Counter-Insurgency and the Dual Logic of American Energy Security', *Review of International Studies*, 33: 245–64.

Stork, Joe 1975, 'US Strategy in the Gulf', *MERIP Reports*, April: 17–28.

—— 1980, 'The Carter Doctrine and US Bases in the Middle East', *MERIP Reports*, September: 3–14, 32.

Sturm, Michael and Nikolaus Siegfried 2005, 'Regional Monetary Integration in the Member States of the Gulf Cooperation Council', at: <http://www.ecb.europa.eu/pub/pdf/scpops/ecbocp31.pdf>.

The Financial Express 2009, 'Travel Trade in Jeopardy as Manpower Export Falls', April 21.

The Institute of International Finance 2007, 'Gulf Cooperation Council Economic Report', 16 January.

—— 2008, 'Gulf Cooperation Council Regional Report', 6 November.

Thomson, Simon 2006, 'Year of the Hypermarket', *RetailME*, January/February: 49–59.

Timewell, Stephen 2006, 'Top 100 Arab Banks – Saudis Remain Unmatched', *The Banker*, November 1.

Tolui, R. 2007, 'Petrodollars, Asset Prices, and the Global Financial System', in *Capital Perspectives*, Newport Beach: PIMCO.

United Arab Emirates Yearbook 2006, London: Trident Press, available at: <http://www.uaeinteract.com/uaeint_misc/pdf_2006/index.asp>.

United Nations Conference on Trade and Development 2007, *World Investment Report 2007*, Geneva: United Nations.

Vassiliev, Alexei 1998, *The History of Saudi Arabia*, London: Saqi Books.

Vitalis, Robert 2007, *America's Kingdom: Mythmaking on the Saudi Oil Frontier*, Stanford: Stanford University Press.

Walt, Stephen 1987, *The Origin of Alliances*, New York: Ithaca.

Walter, Nicole 2009, 'Arabetc Won't Put All Eggs in the UAE Basket', *Property Weekly*, 18 March.

White and Case 2004, 'White & Case Closes Largest Ever Energy Financing', available at: <http://www.whitecase.com/news/detail.aspx?news=632>.

Wilson, Rodney 1983, *Banking and Finance in the Arab Middle East*, New York: St Martin's Press.

—— 1987, 'Financial Development of the Arab Gulf: The Eastern Bank Experience, 1917–1950', *Business History*, 29, 2: 178–98.

World Bank 2009, *Global Development Finance Report 2009*, Washington DC.: World Bank Group.

BRILL

Historical Materialism 18 (2010) 77–96

historical materialism
research in critical marxist theory
brill.nl/hima

Art After Deskilling*

John Roberts
University of Wolverhampton
jorob128@aol.com

Abstract

The absence of would-be palpable skills in contemporary and modern art has become a commonplace of both conservative and radical art-criticism. Indeed, these criticisms have tended to define where the critic stands in relation to the critique of authorship and the limits of 'expression' at the centre of the modernist experience. In this article, I am less interested in why these criticisms take the form they do – this is a matter for ideology-critique and the sociology of criticism and audiences – than in the analysis of the radical transformation of conceptions in artistic skill and craft in the modern period. This will necessitate a focus on modernism and the avant-garde, and after, as it comes into alignment with, and retreat from, the modern forces of production and means of reproduction. Much, of course, has been written within the histories of modernism, and the histories of art since, on this process of confrontation and exchange – that is, between modern art's perceived hard-won autonomy and the increasing alienation of the artist, and the reification of art under the new social and technological conditions of advanced capitalist competition – little, however, has been written on the transformed conditions and understanding of labour in the artwork itself (with the partial exception of Adorno). This is because so little art-history and art-criticism – certainly since the 1960s – has been framed explicitly within a labour-theory of culture: in what ways do artists labour, and how are these forms of labour indexed to art's relationship to the development of general social technique (the advanced level of technology and science as it expressed in the technical conditions of social reproducibility)? In this article, I look at the modern and contemporary dynamics of this question.

Keywords

Skill, deskilling, avant-garde, modernism, readymade, productive labour, artistic labour, value, autonomy, negation, asociality

The idea that there is an absence of discernible skill in contemporary art is something of a commonplace. Indeed, attacks on the skill of the modern artist

* A version of this article was delivered at the Universities of Wolverhampton, Middlesex, and Aarhus, in November 2008, and at the Maryland Institute College of Art, in July 2009. I would like to thank students and staff of these institutions for their comments, and also the comments of the four anonymous referees for *Historical Materialism*.

DOI: 10.1163/156920610X512444

have accompanied the emergence of art in the modern period from Jacques-Louis David onward, and, as such, are indivisible from the origins of modernism as such. In this article, I am less interested in why this should be so – that is a matter for ideological critique and the sociology of audiences – than in the analysis of the radical transformation of conceptions in artistic skill and craft in the modern period. This will necessitate a focus on modernism and the avant-garde, and after, as it comes into alignment with, and retreat from, the modern forces of production and means of reproduction. Much, of course, has been written within the histories of modernism, and the histories of art since, on this process of confrontation and exchange, that is, between modern art's perceived hard-won autonomy and the increasing alienation of the artist, and the reification of art under the new social and technological conditions of advanced capitalist competition. Little, however, has been written on the transformed conditions and understanding of labour in the artwork itself.[1] This is because so little art-history and art-criticism – certainly since the 1960s – has been framed explicitly within a labour-theory of culture: in what ways do artists labour, and how are these forms of labour indexed to art's relationship to the development of general social technique (the advanced level of technology and science as it is expressed in the technical conditions of social reproducibility)? The notion of art as embedded in a prevailing set of technical and social relations – and that art reproduces, subverts or resists – was particularly acute as an issue in the second half of nineteenth century in Europe. This is because the new capitalist social conditions challenged advanced artists to think of themselves as newly modern outside of the prevailing and long-standing academic institutional arrangements, and therefore, as engaged in defining themselves as other to what was seen as holding the artist back technically: a bourgeois academy and culture harnessed to modes of *retardataire* production that fundamentally *de*-subjectivised art and as such de-linked its forms from the appearances of the contemporary world. In this sense, late nineteenth-century European capitalism does not just provide 'new modern subjects' for the artist, but, crucially, transforms the *affective* space in which artists produce their work – how artists materially constitute the problem of representation – and, as such, how their works are received, transforming the questions of artistic value itself. As advanced modernist artists seek to define and resist what they see as their threatened or marginal cultural status, the priority – the *modernist* priority – becomes: *how, with what materials, and to what ends* does the artist labour?

1. The exception being Theodor Adorno. See Adorno 1984. See also Roberts 2007b.

We see this affective and technical shift paradigmatically in the crisis around painterly craft in French modernism between 1848 and 1880. Both Gustave Courbet and Édouard Manet open up painting to new forms of painterly affect that were at odds with the academy and salon. Both artists embraced, in different registers, a 'semi-disorganised' pictorialism, the representation of divers themes and non-bourgeois types, and an indifference to the coherent modelling of form and the production of convincing illusion. Indeed, Courbet and Manet were soon castigated for what was taken to be their formal inchoateness, and lack of technique or *facilité*.[2] In Manet's case, much was made of what appeared to be the incorrigible awkwardness or mis-positioning of his figures, and in the case, famously, of *Olympia* (1863), of allowing a proletarian figure – a naked prostitute – to directly address the bourgeois (male) spectator.[3] For the academic critics of Courbet and Manet, there was good reason for these criticisms: Courbet and Manet's major pictures were, when compared with official canons of taste and aesthetic propriety, undoubtedly ugly, technically deflationary and fragmented. But, of course, few writers and commentators in the 1850s, 1860s and 1870s theorised why this was the case, because few were able to grasp the emerging connection between the development of new forms and technical effects in painting and the demand that art distinguish its interests from those of its patrons, be they state or private. In other words, this is the moment – as artists begin to define their interests in open opposition to the academy and salon – when a gap opens up between art as a bourgeois *profession* – like law or medicine – and its nascent, undefined, unofficial social role as a critic of bourgeois culture.[4] Artists were faced with a crucial choice, then: to continue to throw their lot in with the official culture and its traditional (although weakening) forms of patronage – and, as a consequence, see their art suffer – or work independently in alliance with the newly-emergent private market for art, in order to defend and continue the possibility of the achievements of the past. But, in making

2. For an extended discussion of modernism and *facilité*, see Roberts 2008.
3. See Clark 1984.
4. The critical function of art, of course, does not begin with modernism – even during the Renaissance, the highpoint of state-patronage, artists used art to challenge the authority of their clients. But these moments were invariably moments of individual honour – of hurt pride and revenge – and not attached to a critique of the state or its artistic institutions. Indeed, it would have been incomprehensible for any artist to criticise his patrons on these grounds; for the making of art and of its meanings was a direct extension of the power bequeathed to the artist by those who ruled. With the rise of capitalism, and the emergence of an independent market for art and, as such, the emergence of the independent professionalisation of the artist (a professionalism at odds with the academy and with state-patronage), this direct transmission-belt between ruler and artist is broken.

this break in order to defend the achievements of the past, modernist artists realised they could not rely *on* the achievements of the past. Indeed, artists realised that the emergence of the modern in art required that artists distance themselves from, or revoke, the sureties of artistic tradition.

Consequently, for the first time, artists who sought to define themselves as modern were presented with an unprecedented challenge: in order to defend art and its future, the artist had to first distinguish himself or herself from what the official culture *does to art* in the name of value, quality and tradition (that is, invariably, reduce it to a form of decoration, a social irrelevance, or a self-aggrandising adjunct of the artist and client's social status). Crucial to this modernising move, therefore, is a sense that the inherited languages of academic painting (broadly neo-classicising) are languages of authority and stability, and, as such, inadequate to the representation of new forms of artistic subjectivity demanded by a newly-industrialising, capitalist culture; as Baudelaire was to suggest, in one of the first critical recognitions of this as an emerging problem for art, the need for a new kind of painting – a 'painting of modern life' as he called it[5] – is profoundly at odds with the would-be harmonising spirit, equitable social bonds and idealising charm of classical culture. Accordingly, the great requirement of the modernising artist of this period is the exteriorisation of affect: how do I paint convincing images that express the truth of what it is like to live under these new conditions? As a result, painterly technique becomes a highly contentious matter in the bid for non-academic status and value; technique, it is asserted, is not a neutral skill, something transmittable down the ages, but, rather, historically contingent, and therefore inseparable from the demands of artistic subjectivity and the artist's *mode of vision*. Questioning inherited technique then became a means of questioning the link between academic technique and form in official or salon-painting.

One writer and philosopher during the latter part of the modernist revolution who recognises that art is on a new course is Friedrich Nietzsche. Writing in the 1870s, in his collection *Untimely Meditations*, he argues that the attacks on modern art produce a monumentalism of the past that blocks off the problems, divisions and hiatuses of the present. Because the 'contemporary is not yet monumental, [modern art] seems to them [the official guardians of culture] unnecessary, unattractive and lacking in the authority conferred by history'.[6] The purported defence of tradition against 'relativism' is not so much a defence of quality, as an attack on art *tout court*. 'They

5. Baudelaire 1981.
6. Nietzsche 1997, p. 72.

are connoisseurs of art because they would like to do away with art altogether', he declares.[7] Now, there are clear affinities between Nietzsche here and Baudelaire's writing on the 'painting of modern life': both seek to define art in an active and futural sense. But what Nietzsche introduces is something more profound: the recognition that, under the dissociation of art and artist from the stability and assurances of tradition, the artist has to struggle to assert himself in defiance of tradition. As such, the determining framework of art is of necessity that of negation – of past art, of artistic tradition itself. The modern artist does not just inherit and transform tradition, but is compelled to shatter it, blast it apart, remake it, and as such remake it again. This introduces into the domain of art and art-theory a new relationship between the production of artistic form and artistic judgement. If the transmission of artistic technique is not stable, and, as such, subject to adaptation and reinscription, then artistic form is not able to be assessed from any normative standpoint. Indeed, a reversal of judgement takes place: rather than the spectator adjudicating a work on the grounds of how well it matches or surpasses inherited technique, the assessment of value is based on how well the work, in its creation of new forms, withdraws from, and adulterates, inherited technique. In this sense, Courbet and Manet's negation of inherited technique introduces into modernist painting what we might call a *deflationary logic*, that was to stretch to Picasso and on to Jackson Pollock. The inherited techniques and forms of naturalism and realism are submitted to a radical process of denaturalisation, abstraction and formalisation.

This is the familiar grand narrative of modernism from 1850 to 1950, in which the 'making of the new', in Nietzsche's vision, testifies to the continuous unfolding of painterly achievement and technical reassessment. Moving through Courbet, Manet, Cézanne, Van Gogh, Derain, Picasso, Braque, Miro, Frankenthaler, Rothko and Pollock, modernist painting demonstrates an extraordinary capacity for immanent self-definition and formal transformation. But, confined to painting, this model of negation is itself haunted by its own, and more fundamental negation: namely, the rejection of art's confinement to painterly form and painterly technique as such. Indeed, the confinement of the 'making of the new' to painting begins to break down by the time of cubism and of Picasso's and Braque's paper-collages. For, in the shift from the painterly proto-cubism of Picasso's *Les Demoiselles d'Avignon* (1907) to the cubist paper-collages of the 1910s we see the beginning of the deflation of painterly modernist deflation itself. Thus, when Picasso and Braque introduced collaged elements into the space of painting in, respectively, *Glass, Guitar and*

7. Ibid.

Newspaper (1912) and *Le Quotidian* (1913), the content of modernist negation in art changes; by incorporating found mass-printed materials such as newspaper-mastheads, into these paper-collages, the deflationary logic of modernist anti-classicism is for the first time positioned *against* painting. That is, the introduction of non-painterly elements into the space of painting places modernism's strategies of negation in opposition to the aesthetic self-containment of painting. As a result, artistic deflation becomes embodied in a radical re-orientation and expansion of artistic skill: the introduction of the readymade into painting links negation for the first time to the development of non-artistic techniques, such as collage and assemblage. In turn, the measure of artistic competence shifts from the distribution of painterly marks to the positioning, arranging and conjunction of pre-given elements and prefabricated forms. Now, this compositional shift is very familiar from the histories of modernism.[8] But what is rarely commented upon is the cultural character of this shift.

With the move to a deflationary logic *outside* of painting, the competence of the artist also changes. By breaking and interrupting the surface of the painting – by reaching *into* the space of painting – the artist signals that painting is now historically 'in the way' of art's technical demands, so to speak. That is, what Picasso and Braque introduce in their paper-collages is the notion that paintings – and therefore art – can be made and accomplished without carrying through painting as an *aesthetically-bounded totality*. Paintings can be made of alien, non-painterly, non-artistic things, and consequently can be made with very little labour. Or, rather, painting can easily incorporate non-painterly things without failing as paintings, or as autonomous aesthetic objects.

This objectification of art's deflationary logic in the form of the introduction of the readymade into the artwork is what represents the great seismic shift of twentieth-century art. Modernist art's negations are now directed not just at destabilising the genres and conventions of painting, but demolishing the formal hierarchy in which painting is itself positioned and embedded.[9] Art's negations are now located in tension with, and in opposition to, the tradition of painting itself.

It is Marcel Duchamp, of course, who is the first artist to systematise this shift through the readymade, providing the ground-rules for the deflationary strategies of twentieth-century art. In *Bottlerack* (1914), *In Advance of a Broken Arm* (1915) and *Fountain* (1917) – what he referred to as 'unassisted'

8. See, for example, Krauss 1986.

9. For a discussion of the relations between modernist painting and the readymade, see De Duve 1996 and Joselit 1998.

readymades – he places the readymade outside of the supportive frame of the painting. In this respect, he locates artistic meaning in the act of deliberation. By locating meaning in the aesthetically-chosen found object (that is, the object of artistic discrimination) the artist is no longer bound to the expressive demands of covering a given surface or modelling a given material, but, rather, to the intellectual demands of re-contextualising extant objects in order to change their sign-value. Thus, what is important about Duchamp's early readymades is that they reorder the way hand and eye have, traditionally, determined the form and content of art. The Duchampian readymade disperses the hand and eye to a world of signifiers and materials that require forms of mapping, superimposition and coordination. 'It is a kind of rendezvous', Duchamp said of this function of the readymade.[10] The immediate outcome of this shift is that the deflationary content of art is subject to the thoroughgoing dismantling of the metaphysics of the hand, of handicraft, of the handmade. If the post-cubist painter is compelled to place something into the space of the painting in order to render that space more believable as a painting, the Duchampian artist is free to place any object in any art context (or non-art context) without relying on the organisational discipline of the expressive hand. The production of meaning as the act of placing and arranging becomes fundamentally *indeterminate* in this sense: any readymade, anywhere might have meaning.

Thus, if, in the post-cubist painting, hand and eye are no longer constrained by the dictates of bringing coherence to an orderly progression of mark-making, in the work of the Duchampian artist, this freedom is limitless. This means that the readymade's deflationary logic invites more than a critique of painting's circumscribed sense of artistic craft. Duchampian deflation stands not simply as a negation of the status of painting, but as an actual *extension* of the artist's skills and competences. As Duchamp's notion of the 'rendezvous' suggests, the superimposition and reorganisation of extant forms and materials opens up the category of art to non-artistic technical skills from other cultural, cognitive, practical and theoretical domains: film, photography, architecture, literature, philosophy and science. Indeed, if art is a site of many different disciplines, materials, and theoretical frameworks, art can be made quite literally from *anything*.

Essentially, the Duchampian deflation of painting is the point where modernism's 'make it new' is brought into conjunction with a wider set of historical pressures: the requirement of art to enter the modern division of labour, and align itself with the transformed technical base of twentieth-century mass-production and reproduction. In this sense, in the passage from

10. Duchamp 1975, p. 32.

painting to the readymade, the artist exchanges inherited artisanal skills for an executive role (the directing and organisation of forms and materials produced by others) or a technical role (the use or manipulation of a given technology, as in photography) or, of course, both. As a result, the artist is no longer beholden to actually physically produce her work at all; indeed, in moving from the artisanal to the machino-technical, the artist is able to devolve the work to others, perhaps submitting plans or ideas to specialist technicians for them to execute, or working in collaboration with other artists and technicians as part of an extended division of labour (as in the printing of photographs). But, in 1923, this is precisely what Laszlo Moholy-Nagy did when he ordered three, enamel-covered steel plates from a Berlin sign-factory, which he then duly exhibited under his own name. Known as the 'telephone-pictures', he dictated his instructions for their production over the phone to a foreman, using, as his wife Sibyl Moholy-Nagy writes, a 'color chart and an order blank of graph paper to specify the location of form elements and their exact hue'.[11] In these terms, the artistic act here functions as a form of surrogacy: the artist adopts a conceptualising role, directing the labour and technical accomplishments of others, without actually directly manipulating any materials himself.

There is, of course, nothing historically novel in art about art's place in an extended division of labour. In the pre-Renaissance and Renaissance workshop-system, the workshop-master hired apprentices and wage-labourers to collectively produce works in the name of the workshop, and later in the name of the independent artist.[12] But, under modernism and the avant-garde, and

11. Moholy-Nagy 1969, p. 31.

12. Cennini 1954. This anonymous collective production was mitigated in the workshop by the encouragement of the all-round development of the apprentice and the trained craftsman. In the fourteenth, fifteenth and early-sixteenth centuries, the workshop-artisan had to be skilled in a wide variety of painterly, carving, woodworking and metalworking skills, from casting medals and constructing caskets and chests to painting in tempera and painting frescoes. With the mercantile and ecclesiastical rise of Florence and Rome and the birth of the large private commission, in conjunction with the development of a new model of the artist based on the importance of the concept of drawing from life (to distinguish it from the artisan's working-to-order), this wide skill-base breaks down. That is, with the arrival of the independent artist and the model of *disegno* – the close working from the particulars of nature, by the artist – the workshop has to adapt to the demands of the individual artist rather than the workshop-master's multiple tasks. The result is that the old workshop skill-base is divested of its collective integrity (the apprentices finishing various tasks and completing different processes for the workshop-master as interdependent parts of creative whole), to be given over in support of the 'revealed creation' of the independent artist who, increasingly, is commissioned by court and ecclesiastical authorities, in his own right as an artist, and as such where and when possible seeks to complete the majority of the work himself, and without tutoring apprentices in the process. The diversified skill-base of the workshop, then, becomes subordinate to the commercial dictates of the

the general subordination of craft to general social technique under capitalism, an ideological reversal takes place. Art's place in the social division of labour is increasingly exercised as a critique of the social and cultural division that distances art from 'mere' technique and 'mere' craft. That is, art's place within the social division of labour is no longer the thing that art desires to escape from in the name of the 'revealed creation' of the independent artist, but, is, rather, the site of art's democratic horizons and indebtedness to the collective labour of others. This is because, as I outlined in my introduction, the artist is increasingly forced to measure her own creativity and skills up against her diminished social status under the new market- and social conditions, thereby bringing the ideology of 'revealed creativity' under some kind of critical scrutiny. Indeed, by opening up a gap between the prevailing skills of the academy and the salon, and the need for new skills, this distinction becomes constitutive of how the artist negotiates this loss. That is, certain skills and effects become identifiable *with* inherited cultural power (such as unnecessary ornateness and intricacy, and metaphysical atmospherics and vagaries) and others with an exemplary distance *from* this power (clarity and directness of form and social relationships and an 'unfinished' quality). It is not surprising, therefore, that these 'democratic' effects becomes associated with various anti-bourgeois and progressive functions. Consequently, subsequent to the rejection of received *facilité* in early French modernism, there is an increasing identification between the artistic labour demanded of the representation of 'modern life' and the perceived straightforwardness and honesty of ordinary manual labour,[13] which, after the Russian avant-garde, becomes a flood, as the artist adopts the democratic identity of the technician as a political and self-conscious act.

Duchamp's 'unassisted' readymades and Moholy-Nagy's 'telephone-' – paintings' appropriation of the labour of others, therefore, are a direct provocation to traditional notions of artistic creativity weakened by the artist's loss of social position. By transparently presenting the labour of others as their 'own', Duchamp and Moholy-Nagy deliberately downgrade their own authorial status as artists. And this, precisely, is what was meant in the 1920s and 1930s by the designation 'artist-as-technician'. As one part of an extensive intellectual and technical division of labour, the skills of the artist are held to be of no more significance or value than those possessed by the labourers and

independent artist of exemplary distinction, transforming the workshop-apprentice, eventually, into a studio wage-labourer.

13. For a discussion of this identification in relation to the photographs of Eugène Atget, who was working in Paris directly in the aftermath of this French modernist critique of *facilité*, see Nesbit 1993.

technicians who produce the materials for the work's completion.[14] In fact, although the artist-as-technician and actual technician enter the production process at different points, they share a similar range of skills; they simply bring a different set of accomplishments to the process. This erosion of the distinction here between intellectual labour and manual labour, the creativity of the artist, and the routinised work of the labourer, then, represents more than a fantasy of egalitarianism on the part of artists, it proposes an actual shift in artistic practice. Moholy-Nagy and Duchamp are two of the many artists in the first decades of the twentieth century who, in rejecting the expressive-artisanal model of art, wanted a different account of what art might *do*, what the artist might *become*, and whom the work of art might be destined *for*.

This shift from the artisanal to the executive, nominative, and immaterial in art is the point where the post-Renaissance definition of artistic creativity as the autonomous and expressive rendition of craft-skill is finally destroyed; the deflation of painterly technique in modernist painting from 1850 to 1915 is, in this sense, an internal prefiguration of this crisis. In this respect, it is possible to trace the emergence of the modern artist under capitalism as comparable to the loss of the artisan and 'integral' creativity of labour within the labour-process. The rise of the post-artisanal labourer, through workshop, automated factory and office, parallels the decline of artisanal skill in artistic production; and this, of course, is what both Marx and William Morris generalise as being the overwhelming destiny of human capacities under capitalism: namely capitalism's general diminishment of all-round human creative powers in the interest of narrowly-defined categories of productive labour and free creativity; and, concomitantly, this is why Morris was so interested in the pre-Renaissance medieval workshop as a model of socialised creativity, given the ways in which it brought the possibility of freely-directed creative work into alignment with production.

But, if artistic labour and productive labour are subject to the extension and refinement of the social division of labour, and, in turn, the objectivity of general social technique, this does not mean that the demise of the artisanal in art is reducible to the process of deskilling in productive labour. Indeed, 'deskilling' in art is very different from deskilling in the factory and office. This is because, as Marx also insists, art is not subject to the law of value and therefore to the real subsumption of labour. Some artists may fall under the disciplinary régime of the law of value – working harder, faster; subject to re-routinisation and technical division – that is, those that are engaged in the

14. In his early years in New York, Duchamp participated in a discussion-group on art and labour, mostly influenced by the writings of Max Stirner. See Antliff 2001.

production of mass-produced artistic products, but the majority of artists are not, insofar as they are engaged in the production of *non-reproducible* forms.[15] This means that the artist confronted with the perceived deskilling in modern culture does not suffer the same creative denigration as the productive labour. Whereas the productive labourer experiences an overall loss of autonomy as a consequence of her subordination to the capitalist's control over the labour-process, the artist, as absent from the disciplinary régime of the value-form, does not.[16] Despite the artist's would-be loss of all-around artisanal skills and the enforcement of her social alienation, there is no comparable loss of artistic *autonomy*; other skills directed towards self-motivated and creative ends fill the gap. In other words, the demise of traditional artistic skills is not the result of a coercive process of control and division, which like the value-form, strips autonomy *out of* the production-process.

Now, this is not to say that the objects and events that artists produce are not commodities, but, rather, that the artwork's status as a commodity is not strictly subject to the price-calculation of the law of value. As I.I. Rubin notes: the economist 'L. Lyubimov is completely right when he subsumes the value of a product of a highly qualified laborer under the law of value. But he cannot deny the fact of the monopoly in relation to the individual price of unreproducible objects.'[17] This is why, in the final analysis, Marx makes a fundamental distinction between artistic production and productive labour: certain forms of creative labour are excluded from the law of value because their forms cannot be reproduced *through* socialised labour, and, as such, they remain resistant to, indeed excluded from, the routinisations of the labour-process.[18]

Marx does not discuss the distinction between deskilling in productive labour and deskilling in art, as a consequence of art's relative absence from the law of value, because new forms of autonomy in art were not yet visible. Neither Marx nor Morris anticipated the massive technical transformation of art that was to occur after 1910; in this respect, both Marx and Morris appear, from our twenty-first-century vantage-point, as oddly premodern in their cultural reflections, particularly Morris. Yet, in *Capital*, in the early sections on the discussion of value and passing reflections on artistic labour, there is an implicit revolutionising sense that the future struggle for workers' autonomy is through the *adaptation* of technique, not its abandonment, despite the subordination of general social technique to capital. Reading very much

15. Marx 1969.
16. For an extended discussion of this distinction, see Roberts 2007a.
17. Rubin 1972, p. 166.
18. Marx 1970.

against the artisanal humanism and pastoralism of the classical Marxism of the time,[19] this, essentially, is what Walter Benjamin sees in Marx, in his reconfiguration of the question of skill, artistic production and labour in the 'Author as Producer'. Emboldened by the Russian Revolution, and, as such, the sense that the repossession of traditional artisanal skills was utterly irrelevant to the emancipatory class-dynamic of the Revolution, Benjamin's insistence on the forging of a new identity for the artist out of the critical insertion of the artist into the new technical relations of the relations of production is a defence of the possible new sources of autonomy *within* the demands of general social technique. The new artist becomes a model for the new worker, and the new worker in his or her machino-technical proficiency becomes, potentially, a new artist. In this sense, there is no nostalgia for lost skills, artisanal creative all-roundedness, or any other humanist shibboleth regarding the release of the 'essential creativity of the masses'; in fact, for Benjamin, such things actually get in the way of the pursuit of new forms of autonomy and knowledge.[20]

Consequently, there is a way of linking Benjamin's cultural position with later debates on 'deskilling' in labour-process theory, particularly Harry Braverman's *Labor and Monopoly Capital* (1974).[21] Like Benjamin, Braverman

19. This is not to say that there are elements of Marx's earlier artisanal humanism and pastoralism from the 1844 'Economic and Philosophical Manuscripts' in *Capital*, but this perspective is increasingly subjected to the progressive function of socialised labour, as socialised labour becomes a defining part of Marx's conception of human emancipation and the development of human needs. This is why, in reading *Capital* as a critique of political economy, we need to be careful to read the critique of abstraction (abstract labour) as double-coded with regard to skill and craft: abstract labour is the thing that both destroys all-roundedness as an exemplar of socialised, collective production, but also stands to liberate all-roundedness from its chronic technical and conceptual inflexibility (in the medieval workshop) through splitting the producer away from the need to subordinate all of his creative labours to the performance of a multitude of routine tasks, perfectly reproducible by machines. There is something monstrous about the need for the liberated labourer to recover a multitudinous dexterity as an ideal expression of creative autonomy, as if our emancipation as labourers were bound up with the development of ourselves as multi-tasking *Kraftmeisters*. That is, the meeting between a transformed labour-process and a transformed conception of art in any postcapitalist or communist future, must also allow the disdain for labour, be it necessary labour or creative and intellectual labour. Looking, reading, sharing simple accomplishments might be all we want or need, after the 'specialist' and intellectually-invested activity and sensuous transformations of our necessary labour is done. The retaining or development of a craft-base in any emancipated model of labour, then, must allow space for 'unproductive' and distracted labour. Indeed, this is part of a more substantive debate about whether communism will be more 'complex' (or more complexly varied) than capitalism, or at, an important level, release us in our daily affairs from the demands of complexity.

20. Benjamin 1981.

21. Braverman 1998.

is concerned to defend the *advanced* technical and intellectual role of the worker in the relations of production, in conditions where, historically, the level overall of material and intellectual skill within the working class is in decline. Certain skilled technical workers (and 'knowledge'-workers today) may benefit from the general rise in scientific and technical knowledge under capitalism; the working class as a whole does not.

The mass of workers gain nothing from the fact that the decline in their command over the labour-process is more than compensated for by the increasing command on the part of managers and engineers. On the contrary, not only does their skill fall in an absolute sense (in that they lose craft and traditional abilities without gaining new abilities to compensate for the loss), but it also falls in a *relative* sense. The more science is incorporated into the labour-process, the less the worker understands of the process.[22]

In this light, Braverman's work is crucial in setting workers' struggle over the erosion of productive labour-skills within a wider social and historical setting. Certain workers within certain sectors may win back craft-skills, just as new skills in certain sectors may be forged out of transformations in the technical division of labour, but, overall, the level of technical skill embodied in the labour of the productive and unproductive worker has been radically diminished. Today, for instance, the greater percentage of newly-created 'knowledge'-jobs are largely routine and highly-monitored. Indeed, this sense of class-dispossession actually goes far deeper than Braverman suggests, into the heart of the sexual division of labour. As Ursula Huws argues – in an extension of Braverman's deskilling thesis – that, with the extensive socialisation of labour in the household from the seventeenth century onwards, women have suffered a 'double deskilling': from within the labour-process, and in exclusion from the unsocialised productivity and creativity of the household. In the seventeenth century, all participants in the running of the household

> would have had an understanding of the total process and a high general knowledge of such things as cooking, curing meat, preserving methods, preparation of medical remedies, textiles, brewing, the manufacturing of candles and soap, the caring of animals and so on.[23]

Yet, importantly for Braverman, this radical dispossession is not an invitation to link the emancipation of the working class with the restoration of this world of unsocialised skills (certainly, we should not forget the seventeenth-century unsocialised household was not a haven of women's freedom). On the

22. Braverman 1998, p. 295.
23. Huws 2003, p. 69.

contrary, the development of the forces of production, and the advances in general social technique, increases the revolutionary demand that working-class emancipation is inseparable from the 'return of requisite technical skill to the mass of workers', at a level and in a form in which such skills exert direct control over the labour-process.[24] How this actually has an impact upon the dissolution of the value-form and the release of the autonomy and creativity of the worker is less clear in Braverman.[25] But, without this massive sense of working-class dispossession, the revolutionary transformation and repossession of skills within the labour-process *at an advanced level* is made anodyne.

In this respect, the deflation of the expressive-artisanal model is part of a larger political narrative of negation at the beginning of the twentieth century: the drive of the historic avant-gardes (1917–39) during and after the Russian Revolution to finally depose artistic skill from its artisanal myths and fealties, and release new forms of artistic production from out of the new relations of production. That the tradition of high-modernist painting continued to produce work of value during this period, then, does not alter the fact that, after cubist-collage, after Duchamp's 'unassisted' readymades and Moholy-Nagy's 'telephone-paintings', after the concept of artistic surrogacy and authorship-at-distance, after the assimilation of photography into art, after Soviet constructivism and productivism, and the general transformation of the artist into a technician, the technical base of art is irredeemably changed.

24. Braverman 1998, p. 308.

25. This article is not the place for an extended discussion of recent debates on the value-form, that is for another time, however, suffice it to say though, one of the misplaced assumptions of much of the recent writing on the law of value and the value-process is that the critique of the value-form is somehow internal to political economy alone. For instance Kicillof and Starosta in their critique of I.I. Rubin (Kicillof and Starosta 2007) fail to acknowledge the cultural context in which Rubin wrote his *Essays on Marx's Theory of Value* in 1927–8. Rubin's tendency to confine the law of value to the exchange-process is a conservative and economistic addendum to what had been an extensive and rich debate on value and labour within the avant-garde from 1920 to 1928, a debate that had an impact well beyond the artistic production itself. As Boris Arvatov, the leading productivist theorist, asked at the time: in what ways might artistic labour presage and model emancipated labour, and, as such, in what ways might artistic praxis transform the labour-process itself within and outside the factory? (Arvatov 1972.) Indeed, the Soviet factory was for a while (even under the extended factory-discipline of the NEP with its officious red managers), not only a site of extended debate on the labour-process, but also a place of social-artistic experimentation (Gough 2007). Thus, if the value-form debate has indeed become academicised, divorcing itself from 'political action' (Kicillof and Starosta 2007), this is partially as a result of its separation from cultural and artistic questions. The recent debate on Chris Arthur's theory of value in *Historical Materialism* (viz. the critique of Arthur's Rubinesque separation of exchange and production) is a further indication of this. Thus, if there is a pressing requirement to link the debate on value to political action, there is an equally-pressing requirement to link the value-debate and politics to the emancipatory functions of artistic labour (Roberts 2007b and 2009).

Artistic skill is no longer confined to the manipulation of a given medium within a tradition of discretely crafted works, but is the cross-disciplinary outcome of an ensemble of technical and intellectual skills, embedded in the general division of labour. And, as such, this technical repositioning of art engages and directs a wider process of deflation within this period: the general move towards defining art as a form of *cultural practice* and, therefore, as something that has a direct and possibly transformative presence in the world (as opposed to a contemplative or decorative one). With the massive disinvestment of art from the confines of singular authorship, and from auratic forms of production and spectatorship associated with painting, mechanical production and interdisciplinarity become the motor of art's passage *into* the everyday and collective experience. No longer confined solely to the gallery-wall or to the painterly frame, avant-garde art moves to embed itself, across a variety of social locations, in the material and symbolic fabric of the world. Constructivism, of course, is central to this transformation.[26] The singular-discrete artistic object is dissolved into the functional demands of material transformation of the built environment (architecture, public monuments, propaganda, design). Art-object, art-event and social process coincide. Or, at least, they did in theory. Of course, the heightened expectations of this social role for art were soon curtailed and destroyed by the rise of Stalinism in the Soviet Union and fascism in Europe. By the mid-1930s, the great avant-garde experiment was in retreat, replaced by various forms of artisanal nostalgia. But what remained undefeated was the new cultural and technical dialectic that this period established, and that the new postwar-institutions, under new political conditions, have been compelled to address: the long-range dissolution of art into general social technique (that is, the unification of technology, technique and artistic form).

Since the 1960s, we have seen the deflation of the expressive-artisanal model of artistic skill played out in a number of registers. Conceptual art, post-conceptual photography and text, the appropriationist art of the 1980s, down to relational aesthetics, and the re-emergence of many forms of social functionalism today, all revive and repossess in various ways the notion of the artist as technician, as surrogate, as operator. Indeed, we say might say that the recrudescence of high-modernist painting between 1945 and 1985 – exemplified by the achievements of Gerhard Richter – represents a rupture within a broader historical pattern. Although the historic avant-garde as a social and cultural formation is at an end, avant-garde strategies and forms

26. For a discussion of constructivism and productivism and the avant-garde debate on the redefinition of artistic labour, see Margolin 1997 and Gough 2005.

remain integral – in socially constrained ways, obviously – to how art defines its contemporaneity and critical function.[27] Thus, the repeated attacks on postconceptualism, generally, in the 1980s and 1990s – for pursuing art to a point of inexorable technical and artisanal collapse – are a misrepresentation of the historical evidence. What we see is not a terminal decline of artistic skill, but the re-positioning of the notion of skill within a deeper dialectic: the necessary *interrelationship* between (received) skill, deskilling and *re*-skilling. Technical skill is not something that has been stripped out of art through surrogacy and technological reproduction, but is redefined through the emergence of art, since the 1920s, as a generic form of conceptualisation.

Since the late 1960s, this has also had a profound effect on the sexual division of intellectual labour in art. In the early 1970s, in the wake of the women's movement, one of the direct beneficiaries of the crisis of the artisanal-expressive model were women-artists who rejected painting on the grounds that its histories and expressive protocols inhibited women's artistic access to the representation and structuring of their own lives and experience. In this, conceptualisation offered a significant opportunity for women-artists to reflect on sexual difference, gender and femininity, without expectation. Thus, following Duchamp and Moholy-Nagy, a new generation of women-artists in the early seventies, were able to create compelling, assiduous, exacting, anomalous post-painterly forms that embodied distinctive thought-experiments. This is best represented during this period by Mary Kelly's influential *Postpartum Document* (1973–9), a sequence of panels consisting of hand-written and typed texts, images and objects, tracing and examining the relationship between Kelly and her newly-born son and, as such, his emerging subjectivity. What is distinctive about *Postpartum Document* is twofold: its resolute anti-pictorialism in its depiction of motherhood and domestic labour – the fact that neither the mother nor child's body is figuratively represented – and its resolute, uncompromising intellectualism, that is, its explicit identification of women's authorship with demonstrable theoretical skills.

The general implication of this move (and similar ones) is that skill is definable through the quality of this process of conceptualisation and the intellectual acuity the artist brings to art's material or immaterial forms, and not simply through evidence of the artist's own mastery of a range of technical processes challenging – in this case – women-artists' traditional identification as producers with certain inherited feminine craft-processes. As such, conceptualisation serves to split the judgement of a work's skilfulness from the fetishistic evaluation of technical skills. The artist may choose to be a master

27. See Roberts 2007b.

of a given technical process – the manipulation of digital photographs, for instance, or weaving – but this does not determine our judgement of the artist's skill overall.

Yet, in noting the emergent conceptualisation of art, we should not confuse the new art with the disciplines of intellectual and theoretical production itself, such as science or philosophy. The emergence of art from its historical-artisanal base into the realm of material conceptualisation is not evidence of a unilinear, if uneven, process of art's reskilling, as if art has revivified itself by talking on the languages of science. Art may have become a practice of conceptualisation, but this does not mean that it takes over the positivistic, deductive, and research-programme requirements of scientific investigation. This is because the dialectic of skill, deskilling and reskilling is first and foremost an expression of art's alienated and reified place in the totality of the social relations of capitalist culture. Art may have freed itself from its artisanal bonds, and taken on a conceptual and interdisciplinary identity, but it is also necessary to defend its interests as art against its systematic misuse, assimilation and containment by the culture as a whole. In these terms, we need to see the dialectic of skill, deskilling and reskilling as still very-much embedded in the modernist dialectic of negation that I discussed above. That is, we need to see how the relationship between skill, deskilling and re-skilling is driven by the need for art to assert and define its autonomy as art in the face of these constraints. In this sense, we need to draw up again the question of autonomy and negation in relation to the notion of the 'new', or 'making it new'.

In this respect, Theodor Adorno's theory of autonomy still has exemplary use-value for understanding the situation we are in.[28] Let us recall what Adorno has to say on the issue. For Adorno, autonomy in art is defined as a social relation between art's production and reception. In order to delineate itself as modern, it is imperative that art define itself against those institutional arrangements, social circumstances and traditions in which it *finds itself*. Therefore, there can be no critical future for art without this experience of disjunction with the traditions and institutions that have brought art into being. That is, the dynamic content of art continues to be mediated by its own reflection on the very category of art itself. As such, what drives this process is the very 'asociality' of art under capitalism, the fact that, for art to remain art (rather than transform itself into architectural design, fashion or social theory *tout court*), it must experience itself as being 'out of joint' both with its official place in the world and its own traditions. Thus, we should be clear here about what I mean by 'asociality'. Asociality is not to be confused with its idealist

28. Adorno 1984.

designation in Kant. For Kant, the 'asocial sociability of men' – the nature-determined tendency of humans to generate a state of constant mutual resistance – is that which threatens the dissolution of society, and, as such, is innate to humans and human relations.[29] Here, 'asociality' is, rather, the contingent and shifting space of art's non-identity and resistance within the heteronomous field of its social and institutional operation. Accordingly, it is identifiable with the notion of autonomy as the *produced* function of art's heteronomous emergence under commodity-relations. New forms of commodification are the heteronomous site of new forms of autonomy.[30] In this respect, 'asociality' is certainly worth saving for a theory of negation in art and culture, in the face of any (anti-Hegelian) social ontology that would overplay 'positive real alternatives' in the current period, as in István Mészáros.[31] Consequently, without this drive to autonomy out of the conditions of heteronomy (that is, the emergence of art as something 'other' in respect of the conditions which call it into being), art would cease to exist as a tradition of aesthetic and intellectual achievement, and, more importantly, as a means of resistance to capitalist exchange-value. This is why such a tradition of negation continues to produce work of value and quality, despite the demise of the original avant-garde and the dispersal and assimilation of modernism, and despite art's constant submission to the demands of entertainment and commerce and institutional legitimation and approbation. Art is irreducible to its own histories and institutional arrangements because art is that which *starts* from a position of negation. In fact, art's development and its social constraints are precisely *interdependent*.

Under commodity-culture, the alienation of art and the renewal of art are interwoven with the history of modernism and the modern, and therefore, negation, far from being that which damns art to decline and dissolution, is the very ground of modern art's unfolding and reinvention. This means, in turn, that the cognitive demands of the 'new' and art's openness to new meaning are not in *themselves* in a state of desuetude. For, if this were so, it would imply that, at some previous point, the alienated conditions of art's production and reception were somehow more perspicacious than the alienated conditions of art's production now or yesterday. On these grounds – in order to defend art against the critics of its technical dissolution – we should look for quality and value in periods of relative social stability. This is plainly absurd. In fact, the negations of art are continually able to reanimate themselves because the negations of art are 'inexhaustible' so long as asociality remains the

29. Kant 2001.
30. Martin 2007.
31. Mészáros 2008.

necessary dynamic of art's production, and human beings are capable of finding meaning in this dynamism. To presume otherwise is to believe that asociality is simply a discrete effect of art – the result of what artists *claim* to feel and experience – and not the basis upon which the conditions of art, irrespective of the particular ideologies professed by artists, are produced and enter social relations. Art's negations, therefore, are not something that touch lightly on art, come and go, as if they were a decorative dusting of snow, but, on the contrary, that which actually secures art's conditions of visibility and autonomy, and, as such, give shape to art's unfolding.

So, art's traditions of negation persist, because negation persists, and, if this is so, then the dialectic of skill, deskilling and re-skilling becomes the very means whereby this dynamic expresses itself. That is, reflections *on* skill (as a withdrawal from received skills), as much as the development of new skills become part of the restless, ever-vigilant positioning of art's critical relationship to its own traditions of intellectual and cultural formation and administration.

References

Adorno, Theodor W. 1984 [1970], *Aesthetic Theory*, London: Routledge and Kegan Paul.

Antliff, Alan 2001, *Anarchist Modernism: Art, Politics, and the First American Avant-Garde*, Chicago: University of Chicago Press.

Arvatov, Boris 1972 [1926], *Kunst und Produktion*, Munich: Karl Hanser Verlag.

Baudelaire, Charles 1981, *Art in Paris 1845–1862: Salons and other Exhibitions*, translated and edited by Jonathan Mayne, Oxford: Phaidon Press.

Benjamin, Walter 1981, 'The Author as Producer', in *Thinking Photography*, edited by Victor Burgin, London: Macmillan.

Braverman, Harry 1998 [1974], *Labor and Monopoly Capital: The Degradation of Work in the Twentieth Century*, New York: Monthly Review Press.

Buchloh, Benjamin H. 2003, *Neo-Avant-Garde and Culture Industry: Essays on European and American Art from 1955 to 1975*, Cambridge, MA.: MIT Press.

Cennini, Cennino d'Andrea 1954, *The Craftsman's Handbook*, translated by Daniel V. Thompson Jr., New York: Dover.

Clark, T.J. 1984, *The Painting of Modern Life: Paris in the Art of Manet and his Followers*, London: Thames and Hudson.

De Duve, Thierry 1996, *Kant After Duchamp*, Cambridge, MA.: MIT Press.

Duchamp, Marcel 1975, *The Essential Writings of Marcel Duchamp*, edited by Michael Sanouillet and Elmer Peterson, London: Thames and Hudson.

Gough, Maria 2005, *The Artist as Producer: Russian Constructivism in Revolution*, Berkeley: California University Press.

Huws, Ursula 2003, *The Making of a Cybertariat: Virtual Work in a Real World*, New York: Monthly Review Press.

Joselit, David 1998, *Infinite Regress: Marcel Duchamp 1910–1941*, Cambridge, MA.: MIT Press.

Kant, Immanuel 2001 [1784], 'Idea for a Universal History with Cosmopolitan Intent', in *Basic Writings of Kant*, edited by Allen W. Wood, New York: Random House.

Kelly, Mary 1999, *Postpartum Document*, Berkeley: University of California Press.
Kicillof, Axel and Starosta Guido 2007, 'On Materiality and Social Form: A Political Critique of Rubin's Value-Form Theory', *Historical Materialism*, 15, 3: 9–44.
Kincaid, Jim 2005, 'A Critique of Value-Form Marxism', *Historical Materialism*, 13, 2: 85–120.
Krauss, Rosalind 1986, *The Originality of the Avant-Garde and Other Modernist Myths*, Cambridge, MA.: MIT Press.
Margolin, Victor 1997, *The Struggle for Utopia: Rodchenko, Lissitzky, Moholy-Nagy, 1917–1946*, Chicago: University of Chicago.
Martin Stewart 2007, 'The Absolute Artwork Meets the Absolute Commodity', *Radical Philosophy*, 146: 15–25.
Marx, Karl 1969 [1905–10], *Theories of Surplus Value* Volume 1, London: Lawrence and Wishart.
—— 1970 [1867], *Capital* Volume 1, London: Lawrence and Wishart.
—— 1975 [1844], 'Third Manuscript', *Economic and Philosophic Manuscripts of 1844*, in Karl Marx and Frederick Engels, *Collected Works* Volume 3, London: Lawrence and Wishart.
Mészáros, István 2008, *The Challenge and Burden of Historical Time: Socialism in the Twenty-First Century*, New York: Monthly Review Press.
Moholy-Nagy, Sybil 1969, *Moholy-Nagy: Experiment in Totality*, Cambridge, MA.: MIT Press.
Morris, William 1984, *Political Writings*, edited by A.L. Morton, London: Lawrence and Wishart.
Murray, Patrick 2000, 'Marx's "Truly Social" Theory of Value: Part 1, Abstract Labour in Marxian Value Theory', *Historical Materialism*, 6: 27–65.
—— 2002, 'Reply to Geert Reuten', *Historical Materialism*, 10, 1: 155–76.
Nesbit, Molly 1993, *Atget's Seven Albums*, New Haven: Yale University Press.
Nietzsche, Friedrich 1997 [1874], 'On the Uses and Disadvantages of History for Life', in *Untimely Meditations*, edited by Daniel Breazeale and translated by R.J. Hollingdale, Cambridge: Cambridge University Press.
Roberts, John 2007a, *The Intangibilities of Form: Skill and Deskilling After the Readymade*, London: Verso.
—— 2007b, 'The Avant-Garde After Avant-Gardism', *Chto Delat* [*What is to be Done?*], 17, available at: <http://www.chtodelat.org/images/pdfs/17_vanguard.pdf>.
—— 2008, 'The Amateur's Retort', in *Amateurs*, edited by Ralph Rugoff, San Francisco: CCA Wattis Institute for Contemporary Arts.
—— 2009, 'Productivism and Its Contradictions', *Third Text*, 23, 5: 527–36.
Rubin, Isaak I. 1972, *Essays on Marx's Theory of Value*, Detroit: Black and Red.

BRILL

Historical Materialism 18 (2010) 97–116

historical materialism
research in critical marxist theory

brill.nl/hima

Locating Financialisation

Ben Fine
Department of Economics,
School of Oriental and African Studies, University of London
bf@soas.ac.uk

Abstract

The notion of financialisation as the exploitation or expropriation of workers' wages in the sphere of exchange is taken as a critical point of departure. In this way, financialisation is more deeply rooted in contemporary developments, including the slowdown preceding the current global crisis, and in Marx's own theory of finance. Financialisation is seen to represent the increasing penetration of interest-bearing capital across economic and social reproduction and to be a key defining moment of neoliberalism.

Keywords

financialisation, crisis, Marx

i) Introduction[1]

Literature on the current crisis has been much stronger in charting its origins and course than in identifying deeper causes. Not surprisingly, Marxist and heterodox scholarship and commentary have assumed a more prominent role as orthodoxy has been left floundering. The issue, then, is less to observe than to explain, and to explain requires locating the empirical within a theoretical framework. In particular, three issues need to be confronted. First, the reasons for the slowdown of the past thirty years, particularly – and this cannot be emphasised strongly enough – given conditions that could not on the face of it be more conducive to capital-accumulation: across levels of economic and social wages, weakness of labour and progressive movements at national and international levels, expansion and 'flexibility' of the workforce through Chinese and female participation in the workforce, end of the Cold War, availability of new technologies, and neoliberal hegemony in policy, politics

1. Thanks to Sam Ashman, Jan Toporowski and Alfredo Saad-Filho for comments on parts of an earlier draft, Fine 2009c.

DOI: 10.1163/156920610X512453

and ideology. Without an explanation for the slowdown, it is likely to prove impossible to explain why such a financial crisis should have emerged and been so severe, and to specify the nature of the crisis itself beyond its immediate economic parameters.

Second, how to locate the role of class-struggle in these circumstances when it seems both weak and removed from its classic location at the point of production. Of course, one of the mantras of neoliberalism is 'flexibility' in labour-markets, and that flexibility, in practice, is imposed through state-intervention on behalf of capital through legislation and, where possible and necessary, authoritarianism. These have served as complements to the declining strength of working-class organisation and activism, whilst the presence and interests of organised labour in social reproduction have also been considerably weakened through depoliticisation, privatisation and so on. This all poses both an analytical and a strategic challenge and, well before the crisis, these have been variously addressed in terms of the emergence and salience of new social movements and the demise of the traditional working class under capitalism.

Third, one must unravel the significance of financialisation and its relationship to the real accumulation of (productive) capital. Paradoxically, whilst finance and financialisation have drawn extensive attention from Marxist scholars, there has been relatively little by way of attempt to embed finance within Marx's own analysis or even to relate it to the tradition subsequently laid down by and through Hilferding – not least, no doubt, because the notion of finance-capital seems insufficiently attuned to the diversity and extent of today's financialisation that goes far beyond the relations of conflict or co-operation between banks and industry.[2] Despite the understandable draw to Marxist political economy in light of the crisis, much more attention has arguably been focused on Minsky (and his putative 'moment') than Marx when it comes to the role of finance in the crisis.[3]

My own approach to these issues is to deploy and develop, both logically and historically, Marx's theory of accumulation and base this upon the categories of analysis offered throughout the three volumes of *Capital*.[4] In the case of financialisation, I will understand it as the process by which the various forms of capital in exchange (including financial and other assets and markets) have not only expanded in extent and diversity but become increasingly articulated with one another. And, in particular, interest-bearing capital has

2. See Lapavitsas 2009a and 2009b.

3. For the contemporary arrival of the Minsky-moment in the literature see Tavasci and Toporowski 2010.

4. For some account of how this approach emerged and its application with references, see Fine 2008b.

increasingly appropriated activities that were previously the preserve of other forms of productive and commercial capital (or not capital at all, as in unproductive labour engaged in economic and social reproduction). Consequently, economic activity in general has become subject to the logic and imperatives of interest-bearing capital.

More generally, Marx's theory addresses accumulation as the quantitative expansion of productive capital through its restructuring – generally into larger units, variously organised in the modern world through multinational corporations, for example. Crucially, though, the pace and rhythm of the restructuring of capital is dependent upon agencies other than industrial capitalists themselves, and the restructuring of other forms of capital, in markets and finance, as well as through more general restructuring, or reproduction and transformation, of economic and social life. Each of these elements may be more or less conducive to accumulation by restructuring as well as uneven in their effects; their impact is contingent upon configurations of economic, political and ideological interests and conflicts within the bounds set by their location within the system of accumulation as a whole. And, in particular, the role of the state as an agent of restructuring is paramount across all of the constituent factors involved, including the exercise of force and legitimisation through other means, of the dysfunction, inequities and iniquities of contemporary capitalism.

It is against these briefly-presented perspectives that the contributions of dos Santos and Lapavitsas may be judged. Broadly, my assessment is that they go too far in one respect and not far enough in another. They exaggerate the role of appropriation of working-class revenue as an element in the current crisis. They also underestimate how the process which they themselves highlight is variously integrated into financial and productive accumulation, and economic and social reproduction more generally. For, as will be argued in Section (iii), the expansion of finance has been at the expense of the rate of accumulation and the conditions conducive for its efficacy. This is established through critical engagement with the contributions of dos Santos and Lapavitsas, who acknowledge the significance of financialisation but do so primarily by apprehending its role in the exploitation/expropriation of the working class through provision of financial services (credit) as a major point of departure in defining the current period and the contours of the crisis.[5]

5. See dos Santos 2009, Lapavitsas 2009a and Lapavitsas 2009b. The work of dos Santos and Lapavitsas has gone through a rapid process of evolution in wake of the crisis. I have the benefit of having seen earlier versions of their papers and those that remain unpublished. We also engaged in an extensive debate by email which allowed me to clarify my understanding of their position (which appears to remain incomplete) and how it differed from my own. During the

This is significant for bringing class-relations into account, albeit displaced from the sphere of production into the sphere of exchange. But it does so at two very serious and unacceptable costs. The first is an inability to explain either the period of slowdown or, other than as a purely financial phenomenon, the crisis to which it has given rise. For, further to the unprecedented and favourable conditions conducive to capital-accumulation already laid out, we could also add the exploitation of workers by finance in exchange – US and neoliberal hegemony, stagnant real and social wages, a supplementary basis for (financial) exploitation/expropriation, yet capital is stuck in stagnation leading to crisis? The second cost is to neglect, if not overlook, the broader incidence and impact of financialisation across all areas of economic and social life, not least on the general restructuring of capital (including of finance itself) as opposed to narrow attention to the financial exploitation/expropriation of the working class.

In short, as will be shown in respect of both form and content, dos Santos and Lapavitsas have got both financialisation and working-class exploitation wrong. Looking at this from a different angle, their distorted over-reliance upon exploitation/expropriation is a consequence of superficial treatment of the value of labour-power. For them, financial exploitation/expropriation is purely and simply a deduction from a given value of labour-power that is taken out of wage-revenue by the supply of banking services at abnormal profit. But, if this is generally so and has persisted and strengthened over the past thirty years along with financialisation itself, surely the value of labour-power has become pitched at a lower level, rather than a portion being stolen away, as it were? At a deeper level, this raises serious questions about what we mean by the value of labour-power and how we understand it as being determined (its moral and historical elements). I have addressed these issues at length elsewhere by arguing, in part through a 'system-of-provision' approach to (working-class) consumption,[6] that each element in the value of labour-power (housing, clothing, transport, food) is differentially determined in how it is provided *and* that levels of consumption (and modes of delivery) across the working class are also differentiated. In other words, modes and incidence

evolution of their stance, the notion of expropriation has gradually, if not completely, displaced the notion of exploitation in their work in deference to strong objections from Marxist commentators to the location of exploitation within the sphere of exchange, something that appears to remain their intent. For this reason, we deploy the hybrid 'exploitation/expropriation' to indicate both the ambiguity and origins of how they address the financialisation of wage-revenue.

6. See Fine and Leopold 1992 and Fine 2002, 2005 and 2007c. This is complemented by a theory of differentiated labour-markets which is not taken up here. See Fine 1998, 2007b and 2008a.

of provision of working-class consumption are differentiated (and are not simplistically reducible to monetary or labour-time equivalents other than at the most abstract level of confrontation between capital and labour as a whole at the point of production). This is all crucial in taking forward the nature and role of credit in serving working-class consumption and, in particular, implies that it is at least as important to differentiate the impact of credit upon what is provided, how and to whom, rather than confining it to a generalised deduction from wages. This point is briefly illustrated below by reference to housing which, unsurprisingly, occupies a prominent position in the account of exploitation/expropriation.

ii) Financial exploitation/expropriation

For dos Santos and Lapavitsas, the major but not exclusive novelty in the current period of capitalism has been the growing incidence of exploitation or expropriation of workers' wages through banking provision of personal services to them. In particular, a portion of workers' wages and salaries have been extracted directly with the result that banking profits have been abnormally high. Moreover, in the light of stagnant real wages (especially in the United States), and credit-fuelled consumption to compensate for this, the crisis was unavoidable once mortgage-defaults inevitably materialised. In short, for them, banking capital has been able systematically to appropriate, as part of the process of reproduction of the working class under neoliberalism, a portion of wage-revenue at higher than normal profit, and this is presumed to take place more or less independently (both in reality and for the purposes of their argument) of the processes of production and circulation that otherwise generate and distribute surplus-value in the normal course of events.

A number of factors are offered in support of this position, but they present difficulties even on their own terms. First, for example, the parallel, or even precedent is drawn with usury and trucking, with the financial system having allegedly generalised these socially and on a huge scale. A major problem with this argument by analogy, torn out of analytical and historical context, is that usury and trucking are proto-, even pre-capitalist, highly individualised, not open to generalisation, and the exception rather than the rule. Is it possible that usury and trucking can be *generalised* across workers in the context of *developed* capitalism? And, of course, usury in the past (and consumer-indebtedness in the present) is not confined to the working class. Indeed, for the past at least, there are at least two clichés attached to usury – the impoverished, indebted, even tied worker and the libertine-squanderer of an anticipated inheritance.

Second, appeal is made to the idea that, for the rise of financialisation in the form of direct financial exploitation/expropriation, deeper causal explanations can be found by reference to the forces and relations of production as with classical Marxism. For the forces, reference is made to the significant revolution in information-processing and telecommunications. This is subsequently finessed in terms of slow productivity-growth across both industrial and financial sectors over the period of financialisation. But, apart from an unduly crude flavour of technological determinism, at most tempered by appeals to deregulation (that applies equally to industry over the period concerned), there is no reason why such a shift in technology in and of itself should either lead to a change in the proportion of financial activity (the more productive sector could simply decline in weight) nor in its extension. In addition, in this respect at least, the evolution of industrial and financial sectors is unjustifiably, if not inevitably, treated as independent of one another rather than as symbiotic in mutual reliance upon the production of surplus-value (although, of course, that independence is mooted in terms of financial exploitation/expropriation). In other words, the technology as productive-forces argument is unconvincing (although this is not the same thing as saying that such material developments have no influence or relative impact). To put it metaphorically, it is as if electronic banking had turned us all into proto-serfs and we deduct a part of our wages and hand them over, directly or indirectly, to the banking system to source their super-normal profits. By way of parody, if genetic engineering allows for the generalised breeding of racehorses, that is no reason to believe the working class would be forced to stable them in their backyards at huge personal expense whilst industry proceeds to deploy more advanced forms of transport.[7]

Third, there must be similar reservations over reliance upon transformed relations of production in explaining financial exploitation/expropriation. These are specified in terms of the triumph of neoliberalism and the deregulation of labour- and financial markets, with an additional boost through female labour-market participation. Once again, the problem here is that there is no reason why any of this should be particularly associated either with the expansion of finance or with its particular forms, especially exploitation/expropriation. Industry or other activities are just as likely to benefit.

Fourth, this is all indicative of a substantial asymmetry in the treatment of industry and finance as well as with the working class. This is not to deny the

7. For a more fruitful, if still somewhat mechanical approach, see Perez 2009 and the idea that the new-technology origins of subsequent bubbles doubled up in the case of finance for the current crisis.

presence of such asymmetry, but whether it has been grasped correctly. The disproportionate rise of finance cannot be explained by conditions which are equally favourable to industry. Moreover, the difference between workers and industrialists (who are not, it seems, subject to exploitation/expropriation) is founded less on specification of class-position than on the individualised working-class consumer forced into relations of usury with the banking sector in order to access the credit necessary to fund consumption. Such arguments do not differ much from those that would be offered by the mainstream information-theoretic (market-imperfection) approach to credit-markets. The problem here, though, is that, as an individualised account of asymmetry, the advantage to either side is contingent. And there are plenty of consumers (workers even) who take advantage of the credit-relations on offer rather than being subject to exploitation/expropriation. I count myself as one of them, and suspect dos Santos and Lapavitsas do too. To pursue the pastiche, I do not keep a racehorse but I do own a motor-car. This raises doubts again over the extent to which financial exploitation/expropriation can be generalised insofar as it is understood in terms of deductions from the value of labour-power (see below).

Fifth, though, there is a potential appeal to a deeper understanding of asymmetry in drawing the contrast between the credit-relations by banking with corporations, as opposed to workers. No-one doubts that corporations have a different relationships with banks than with workers, for all sorts of reasons relating to material practices, customary position, networks, and so forth. But why should these leave corporations free of the mercy of disadvantageous credit-relations? Here, an answer is provided in terms of the heavy emphasis stressed by dos Santos and Lapavitsas upon the growing financial independence of the non-financial from financial corporations, not least through corporate self-funding and their own engagement in financial operations. This is stressed throughout their work in order both to place financial exploitation/expropriation in a more prominent position and to liberate the Marxist (and other) traditions, in the spirit of Hilferding, from the false notion of increasing integration of industry and finance under the dominance of finance.

But their own argument fails to move to a more systemic level of understanding (being based on asymmetry between individual agents in circulation) and is beset by two major problems irrespective of the other issues raised above or below and, to a large extent, independent of how they are resolved. On the one hand, how is it possible to explain the persistence, over such a long period as the era of financialisation, of both financial exploitation/expropriation and, whether accepting this specification or not, consequently abnormally high profits within the personal banking sector. To put it bluntly, why has capital not flowed into the sector of personal finance and reduced profitability to normal levels? This is particularly salient in view of the stance taken by dos Santos and Lapavitsas on the relative independence of, and capacity for, not only self-finance but deployment of financial instruments within the corporate sector more generally. Given this, and abnormal profits in personal finance, the way would appear to be open for abnormal profits to be eroded to normal levels by competitive entry of other sources of credit, thereby presumably eliminating financial exploitation/expropriation across the working class, not least as normal profits would be expected across all capitals whether working within production or exchange.

In other words, why have financially independent, self-financing corporations themselves been unable to offer horses, or even more advanced forms of transport than they themselves deploy, to the working class (as, indeed, there has been some degree of competitive entry into consumer-credit markets)? On the other hand, the slowdown itself becomes even more impenetrable. For, apart from the most conducive conditions for capital that anyone could wish for (with financial exploitation/expropriation added to a favourable balance of class-forces, US hegemony, neoliberalism, etc.), industrial corporations are deemed to be financially independent.

I will offer an alternative explanation for these abnormal profits and the slowdown later. But, before doing so, I will now turn to the issue of the value of labour-power. For dos Santos and Lapavitsas, financial exploitation/expropriation has nothing to do with its determination, which is taken as given by other factors, with banking's provision of personal financial services independently and directly appropriating a part of that value of labour-power and in the form of abnormal profits from within the sphere of exchange.[8] Interestingly, even at the most direct empirical level, this appeal to direct exploitation/expropriation is not valid. For some of the exploitation/expropriation attached to (working-class) consumption takes place at the direct expense of retailers, not least those (the majority and/or bulk) who are charged a fee when a sale is made (leading predominantly discount-stores, internet and other traders to charge extra for credit-card as opposed to debit-sales), rather than their customers. This raises the issue of how such credit-

8. The logic of their position, and the rigidity with which it is held, is evident from the total dismissal of the alternative offered in the earlier version of this paper (Fine 2009c). When, subject to their formal (refereeing) review, its arguments are dismissed as 'undeveloped for reasons of structure, empirical content, theoretical analysis *and* relevance', emphasis added.

relations relate to the revenues and profits of retailers and, consequently, producers.

Significantly, though, and paradoxically as will be seen, dos Santos, Lapavitsas and Dymski refer to one another for further elaboration of financial exploitation/expropriation, and it is with Dymski's account that we encounter further difficulties in this respect, at least as a *general* theory of exploitation/expropriation, which he does not provide, as opposed to a very specific (part of) one. For he is concerned with the way in which sub-prime emerged as a result of enforced inclusion of redlined racially-segregated housing into private ownership with corresponding over-selling of unsustainable and dishonest mortgages, their incorporation into sold-on derivatives, and the resultant collapse of the financial system once a combination of falling housing prices and defaulted payments arose, as they inevitably did.

But, for the dos Santos and Lapavitsas story, this raises serious obstacles to its status as a *general* account of financial exploitation/expropriation. This is so for two very transparent reasons. The first is that it is specific to a *particular* section of the *housing* market that was previously excluded from mortgaging by the actions of the lenders themselves. The second is that it is a reflection of systemic racism in this respect. The point is that neither of these is characteristic of the housing market as a whole or the extension of (working-class) credit as a whole. Irrespective of whether the attempt to break down the barriers to private (mortgaged) ownership of housing in previously ghettoised neighbourhoods involves what might be termed financial expropriation or not, it does not serve as an exemplary illustration of the more general argument concerning the extension of credit to the working class as a whole across all items of consumption. Similarly, sub-prime as a whole, whatever its role in causing and triggering the current financial crisis, is unlikely to serve as an ideal example of generalised financial exploitation/expropriation.

As it stands, this however is not a devastating blow to the hypothesis of financial exploitation/expropriation, as it could be seen as both pervasive and differentiated by sector and socio-economic status. Indeed, dos Santos and Lapavitsas argue that the displacement of public by private provision across housing, health, education, pensions and so on, is what has driven financial exploitation/expropriation. This, then, has to be explained in terms of how credit differentially pertains across sectors *and* consumers (always, it seems, treated as undifferentiated members of the working class subject to financial exploitation/expropriation). The (shifting) role of credit-relations in serving working-class consumption will be differentiated from one item of consumption to the next both in terms of its level and the way in which it is present. You do not, for example, buy a house on a credit-card, but, on the other hand, it is very hard to hire a car (and possibly a horse) without one. As a result, the role of credit is not simply the form in which the value of labour-power is realised (or subject to deduction through exploitation/expropriation by finance), it is positively constitutive of the value of labour-power itself, certainly through its so-called 'moral and historical' determination.

This has particular implications for understanding the role of credit in the housing market, and for the 'financial expropriation' which Dymski examines and upon which dos Santos and Lapavitsas approvingly draw. For, significantly, my own, more general, 'system-of-provision' approach to consumption was inspired to some degree by work on the UK housing system.[9] In this, as is well-known, the role of credit (and mortgages) is heavily linked to the appreciation in house-prices, which is itself then underpinned by inflated land-prices as well as the insertion of intermediaries in the buying and selling of housing, with a corresponding impact on the provisioning of housing whether in new build or repair.

The details of this need not detain us, and they will be different in one location (within and across countries) as opposed to another. But what this means is that the provision of housing is necessarily intimately related, unlike most other commodities, to the role of landed property, by which is meant the terms and conditions of access to land (and the housing located upon it).[10] The economic form taken by such a relationship is usually rent.[11] It is also highly contingent upon how the construction-industry and other agents in the process are integrally related and structured in the social reproduction of housing and the social construction of the built environment (what is redlined and what is not, and why, for example). In case of the pressure upon financial

9. See Ball 1983, Ball 1988 and Fine 2004 for an account of its influence.

10. It is unfortunate that the combination of housing and financial crises has induced radical geographers to shift focus away from the (re)construction of space as the built environment to the reconstruction of financial assets without reference to the corresponding material factors involved in housing supply. This is sharply illustrated by the special June 2009 issue of the *International Journal of Urban and Regional Research*, to which Dymski provides a commentary (Dymski 2009b).

11. Indeed, this would appear to represent a classic application of Marx's theory of landed property with slow increases in productivity complemented by higher prices to allow for (absolute) rent. See Fine 1979. See also the contribution from Wyly et al 2009 in the collection cited in the previous footnote, 'In the subprime market, homeowners are simply paying rent to the new landlord, subprime mortgage capital. In these circumstances, the cultural symbolism of homeownership is nothing more than a deceptive illusion', p. 338. They continue, 'analysis of class-monopoly rent provides a compelling theoretical and strategic alternative that emphasizes the social relations of the rights of property, ownership and profit – against the use values of home, community and security', p. 351, but get no further in examining the production of housing (and why inflated prices do not increase supply).

institutions to grant mortgage-finance to previously redlined areas, as reported in Dymski,[12] this implies a shift in the nature of landed property attached to the corresponding housing, with enhanced access to owner-occupation within redlined areas as opposed to dependence on slum-landlords. Insofar as 'interest' accrues to finance-companies out of arranging those mortgages, it is at least in part and potentially a form of rent that derives from the capital-gains attached to the housing (and can only continue as long as such capital-gains accrue as well as mortgage-repayments).

Two important implications follow from this. First is the potential conflation of economic categories, by reason of which it is necessary to probe a little deeper into the source of forms of revenue other than the way in which they happen to present themselves. As dos Santos and Lapavitsas have correctly emphasised, the proximate source of (some of) banking's profits from the provision of personal finance are deductions from wages. But, as suggested, these may merely be the way in which capital-gains in housing are passed on through intermediary of the wage-earner. Some understanding of this may be offered by way of analogy. The state, for example, differentially taxes each wage-earner according to a number of criteria through deduction from gross wages. Does this mean that the state exploits or appropriates from the wage-earner? The answer is no, for, as argued by Fine and Harris,[13] all taxes are paid out of surplus-value as the value of labour-power is determined by what the wage-earner receives, not by what is not received, although this does make for a change in forms of conflict over real wages as labour seeks to defend or promote them (against taxes and inflation).[14]

The point here is not to make an exaggerated virtue out of false appearances and to look for a deeper reality behind every empirical outcome. But it is important to acknowledge that there is something different about housing markets (or systems) and, correspondingly, the credit-markets to which they are attached. This is to return to the theme of the nature and determinants of the value of labour-power, the differentiation between the systems of provision that underpin working-class consumption to which credit-relations are differentially attached. It is – at least currently, although the same may have been said about such housing in the past right up to the crisis itself – inconceivable that speculation in financialised working-class consumption of

12. Dymski 2009a.

13. Fine and Harris 1979.

14. Similarly, to illustrate the conflation of categories, but not to impose this instance as identical, see Bhaduri 1977 for his classic study of peasants' usurious interest-payments as representing rent in another form (and not expanded possibilities as idealised by orthodox economics).

education or health could have been the trigger to the crisis (or even oil and food, both items of working-class consumption and subject over the most recent period to extremes of speculative volatility).

Yet, with dos Santos and Lapavitsas, these are all rounded up into the same undifferentiated category of financial exploitation/expropriation. Consider credit-card (ab)use. Here, once again, there is an enormous difference, both within the working class and among consumers more generally, as has long been recognised by those who have campaigned against usurious interest-rate exploitation of a minority (and there is a simple failure of many of those at the extremes of exploitation to manage their financial affairs efficiently in some sense).[15] An interesting dynamic has been involved in this around the formal/informal structural division between those who are creditworthy and those who are not, in that informal lines of credit which are far more expensive (i.e. usurious) occupy the space left by their formal counterpart. But such informal lines of credit are increasingly integrated with, and even absorbed within, the formal, and are contingent upon (and calculated as) a balance between higher charges and higher defaults. We, who use credit responsibly, pay in overheads for the defaults of others who are, nonetheless, even more penalised than we are. So, if there are abnormal profits in the (consumer)-credit sector, it is because of this systemic structure and dynamic in which there is some averaging of gains and losses taken as a whole, albeit with differential performance across individual agencies on both sides of the market. This still leaves open, however, how abnormal profits can persist in banking and the provision of financial services, and the broader significance of this in addressing the crisis.

This has broader relevance for understanding the nature of contemporary capitalism, and my position would appear to differ from that of dos Santos and Lapavitsas (although I suspect these differences do not necessarily depend on those drawn over financial exploittion/expropriation). As argued elsewhere in some detail, the relationship between neoliberalism and financialisation is direct and integral, with the latter underpinning the persistence of the former (and not vice-versa) through different phases and reflecting a relationship of contradiction and tension between rhetoric, scholarship, policy in practice and the representation of reality.[16] In other words, financialisation is, in a sense, (shorthand for) neoliberalism, and not merely one of its consequences.

---

15. See, for example, Manning 2000. Note that my own (analytical) exposure to contemporary exploitative credit-relations derives from consumer-studies where the emphasis is upon a minority of those who suffer credit-abuse whether by necessity, disposition or 'irrationality'. See also Montgomerie 2009 for an account of the differentiated (mis)fortunes of the US middle classes in terms of their use and dependence upon credit-relations.

16. Fine 2009a and 2009b.

This does, however, require that financialisation be understood as also incorporating the shifting appropriation of activity across and within different fractions of (industrial and financial) capital, in contrast to the view that it is primarily a shift in the balance between production and circulation, as suggested by the forces-and-relations of production argument that putatively underpins the explanation for financial exploitation/expropriation. Further, nor is it simply that financialisation is a *reflection* of continuing difficulties in production. On the contrary, as I have argued elsewhere,[17] financialisation is itself the major causal factor in low levels of real accumulation and in undermining conditions of economic and social reproduction conducive to such accumulation. Thus, by deploying the erroneous notion of exploitation/expropriation to signal, correctly, the financialisation of the value of labour-power (and economic and social reproduction more generally), dos Santos and Lapavitsas mis-specify the nature of financialisation itself and its broader location within contemporary capitalism. But, this is to anticipate the following section.

iii) Towards an alternative

Irrespective, then, of the role of working-class credit and abnormal banking profits in the determination of the value of labour-power, as already emphasised dos Santos and Lapavitsas offer no explanation as to why such credit should command abnormal as opposed to normal profits and why the crisis should have been preceded by a slowdown. And this is not simply a matter of the status of the notion of financial exploitation/expropriation, but how this relates more fundamentally to the Marxist theory of finance. Dos Santos and Lapavitsas do take some trouble to locate themselves in this respect, not least with regard to a favourable view of Hilferding, even if his characterisation and influence are perceived to be outdated in view of the current relative independence and lack of subordination of industry to finance, whatever their past significance. But what is strikingly absent is the grounding of their analysis in the theory of finance, and the corresponding concepts offered by Marx himself.

In particular, I would put forward the following propositions concerning Marx's theory of finance, each to be found elaborated and justified in more detail in earlier work (see my bibliography for the appropriate references). First, Marx divides the capital functioning within exchange into two sorts, merchant-capital and interest-bearing capital. It is easiest to begin with

17. Fine 2007a.

merchant-capital as it typically involves trading, such as retailing and wholesaling (or commercial capital), and, apart from its location within the sphere of exchange, is *logically* defined by its not producing (surplus-) value whilst being subject to competitive entry and exit in the same way as industrial capital. As a consequence, it is subject to a tendency to equalised profitability. Further, such merchant-capital is not confined simply to buying and selling but also involves a variety of credit and other monetary relations and functions which, nonetheless, tend to attract equal profitability. For convenience, I refer, to some extent in parallel with Marx, to such non-trading merchant-capital as money-dealing capital. Once again, it is a logical category defined by the necessity of circulation for economic reproduction but in which the corresponding activities are undertaken by what is possibly a specialised capital dedicated to that purpose.

Second, and in contrast, interest-bearing capital involves the borrowing and lending of money-capital for the purposes of making an advance in pursuit of the production of surplus-value. It potentially earns interest as a result, with a simple division of surplus-value between such interest and 'profit of enterprise' that is distributed across capital subject to rate of profit-equalisation. Once again, interest-bearing capital is a *logical* category, signifying that the competitive accumulation of capital is mediated by access to money-capital for the purposes of producing surplus-value and the corresponding restructuring of capital. The division between profit and interest is not predetermined by the value-system as such but by the outcome of the accumulation-process, both in terms of how much surplus-value is realised in practice (as the advance of money-capital is a precondition but not a guarantee of successful accumulation) and how it is divided with industrial (and merchant-) capital. This division bears no relation as such to the determination of the rate of interest. Nonetheless, differences between rates of interest in borrowing and lending and fees etc. incurred in circulation are mechanisms through which interest-bearing capital appropriates interest. So, the surplus-value appropriated as interest by interest-bearing capital, as mentioned, is variable and not pre-determined by the value-system just as the surplus-value produced by labour-power is itself variable.

Third, and by the same token, this does not mean that the division is not subject to systematic forces and factors such as the nature and rhythm of the accumulation-process. Logically, the capacity to appropriate surplus-value as interest derives not simply from interest-bearing capital as a logical category but in its role as the lever of competition in capital-accumulation in which interest-bearing capital is differentially situated in relation to itself as opposed to industrial and merchant-capital. A financial institution may be willing to lend to an industrialist to compete with another in the same sector but is less likely to set up another financial institution to do so and thus compete with itself. This does not mean there is no competition within or with the financial sector, only that it is of a different nature than for the rest of the economy. And this is precisely why the interest attached to interest-bearing capital is *not* competed away to the normal rate of profit on capital deployed.

Fourth, because each of the categories discussed is both logically and abstractly derived, their concrete existence must be addressed through closer theoretical and empirical analysis, discovering the reproduction of the real but abstract in thought at more complex levels. For, in practice, the functioning of interest-bearing capital and money-dealing capital (and commercial capital, for that matter) are inextricably integrated with one another (like constant and variable capital, or absolute and relative surplus-value, or the three types of rent) in the sphere of circulation, most notably in the market for loanable money-capital (a category deployed by Marx to signify the co-existence of the two in money-markets) where, in principle, all idle money is placed for the purposes of borrowing and lending irrespective of its origins and destinations.

Fifth, it follows that the real existence of, and distinction between, interest-bearing capital and money-dealing capital are not entirely the consequence of the intentions of those engaged in the corresponding activities, as outcomes are contingent upon the movement of capital as a whole. Historically, financial institutions have emerged to cover the specialised functions associated with the separate categories of capital within exchange. But, and this is crucial, even in a world in which there is absolute regulatory or de facto division between investment- and retail-banking (for want of better terms), concrete outcomes do not correspond to their distinct spheres of operation either individually or in toto. An advance of interest-bearing capital that fails will, nonetheless, expand commercial credit and realise surplus-value for others out of the expenditure of the constant and variable capital advanced. On the other hand, state-expenditure, on pensions for example, or credit extended for personal consumption will potentially realise surplus-value in commodities purchased, underpinning the capacity to sustain surplus-value appropriated by corresponding interest-bearing capital.

Sixth, it follows that what is or is not interest-bearing capital or money-dealing capital is only loosely constrained by the particular functions involved, and depends upon how corresponding capitals are situated within the accumulation and circulation of capital as a whole. Marx himself worried over this in terms of interrogating the relationship between the real and fictitious accumulation of capital, something which cannot be (pre-)determined by the capitals themselves. He also addressed the issue, in the slightly different context, of merchant-capital, of whether transport of commodities is a productive or unproductive activity, something which can only be determined by the way in which such capitals are differentially attached to industrial as opposed to merchant-capital.

Seventh, then, this implies that the issue is not whether interest-bearing capital and money-dealing capital are empirically separate or not to a greater or lesser degree, but rather how they are articulated concretely. In addition, this very much involves the extent to which the different fractions of capital appropriate, or are attached to, activities that might otherwise fall under the command of other fractions of capital or outside capitalist circulation altogether other than as expenditure of revenue. Do industrialists access their own finance, transport, marketing, etc.? Or, at the opposite extreme, are more general activities associated with capital in exchange falling under the command of, or being integrated with, interest-bearing capital?

Eighth, the current era of financialisation is precisely one in which there has been not only a disproportionate expansion of capital in exchange, through extensive and intensive proliferation of financial derivatives but also the extension of finance into ever more areas of economic and social reproduction, of which personal finance is a leading example. But, at this point, I would appear to begin to part company with dos Santos and Lapavitsas. For, in my view, such financialisation is consistent with the application of Marx's method and categories as outlined above, with an understanding based upon acknowledging the increasing shift of capitalist activity along the productive, commercial, money-dealing, interest-bearing continuum, as well as a heavy degree of hybridity across these. In other words, an increasing range of activities has come under the auspices of interest-bearing capital, not least sub-prime itself as mortgages have been sold on. As a result, it does become possible, at least in principle, to explain why abnormal profits should be able to persist in personal finance since this has become increasingly attached to interest-bearing capital as opposed to merchant-capital.[18]

In addition, as hinted earlier, personal finance (as exploitation/expropriation of working-class revenue), does not begin to get to grips with, even precludes, an account of how such provision is integrally attached to the functioning of retailing (or, rather differently, mortgaging) and their own differentiated attachment to other forms of capital in exchange and the productive capital upon which they depend (for surplus-value). Pointing to abnormal profitability

18. Although not addressed in these terms, the account by Treganna 2009 of abnormal profits in US banking as applying both to large and small firms (and hence structurally systemic and not individual market-power specific), would support the stance adopted here.

aside (and spurious notions of forces and relations of production as underpinning them within finance), dos Santos and Lapavitsas offer a limited account of competition within the banking sector (and the restructuring across credit-card providers, for example) and how this is itself integral to financialisation more generally (although they do acknowledge that banking has diversified into a range of services and markets, whilst treating exploitation/expropriation as more or less independent of these).

Ninth, then, and this is crucial to the explanation of the slowdown, the secular expansion of interest-bearing capital is not confined to the abnormal profits arising from the exploitation/expropriation of workers but is generalised across the economy as a whole, including the financial operations of putatively independent industrial corporations. Indeed, as the financialisation-literature has established, these have themselves been engaging in financial-speculative activities as opposed to industrial investment as an increasingly important source of profits. In short, to return to the theme raised in the introduction, financialisation is underpinned by the quantitative expansion of interest-bearing capital and its extension across the economy at the expense of restructuring of industrial capital both directly and indirectly through the broader modes of neoliberal impact upon economic and social reproduction (as with financialisation, public-private partnerships, etc.).

iv) Concluding remarks

For obvious reasons, the notion of financial exploitation/expropriation offers a compelling critique of certain aspects of contemporary capitalism. But it is one that is, in many respects, far from controversial both in substance and strategic implications. That finance has been over-rewarded at our expense and that the remedy is to be found even in terms of nationalisation of banking are already accepted in major part as establishment-views and policy. What remains unaddressed in such perspectives is the systemic effects and the particular and variegated uses to which financialisation has given rise. If it were possible, eliminating financial exploitation/expropriation would scarcely remedy the crisis, let alone the slowdown that preceded it. This is not to suggest that dos Santos and Lapavitsas would draw back from making radical proposals for alternative organisation and use of finance, but these do not follow from their analytical postures, for which elimination of excess financial exploitation/expropriation would appear to suffice, not least because they construe it as being in large part independent with respect to the broader functioning of the financial, let alone the productive, system.

The alternative offered here has two crucial components. The first is both to deny financial exploitation/expropriation as such as a systemic and pervasive aspect of contemporary capitalism, whilst accepting that economic and social reproduction (of the workforce) has become increasingly articulated with the financial system as part and parcel of a broader process of financialisation. Second are the implications for locating class-struggle in the current conjuncture. For, with the general, if not universal, weakness and disorganisation of working-class and progressive movements, despite the de-legitimisation of finance in particular and of neoliberalism in general, the latter has not been matched by the posing of prominent alternatives in practice and through struggle. With the global recession, however, these struggles and alternatives will emerge in response to the shifting of its incidence onto those who are generally recognised to be blameless for its occurrence, whether through 'market-forces' or policy itself (especially in light of obscene levels of support offered to finance). The challenge will be both to further these struggles by extending them from the financial logics to which they are most immediately attached to the processes of production and provisioning that underpin them and to draw such struggles together to build unified and systemic resistances and programmes for change. For these, 'financial exploitation/expropriation' is, at most, a first and fractured pointer with differentiated impact and potential for highlighting change across health, education, housing, standards of living, employment and so on. By contrast, it is necessary to frame the way in which strategic alliances might be formed that strengthen, broaden and transform individualised, often financialised, struggles for more and different modes of provision than those confined to exchange alone.[19]

References

Arrighi, Giovanni 2009, 'In Retrospect', *New Left Review*, II, 56: 61–94.

Ball, Michael 1983 *Housing Policy and Economic Power: The Political Economy of Owner Occupation*, London: Methuen.

—— 1988, *Rebuilding Construction: Economic Change in the British Construction Industry*, London: Routledge.

Bayliss, Kate and Ben Fine (eds.) 2008, *Whither the Privatisation Experiment?: Electricity and Water Sector Reform in Sub-Saharan Africa*, Basingstoke: Palgrave Macmillan.

19. See Fine 2005 and 2009d for a discussion of the way in which struggles over consumption, for example, are self-limiting both in and of themselves and as they evolve to become transformed into something else (such as for public provision, for decent wages and working conditions, or for attention to the environment).

Bhaduri, Amit 1977, 'On the Formation of Usurious Interest Rates in Backward Agriculture', *Cambridge Journal of Economics*, 1, 4: 341–52.

dos Santos, Paolo 2009, 'On the Content of Banking in Contemporary Capitalism', *Historical Materialism*, 17, 2: 180–213.

Dymski, Gary 2009a, 'Racial Exclusion and the Political Economy of the Subprime Crisis', *Historical Materialism*, 17, 2: 149–79.

—— 2009b, 'Afterword: Mortgage Markets and the Urban Problematic in the Global Transition', *International Journal of Urban and Regional Research*, 33, 2: 427–42.

Fine, Ben 1979, 'On Marx's Theory of Agricultural Rent', *Economy and Society*, 8, 3: 241–78 [reprinted in Fine (ed.) 1986].

—— 1998, *Labour Market Theory: A Constructive Reassessment*, London: Routledge.

—— 2002, *The World of Consumption: The Material and Cultural Revisited*, London: Routledge.

—— 2004, 'Debating Production-Consumption Linkages in Food Studies', *Sociologia Ruralis*, 44, 3: 332–42.

—— 2005, 'Addressing the Consumer', in *The Making of the Consumer: Knowledge, Power and Identity in the Modern World*, edited by Frank Trentmann, Oxford: Berg.

—— 2007a, 'Financialisation, Poverty, and Marxist Political Economy', available at: <https://eprints.soas.ac.uk/5685>.

—— 2007b, 'Rethinking Critical Realism: Labour Markets or Capitalism?', *Capital and Class*, 91: 125–9.

—— 2007c, 'From Sweetness to McDonald's: How Do We Manufacture (the Meaning of) Foods?', *The Review of Social & Economic Studies*, 29, 2: 247–71.

—— 2008a, 'Debating Lebowitz: Is Class Conflict the Moral and Historical Element in the Value of Labour-Power?', *Historical Materialism*, 16, 3: 105–14.

—— 2008b, 'Engaging the MEC: Or a Lot of My Views on a Lot of Things', paper for the June 2008 MEC workshop at University of KwaZulu-Natal, Durban, available at: <https://eprints.soas.ac.uk/5813/>.

—— 2009a, 'Social Policy and the Crisis of Neoliberalism', available at: <http://www.networkideas.org/ideasact/jan09/PDF/Fine.pdf>.

—— 2009b, 'Looking at the Crisis through Marx', *International Socialist Review*, 64: 40–7.

—— 2009c, 'Financialisation, the Value of Labour Power, the Degree of Separation, and Exploitation by Banking', available at: <https://eprints.soas.ac.uk/7480>.

—— 2009d, 'Political Economy for the Rainbow Nation: Dividing the Spectrum?', prepared for 'Making Sense of Borders: Identity, Citizenship and Power in South Africa', South African Sociological Association, Annual Conference, June/July, Johannesburg, available at: <https://eprints.soas.ac.uk/7972/1/sasa_benfine.pdf>.

—— (ed.) 1986, *The Value Dimension*, London: Routledge and Kegan Paul.

Fine, Ben and Laurence Harris 1979, *Rereading 'Capital'*, London: Macmillan.

Fine, Ben and Ellen Leopold 1992, *The World of Consumption*, London: Routledge.

Lapavitsas, Costas 2009a, 'Financialised Capitalism: Crisis and Financial Expropriation', *Historical Materialism*, 17, 2: 114–48.

—— 2009b, 'Financialisation, or the Search for Profits in the Sphere of Circulation', available at: <http://www.soas.ac.uk/rmf/papers/file51263.pdf>.

Manning, Robert 2000, *Credit Card Nation: The Consequences of America's Addiction to Credit*, New York: Basic Books.

Montgomerie, Johanna 2009, 'The Pursuit of (Past) Happiness?: Middle-Class Indebtedness and American Financialisation', *New Political Economy*, 14, 1: 1–24.

Perez, Carlota 2009, 'The Double Bubble at the Turn of the Century: Technological Roots and Structural Implications', *Cambridge Journal of Economics*, 33, 4: 779–805.

Tavasci, Daniela and Jan Toporowski (eds.) 2010, *Minsky, Crisis and Development*, Basingstoke: Palgrave Macmillan.

Tregenna, Fiona 2009, 'The Fat Years: The Structure and Profitability of the US Banking Sector in the Pre-Crisis Period', *Cambridge Journal of Economics*, 33, 4: 609–32.

Wyly, Elvin, Markus Moos, Daniel Hammel and Emanuel Kabazi 2009, 'Cartographies of Race and Class: Mapping the Class-Monopoly Rents of American Subprime Mortgage Capital', *International Journal of Urban and Regional Research*, 33, 2: 332–54.

BRILL Historical Materialism 18 (2010) 117–122
historical materialism
research in critical marxist theory
brill.nl/hima

Response to Henry Heller's 'The *Longue Durée* of the French Bourgeoisie'

William Beik
Emory University
wbeik@comcast.net

Abstract
Beik criticises Heller's mechanical view of the dynamic role of the bourgeoisie in the rise of capitalism in early-modern France. While they agree that the primary class-conflict was between the nobility and the peasantry, Beik stresses the slow emergence of genuine capitalist social relations and the cooptation of the bourgeoisie by a monarchical state which was still propping up the feudal régime, whereas Heller views mercantile activity and production increases as evidence of rising capitalism.

Keywords
Bourgeoisie, Dobb, Sweezy, transition, feudalism, capitalism, France

In 'The *Longue Durée* of the French Bourgeoisie'[1] Henry Heller devotes an entire article to criticising David Parker, Robert Brenner and myself for our approaches to social relations in early-modern France. I am pleased to be invited by this journal to respond. I will leave it to Parker and Brenner to speak for themselves. In the interest of full disclosure, I should note that, while I am honoured to find myself in the company of distinguished Marxist scholars such as Parker and Brenner, I cannot myself claim to be a Marxist. Class-analysis and the insights of Marxist historians have been central to my thinking, but I have not studied the principal works of Marx, nor have I consistently adhered to Marxist methodology in my work.

Heller charges that I have undervalued, indeed eliminated altogether, the crucial role of the bourgeoisie in the evolution of class-relations leading up to the triumph of the bourgeoisie in the French Revolution: 'For [Beik] the bourgeoisie did not exist.'[2] He argues that, in distancing myself from

1. Heller 2009.
2. Heller 2009, p. 35.

 DOI: 10.1163/156920610X512462

'classical-Marxist interpretations',[3] I have joined the ranks of the so-called revisionists who deny the bourgeois origins of the French Revolution. I have also misunderstood Le Roy Ladurie's discussion of feudal rents and land-rents. I have ignored the insights of Soviet historians Boris Porchnev and A.D. Lublinskaya.[4] I have rejected the class-struggle between nobility and bourgeoisie, and thereby lost a sense of 'dynamic development'. I have abandoned the concept of a 'nascent bourgeoisie and capitalism within the ancien régime' along with 'any notion of simple-commodity production or primitive accumulation'.[5] Moreover, I have missed the importance of markets, merchant-capitalists and international trade, and failed to understand the rise of 'profit-minded rural capitalists' exploiting 'operating capital and wage-labour'. I also need to be reminded that 'the age of merely feudal rent had long since passed'.[6]

Henry Heller deserves commendation as one of the few historians who has continued to defend the merits of a Marxist approach, most recently in his provocative history of the French Revolution.[7] But his charges here are way off the mark and surprisingly old-fashioned. His evidence for my neglect of the bourgeoisie is based almost entirely on my 1985 book *Absolutism and Society*, which was about something quite different – the channels of political power and shared influence that linked the royal government and the ruling class of the province of Languedoc.[8] Seen in this context of political influence, the bourgeoisie had hardly any influence. The towns were run by oligarchies of royal officers either enjoying nobility or on the way to acquiring it. Taxes and public expenses were run by the provincial estates, which were, in turn, dominated by twenty-two bishops and a handful of locally-based noble potentates. Of course, Languedoc had markets, merchants, entrepreneurial farmers, even rural manufactories. But those involved were relatively powerless, except in matters of commerce and some local governance. The province was run by noble commanders with delegated powers of command, by an array of top churchmen, and by a circle of élite-families who controlled the principal royal offices and profited from the royal fiscal system. Similar situations prevailed in other provinces.[9] Those who made their fortunes in manufacturing or commerce usually abandoned their businesses after one or more generations and purchased offices for themselves or their sons in order to gain privileged

3. Heller 2009, p. 33.
4. Porchnev 1963; Lublinskaya 1968.
5. Heller 2009, p. 36.
6. Heller 2009, p. 39.
7. Heller 2006.
8. Beik 1985.
9. Collins 1994; Swann 2003.

status. These power-brokers were landowners who mostly drew their wealth from the labour of the peasants who paid them rent and dues. This was indeed a 'feudal' situation inherited from the distant past, but it was not static. On the contrary, the tenants continued to resist and obstruct from below, while, within the nobility, a long-term struggle was going on between regional magnates and the centralising royal state over distribution of the agricultural surplus, which came directly from rents and indirectly from taxes. I am in agreement with Porchnev about the fundamental class-orientation of this society, although I have criticised him for overstating the influence of the bourgeoisie.[10] Heller has no grounds for claiming that I 'deny an initial period of petty-commodity production and primitive accumulation', since this topic was beyond the scope of my project and consequently was not discussed.

Heller concedes that he 'basically agrees' with me that France was 'ruled by a nobility which exercised its hold over the peasantry through the absolutist state'.[11] Where, then, is the problem? It lies in our differing approaches to the agents of change. In a sense, our discussion recapitulates the old Dobb-Sweezy debate of the 1950s.[12] What was behind the dynamic and dramatic transition from feudalism to capitalism? For Sweezy, it was the external push of international trade and the circulation and accumulation of merchant-wealth. For Dobb, it was class-conflict emerging within the system from contradictions between social forces and relations of production. Heller, closer to Sweezy, continues to see evidence of capitalism in every economic fact. Wherever he finds merchants, manufacturing, markets, extensive wage-labour, agricultural consolidation or technological improvement, he declares that capitalism is on the rise.

To be sure, all these economic and social facts can loosely be designated 'capitalistic' and be attributed to the rising middle class. No-one denies that the economy was developing in early-modern France. But how was their profit-making different from that of the ancient Greeks or the merchants of any other society? A good Marxist definition should indicate what is distinctive about a given form of class-exploitation and explain its dynamic capacity to transform social relations. We need to know how labour was managed by the dominant class and how the fruits of that labour were distributed. Merely citing merchants or profit-making does not fill the bill.

Heller can certainly cite progressive forces at work here and there, such as the landlord who invests his revenues back into farm-improvements and raises production by hiring cheap labour, the merchant-partners who take over and

10. Porchnev 1963.
11. Heller 2009, p. 38.
12. Harman 2008; Sweezy et al. 1976.

transform the market for a product, say woollens, by employing cheap cottage-labour and taking advantage of economics of scale to produce larger quantities at lower cost; or the banker whose international contacts enable him to transfer money on paper over long distances without moving actual coins, thus lowering transaction-costs. All these techniques existed in France, although the French often lagged behind other countries. But the big question is how widespread these new practices were and how much impact they had on social change. We need the whole picture rather than focusing only on certain dynamic elements. And it is equally important to ask what obstacles kept the innovators from achieving their potential and what contradictions kept the society from reproducing itself without mutating into something else.

Heller claims that I have missed Le Roy Ladurie's depiction of the 'offensive of rent against profit'. Heller takes 'rent' as signifying traditional payment to the owner for the use of the land, an archaic payment which he at one point assimilates with seigneurial dues, and 'profit' as the net proceeds of a farmer's rural capitalist enterprise. Rent and profit then become stand-ins to measure the struggle of the two sides – the landed nobility and the bourgeoisie. The enterprising farmer gains in the sixteenth- century, falls back in the seventeenth century, and triumphs in the eighteenth century. But Le Roy Ladurie is not speaking in Marxist terms. He is talking in market-terms about a conjunctural balance-sheet comprised of land-rent, taxes, wages, and what was left – profit. The changes in rent and profit were determned largely by demographic and political factors, which, in turn, affected supply and demand. Left out of the equation is any consideration of whether the profits were invested in growth which brought fundamental change in yields or in class-relationships. In other words, the process describes the relative prosperity of owner, tenant, and hired employee, but not necessarily the progress of the rural bourgeoisie.

Heller consistently elides the meaning of his terms, seeing a bourgeois under every bush. He finds evidence of a growing bourgeoisie in 'a proliferation of markets', 'merchant-capitalism', 'peasant-expropriation', 'dependence on wage-labour', the 'strengthening of the middle class by the religious wars', 'the growing assertiveness of the bourgeoisie' in Dauphine and Languedoc in the 1570s, the strength of the Catholic leagues in the 1590s, the demands of the Third Estate in 1588, the quarrels of the Third and Second Estates in 1614, the 'democratic commune' of La Rochelle, and the Huguenots' extensive business-dealings. In the popular revolts of the seventeenth century, he speculates, 'there surely were peasants or merchants who rebelled as a result of a squeeze on profits'. He argues the same for the Ormée-rebellion in Bordeaux in 1651–2.[13] There were indeed merchants involved in the Ormée-movement,

13. Heller 2009, p. 50.

along with a cross-section of artisans, legal functionaries and a few nobles, but their grievances were about representation, good government and popular control. There was no hint of concern over profits, or even foreign trade. The more characteristic seventeenth-century tax-riots were conducted largely by the *menu peuple* over illicit taxes. The merchants were usually targets, not participants.[14]

With these issues in mind, I see much of Heller's evidence as problematic. First, it is no longer adequate to speak of the bourgeoisie, or indeed any class, as a unified force playing a single-purposeful role in history. Second, it is crucial to weigh the forces of resistance and blockage as well as the influence of change. Evidence of an urban investor who was consolidating rural properties does not necessarily show that he was shifting to intensive cultivation of capitalist crops, if the landlord was absentee and the farms were leased out in small plots to local peasants, as we see in Jacquart's study of the Hurepoix.[15] Evidence of growing masses of landless villagers does not necessarily indicate the emergence of capitalist wage-labour. Merchant-successes and active markets do not necessarily demonstrate a rise in the rate of production due to improved methods. The rise of new wealth does not automatically transform the system if it is sunk into royal offices and into ownership of traditional farms leased out to traditional peasants. My contention is that much of the potential progress was absorbed into the existing social system, even while new forces were growing and influences from abroad were provoking change. The bourgeois were on the stage but they still had a relatively small role.

Formulae drawn from the *Communist Manifesto* or the writings of Engels do not provide adequate tools for a thorough analysis of the early-modern period, which was not, after all, their central concern. A reflective Marxism needs to delve deeply and critically into the forms of exploitation and the uses of capital. Recent scholarship provides ample evidence of the subordinate role played by the bourgeoisie in early-modern France. It appears that, contrary to Heller's 'classical-Marxist' focus on the dynamic leadership of the bourgeoisie, this class was not strong enough or conscious enough to seize power. This loosely defined 'middle class' was still made up of groups with contradictory interests. Many were royal officials, professionals of various sorts, craftsmen and artisans with distinctive skills. Many of those who could be defined as bourgeois were still deeply tied to the existing power-structure, and, as a group, were not yet strong enough to bring about revolutionary change.

Stating this does not put us in the ranks of the revisionists. There are other ways to think of class-conflict in the Revolution. The dramatic development of capitalist forces in the later eighteenth century may have altered the situation

14. Beik 1997.
15. Jacquart 1974.

by 1789. The Revolution might be seen as being made not *by* the bourgeoisie but *for* the bourgeoisie. One might postulate that the Revolution was caused by the collapse of the old system under the weight of its own contradictions: a new study by Steven Miller on eighteenth-century Languedoc, for instance, finds the collaboration of royal and noble forces still in place.[16] The provincial nobles were still allied with the crown in defence of their privileges, but they were becoming alienated from other aspects of the royal administration and some were leaning towards constitutional resistance. They would both generate demands for change and lead the resistance to change, as the Revolution approached.[17]

In the end, Heller and I agree that French society was structured by the class-conflict between landlords and peasants and that the bourgeoisie was growing more powerful within it. In his recent book on the Revolution, Heller describes these conflicts better. Here, in his haste to defend the concept of a rising bourgeoisie, he holds on to weak equivalencies and overly-simplified notions.

References

Beik, William 1985, *Absolutism and Society in Seventeenth-Century France: State Power and Provincial Aristocracy in Languedoc*, Cambridge: Cambridge University Press.

—— 1997, *Urban Protest in Seventeenth-Century France: The Culture of Retribution*, Cambridge: Cambridge University Press.

Collins, James 1994, *Classes, Estates and Orders in Early Modern Brittany*, Cambridge: Cambridge University Press.

Harman, Chris 2008, 'An Age of Transition? Economy and Society in England in the Later Middle Ages: The Field and the Forge: Population, Production and Power in the Pre-Industrial West', *Historical Materialism*, 16, 1: 185–99.

Heller, Henry 2006, *The Bourgeois Revolution in France 1789–1815*, New York: Berghahn Books.

—— 2009, 'The *Longue Durée* of the French Bourgeoisie', *Historical Materialism*, 17, 1: 31–59.

Jacquart, Jean 1974, *La Crise rurale en Ile de France, 1550–1670*, Paris: Publications de la Sorbonne.

Lublinskaya, A.D. 1968, *French Absolutism: The Crucial Phase 1620–1629*, translated by Brian Pearce, Cambridge: Cambridge University Press.

Miller, Stephen 2008, *State and Society in Eighteenth-Century France: A Study of Political Power and Social Revolution in Languedoc*, Washington DC.: The Catholic University of America Press.

Porchnev, Boris 1963, *Les soulèvements populaires en France de 1623 à 1648*, Paris: SEVPEN.

Swann, Julian 2003, *Provincial Power and Absolute Monarchy: The Estates of Burgundy, 1661–1790*, Cambridge: Cambridge University Press.

Sweezy, Paul M. et al. 1976, *The Transition from Feudalism to Capitalism*, London: NLB.

16. Miller 2008.
17. Miller 2008.

BRILL

Historical Materialism 18 (2010) 123–131

historical materialism
research in critical marxist theory
brill.nl/hima

Henry Heller and the '*Longue Durée* of the French Bourgeoisie'

David Parker
Professor Emeritus University of Leeds
D.Parker@Leeds.ac.uk

Abstract
This short article shows that Heller's assertion that I have announced the death of the early modern French bourgeoisie is misplaced. At the same time, it defends the view that a prolonged period of economic stasis together with the low level of bourgeois classness make it impossible to sustain Engel's view that absolute monarchy rested on a supposed balance between it and the nobility. In conclusion, it is suggested that Marxist analysis cannot be reduced to a treatment of class-anatogonisms.

Keywords
France, absolute monarchy, bourgeoisie, economic development

Heller's central argument is that Beik and I have underestimated the weight of an 'independent', that is *capitalist* bourgeoisie in France. He believes that my treatment of the trading and manufacturing class is 'cursory and dismissive'[1] and amounts to no less than a declaration of the 'death of the bourgeoisie in the seventeenth century'.[2] Yet, in the passages to which Heller alludes, I observed that, despite the relatively depressed economic conditions of the seventeenth century, maritime trade continued to expand even if more hesitantly than during the preceding hundred years; notwithstanding significant geographical and institutional obstacles there were, I wrote, identifiable successful 'merchant capitalists' who contributed to a slow integration of local, regional and international-commercial networks.[3]

Heller's view that I have killed off the bourgeoisie is buttressed by the further claim that I have 'failed to notice the process of primitive accumulation, social

1. Heller 2009, p. 52.
2. Heller 2009, p. 55.
3. Parker 1996, pp. 31–2, 36–7.

DOI: 10.1163/156920610X512471

differentiation and growing bourgeois strength in the French countryside'.[4] This involved the expropriation and pauperisation of a substantial proportion of the peasantry and the concentration of land into the hands of a bourgeoisie both urban and rural. It is Heller himself who is guilty of not noticing. I dealt at some length with these developments in twenty or so pages devoted precisely to 'The Dispossession of the Peasantry' and 'Agrarian Class Relations'.[5] I even observed, as many others have done, that, despite the remorseless fragmentation of peasant-landholdings over the best part of two centuries and the well-documented decline in the number of substantial peasant-holdings, every community still contained a small group of rural notables who occasionally founded farming dynasties which lasted into the twentieth century.

In similar vein, Heller asserts that I concluded that 'there was no participation by substantial merchants' in the extraordinarily successful revolt at La Rochelle of the lesser bourgeois in 1614, a view, he says, disputed by the later work of Kevin Robbins.[6] If I had actually reached such an unqualified conclusion, Robbins would undoubtedly have put me right. In fact, I had been very careful to say that a definitive view of the social composition of leaders of the revolt would require a systematic investigation of the notarial records at La Rochelle.[7] Robbins subsequently carried out the necessary research and was indeed able to reveal the significant role played by some wealthy merchants in directing and sustaining a movement rooted in the middling groups of the Rochelais community. The coalition of forces which he describes has a striking similarity to those which contributed to the earlier establishment of the Dutch Republic and the imminent revolution in England. Heller might have made more of this, but he was perhaps aware that Robbins's analysis contained a significant rider. 'After 1614', he observed, 'La Rochelle became even more anomalous among French provincial cities, combining a majority of religious schismatics with a substantial influential number of innovative political actors drawn from the middle ranks of urban society'.[8] In other words, developments at La Rochelle during the fourteen years in which the lesser bourgeois secured a leading role in the municipal government were not typical of French towns in general; except, it should be stressed, in the sense that the rebellion of the lesser bourgeoisie was itself a reaction to the emergence of a self-perpetuating, increasingly venal, urban patriciate – a process replicated virtually everywhere. No doubt, Heller is right, though he produces no evidence, in suggesting that merchants also played a part in the most celebrated urban revolt of all in

4. Heller 2009, p. 43.
5. Parker 1996, pp. 51 ff.
6. Heller 2009, p. 47.
7. Parker 1980, p. 44 & note 3.
8. Robbins 1997, p. 329.

mid-century Bordeaux. Antipathy to the office-holding élite was again a significant factor.

In presenting a caricature of my view of French economic and social developments, Heller misses the point. The existence of those whom we may describe as capitalists or bourgeois is not and has never been in dispute. The picture I offered is sufficiently nuanced to accommodate both the discovery of merchants who were not only wealthy but hostile to authority and the existence of the hundred or so *gros fermiers* of the Ile de France identified by Moriceau to whom Heller appeals. Whether they formed part of a bourgeois class is another question. If one assumes, as Heller appears to do, that it is sufficient to define a class by virtue of a common relationship to the means of production, then both merchants and *fermiers* may be said to form two identifiable classes by the mere fact of their existence. But this is clearly inadequate if we wish to be more precise about either the progress of the bourgeoisie or the extent of capitalist development. The key questions are what happened to the bourgeoisie in the seventeenth century, what role did they play in the formation of the absolute state and what merit was there in Engels's view that the monarchy was able to achieve a certain independence because the bourgeoisie now offered a counterpoise to the traditional nobility. On the first of these questions, it transpires that Heller and I are at least in agreement about the way in which capitalist development was arrested in the seventeenth century. He accepts that 'as a class the bourgeoisie was clearly in retreat' and that 'its most advanced elements were co-opted to the side of the state'.[9]

Yet there is more to be said about the way in which the political autonomy and economic vitality of France's urban communities was subverted and constrained by the drive to restore the integrity of the monarchical régime after decades of civil strife. To this end, the crown employed a combination of strategies depending on local circumstances: direct military or political intervention, fiscal pressure and the sale of offices on a vast scale. The latter diverted productive capital to an incalculable extent, offering thousands of willing purchasers the prospect of greater status, influence and security. The bourgeoisie had neither the resolve nor the means to resist what proved to be a very effective combination of carrot and stick. Their unco-ordinated and often sectional responses reflected the low level of economic integration and the fragmented character of France's political institutions. Local interests were paramount and, as the capitalist thrust of the sixteenth century stressed by Heller ebbed away, they remained a formidable obstacle to the formation of the bourgeoisie as a class with a clear sense of its own identity. The rebellious Rochelais bourgeois did not constitute part of a cohesive class but a highly

9. Heller 2009, p. 51.

localised – indeed isolated – movement within the confines of an exceptionally privileged urban enclave which wanted nothing more than to preserve this position. Of course, in the right circumstances, as in the Low Countries, defence of traditional privileges could acquire a more radical character but France was not Holland – although the royal apologists found it useful to castigate the Huguenots as would-be republicans.

It is nonetheless true that the social and political stresses of the sixteenth century had encouraged a certain development of constitutional ideas and a critique of noble mores and values. Heller cites Louis Turquet de Mayerne's *La Monarchie aristodémocratique*, written in 1591 and published in 1611, as an expression of bourgeois aspirations.[10] Given that Heller takes me to task for underestimating the bourgeois thrust of the sixteenth century, it is surprising that he has nothing to say about my own discussion of Turquet, which acknowledged its significance in unambiguous terms. Turquet's ideas, I said, could 'be seen as a manifestation of the dynamic economic and social impulses of the sixteenth century before they faded away and the implementation of which would have destroyed the *ancien régime*'.[11]

I went on to discuss the 'hegemonic tour de force' by which the nobility recovered the ideological high-ground. If this is what Heller means by 'class-war from above'[12] then there is little between us; but it might be thought that a class-war really requires two sides. Urban oligarchs, though often vexed by the threats to their privileged position, showed less and less inclination, once the Protestant towns had been defeated or isolated, to join either dissident nobles or artisans and peasants in their endemic resistance to the crown. In the end, not being able to produce much more than stray and tenuous references to a rebellious bourgeoisie, Heller virtually concedes as much, declaring that the involvement of the bourgeosie in popular uprisings is not really an appropriate test of class-conflict.[13]

Given that Heller agrees that the seventeenth century was, on the whole, one of relative economic stagnation with the bourgeoisie in retreat, its upper layers absorbed into the state-machine, and the nobility on the offensive, it is difficult to understand why he persists with the notion that absolute monarchy was in some way the product of a balance between two contending classes. His conclusion is indeed hesitant, defending the classical-Marxist view 'only in part' and acknowledging that the equilibrium was tipped in favour of the nobility. This is very wise, given that no-one has ever been able to show that an independent, capitalist bourgeoisie possessed anything like the same social

10. Heller 2009, p. 47.
11. Parker 1996, p. 139.
12. Heller 2009, p. 51.
13. Ibid.

and political clout as the nobility. The only Marxist analysis which attempted to do this in any depth was produced by Lublinskaya, who argued that the recovery of monarchical authority in the early seventeenth century and its success in overcoming the Huguenots depended on the support of the towns. The bourgeoisie, she suggested, was grateful for the government's programme of economic protectionism. This interpretation founders on objections which I set out at some length.[14] The critical one is that it was the defection of the Huguenot nobility, rather than that of the principal Huguenot towns, which resulted in the royal victory. Despite the social and political conservatism of the urban élites, which may, as at La Rochelle, have been under pressure from the middling sort, the major towns continued to resist after having been abandoned by the great nobles. In any event, such conservatism had little to do with gratitude for the government's mercantilist policies which were rightly perceived to be a threat to urban autonomy. These were certainly not developed at the behest of, or in conjunction with, the merchant-community.[15] Heller, though evidently convinced that Beik treats Lublinskaya in a dismissive fashion, makes no attempt to engage with these questions. What precisely, we are justified in asking, is the evidence to support the view that the trading and industrial bourgeoisie had sufficient influence 'to push the state towards developments which prepared the way for the rise of capitalism'?[16]

Heller introduces Engels's view of the class-equilibrium, which supposedly made possible the rise of absolute monarchy in one brief sentence. The following one moves on to Engels's picture of the dissolution of serfdom, the growth of petty-commodity production and primitive accumulation.[17] Heller does not elucidate the connection between the first and the second, although we might reasonably infer that he sees the latter as a basis for the former. He certainly gives the impression that he sees the dispossession of the peasantry, accompanied by a growing bourgeois strength in the countryside and creating a pool of wage-labour, as fundamental. Far from ignoring this development, as Heller claims, I explicitly recognised that the proletarianisation and expropriation of the peasantry was an essential precondition for the development of capitalism.[18] Nonetheless, because of the immense burdens placed on the productive population and the inability of French manufacture to absorb more than a fraction of the potential labour-force, the net result was not a rapid development of capitalism but a period of stasis. Le Roy Ladurie's famous study of the Languedocian peasantry, to which Heller mistakenly

14. Parker 1971.
15. Parker 1980, pp. 71–80; 1966, pp. 29–31.
16. Heller 2009, p. 34.
17. Heller 2009, p. 33.
18. Parker 1996, p. 58.

appeals in order to buttress his view of the progress of rural capitalism, was a major influence in leading to me this conclusion. Le Roy Ladurie was unambiguous about the consequences which flowed from the polarisation of rural landholding and the concomitant decline of the middle-ranking peasants, stressing that 'capitalism is not built on poverty'.[19]

Nor did the concentration of larger properties in the hands of aspiring urban bourgeois and officeholders of itself introduce capitalism, because these were frequently broken up into smallholdings manageable by their tenants, the use of wage-labour was frequently partial and intermittent, whilst capital-investment was low. The *gros fermiers*, to whom Heller refers, undoubtedly displayed entrepreneurial qualities, managing the holdings which they rented with an eye to the profits to be made from selling produce to nearby urban markets. But they were a tiny fraction of a rural population overwhelmingly devoted to subsistence-farming within the constraints imposed by both seigneurial and communal régimes. There was no equivalent in seventeenth-century France to the English yeomanry and resident gentry who were the driving force behind a significant rise in agricultural productivity which left most French regions lagging far behind. In the following century, there were greater signs of agricultural progress which Heller has assembled to much better effect in his recent study of the French Revolution. Even then, however, he notes that productivity remained low, that most peasants had small amounts of land or none at all and that progress towards capitalist relations was generally 'halting and tentative'.[20]

Absolute monarchy in France emerged at a time when economic conditions make it impossible to explain this by reference to a rising bourgeoisie endowed with the social and political weight to perform the function attributed to it by Engels. Heller, however, is concerned that by denying the central importance of conflict between nobility and bourgeoisie we have deprived seventeenth-century France of 'a sense of dynamic development'.[21] This is a telling comment, indicative of Heller's attachment to a reductionist Marxism which seeks to make the evolution of the French state directly dependent on the balance of class-forces. The French state undoubtedly fulfilled a class-function, draining the countryside and towns of their surplus-wealth to the benefit of those with power, influence and status. But this function does not, of itself, explain the forces which brought absolute monarchy into being. I have set out in various publications, and at some length, the dynamics which pushed

19. Le Roy Ladurie 1969, p. 163.

20. Heller 2006, pp. 28, 29, 31. Doyle estimates that, in the eighteenth century, the peasant-élite numbered at most 600,000 that is less than 3% of the population. Doyle 1997, p. 197.

21. Heller 2009, p. 38.

France in an absolutist direction, so, here, a rather mechanical list will have to suffice: tension between the decentralising and centralising elements in a feudal body-politic; the pressures of large-scale warfare on an inelastic economy; the drive to religious conformity; economic nationalism and *dirigiste* economic policies; the intense competition for place, influence and a share of the wealth channelled in ever-increasing amounts through the growing state-apparatus. The dialectics of this competition lead both to a concentration of power in the hands of the great royal favourites and then to an appreciation of the need for a ruler who could rise above the fray. The endemic rebellions of the populace further reinforced the willingness of the upper classes to settle their own differences. How convincingly I managed to develop these arguments and how successfully they were incorporated within a Marxist conceptual framework is for others to judge. But it is absurd to suggest that I have ended up with an immobile seventeenth century denuded of dynamics.

By comparison with the seventeenth century, the following one was economically much more dynamic, and, in some areas, notably overseas-trade, the rate of growth was truly remarkable. Heller is therefore on stronger empirical ground in his recent work which seeks to rescue the idea of bourgeois revolution. Economic growth there certainly was and its relationship to the Revolution is far from settled, despite the efforts of those who would gut it of its social and economic content. Bourgeois culture and ideas, both political and economic, were increasingly evident, particularly from the 1760s, and affected the thinking of many who were certainly not merchants or manufacturers. Nonetheless the allied question of whether a bourgeois class made the revolution in 1789 remains deeply problematic. Right until the last, the bourgeoisie aspired to join the nobility rather than destroy it, whilst the feudal property-régime was abolished only under duress from an insurgent peasantry. Although the capitalist bourgeoisie grew in numbers and wealth over the course of the eighteenth century, they formed only part of the six per cent of the population who could be classified as bourgeois.[22] If the outbreak of Revolution had been dependent upon a capitalist bourgeoisie chafing at the limitations of an aristocratic polity, it would not have occurred in 1789. It was the crisis itself and what followed which crystallised latent values and pushed the bourgeoisie into a sense of its own identity. Yet, even when the bourgeois revolution was won, the hegemony of the bourgeoisie remained fragile, its rule subject to fracture and instability for many decades to come. In contrast, the British ruling class first absorbed demands for political reform and then successfully avoided the revolutions which swept across Europe in 1848.

22. Doyle 1999, p. 122.

All this may confirm Heller in his conviction that revisionism has swept the board, disfiguring Marxism in the process. In response, I would simply say that Marxism does not presuppose that class-antagonisms are the only contradictions to be addressed, either when explaining the formation of absolute monarchy or when analysing its demise. As Lenin (who knew more than most about making a revolution before the 'objective' conditions had matured) observed, a revolution happens when the old order cannot carry on in the old way. By the 1760s, many Frenchmen, and not just the bourgeoisie, were coming to understand that the monarchy could not carry on in the old way. Central to this realisation was the experience of defeat in their colonial rivalry with Britain, which not only bankrupted the régime but reinforced awareness of the latter's economic superiority. Such awareness stretched back to the mercantilist writers of the early seventeenth century, but now the idea that protectionism offered a solution was discarded in favour of *laissez-faire*. English agriculture and industrial techniques set the benchmark. In a significant sense, it was the comparative backwardness of French capitalism that precipitated the crisis of 1789 rather than the collision of a rising class with the limits of the existing order. This is not a new idea.[23] Here is what Marx and Engels wrote in 1845, although not specifically about the French Revolution:

> ... [A]ll collisions in history have their origin, according to our view, in the contradiction between the productive forces and the form of intercourse. Incidentally to lead to collisions in a country this contradiction need not necessarily have reached its extreme limit in that particular country. The competition with industrially more advanced countries is sufficient to produce a similar contradiction with a less advanced industry.[24]

References

Doyle, William 1999, *Origins of the French Revolution*, Third Edition, Oxford: Oxford University Press.

Heller, Henry 2006, *The Bourgeois Revolution in France 1789–1815*, New York: Berghahn Books.

—— 2009, 'The *Longue Durée* of the French Bourgeoisie', *Historical Materialism*, 17, 1: 31–59.

Le Roy Ladurie, Emmanuel 1969 [1966], *Les paysans de Languedoc*, Abridged Edition, Paris: Flammarion.

23. Cf. Skopcol 1979; Parker 1996; Teschke 2002.
24. Marx & Engels 1975, pp. 74–5.

Lublinskaya, A.D. 1968, *French Absolutism: the Crucial Phase 1620–29*, translated by Brian Pearce, Cambridge: Cambridge University Press.
Marx, Karl and Friedrich Engels 1975 [1845/6], *The German Ideology*, in *Collected Works*, Volume 5, London: Lawrence and Wishart.
Parker, David 1971, 'The Social Foundation of French Absolutism 1610–30', *Past and Present*, 53: 67–89.
—— 1978, 'The Huguenots in Seventeenth Century France', in *Minorities in History*, edited by A.C. Hepburn, London: Edward Arnold.
—— 1980, *La Rochelle and the French Monarchy: Conflict and Order in Seventeenth Century France*, London: Royal Historical Society.
—— 1996, *Class and State in Ancien Régime France: The Road to Modernity?*, London: Routledge.
Robbins, Kevin 1997, *City on the Ocean Sea, La Rochelle 1530–1650: Urban Society, Religion and Politics on the French Atlantic Frontier*, Leiden: Brill.
Skopcol, Theda 1979, *States and Revolutions*, Cambridge: Cambridge University Press.
Teschke, Benno 2003, *The Myth of 1648: Class, Geopolitics and the Making of Modern International Relations*, London: Verso.

BRILL

Historical Materialism 18 (2010) 132–142

historical materialism
research in critical marxist theory
brill.nl/hima

Response to William Beik and David Parker

Henry Heller
University of Manitoba, Winnipeg, Canada
heller@cc.umanitoba.ca

Abstract
This debate with William Beik and David Parker concerns whether a capitalist bourgeoisie developed in the *ancien régime*. Parker asserts that, in 1789, this class at best was new and unfledged. Beik claims that it is unhistorical to speak of its existence. Addressing their arguments, I re-iterate that the existence of a capitalist bourgeoisie was of long standing. It emerged from the sixteenth century onwards, buoyed by primitive accumulation and strengthened itself even in the face of the so-called offensive of rent under seventeenth-century absolutism.

Keywords
Capitalism, class, rent, profit, bourgeoisie, primitive accumulation, revisionism, French Revolution, Le Roy Ladurie

In 'The *Longue Durée* of the French Bourgeoisie' I argued that, despite the ascendancy of the Bourbon monarchy and nobility, a capitalist bourgeoisie continued to exist in seventeenth-century France.[1] As the title of the article suggests, what is in question is the long-term development of a capitalist bourgeoisie through the three centuries of the *ancien régime*. What is at stake is the notion of the Revolution of 1789 as a bourgeois and capitalist revolution culminating this long-term development. Such a view represented the standard interpretation of early-modern French history among liberal and Marxist historians of the nineteenth and twentieth centuries. According to this interpretation, the Revolution cleared the way for capitalism to flourish in the nineteenth century.

In the last generation, this narrative has been challenged by revisionism. Strongest in the English-speaking countries, this tendency has its followers in France as well. Mercurial in its approaches, revisionism's main focus is to attack the idea that the Revolution was a bourgeois and capitalist revolution.

1. Heller 2009.

 DOI: 10.1163/156920610X512480

It has become my project to argue against such revisionism from a Marxist point of view by reasserting the old view of the rise of a capitalist bourgeoisie through the history of the *ancien régime*.

The first part of this plan emerged in the course of researching a book entitled *Labour, Science and Technology in France 1500–1620*.[2] In that work, which was published in 1996, I offered a new interpretation of the religious wars that shook France in the late sixteenth century (1562–98). That period was, for the most part, interpreted as a complex period of fanatical and irrational violence which led to a serious demographic and economic regression. While not completely rejecting this consensus on the religious wars, I highlighted the role of class-conflict in the form of noble reaction, but also of bourgeois and popular resistance. More importantly, I argued that the violence, heavy taxes, usury and economic decline of that period provoked an acceleration of primitive accumulation which led to a substantial decline in landholding by the poorer peasantry and the transfer of much of its property into the hands of rural and urban élites. The consequence was a notable increase in the availability of wage-labour and an unprecedented spurt of interest in both technological innovation and agricultural improvement.

My findings were reinforced by the pioneering research of Jean-Marc Moriceau who found that it was precisely in this period that an élite of wealthier peasants consolidated itself as a stratum of capitalist tenant-farmers in the Ile-de-France. Already endowed with some land, fixed capital and cash-reserves, rich peasants were able to lease the farms controlled by the nobles, urban bourgeoisie and Church while using the wage-labour of their hard-pressed neighbours.[3] In other words, far from simply being a period of mere economic regression, the late sixteenth century in France was a period of primitive accumulation quite comparable to what occurred in England in the sixteenth century as classically outlined by Marx in the concluding chapters of the first volume of *Capital*.[4] In those chapters, Marx demonstrated that as a result of such processes the sixteenth century must be regarded as the founding moment of English capitalism. My work, in addition to that of Moriceau, led me to the conclusion that the late sixteenth century must be regarded as a comparable period in France.

The second part of my plan was completed with the recent publication of *The Bourgeois Revolution in France: 1789–1815*.[5] In that work, I analysed the

2. Heller 1996.
3. Moriceau 1993.
4. Marx 1977, pp. 874–913.
5. Heller 2006.

current historiography on the French Revolution and showed that, despite the arguments of the revisionists, an analysis of the evidence overwhelmingly pointed to the fact that the French Revolution was a bourgeois and capitalist revolution. In the Revolution, the upheavals in the agrarian sector proved to be crucial. Pushed by mass-protest from below, capitalist farmers assumed leadership over the rural revolution which saw the overthrow of feudalism.

The third part of this triadic design is found in the article in question. It seeks to tie together my findings on the late sixteenth century with my analysis of the French Revolution. It argues that, since there was a capitalist bourgeoisie in the sixteenth century, and an even stronger one in the eighteenth century, it is likely that there was continuity in the development of this class in the intervening period. My hypothesis was reinforced by the doctoral thesis of Moriceau, which showed, not only that a rural bourgeoisie took root in the sixteenth century, but that it persisted though the seventeenth century, getting stronger rather than weaker through its engrossing of the land and the rationalisation of its operations.[6] At the same time, I argued that merchant-capital also held its own during the seventeenth century. As a result of this persistence of the bourgeoisie, it was in a position to resume its progress during the boom of the eighteenth century. In consequence of this analysis, I re-asserted the view that the dominant role played by the bourgeoisie in the Revolution was the outcome of a long period of gestation over the three centuries of the *ancien régime*.

In the course of advancing this argument, I challenged some of the principal contentions of the prominent English-speaking historians William Beik and David Parker.[7] Beik and Parker claimed that a capitalist bourgeoisie barely existed or existed not all in seventeenth-century France. In the light of this class's weakness, Beik and Parker inferred further that, although there was a considerable amount of popular unrest in seventeenth-century France, class-war was largely absent. Beik denied that there was a period of petty-commodity production or primitive accumulation prior to the seventeenth century in France, in contrast to England. Parker acknowledged a decline of feudalism in the late middle ages, but insisted that no capitalism emerged in the sixteenth century. According to both Beik and Parker, a mercantile and manufacturing bourgeoisie was scarcely evident in the seventeenth century. In other words, both Beik and Parker denied the existence of a bourgeoise as a class-in-itself (an economic class) let alone a class-for-itself (an economically-formed and conscious class). Indeed, Parker

6. Moriceau 1994.
7. Beik 1985; Parker 1996.

took this a step further, arguing that it was difficult to identify a capitalist bourgeoisie in eighteenth-century France, thus throwing doubt on the notion that the French Revolution could have been a capitalist revolution.

The point of departure of my objections to the views of Beik and Parker was their neglect and underestimation of the achievements of the sixteenth century. Basing my analysis on the work of Emmanuel Le Roy Ladurie,[8] Moriceau and others, I claimed that the two historians had ignored or dismissed the emergence of a rural and urban capitalism and capitalist bourgeoisie in the sixteenth century, bolstered particularly by the consequences of primitive accumulation. Indeed, I asserted that not only was there evidence of the existence of a bourgeoisie as a class-in-itself, but also one-for-itself, reflected in urban and peasant-protest, demands of the third estate at the Estates-General of 1588 and the anti-feudal writings of figures such as Turquet de Mayerne. This so-called offensive of profit lasted until the late sixteenth or even the early decades of the seventeenth century. On the other hand, the seventeenth century was to be mainly characterised by an offensive of rent.

It is this notion of an offensive of rent derived from the work of Le Roy Ladurie, upon which Beik and Parker depend as the basis of their interpretation of the seventeenth century. But such an offensive of rent, I argued, has to be understood as coming at the expense of profit, which continued to exist although in retreat. In other words, a capitalist bourgeoisie endured, albeit thrown on the defensive by a class-war carried on from above by the nobility and Bourbon state. Indeed, based on the work of Moriceau, which was admittedly founded on research confined to the Ile-de-France, I pointed out that capitalist farmers successfully adapted to this assault by rationalising and improving their operations, emerging stronger than ever at the beginning of the eighteenth century.[9] At the same time, I brought forward a growing body of research reflecting the continued existence of a mercantile and manufacturing bourgeoisie. In short, whilst agreeing that the sense of a bourgeoisie as a class-for-itself faded in the seventeenth century, I insisted that the bourgeoisie as a class-in-itself continued to exist. It constituted the soil out of which grew the increasingly large and powerful bourgeoisie that developed in the eighteenth century and which eventually assumed leadership over the revolution of 1789.

In his response to my article, Beik claims that his book was not about the bourgeoisie, but rather 'the channels... that linked the royal government and the ruling class of... Languedoc'. This is fair enough, as this nexus is

8. Le Roy Ladurie 1966.
9. Moriceau 1994.

fundamental to understanding the political structure of the *ancien régime*. But, in the course of making the argument for a virtual symbiosis between the civil society of the *ancien régime* and the Bourbon state, Beik made a point of dismissing the existence of a capitalist bourgeoisie living off profit. He was perfectly correct to discount the influence of the bourgeoisie politically, but, in doing so, he wrongly erased its continuing economic existence.

As part of his argument he wrote that 'Heller has no grounds for claiming that I "deny an initial period of petty-commodity production and primitive accumulation" since this topic was beyond the scope of my project, and consequently was not discussed'. Yet, in noting the development of Marxist views of the *ancien régime*, Beik approvingly observed that

> once serfdom, which was intimately associated with feudalism, disappeared, a new mode of production was called for – if not capitalism directly, then a period of 'petty commodity production' or 'primitive accumulation'. This association of the early modern period with the rise of the bourgeoisie and the rise of capitalism made considerable sense for England, where most attention was directed, but not for France, where the society of lords and dependent peasants persisted for centuries, the aristocracy consistently renewed itself, and absolutism became a powerful force instead of a hollow shell.[10]

Beik asserts that the difference between us rehearses the old debate between Paul Sweezy and Maurice Dobb, in which the former invoked trade as the external prime mover and Dobb insisted on the importance of class-struggle. Beik intimates that he somehow stressed Dobb's relations-of-production approach (class-struggle?) while I mistakenly emphasised the importance of trade which Dobb regarded as a regressive force. Actually, Dobb regarded primitive accumulation on the land and the changes in the social relations of production that came with it as fundamental to capitalist beginnings. As noted above, Beik dismissed primitive accumulation in France, while I regard it as the starting point of capitalist origins in France as well as England. It is true that I highlight the evidence for the existence of a trading bourgeoisie as Beik noted. But this is because, once capitalist production begins, exchange is essential to the realisation of surplus-value as capitalist profits. Trade is two-sided, playing a regressive role reinforcing feudal relations of production and blocking innovation, but, once capitalism has entered productive relations, market-exchange is necessary to the realisation of profits and eventually to the emergence of capitalist competition. Of course, Dobb fully understood this.

10. Beik 1985, p. 21.

Beik asserts that my claims of an early-modern French capitalism are superficial and that I need to probe deeply into the relations of production that existed under the *ancien régime* if I want to show that a real agricultural capitalism existed. If he read my analysis of Olivier de Serres's *Le théâtre d'agriculture et mesnage des champs* (1600) in *Labour, Science and Technology* he would realise that I have offered just such an analysis.[11] In Serres, who was reprinted many times and widely read down to the Revolution, he would have discovered the reality of a French rural capitalism which has eluded him.

In criticising Beik and Parker, I counterposed their notion of an unopposed seventeenth-century offensive of rent with Le Roy Ladurie's conception of a struggle between rent and profit, stressing that the advance of the one was always relative to the other. As such, profit and a rural-capitalist class certainly survived in the seventeenth century, although put on the defensive. In response, Beik claims that the neo-Malthusian Le Roy Ladurie deployed the terms rent, profit and wages in a way that has nothing to do with the vocabulary of Marxism. But the fact is that classical political economy starting from Adam Smith and continuing through Thomas Malthus, David Ricardo and Karl Marx used a common terminology with respect to rent, profit and wages, although they differed with respect to the historical premises and the consequences of their inter-action.

It is true that Le Roy Ladurie in the past expressed intense hostility to Marxism, as was the wont with some former members of the French Communist Party. But the intensity of the Cold War having dissipated, Le Roy Ladurie has called for reconciliation with Marxist colleagues and has expressed admiration for the work of eminent Marxist historians such as Albert Soboul and Guy Lemarchand.[12] Even in the 1970s, the then-Cold Warrior Le Roy Ladurie found it possible to give high marks to the doctoral thesis of the Marxist Guy Bois on late-medieval and early-modern upper Normandy. In his review of Bois in the pages of *Annales*, he makes clear that he and Bois are speaking about the same thing and from a congruent perspective:

> Under the cloak of a Marxist vocabulary which speaks to us of feudalism and even of centralised feudalism (the name ascribed to the modern royal state) we arrive with Guy Bois finally at the basic facts: they imply a Ricardian-Malthusian (or neo-Malthusian) equilibrium of the eco-system in a more than two centuries *longue durée* and at one and the same time the drift of the said eco-system towards

11. Heller 1996, pp. 168–73.
12. Le Roy Ladurie, Lemarchand and Rance 2008.

> a family-based capitalism. This is what makes this powerful and frequently admirable doctoral thesis truly interesting.[13]

The idea that Le Roy Ladurie employs a terminology which has no relation to Marxism therefore holds no water.

Beik denies that we can see the urban and peasant-unrest of the religious wars and the immediately following decades in class-terms. As for the French Revolution, Beik claims that the Revolution might be seen as being made not by the bourgeoisie but for the bourgeoisie. This is but part of his larger view that '…it is no longer adequate to speak of the bourgeoisie, or indeed any class, as a unified force playing a single-purposeful role in history'. It is interesting, in this regard, that Beik has had no problem speaking about the nobility as a class. Rather, it is the notion of a class that is an agent of change which appears problematic.

Early in his writings on history and politics, Marx made the distinction between the existence of such a class in terms of its relation to the means of production and the degree to which it has consciousness of itself. The former notion of a class-in-itself, in my view, continues to be a fruitful and important one in both historical and economic analysis. From the perspective of history, the notion of a class-for-itself and its relation to that of a class-in-itself appears more problematic. Yet it seems to me that the notion of a class-for-itself can be usefully applied to particular historical conjunctures. The three centuries of the *ancien régime* each have their concrete and particular characteristics which must be carefully taken into account. But the relationship of these phases to their denouement in the French Revolution must also be borne in mind.

In the French Revolution, the dominant discourse became that of *sans-culotterie* and classical republicanism. Nevertheless, it is significant that some revolutionaries did interpret the Revolution as a revolution of the bourgeoisie, the middle class and even the capitalist class. Such a discourse did not take hold because it was regarded as too divisive by the revolutionary élites attempting to establish leadership over the common people. The populist idea of the common people united against the aristocrats and of republican virtue appeared more appealing and politically palatable.[14] But it cannot be denied that the notion of a bourgeois revolution was certainly present in the minds of revolutionaries. This was because the revolution of 1789 was, in fact, a revolution in which a bourgeoise based on a growing capitalism took state-power. In other words, there was a convergence between the sense

13. Le Roy Ladurie 1978, p. 124.
14. Heller 2010.

of a class-in-itself and class-for-itself. In this light, it seems appropriate to examine the ferment of the late sixteenth century when, in more tentative and less organised fashion, an emerging capitalist bourgeoisie expressed itself politically, or as a class-for-itself. Le Roy Ladurie, for example, unselfconsciously compared the call of the third estate of Languedoc for confiscation of the temporalities of the Church in 1560 with the passage of the Civil Constitution of the Clergy by the National Assembly in 1791.[15] In seeing the one event as a prefiguration of the other, Le Roy Ladurie, like any good historian, was pointing to the common underlying social dynamic active in both periods.

With respect to the French Revolution, Parker asserted in his book that it was difficult to find a bourgeoisie in eighteenth-century France.[16] But, in light of my work, Parker now grudgingly concedes that a bourgeoisie, however feeble, took power in 1789. Yet he insists that this class was not the product of the long evolution of the *ancien régime* but only of its last years. On the contrary, I assert that great events like the French Revolution have proportionally deep causes, in this case the *longue durée* of the bourgeoisie. Parker complains that I ignored his treatment of maritime trade and references to primitive accumulation and social differentiation in the countryside. In fact, his references to maritime trade were cursory. Furthermore, his notion of a *dirigiste* state overriding the views of local entrepreneurs does not square with the emerging consensus on the way that seventeenth-century French mercantilism operated.[17] As for his discussion of primitive accumulation and social differentiation, I did not ignore them, but complained instead that '...Parker's approach is to underline all those factors which inhibited the development of capitalism in agriculture, while minimising those aspects which favoured its growth'.[18] Parker eventually admits this by noting that, despite the expropriation of the peasantry and their proletarianisation that 'because of the immense burdens placed on the productive population and the inability of French manufacture to absorb more than a fraction of the potential labour-force, the net result was not a rapid development of capitalism but a period of stasis'.

In drawing these conclusions, the authority of Le Roy Ladurie looms large in the eyes of Parker. Indeed, as the absolute master of the history of the *ancien régime*, it could hardly be otherwise. In any case, Parker invokes Le Roy Ladurie as 'a major influence in leading me to this conclusion', i.e., the

15. Le Roy Ladurie 1966, pp. 360–1.
16. Parker 1996, p. 280.
17. Reynard 1999.
18. Heller 2009, p. 44.

non-development of capitalism. But we have already cited Le Roy Ladurie to the effect that there was in fact a slow drift to capitalism throughout the course of the *ancien régime*.

Le Roy Ladurie's definitive statement on this question is found in his great summing up of 2002, the *Histoire des paysans français de la peste noire à la Révolution*.[19] Much of this enormous work simply reprints his earlier contribution to the *Histoire de la France rurale* and the *Histoire économique et sociale de la France*.[20] But about a third embodies new material including an up-to-date bibliography. In a quite dialectical way, Le Roy Ladurie points to the role of the nobility in creating large farms while underscoring the role of the tenants of these farms in the development of agrarian capitalism:

> ...[T]he accumulators of land of the classical age of the sixteenth and seventeenth centuries played the role of sorcerers's apprentices. In creating large domains they saw fit at the same time to create tenants who one day, in the eighteenth century, would challenge their descendants. From the midst of the peasants the amassers of land singled out an élite of farmers who for the times were already modern. In the very long term the latter traversed the French route toward agricultural capitalism, a route which itself preceded the 'agricultural revolutions' in the French mode. It is true that this 'route' was especially characteristic of northern France in which grain-farming on its fertile and muddy open fields dominated.[21]

Based on recent scholarship, including the work of Moriceau, Le Roy Ladurie ascribes this evolution towards capitalism to the whole of the north, the most productive agrarian region of France. In contrast, Parker defends his view of a non-capitalist France by falling back on Le Roy Ladurie's thesis of 1966, whose findings were explicitly limited to Languedoc, to the effect that capitalism failed to consolidate itself in that region. Forced to address the research of Moriceau on the capitalist tenant-farmers of the Ile-de-France, Parker attempts to minimise its import for the rest of northern France by noting their relatively small number, which he compares unfavourably to the in-depth strength of the capitalist gentry and yeomen of England. That the gentry or even the yeomen were in the vanguard of English rural capitalism is questionable. But, in any case, an acknowledged expert on English agriculture, J.P. Cooper, has noted that the number of large farms in northern France was entirely comparable to the number in lowland-England.[22]

---

19. Le Roy Ladurie 2002.
20. Le Roy Ladurie 1975; Le Roy Ladurie 1977, pp. 483–865.
21. Le Roy Ladurie 2002, p. 391.
22. Cooper 1985, pp. 143, 152.

In challenging Beik and Parker, my primary purpose has been to re-assert the old view that, from the sixteenth century onwards, there existed a capitalist bourgeoisie in France. Moreover, it eventually provided leadership to the mass of the population during the Revolution, assuming control over the state. The leadership and hegemony of such a bourgeoisie was particularly decisive in the crucial revolution in the countryside. But my purpose extends beyond this question to the history of capitalism itself. Far too often, the early history of capitalism has been seen to be an exclusively English affair. This is a mistakenly parochial approach. Capitalist relations of production began at more-or-less the same time in England and France. In the one case, such relations were able to advance as a result of the success of the Puritan Revolution. In the latter case, feudal and absolutist reaction under the Bourbons was able to hold back, if not extinguish, capitalism in the seventeenth century, delaying its advance until the next century. It is important to note that capitalism, which always was a single system, in fact began in Italy in the late middle ages and extended into Germany, the Netherlands, France and England in the sixteenth century. Robert Brenner has recently demonstrated the particularity of the Dutch route to capitalism.[23] The responsibility of European historians is to appreciate that there were different paths to the development of capitalism in the various states of Western Europe. The strengths and weaknesses of its development in each case has to be taken into account if we are to do justice to capitalism's development and to the concrete history of separate states.

References

Beik, William 1985, *Absolutism and Society in Seventeenth-Century France: State Power and Provincial Aristocracy in Languedoc*, Cambridge: Cambridge University Press.

Brenner, Robert 2001, 'The Low Countries in the Transition to Capitalism', in *Peasants into Farmers? The Transformation of Rural Economy and Society in the Low Countries (Middle Ages–19th Century) in Light of the Brenner Debate*, edited by Peter Hoppenbrouwers and Jan Luiten van Zanden, Turnhout: Brepols.

Cooper, J.P. 1985, 'In Search of Agrarian Capitalism', in *The Brenner Debate: Agrarian Class Structure and Economic Development in Pre-Industrial Europe*, edited by T.H. Aston and C.H.E. Philpin, Cambridge: Cambridge University Press.

Heller, Henry 1996, *Labour, Science and Technology in France 1500–1620*, Cambridge: Cambridge University Press.

—— 2006, *The Bourgeois Revolution in France 1789–1815*, New York: Berghahn Books.

—— 2009, 'The *Longue Durée* of the French Bourgeoisie', *Historical Materialism*, 17, 1: 31–59.

23. Brenner 2001.

—— 2010, 'Marx, the French Revolution and the Specter of the Bourgeoise', *Science & Society*, 74, 2: 184–214.

Le Roy Ladurie, Emmanuel 1966, *Les paysans de Languedoc* Volume 1, Paris: SEVPEN.

—— 1975, 'De la crise ultime à la vraie croissance', in *Histoire de la France rurale*, edited by Georges Duby and Armand Wallon, Volume 2, *L'âge classique 1340–1740*, edited by Hughes Niveux, Jean Jacquart and Emmanuel Le Roy Ladurie, Paris: Seuil.

—— 1977, 'Les masses profondes: La paysannerie', in *Histoire économique et sociale de la France* Volume 2: *Des derniers temps de l'âge seigneurial aux préludes de l'âge industriel (1660–1789)*, edited by Fernand Braudel and Ernst Labrousse, Paris: PUF.

—— 1978, 'En Haute-Normandie: Malthus ou Marx?', *Annales: Économies, Sociétés, Civilisations*, 33, 1: 115–24.

—— 2002, *Histoire des paysans français. De la Peste noire à la Révolution*, Paris: Seuil.

Le Roy Ladurie, Emmanuel, Guy Lemarchand and Karine Rance 2008, 'Regards croisés: historiens et révolutions. Vers une "paix des braves"', *Annales historiques de la Révolution Française*, 351, 1: 177–96.

Marx, Karl 1977 [1867], *Capital*, Volume 1, translated by Ben Fowkes, New York: Vintage.

Moriceau, Jean-Marc 1993, 'Le laboureur et ses enfants. Formation professionnelle et mobilité sociale en Ile-de-France (seconde moitié du XVIe siècle)', *Revue d'histoire moderne et contemporaine*, 40, 3: 387–414.

—— 1994, *Les fermiers de l'Ile-de-France: l'ascension d'un patronat agricole, XVe–XVIIIe siècle*, Paris: Fayard.

Parker, David 1996, *Class and State in Ancien Régime France: The Road to Modernity?*, London: Routledge.

Reynard, Pierre Claude 1999, 'Early Modern State and Enterprise: Shaping the Dialogue Between the French Monarchy and Paper Manufacturers', *French History*, 13, 1: 1–25.

BRILL

Historical Materialism 18 (2010) 143–207

historical materialism
research in critical marxist theory

brill.nl/hima

Review Articles

Sciences et dialectiques de la nature, edited by Lucien Sève, Paris: La Dispute, 1998.

La nature dans la pensée dialectique, Eftichios Bitsakis, Paris: L'Harmattan, 2001.

Abstract

Dialectics, especially Engels's dialectics of nature, is nowadays mostly held in low esteem, even by Marxist scholars because of its Stalinist dogmatisation over the past century. The aim of this comparative review is to show some stakes and prospects, *in* Marxism and *for* Marxism, of the debate: the two reviewed books show how the dialectics of nature could, and why it should be considered in a renewed materialist approach to the natural sciences, and provides the reader with complementary outline from the cognitive sciences to physics, via mathematics.

Keywords

Dialectics, dialectics of nature, epistemology, history, laws of nature, logic, mathematics, materialism, objectivity, reflection

Dialectics of Nature: The Stakes and Prospects of the Current Debate

> Dialectics, so-called *objective* dialectics, prevails throughout nature, and so-called subjective dialectics, dialectical thought, is only the reflection of the motion through opposites which asserts itself everywhere in nature, and which by the continual conflict of the opposites and their final passage into one another, or into higher forms, determines the life of nature.
>
> Friedrich Engels, *Dialectics of Nature*[1]

> The Marxist theoretical practice of *epistemology*, of the history of science, of the history of ideology, of the history of philosophy, of the history of art, has yet in large part to be constituted.
>
> – Louis Althusser, *For Marx*[2]

By now it is well known,[3] or at least it should be, that the loosely ordered folders of manuscript-pages by Engels that were later assembled under the title *Dialectics of Nature* underwent, beginning in the early twentieth century, a fossilisation that elevated this

1. Engels 1977b, p. 213.
2. Althusser 1996, p. 170.
3. See, above all, Pierre Macherey's overview, 'Dialectique de la nature', in Bensussan and Labica (eds.) 1985.

DOI: 10.1163/156920610X512499

unfinished work into an integral, dogmatic founding doctrine. This process was, in part, motivated by a politically-inspired need for a complete and structured ideology. Although we, unfortunately, do not yet have a scholarly edition of these texts, their ambiguity is patent. Many passages, exemplified by the one quoted above, clearly betray the intention to produce a systematic, ontological theory. From this standpoint, the status of a new 'system of nature' is conferred upon this dialectics of nature: it becomes a totalising encyclopaedia based literally on a reduction, with heavy neo-Hegelian overtones, of reality to the set of 'laws' of the dialectic.

Yet Engels's enterprise, which is premised on the validity of Marx's critique of political economy, is also, and above all, programmatic and critical (this is patent in the *Anti-Dühring*). It materialised in the context of a struggle against the idealism of the *Naturphilosophen* and the vulgar materialism of the sciences of the day. It sought to conceptualise and then resolve the contradiction between the philosophical need for theoretical systematisation and a properly scientific attention to the local specificity of the different types of natural processes and movements, while rejecting the simplistic mechanicism that distorted them. The dialectics of nature is first and foremost a dialectical synthesis of the natural sciences; as such, it advertises its eminently paedagogical and/or critical function and its epistemological status. Taking the concept of *the form of matter and movement* as his guiding thread, Engels brings the laws of nature and historical processes into relation against the backdrop of an integral materialism. But this critical project takes a dangerous turn that paves the way for its later dogmatic transformation when it attempts to work out the general laws of the dialectic, in which the analogy between nature and history is rooted.

In what follows, I begin with a comparative, that is, structural and then thematic review of two books by the philosopher Lucien Sève and the philosopher and physicist Eftichios Bitsakis. Both attempt to develop a rigorous problematisation of this internal tension in Engels's project. They break with most previous interpretative traditions (overall, albeit not across the board),[4] which are fundamentally ideological in that they reject or accept this project as a whole in ultimately uncritical fashion. That is, they do not engage in a genuine internal and external examination of its content and structure. If only because they carry out this interpretative break, the books under review here deserve close attention.

1. The structure of the two books

1.1 *Sciences and dialectics of nature*

Sciences et dialectiques de la nature has two parts. The first (pp. 11–247), by Sève, takes the form of a manifesto. It is a defence and illustration, informed by both Marxist and non-Marxist epistemological traditions, of the dialectic in what are called the 'hard' sciences, as opposed to the humanities or political economy. After acknowledging that the dialectic

4. See the references given in Tosel 1995 and the quotation from Pierre Macherey in n. 50 below.

has been widely rejected as a result of the scientific discredit into which it fell in the twentieth century, Sève sets out from the hypothesis that we need to 'have done with anachronism' without 'throwing the baby out with the bath-water'. In other words, the dialectic, which can no longer be understood as a perfected, fully-constituted, immediately utilisable method or system of concepts, should be publicly identified as a topic that a theory of the sciences inspired by Marx needs to address again in order to ensure its future development – notwithstanding the kind of systematic denigration that is based on the spurious equation dialectics = Marxism = USSR = failure = past and, above all, *passé*.

The first section of this part of the book, entitled 'Deux siècles d'élaborations dialectiques controversées' ['Two centuries of controversial dialectical arguments'] presents a detailed reconstruction of the Hegelian-Marxist tradition that is informed by a demand for conceptual rigour in the definition and use of the word 'dialectic'. Here, Sève is concerned to mark out, but also to problematise, the general limits of the field where we need to 'start digging' again. The objective and stake of this section is to locate and bring to light the objects upon which future examination should bear: that is, plainly to identify the pertinent problems with a view, if not to clearing them up, then at least to shedding some light on them. For Sève, the essence of this first part of his undertaking consists in laying bare the context in which dialectics, especially the dialectics of nature, has been discredited, and in explaining the reasons for its waning fortunes, whether what is involved is the form of the logic of contradiction associated with Hegel/Marx/Engels, or the de-ontologised or purely ideal-subjective forms that have been divested of the rational core constituted by *negativity*.

In early twentieth-century France, the academic establishment ignored these intellectual traditions in favour of the various brands of neo-Kantian spiritualism which more-or-less consciously reduced dialectics, in line with an ancient tradition running from Aristotle to Kant, to the simple capacity to reason about appearances or probabilities. Although, in the 1930s, Alexandre Kojève's well-known courses once again conferred respectability upon Hegelian thought, the generation educated by Kojève (which included Sartre, for example) perceived Hegel's philosophy of nature as irrational and irrelevant. It was excluded from Kojève's teaching from the outset; the forms of the dialectic that were revived in the years preceding the Second World-War (responsible, after the War, for the founding of the journals *Dialektik* in Germany and *Dialectica* in Switzerland, among others) were rather those directly inherited from the methodologies of correlation and complementarity (of synthesis rather than contradiction) due mainly to Brunschvicg, Renouvier and Hamelin. They were, to be sure, rigorously brought into confrontation with the theoretical and experimental innovations of the day: in Bachelard, with the crisis of the mechanicism of physics; in Cavaillès, Lautman and Gonseth, with the very disparate forms of progress made in formal logic, the axiomatic method, and other, more classical fields of mathematics. The contemporary heir to this tradition is Gilles-Gaston Granger. Here, dialectics is above all an epistemological stance, the (self-)dialecticisation of a knowing-subject who, in a search, involving endless rectification, for truths that are now epistemologically 'regional', acknowledges the fact that his rationality takes the form of a general process. Even such subjective, open dialectics, however – these 'philosophies of the no' in which the 'no' is external to what is negated, not a product of the differentiation of an element that is initially one and undivided – came under sharp attack in the immediate postwar-period, in part because of the thematic and semantic affinities between this neo-Kantian school of dialectics and dialectical materialism.[5]

Dialectical materialism, despite the rich work that appeared in the journal *La Pensée*, founded in 1939,[6] was, for the most part, subject, especially in institutions and theoretical organs dominated by the French Communist Party, to a thoroughgoing Stalinisation. The result was that even in the work of scholars influenced by Marx, such as Paul Langevin, or scientists who 'flirted with dialectics', such as Niels Bohr, Engels's programmatic theses on the dialectics of nature, elevated into a system that grounds the laws of history in the (dialectical) laws of nature, still have to regain their full legitimacy. Beginning in 1948, the Lysenko-affair sealed the discredit into which dialectics, in particular the dialectics of nature, had fallen as a result of this development.

Sève's key thesis is that the collective reasons for promoting and denigrating 'the' dialectic were, in the twentieth century, by-and-large ideological. With the exception of work and interpretations that ultimately remained individual, the categorial content of the dialectic was considerably impoverished. This was so despite the fact that scholars and thinkers who explicitly acknowledged their debt to the categories of the dialectic or to dialectical categories (whether broadly defined and objectively 'charged' or more narrowly circumscribed), such as Langevin or Henri Wallon, took pains to mobilise these categories without neglecting their problematic nature or the fact that they often carried different meanings.

Sève next insists on the recent revival, not of the whole set of dialectical *theses* on natural phenomena, but rather of the *theme* of dialectics. This theme emerges in Henri Atlan's studies of the biological phenomena of self-organisation, Jean-Marc Lévy's work on contemporary physics, and in the work of US biologists such as Stephen Jay Gould, Richard Levins and Richard Lewontin.[7] Sève further discusses the resurgence, independently of the writers just named, of studies of the most classical-dialectical culture, the Hegelian philosophy of nature,[8] and Marx[9] and Engels's[10] scientific work.

All this work has contributed to creating a more receptive intellectual climate for collective studies of this aspect of dialectics.[11] Conceptually, Sève distributes the work to be done along two axes. First, what philosophical-epistemological status can we reasonably confer upon a dialectics of nature? Second, and correlatively, what kind of categorial system should we reconstruct: is a formalisation of the dialectic possible, and, if so, will it be able to generate inferences or knowledge that the many existing systems of formal logic cannot? How should we reconceptualise, along Marxist or Marxian lines, contradiction,

5. See the indispensable critical review of this subject in Tosel 2001.

6. See Sève 1989 for an account of the context in which *La Pensée* was launched in Spring 1939. This account offers an overview of the problematics later developed in Sève (ed.) 1998.

7. Levins and Lewontin 1985.

8. See the monumental collective work in Petry 1993.

9. Based mainly on Engels 1977a and 1977b, and Engels and Marx 1973.

10. See Delbraccio and Labica (eds.) 2000, in particular Sève's text, which provides an overview of the ambiguities in Engels's programme.

11. The fact remains that in France in particular, we are still far from overcoming the political and ideological obstacles to creating the institutional and academic conditions required to sustain genuine research-projects or study-groups on this subject.

the negation of the negation, the relationship between quantity and quality, and the identity of opposites (Engels's three 'laws' of the dialectic) in such a way as to show that they are useful or even indispensable – if not exactly as laws, then as philosophical theses that can help us grasp natural phenomena or certain scientific aporiae without pre-forming or de-forming them? In other words, how shall we conceptualise the rational kernel of an objective dialectics of nature without laying it open to the objection – to be sure, often simplistic (as in Popper), yet surely legitimate – to the effect that it is a projection of concepts onto reality, a 'reification' of categories into active phenomena, or, in short, a patent illustration of 'the transcendental illusory appearance' of reason, long since deconstructed by Kant, which consists in claiming to find in reality what we have previously projected onto it?[12]

Sève revives this project of conceptual definition in the second section of Part One of his book, 'Pour un nouvel esprit dialectique' ['For a New Dialectical Spirit']. This section, which follows on from his historical account of the concept of dialectics, begins with a paraphrase of Bachelard's phrase 'the new scientific spirit', and goes on to make a systematic study of the three main groups of problems: Can dialectics generate formalisable inferences that would guarantee the foundation of a dialectical *logic*? Under what conditions can there be a dialectics *of* and *in* nature? And, if we take these themes as our point of departure, what are the *moments* of the dialectic, that is, what are the semantics of these moments and their ontological and epistemological status?

The second part of Sève's book is made up of a number of contributions by scientists concerning their own theoretical conceptualisations. We find, first, an exchange between Sève and the biophysicist Atlan, the main subject of which is the status of contradiction, the constitutive-conceptual nexus of the notion of dialectics from both the historical and epistemological standpoint. Next, Gilles Cohen-Tannoudji, an eminent specialist in quantum-mechanics, presents a dialectical problematisation of the central concepts in his field of research (primarily 'entropy', 'field', and 'symmetry and symmetry-breaking'); he pays particular attention to the fecundity of the concept of the 'horizon of reality' that he borrows from the Swiss mathematician Ferdinand Gonseth. Offering a more general view of the notions of object, time-space, and matter, Pierre Jaeglé, an epistemologist working on particle-mechanics, concentrates, for his part, on the central dialectic of the interaction between objectivity and subjectivity in the construction and validation of scientific knowledge of reality; it is incumbent on anyone who claims to elaborate a true discourse about the real to arrive at a precise understanding of this interaction.[13] If there is a dialectics of nature that needs to be more closely determined, there exists, first and foremost, the need to examine a dialectics of the *knowledge* of nature. Levins and Lewontin, respectively professors of population-science and zoology, endeavour to show, in a chapter based on their conclusion to the book they have dedicated to Engels, *The*

12. The 'only dialectic one will find in Nature is a dialectic that one has put there oneself' (Sartre 2004, p. 31). Nevertheless, Sartre's *Critique of Dialectical Reason* is, in my view, a (or perhaps *the*) work of fundamental importance for the renewal of Marxist dialectics, and – whether one argues for or against it, for the renewal of the dialectics of nature itself. See Barot 2002.

13. Jaeglé seems to have taken a certain distance from his rather classic utilisation of Engels's theses in the study of the concept of reversibility in physics developed in Jaeglé 1977.

Dialectical Biologist,[14] that the different strands of Cartesianism as well as the various brands of biological reductionism miss the specificity of the organic living being.[15] A living creature is a reality in constant movement, the dynamic of which constantly recreates the dialectically-organic being of a living thing: it is reflected in the fact that the sum of the analyses of the parts of such a being remains incomplete, and, further, in the unreality of this whole whenever it is conceived of as anything other than the reciprocal expression of those parts; such an organic being is regulated and developed under endogenic constraints quite as much as in reaction to, and action upon, the environment. The last section, which crowns the book's polyvalence, is about the significance and functions of the dialectic in mathematics. The mathematician José-Luis Massera shows that it can be conceived of as a tool for the (retrospective) exposition of the construction of theories, or as an operative mode intrinsic to that construction; he adds that its heuristic relevance emerges when we reflect on the status of mathematical objects and also on the procedures and methods of theories. This does not hold only at the level of the gaze brought to bear on the historical-conceptual evolution of mathematics as a form of disciplined thought.[16]

The ambition, not to totalise, but to *globalise* scientific fields which this brief resumé evinces bears witness to the enormity of the domain opened up for research here, and thus to the scope of 'the dialecticians'' ambition. If there is plainly at least one problem in this connection, it its the polysemousness of the term 'dialectic'; one might note that not all of the various authors explain with the same clarity the meaning that they assign the term, although it is obvious that, from Engels to Gonseth, the meaning varies a great deal. Sève's own contribution is helpful in this regard: he does a good job of presenting and clarifying the semantic and conceptual relations between the authors who follow him. If this introductory section finally reminds us of the heuristic and critical function of the dialectic

---

14. 'Dialectical philosophers have thus far only explained science. The problem, however, is to change it' (Levins and Lewontin 1985, p. 288).

15. In all its forms, reductionism proceeds from the strict reduction of the laws governing a phenomenon to the set of laws governing that which constitutes it. The significance of such reduction resides in the fact that, every time, the laws of the level that has been reduced disappear *qua* laws; this makes it easier to perceive them as mere descriptive, heuristic elements. For example, cognitive eliminativism (Changeux's theses, the neurophilosophy of the Churchlands) traces the nomic correlations of the psychology of mental states back to physical-chemical laws, the laws of the neuronal or directly infra-neuronal, molecular level. See the critique of reductionism as a 'manifestation of mechanistic thought' in Bitsakis 2001, pp. 353–4.

16. In my view, Massera forgets an essential dimension of the dialectical conceptions of mathematics from Hegel and Marx and Engels to contemporary non-Marxist dialectics: namely, the critique directed against naive or Platonic realism, the demystification of logical/mathematical objectivity, and the corresponding endeavour, which might be described as constructive or constructivist in the strict sense of the word, to re-inscribe all these objects in the regulated process by which they were instituted. Infinitesimals, and more generally, the differential elements and methodological premises of calculus interested Hegel, in particular, in the 'Doctrine of Being' of his *Science of Logic*, and also Marx (see Alcouffe (ed.) 1985, especially pp. 113–39). Engels 1977b, pp. 272–8, insists on the fact that mathematical infinities are derived by abstract, *a posteriori* analogy, and that the 'prototypes' of these infinities are to be found in the real world.

in the general constitution of different forms of knowledge, their reciprocal relations, and in their relation to the real, it also underscores the necessity of a strict conceptual determination of the term and its moments.

1.2 *Nature in dialectical thought*

In his book, Eftichios Bitsakis writes a partial history of the concept of the dialectic from antiquity to the present by way of a survey of the conceptions of nature forged by the major instances of dialectical thought in history. The first two chapters review the naïve cosmogonies, the Heraclitean and Ionian cosmogonies, and, of course, Aristotle's cosmology and hylomorphism. In the next chapters, the thought of Hegel, Marx, Engels, Lenin and Langevin is examined and set in its intellectual and cultural context. In the concluding chapter, Bitsakis presents a sustained reflection on the scientific practice that he teaches. Grounding what he says in his own adaptation of the perspectives defined by Langevin, he reviews his widely-acknowledged work on theoretical physics, the crisis of mechanicism (rather than determinism), and, more generally, the dialectic of the hierarchised forms of matter and movement.[17]

Bitsakis's introduction, entitled 'Sciences, idéologie et philosophie', offers an extremely close contextualisation of his intentions in this book. To examine, as he does in the last section of the introduction, 'new perspectives on the dialectics of nature', presupposes a critical re-appropriation of dialectical cultures and bodies of thought. Anyone who proceeds in this way must also, however, be able epistemologically to situate what he says with regard to scientists' theoretical production and positive knowledge, on the one hand, and philosophical discourses in their traditional generality and functional vocations, on the other; and he must address, in the process, the problem of the criteria and nature of the scientificity of his own method. If rational thought or the thought that is productive of positive knowledge is always a collective activity that depends on the social and political context in which it is developed, its ideological dimension must be brought out and taken into consideration. That dimension does not just involve an enterprise of mystification – although that is, of course, a clear possibility, attested by the 'dialectical-materialist' fossilisation of Engels's theses, the opposite of a critical theorisation of new knowledge (which requires the kind of guidance provided, notably, by experiment). It also instantiates what Gonseth calls 'previous doctrine', the necessary pre-conceptualisation that combines the intuitive with the conceptual (a sort of hermeneutical 'pre-comprehension') and orients theoretical developments properly so-called. In other words, the ideological dimension displays an essential epistemological character that has already been elaborated, yet is spontaneous (in the sense in which Althusser speaks of the 'spontaneous philosophy of scientists'). As such, it has to become an object of the kind of in-depth discussion that makes it explicit. This is a condition of possibility for its epistemological relevance.

To put it differently, any new perspective on the dialectics of nature has to be based on a redefinition of the relationships between philosophy, science and ideology. This, in turn, calls for a new examination of the categories of historical and dialectical materialism. Accordingly, Bitsakis repeatedly insists on the need for a new thematisation of the relations

17. See Bitsakis's and Sève's bibliographies, which are extensive, and also Tosel 1995, which provides an extremely precise treatment of this subject.

between thought and matter (the matter of nature, but also, of course, matter that has been socially transformed or, as Sartre says, 'worked up').

The history that Bitsakis presents is partial. One reason for this is the deliberate leap from Aristotle to Hegel. Another is his focus, for the post-Engelsian period, on the dialectics that issued directly from Marx and Engels's system; the 'subjective' or non-Marxist dialectics, such as Bachelard's or Gonseth's, that recur throughout twentieth-century French rationalism[18] are not discussed (again, with the exception of Langevin's 'case', since Langevin has, in certain respects, a foot in each tradition). Bitsakis makes this theoretical choice clearly and assumes its consequences. In an already voluminous book, it allows him to zero-in on his objective – a reconstruction of dialectical materialism and the dialectics of nature – while avoiding the pitfalls of a dogmatic, closed system. Thus, the chapters that treat of the period from Hegel to Langevin go beyond mere historical reconstruction: *en route*, the key categories of this indispensable *dispositif* are enriched, and the author's main theses are made more precise. Globally, they bear, perhaps unsurprisingly, on the same sets of problems that Sève also singles out for consideration (with the exception of logical formalisation, which is less directly related to the central themes of Bitsakis's book): the status of dialectical discourse and categories vis-à-vis scientific objectivations as well as natural phenomena; semantic content; operational modes; and the reciprocal links between these categories.

2. The main theses shared by the two books

Bitsakis's book, like Sève's, repeatedly underscores the ambiguity in Engels's texts, which I mentioned at the start. If the 'dialectics of nature' is open to attack on its ontologically-doctrinal side, both books insist on what makes it a critical *dispositif* whose vocation is to think the relations between the concepts of scientific theories, and to think the way in which these concepts can and must be re-articulated in order to grasp the power of formal differentiation *of* nature and at work *in* nature. De-ontologising dialectics: there we have a first principle. But this dialectics remains bound up with an ontology, a materialist theory of natural and social being that belongs, not to science, but to philosophical discourse.

2.1 *Philosophical categories, semi-philosophical concepts and scientific concepts*

In order to think the relationship between philosophy and science, Bitsakis draws concrete distinctions between three discursive instances: the universal propositions and ontological categories of philosophy, semi-philosophical concepts, and scientific concepts.[19] The first, obtained by generalisation and extrapolation (for example, 'motion is the mode of existence of matter') do not, as such, fall under the jurisdiction of the proof:[20] one examines their accuracy [*justesse*] and verisimilitude rather than their truth by comparison with positive knowledge acquired elsewhere. Scientific concepts always stand in a relation

18. The exchanges between this dialectical rationalism *à la française* and dialectical materialism were rich and diverse; see Tosel 2001.

19. On this point, see Bitsakis 2001, pp. 26–40.

20. Lenin already explicitly made these distinctions in Lenin 1976. On this point, see Althusser 1982, pp. 28–30 and Macherey 1999, pp. 271–2.

to concrete forms of materiality, causality, determination, movement, and so on; the chemist or physicist does not study matter or movement in general, but, rather, always certain of their specific forms.

There is a partial overlap between these categories of concepts. Thus the second make up the specific class of philosophical categories that are also utilised by scientists: matter, movement, energy, space, time, etc. These semi-philosophical concepts (in the sense that they are intra-scientific and meta-scientific) serve as dialectical mediators between science and philosophy, because they are a unity of difference, conceptual concretions that conjoin the universality of the categories to the particularity of science. For instance, mass (a scientific concept) is not matter (a philosophical category), but the measure (that is, in reality, a mediating operative-conceptual network involving semi-philosophical concepts, such as that of quantity) of its inertia (likewise a scientific concept), a specific attribute of matter.

Hence one must always spell out the use to which these (philosophical or scientific) mediators are put and what they designate: integral realities (matter, phenomenon, etc.), relations (causality, interaction, etc.), material properties (conservation, transformation, etc.), and their nature, and the general type of category on the basis of which this designation and use are realised, whether ontological (energy, matter, space, time, etc.), interdisciplinary (structure, information, etc.), or epistemological (consciousness, reflection, etc.). Thus, one has to distinguish, in making use of the concepts of object and representation, between the ontological point of view that posits their unity (a materialist thesis) and the epistemological point of view that posits their opposition or, at least, difference, and, consequently, mandates study of the mode by which representation attains the object. The basic idea is always to know what one is talking about, using what instruments, and in line with what uses of those instruments.

It will be seen, then, that one has to distinguish the *dispositif* and the dialectical relations of philosophical categories and scientific objects from dialectical concepts as such. A dialectics of nature is, first of all, a set of philosophical theses structured around a principle, which cannot be proven, of the ontological monism of matter, and also a set of semi-philosophical concepts which ensure that the general-philosophical discourse is commensurable with already-constituted scientific theories. It is at this intermediate level that dialectical categories as such operate. In other words, even while laying claim to objectivity, a dialectics of nature is not a scientific discourse,[21] but a discourse about

21. Sève (ed.) 1998, pp. 140–1: 'In a dialectical materialist perspective, categories are… defined as the *universal determinations-of-meaning of our cognitive and practical relations with it.* Wholly derived from categorical knowledge – second-degree knowledge – dialectics is philosophical. There can therefore be no more radical error than to identify it with *science*… A theory belonging to a specific order, it has a primarily critical function.… To be sure, the categories emerge from [*sortent de*] scientific concepts, in the twofold sense of the term: they come from them, and they detach themselves from them.… [T]he vocation of the categories is to be put back to work in science and *knowledgeable practice* [*pratique savante*]. That is where they operate, under the name of categories or, much more often, under that of the scientific concepts by means of which they fulfill their function. Should we see, from the outset, the unity of opposites in the combination of truth and falsehood constituted by an approximate truth, and the negation of the negation in the negentropic process known as organisation? Every science, whether it knows it or not, *philosophises*'. What Sève says here is not, theoretically, as

scientific discourse that thinks natural reality indirectly, by virtue of the fact that it has acquired the means to inflect and enrich the semantics and utilisation of the concepts of the sciences themselves. Plainly, one has to assume that concepts, semi-concepts, and categories vary with social and historical conditions: they are not valid a priori, but, rather, they are diachronically-implicated in an ideologically-oriented (rather than determined) historical process through which philosophy and science (or the sciences) think the real by way of already-acquired local knowledge (even if it is transitory).

2.2 *What is the logic of the categories of the dialectic?*

Both Sève[22] and Bitsakis closely examine the central categories of the dialectic. Sève proceeds essentially by recapitulating Marx and Engels's basic theses on the question; Bitsakis deepens and differentiates his analysis by taking account of the evolution of conceptualisations of the dialectic from Marx to Langevin, reconstructing them by correlating the concepts developed over time with the scientific problems and objects that they had to confront. This complementarity only makes sense, in my view, in the context of Bitsakis's own work. Bitsakis takes over the traditional categories, complete with their dyadic or triadic associations, while rigorously rethinking their mode of operation with respect both to each other and to natural phenomena. Thus interdisciplinary and relational categories (the main ones are unity and diversity, identity and difference, opposition and contradiction, quality and quantity, and interaction) as well as semi-philosophical concepts (structure and movement, thing and relation, symmetry, dissymmetry and asymmetry, conservation and transformation, continuity and discontinuity) are put to work in an internal examination of scientific concepts in the proper sense of the term. Bitsakis's guiding principle here is always to base the movement of the categories on the specificity of the scientific concepts under consideration – and therefore, indirectly, on the specificity of the phenomenon that the scientific concepts are supposed to make intelligible.

Since we lack the space for a full-length exposition here, let us limit ourselves to a few illustrations. In the physics of elementary particles, interaction is a relation between particles that engenders motion, but it is also brought about by motion. In other words, interaction is simultaneously the source and the product of motion. Mesons, for example, and, more generally, bosons, as opposed to the more 'material' fermions, seem to be nothing more than the mediating function that they play as particles of interaction (insofar as they are the vectors of nuclear forces between the constituent parts of the atomic nucleus); they remain, however, particles.[23] In the same context, protons and neutrons are effectively identical when they are studied without regard to electromagnetic interaction; however, their symmetry or identity is shattered and their difference revealed when we take this interaction

---

finely-shaded as Bitsakis's arguments – although his points are perfectly convergent with Bitsakis's – because Sève applies these categories to very diverse scientific questions, and must therefore inevitably proceed allusively. In principle, Bitsakis *does* what Sève describes or says that one would *have to do*.

22. Above all in Sève (ed.) 1998, pp. 164–203.

23. Bitsakis 2001, pp. 274–5. Sève quite rightly notes that the concept 'particle of interaction' is utterly obscure for everyday understanding and insists on the fact that it designates a relation that *seems to become a thing*, and vice-versa (Sève (ed.) 1998, p. 195).

into account. Thus there exists a difference within the unity and identity of the forms of matter, and this difference is the source of a process. The (non-antagonistic) opposition between mass and energy is cancelled by the theory of relativity to the extent that their direct proportionality is established by means of the square of the coefficient of the speed of light. Laws of conservation always make themselves felt in processes of transformation, and so on. It can be readily seen here that the epistemological dimension (abstraction, theoretical extension, experimentation) makes the movement of categories possible.[24] Bitsakis nevertheless insists, after Engels and Lenin, that contradictions really exist in natural phenomena: if, in nature, opposition is the dominant form, it 'can become [antagonistic] contradiction under the right circumstances' (p. 275).[25] It is at this point that one speaks of 'dialectical transition', that is, a change inducing a qualitative break, a leap[26] at the heart of a continuous process presupposed by the break, a leap that possesses its own temporal density. Witness, says Bitsakis, the discontinuous character of quantum-interactions, especially at the level of the emission and absorption of rays between subatomic particles.[27]

Sève also focuses what he says on contradiction, which is indeed the main subject of his exchange with Atlan, entitled 'L'illogique de la contradiction'.[28] Sève, who is as convinced as Bitsakis that there exist real contradictions, takes up the debate with an interlocutor who, although he acknowledges the dynamic virtues of dialectical thinking, rejects the idea that there exists anything other than real oppositions, in a way reminiscent of Granger's vehement critique of the dialectic in general.[29] Sève devotes a passage to, precisely, the restrictions that Granger imposes on the relevance of dialectics and the fields to which it can legitimately be applied. His argument is instructive because it offers a fresh restatement of the problem, which Bitsakis does not consider, of the formalisation of dialectics, that is, of dialectics as a logic that has its own inferences. This is a central question, since it bears on something that would provide a particularly solid rational kernel for a scientific dialectics.

---

24. On this subject, see Bitsakis 2001 pp. 349–53, which provides a detailed summary (with cross-references to Bitsakis's book).

25. See also Bitsakis 1983, pp. 99–122: the phenomena of symmetry and dissymmetry in physics, and even in the mathematical theory of abstract spaces, reveal the presence of contradictions in 'the essence of things themselves'.

26. This should clearly be compared to contemporary developments in qualitative physics that exceed Leibniz's principle *natura non facit saltus* and have led to a revival of certain intuitions of Aristotle's (the principle that there are no leaps in nature, Leibniz says, has to be thought from God's point of view; from man's, such continuity is difficult to grasp, since the leaps are easier to see). Consider René Thom's and Jean Petitot's morphogenesis-physics or Raymond Ruyer's neo-finalism.

27. Bitsakis 2001, p. 276.

28. Sève (ed.) 1998, pp. 249–86. This exchange is most instructive, not least because Sève, who interprets Atlan's work in terms of the dialectic, manages to make him say: 'If I'm producing dialectics in my scientific work, it's in the sense in which Monsieur Jourdain produced prose: quite without being aware of it. And if you can show me in what sense I'm producing dialectics in this way, I'd be quite pleased' (Sève (ed.) 1998, p. 251). But this remains anecdotal.

29. Sève (ed.) 1998, pp. 124–44. Cf. Granger 1979, 1980, and 1988.

2.3 *Logic and dialectical inferences*

Sève begins by reviewing Granger's representative critique. Granger distinguishes between the dialectic as the *movement* of the creation of contents (of 'formal contents' by empty forms, as in Hegel, or as the creation of real things by specific-new laws, as in Hegel and Engels) and the dialectic as *science*, that is, as a discourse about such creation. His central criticism of dialectical discourse is that it confuses itself with real creative movement, assimilating such movement to itself. This 'disappointing illusion' stems from the *a posteriori* 'ontologisation' of a dialectic that originally consisted of a set of 'maxims' adopted by researchers to help resolve the problems encountered in the course of their research. This is tantamount to complete rejection of any dialectics of nature that would have nature developing by the negation of the negation: the thesis that natural objects are in and of themselves dialectical comes down to making negation and contradiction, in the strict sense, into rules governing the objective production of effects in the domain studied by the empirical sciences. The 'dialectical movement' apparently perceived in natural processes is always, according to Granger, exported by thought *a priori*; it is simply the product of a disguised empirical imagination that does not see through its own disguise. No objective logic dialectically governs the movement of 'things': while certain natural facts can be conceived of as contradictory, the contradiction finds expression at the level of thought alone, not at the level of reality. Any dialectic of nature is always only metaphorical interpretation, an unwarranted projection of subjective categories onto reality.[30]

The dialectic is not the logic of the thing, because negation, like contradiction, is conceptual, not 'in itself'. Yet dialectic cannot be a logic *tout court*; either, that is, it cannot be formalised; the various attempts to formalise it, says Granger, have failed (examples are André Doz and Dominique Dubarle's attempt in their 1972 *Logique et dialectique*, Henri Lefebvre's work,[31] or, more recently, Newton Da Costa's). What justifies the contention that they are failures is the fact that the 'dialectical inferences' sought (such productive inferences alone can legitimate the claim that this formalisation is innovative) are ultimately only reformulations of statements possible in classic-symbolic logic, even if the restatements in question are not based on such logic. 'A dialectic', Granger says, 'can only be a pseudo-logic, and the contents that it exhibits can come from only one of two sources. They are either illegitimately imported empirical contents disguised as formal contents, or they are in fact taken from the stock of natural languages... and can in no way be reduced to the logical-mathematical level.'[32] This need to import contents from the outside derives, again, from the fact that, basically, dialectical negation is not capable of serving as the main generator of valid, fruitful inferences, since, whether such negation is taken in a radical sense or restricted to specifically-defined domains of objects, its significance and uses are correlatively well-defined in analytical fashion, because we are in the field of operation of logical discourse.

30. This is Sartre's thesis, cited above.

31. See Lefebvre 1947, the classic work here, but also Lefebvre 1986, pp. 59–74, and Lefebvre 2002, Chapters 2 and 3, which recapitulate the various dimensions of the author's work on the formal and experimental sciences.

32. Granger 1980, in Granger 1994, p. 51.

It is nevertheless important to recall, in response to Granger's condemnation, that the possible uselessness of a formalised-dialectical logic is no argument against its possible validity (its consistency and completeness, and its ability to produce something new). Accordingly, the project of a new formalisation, in the sense of the 'logic of [objective] becoming' that Bitsakis proposes, is in no way disqualified from the outset. Moreover, the categorial logic – which is, in a sense, what the re-elaboration of the dialectical *dispositif* evoked in the previous paragraph comes down to – could serve as a guide in this attempt, especially in virtue of the dynamic, temporal dimension of the relationship sustained by its concepts.[33]

2.4 *General and regional dialectics*

As we can see, the formal sciences or disciplines (mathematics, logic), the sciences of inert matter (chemistry, physics, astrophysics), and, finally, biology cannot be reduced to one and the same law-governed dialectical scheme. Each field calls for an epistemology of its own, that is, the mobilisation of semi-philosophical concepts that are adapted to it, not the products of prior judgements. It makes sense to talk about 'the' dialectics of nature, if at all, only insofar as that dialectics consists, not of a body of laws, but of a set of philosophical theses that cannot be proven, although they are not arbitrary. The ideological pre-orientation of these theses and their critical, intra-theoretical thematisation makes them a discourse that aims at heuristic relevance and scientific verisimilitude. 'Thus the theses of a dialectics of nature may be exact or in conformity with the natural sciences'; however, 'on the basis of what has been acquired by the sciences, we can affirm that there exist local and regional dialectics, dialectics corresponding to the specific laws of matter' (pp. 368–9). This regionalisation, Bachelardian in principle and spirit (as is Sève's style and the very structure of the book that he has edited) shows that Bitsakis has assimilated the legitimate criticisms and restrictions to which 'the' dialectics of nature is subject. These local dialectics are nevertheless not mere epistemological attitudes or, *pace* Granger, simple, purely subjective, retrospective 'dialecticisations'. The reason is that they are based on, and objectively correlated with, a set of *materialist* principles.

3. The place of materialism

3.1 *Divergences*

There are two kinds of divergences between Sève's book and Bitsakis's. One is methodological, the other conceptual. The book edited by Sève is a broad-ranging historical and theoretical panorama of the themes it treats and the perspectives from which it treats them. For diverse reasons, Atlan, Jaeglé, Cohen-Tannoudji, and Massera bring

33. Anyone undertaking such an enterprise would, of course, have to be well-versed in a broad array of non-classical analytic logics, especially modal and paraconsistent logics, but also those that seek to produce models of temporal structures. The work of the mathematician William Lawvere on the theory of categories should also be tapped; Lawvere's explicit aim is to formalise the Hegelian dialectic of the unity of contradictory opposites.

Marxist and non-Marxist traditions into play and, as a rule, present and develop a few philosophemes linked to specific questions (thus Cohen-Tannoudji discusses the philosopheme of the 'horizon of reality', which he takes from Gonseth).[34] But these authors' contributions, like Sève's, are above all programmatic. Is this something to be regretted?[35] To the extent that Bitsakis's book, like the rest of his work, represents an attempt to concretise the programme outlined in Sève's, we may once again point to the way that the two complement each other. It seems to me valid to read the book edited by Sève as an informed contextualisation of the problem of a dialectics of nature, and Bitsakis's as a detailed 'regional' realisation (in the field of theoretical physics) of this programme, which makes Sève's more meaningful and intelligible.

Above and beyond this difference in the nature of the two books, however, a conceptual divergence also makes itself felt. It is, moreover, one to which Bitsakis regularly returns, in order, precisely, to criticise Sève. Whereas Bitsakis defends a strictly materialist thesis, Sève, despite his claims to the contrary, seems to dissolve an underlying materiality into a system of relations traceable, first and foremost, to discursive thought – a mode of procedure which is in sum quite Hegelian.

3.2 *The self-sufficiency of nature and the objectivity of knowledge*

Bitsakis's rigorous materialism is reflected in an alliance of a principle of the objectivity of nature with a principle of its self-sufficiency.[36] For him, reality exists in-itself; it is uncreated (Engels defended the same thesis); it is independent of the subject (self-sufficiency); and, contrary to the Kantian idea of an unknowable in-itself, it is, *de jure*, fully-knowable (objectivity), although in fact this objectivity is merely 'ontic' – that is, in the absence of an 'ultimate reality', can never be fully-known. The objectivity of knowledge is relative to the historical and experimental determinations in which and through which knowledge is produced. Knowledge is incapable of judging its object in advance, which reveals its complexity with each new technical innovation and, thereby, its resistance to totalising, objectivising ambitions, a resistance that can almost be identified as insurmountable. This 'in itself' of nature is, 'for us', the object of scientific research, which explains why Bitsakis labels his theoretical *dispositif* 'scientific realism'. We should not be deceived by the seemingly naïve appearance of such a realism: it is based, as Russell would say, on a 'solid sense of reality'. 'Let us therefore admit, as both common sense and science would have it, that matter exists' is a fundamental, eminently-philosophical theoretical decision;[37] it reaffirms Lenin's rejection of Machian phenomenalism, with its idealist

34. See, for instance, Cohen-Tannoudji 1990.

35. That is, in any case, André Tosel's general criticism of Sève's work, raised in passing, but repeatedly (for example in Tosel 1984, especially the introduction and epilogue).

36. Bitsakis 2001, for example, pp. 41–5 and 345–6.

37. See also Geymonat 1972, pp. 11–12, where, in like fashion, scientific realism and the historicity of epistemology are associated in principle. See also Quiniou 1987, especially pp. 9 and 22, where the status of both is radicalised ('the only presupposition of scientific physics – or, if one likes, its only implication – is the affirmation of the objectivity of its object: the existence of a material, inanimate nature distinct from the knowing subject and offering itself up to knowledge in an indefinite process', p. 9) and the problem of their articulation is studied at length in Chapter 1.

propensities. One could trace this decision back to Gonseth's 'previous doctrine', or to the self-critical ideology that orients semi-philosophical discourse (in the specific sense applied above to semi-philosophical concepts). As such, it offers an altogether fundamental bulwark against the charge of relativism or idealism that a non-dogmatic dialectics of nature will/would have to confront.

Bitsakis's project is, however, marked by an internal tension. We are repeatedly reminded of a thesis which, it seems to me, should have been clarified: that of the historicity of natural laws. For instance, Bitsakis writes in his last chapter that there are

> natural laws, that is to say, necessary, genetic internal relations between cause and phenomenon. A law is the formal expression of processes that determine the emergence of novelty. Physics and astronomy have demonstrated the historicity, from the ontological point of view, of natural laws. Indeed, the basic forms of matter have a history, as do the more complex, macroscopic forms. Correlatively, natural laws are not eternal, but historical. But the other aspect, too, the epistemological aspect, is affected by historicity. (p. 357.)[38]

This is a classical thesis, for the expression of such laws varies according to the knowledge that is historically and socially available. However, to say that the forms of matter have a history is by no means equivalent to saying that natural laws are historical: the intervention of contingency and chance in the necessarily law-governed actualisation of the possible (for example, in the evolution of species and the phenomena of mutation) is not the sign of a historicity of natural laws, but, rather, of the complexity and multiplicity of the factors that determine this 'emergence of novelty'. Therein resides, as we see it, at best an ambiguity, if not, indeed, a thesis that in this respect deserves to be hedged round by a particularly solid theoretical arsenal. Such an arsenal would have to include, in particular, an explicit definition of the concept of history, a category that is *both* philosophical *and* semi-philosophical, the comprehension (intension) of which would have to be specified here.

Bitsakis's scientific realism, which is grounded in dialectical materialism, yet does not reduce reality to a set of 'things' or unitary phenomena that can be assigned various attributes as predicates (in the Aristotelian mode of substance-predicate, which is obsolete here), makes it possible not to dissolve entities (from elementary particles through molecules to organised bodies, whether living or inert) in an ensemble of relations possessing a status that is, by definition, far too opaque. For some time now, Sève's work, from *Introduction à la philosophie marxiste* to his text in the book under review, has reintroduced this ambiguity. Thus he writes that 'to think dialectically is, from the outset, radically to reverse the relationship between things and relations; it is to posit relations as primary and constitutive of things'.[39] To this, Bitsakis responds, in his discussion of this thesis, that

---

38. See also pp. 281–4.

39. Sève 1980, p. 69. In Sève (ed.) 1998, p. 42, the author, in his discussion of Hegel, distinguishes poorly between what he quotes from Hegel and his own appropriation of him when he writes: 'In the relationship between two opposites, there is a confrontation between the positive – the immediate, which is already contradiction in itself – and the negative – the

> the relations between the parts that are constitutive of the thing are realised thanks to physical interactions, material agents that have their source in the thing and are, at the same time, constitutive of it. The thing is constituted by a material support, internal and external interactions, and relationships. All these aspects are inseparable. (p. 368.)

He also responds, however, from the physicist's standpoint, which is that of the common man and *should also be* that of the philosopher, that 'the thing, present here, is constituted of elements of reality: mass, charge, energy, spin, etc., which are not mere relations, but aspects of a materiality, of a material "ground", the source of relations' (p. 369). A spontaneous, but also a 'posited' materialist, Bitskakis clearly shows the continuing relevance of Lenin's critique of the attempts to dematerialise matter: it is not because matter 'eludes us' that it does not exist. Thus, if there is an ideological break between spontaneous doctrine and epistemological and scientific discourse, it clearly is not situated at this level, but, rather, in the articulation and use of semi-philosophical concepts, which is radically different from a naive mode of analysis.

The fact remains that Sève, as Bitsakis acknowledges just after making this remark, defends, globally speaking, a dialectical-materialist position. 'To understand', he affirms,

> that the objectivity of things can be reproduced by a subjective dialectic of concepts... is conceivable only in the light of an integral materialism in which cognitive processes – the objective contents as well as the subjective activities of knowing – are recognised as being originally *natural* in themselves, and continue to be natural even in their most complex historical-cultural forms. (p. 74.)

3.3 *Refounding a materialism of 'reflection'*

Here, Sève and Bitsakis converge, although they use different terminologies: a materialist refoundation of the dialectic(s) of nature has to take a keen interest in the nature of this dialectical reproduction of real phenomena by means of concepts. But, whereas Sève, adopting Engels's schema, talks, in classical terms, about the objectively-dialectical character of subjective thinking and the dialectical character of nature, insisting on the variety of the forms of the dialectic, Bitsakis, for his part, talks about the 'morphism' between reality, the elements of reality and process, and conceptual representation. In so doing, he indicates – despite himself? – that he has borrowed something from Piaget's genetic epistemology. It is in connection with this point that Bitsakis's remarks about

---

mediated, by which the contradiction is *posited* as such. These two terms are nothing outside their relationship. This is a crucial point for philosophy: every thing has a relationship for its ground, and the relationship, a process, of which the thing is the sedimentation'. Is Sève here tempted by the idealism of process or of something resembling a basic energetics of nature? It would be going too far to say so. Let us not forget that Sève is on the same side as Bitsakis, *pace* Bitsakis, even if Bitsakis is right to point up the ambiguity on a question as fundamental as this one. See Bitsakis 2001, p. 369.

Lenin's return to Marx's and Engels's category of 'reflection'[40] are important and should be confronted with arguments in the cognitive sciences and the philosophy of mind: to establish a structural, 'morphic' correspondence between thought and reality is to call for an examination of the neurological and psychological modalities of the genesis of this correspondence. Whence the need for a two-fold study, both synchronic and diachronic, of the relation between the brain and thought,[41] and, more generally, of the philosophical category of matter.[42]

Reflection is not mechanical, not even for Lenin: concepts are the most abstract products of a cerebral organ that is very highly developed and phylogenetically and ontogenetically determined in multiple ways by genetic and social factors. It is because there is reflection in one sense or another that there exist, simultaneously, the possibility of knowing and the possibility of erring; both possibilities attest to the non-immediacy of the representative process. Lenin was already aware that this process, – studied since his time by Wallon, Vygotsky, in the genetic epistemology founded by Piaget and in the contemporary cognitive sciences, – is complex and corresponds to distinct-theoretical registers: if there is a genetic relation, there is also a difference between reality and thought that is not ontological, but rather ontic and epistemological. This is anything but empiricist;[43] Lenin clearly affirms – Bitsakis follows him without qualification on this point – that approaching objective reality does not mean 'sticking' to sense-experience, but, rather, proceeding from the concrete to the abstract, and constructing conceptually, which

40. Bitsakis 2001, pp. 263–7. See, besides Lenin 1976 – a polemical work, to be sure, but one that thinks the inflection of materialist and dialectical-philosophical principles into politically (and scientifically) operational concepts, or, at least, crucially leaves room for the possibility of thinking this inflection (in the mode of the categorical mediation analysed above) – Lenin's *Philosophical Notebooks* and the contributions to CERM (eds.) 1974, for example: Sève 1974; J.-P. Cotten, 'Quelques réflexions sur la catégorie d'essence chez Lénine', pp. 269–85; J.-C. Michéa, 'Sur la "science de la pensée" ', pp. 571–85; and Jaeglé 1977. See also Quiniou 1987, especially Chapter One, which is about the question of reflection and, more generally, that of the refoundation of materialism.

41. See Barot 2002, pp. 59–60. In this article, I analyse the relations between morphism in the sense that the mathematical theory of categories assigns the term and morphism in the sense in which one puts objects in a relation of correspondence in Piaget. The framework for this analysis is a study of the modelling of the emergence of mathematical cognition that sets out from neuronal matter and makes use of both Marxist and non-Marxist dialectics. I attempt, more generally, to bring Engels's *Dialectics of Nature* up-to-date at a regional level, that of the progress of the cognitive sciences, taking my inspiration from Sartre's materialist ontology. I defend the thesis that a dialectical construction, proceeding by way of qualitative differentiations and the overcoming of contradictions, allows one to understand the genesis of meaning, and, from there, the emergence of logical-mathematical thinking, beginning with the self-organisation of components of the brain. The instruments I use are, first, mathematical theories of recursiveness, and, second, contemporary constructivist theories and theories of information. Ultimately, I defend a particular form of intentional realism (that is, a form of the thesis of the scientific irreducibility of mental contents to physical-physiological brain processes).

42. See Quiniou 1987, pp. 47–51.

43. See Verret 1967, p. 130.

is to say abstractly, the concrete-in-thought that is best able to apprehend reality – as Marx taught. Aside from the fact that reflection, an extremely dynamic philosophical category, condenses the anti-idealist primacy of matter over thought, it plainly designates, in Dominique Lecourt's summary,[44] 'an (active) *practice* of appropriation of the external world by thought'. This is reflection 'without a mirror', in the sense that it only comes about in 'a historical *process* of knowledge acquisition'.[45]

4. The dialectics of nature as a 'theoretical practice of epistemology'

In 1963, Althusser wrote:

> The Marxist theoretical practice of *epistemology*, of the history of science... has yet in large part to be constituted.... Their practice is largely *in front of them* [the Marxists], it still has to be developed, or even founded, that is, it has to be set on correct theoretical bases so that it corresponds to a *real* object, not to a presumed or ideological object, and so that it is a truly theoretical practice, not a technical practice. It is for this purpose that they need Theory, that is, the materialist dialectic, as the sole method that can anticipate their theoretical practice by drawing up its formal conditions. In this case, the utilisation of Theory is not a matter of *applying* its formulae (the formulae of the dialectic, of materialism) to a pre-existing content.[46]

We are still in the early stages of the elaboration of the new *praxis*, yet we can already glimpse the 'real object' of which Althusser speaks. The dialectics of nature, which is neither 'scientific practice'[47] (that is, practice that thinks the limits of the empirical techniques that give rise to it as a scientific application of a given science) nor

44. Lecourt 1973, p. 43.

45. Lecourt 1973, p. 47. Geymonat 1972 and 1976 recall the stakes and importance of the flexible category of reflection.

46. Althusser 1996, pp. 169–70. What Althusser goes on to say recalls Lenin's criticism of Plekhanov and Engels: they applied the dialectics of nature to examples in this fashion – in an analogical mode, a mode that, in my view, Sève would have done well to discuss at greater length. See also the Leninist legacy which is common to Bitsakis and Althusser, and doubtless helps explain this affinity. I here rely mainly on Althusser 1996, pp. 164–73. Althusser's aim in this essay is to give 'an answer with a theoretical basis' to the question: 'what is the use of a theoretical expression of a solution which already exists in a practical state?' (p. 168). Better than anyone else, Pierre Raymond has put Althusser's theses to work in the field of the epistemology and history of mathematics (in *Matérialisme dialectique et logique, Le passage au matérialisme, L'histoire et les sciences*, and *Philosophie et calcul de l'infini*, all published by François Maspero in the 1970s). See also Verret 1967, 'Sur la notion de pratique théorique'.

47. The scientific practice of geometry, although it derives from surveying techniques or architecture, was constituted in a break with them. But the knowledgeable practice [*pratique savante*] of geometry, erected on the basis of this scientific practice, is capable of producing truths (theorems) independently of the scientific application (that is, of this scientific practice) of geometry. See Verret 1967, pp. 140–2, for this example and an analysis of the fundamentally-important distinction between these two practices.

'knowledgeable practice [*pratique savante*]' (that is, the practice of a science that produces exact knowledge, which is true in that it is adequate to its object), should therefore be characterised as a practice of the semi-philosophical concepts that irrigate the networks of scientific concepts and their articulations. Scientific theories objectify phenomena, while also mediating and interrogating the modes and the various instruments of this objectification itself. Hence, the dialectics of nature is invested with a critical, not an ontological dimension.

5. The stakes

What is at stake in the ongoing construction of a dialectics of nature is, first of all, contemporary Marxism's capacity to take charge of the problem of the modes of objectification at work in the sciences of matter, its capacity to think their concepts without paying undue tribute to a comfortable, because sterilising, corpus. This is a key element in the transformation of Marxism and a key to the long-term success of its contemporary renaissance, because its overall theoretical and practical credibility will largely be measured by this capacity. To accomplish the task, we shall have to draw on non-Marxist dialectical schools of thought, as Sève and other contributors to the book published under his editorship invite us to do, rather than limiting ourselves to the Marxist tradition *à la* Bitsakis. This recalls – and it is not the least of Bitsakis's merits to have reminded us of the fact and studied it in depth, where Sève offers only extremely vague general remarks – the need to refound dialectical *materialism* as such, a task that implies, notably, confronting and utilising contemporary work in psychology and the cognitive sciences. Precise knowledge of the neuro-physiological mechanisms of the emergence of thought, especially discursive thought, and the interpretation of this knowledge can provide us with the means of renewing the concepts and, thus, the main problematics bound up with the thesis of reflection, which is already very complex in Lenin. We thus face a two-fold task. First, we must acquire the theoretical means of constructing an authentic dialectical materialism and dialectical psychology, which would lend consistency to the legitimately but too-easily repeated criticism of the subject-object dualism, and, correlatively, revive the study of the ideal nature [*idéalité*] of knowledge as a symbolic form of materiality. Second, we must, by extension, once again apply the historically-determined, ideologically-overdetermined criterion of social practice to the scientificity produced by thought that is necessarily collective.[48]

In other words, what is at stake in the ongoing construction of a dialectics of nature is not purely epistemological, but bears on all the different fields of what is called 'Marxism'. Hence, the dialectics of nature demands – since, even within Marxist thought, it is sometimes regarded as obsolete[49] – attention and respect of the most serious kind, which

48. See Ollmann 2003.

49. With the benefit of hindsight, we can see, for example, that, in 1997, Pierre Macherey clearly, if critically, rejected his own 1982 theses (the substance of the article entitled 'Dialectique de la nature' in Bensussan and Labica (eds.) 1985). His point is that the dialectics of nature has been overcome today, and that it is impossible to be a Marxist in the same way as before. The risk is that one will end up no longer being a Marxist at all. Nevertheless one clearly

the two books discussed here pay it. I hope to have shown that both deserve to become widely read and discussed classics.

As hardly needs be said, we can no longer content ourselves with historical syntheses, but need to move very concretely toward realising this programme.[50] Without lapsing into scholasticism or an eclecticism that would merely conjure up the illusion of renewal, we should also acknowledge the multiple affinities between the various theoretical traditions that, as we have seen, are (or ought to be) involved in this work-in-progress. What are required, then, are research-projects and long-term research-groups, the only practical means of assessing the work to be done.[51] Beyond quarrels between competing schools, which often lead to confusion between rememoration and commemoration, the time is ripe for a new transition to the concept. A critical edition of the manuscripts comprising Engels's *Dialectics of Nature* would constitute an official, and symbolic, first step on the way to this transition to practice.[52]

Emmanuel Barot
University of Toulouse II – Le Mirail
emmanuel-barot@orange.fr

Translated by G.M. Goshgarian

References

Alcouffe, Alain (ed.) 1985, *Les manuscrits mathématiques de Marx*, Paris: Economica.

Althusser, Louis 1982 [1968/9], *Lénine et la philosophie suivi de Marx et Lénine devant Hegel*, Paris: Maspero.

—— 1996 [1963], 'Sur la dialectique matérialiste', in *Pour Marx*, Paris: La Découverte.

Barot, Emmanuel 2002, 'Dialectique de la nature pensante: la construction de la cognition mathématique', *Philosophia Scientiae*, 6, 1: 33–72.

—— 2004, *L'aventure mathématique de la dialectique depuis Hegel*, doctoral dissertation, University of Paris X, Nanterre, France.

detects in 1997 (and further) the still-pronounced influence of Althusser on Macherey, even if it has now been passed through the filter of Spinozist anti-theoreticism.

50. See Barot 2004 and 2009. Some of my current researches concern: (1) the meaning, potency and limits of certain attempts at formalising dialectics (paraconsistency, category-theory) and (2) what I call the 'fetishism of mathematical object and objectivity' and its ontological illusions, by analogy with commodity-fetishism. I use the concepts of 'objectivation' and 'alienation' that Sartre rebuilt in his *Critique of Dialectical Reason*, in close relationship to his categories of 'praxis' and 'practico-inert', to show, for example, in what way standard-formal logic plays a transversal role which justifies assimilating it to the 'currency of the mind', following Marx's approach to Hegel's logic in his *1844 Manuscripts*.

51. On this topic, see Sève and Guespin-Michel (eds.) 2005, which deals with dynamic systems in relationship to the bio-cognitive question of 'emergence', and Barot 2002.

52. A first and different version (translated into Greek) of this text was published as Barot 2003.

—— 2003, `Διαλεκτική της φύσης: Το διακύβευμα ενός εργοταξου. Στοιχεία για το περασμα στην έννοια', *Utopia*, 57, 11/12: 129–52.
—— 2009, *Lautman*, Paris: Les Belles-Lettres.
Bensussan, Gerard and Georges Labica (eds.) 1985, *Dictionnaire critique du Marxisme*, Second Edition, Paris: PUF.
Bitsakis, Eftichios 1974, 'Symétrie et contradiction', in CERM (ed.) 1974.
—— 1983, *Physique et matérialisme*, Paris: Editions Sociales.
—— 1997, *La nouveau réalisme scientifique*, Paris: L'Harmattan.
—— 2001, *La nature dans la pensée dialectique*, Paris: L'Harmattan.
CERM [Centre d'Etudes et de Recherches Marxistes] 1974, *Lénine et la pratique scientifique*, Paris: Editions Sociales.
Cohen-Tannoudji, Gilles 1990, 'La pertinence du concept d'horizon de réalité en physique théorique contemporaine', *Dialectica*, 44: 323–32.
Delbraccio, Mireille and Georges Labica (eds.) 2000, *Friedrich Engels, Savant et révolutionnaire*, Paris: PUF.
Engels, Friedrich 1977a [1875], *Anti-Dühring*, translated by Emile Bottigelli, Paris: Editions Sociales.
—— 1977b [1883], *Dialectique de la nature*, translated by Emile Bottigelli, Paris: Editions Sociales.
Engels, Friedrich and Karl Marx 1973, *Lettres sur les sciences de la nature (et les mathématiques)*, translated by Jean-Pierre Lefebvre, Paris: Editions Sociales.
Geymonat, Ludovico 1972, 'Néo-positivisme et matérialisme dialectique', translated by B. Eisenchitz, *Recherches Internationales*, 73, 4: 1–17.
—— 1974, 'Primi lineamenti di una teoria della conoscenza materialistico-dialettica', in *Attualità del materialismo dialettico*, edited by E. Bellone, L. Geymonat, G. Giorello and S. Tagliagambe, Rome: Editori Riuniti.
—— 1976, 'Premiers éléments d'une théorie matérialiste dialectique de la connaissance', *Recherches Internationales*, 86, 1: 98–124 [French translation by F. Persiaux of Geymonat 1974].
Granger, Gilles-Gaston 1979, 'Y a-t-il des dialectiques internes du développement scientifique?', in *Rationality Today*, edited by T. Geraets, Ottawa: University of Ottawa Press [reprinted in Granger 1994].
—— 1980, 'La notion de contenu formel', *Information et signification*, November: 137–63 [reprinted in Granger 1994].
—— 1988, 'La contradiction', *Travaux du Centre de Recherches Sémiologiques*, 'La négation', 56: 39–54 [reprinted in Granger 1994].
—— 1994, *Formes, opérations, objets*, Paris: Vrin.
Jaeglé, Pierre 1977, 'Dialectique de la nature: sur quelques concepts (qualité, quantité...)', in *Sur la dialectique*, edited by the Centre d'Etudes et de Recherches Marxistes, Paris: Editions Sociales.
Lecourt, Dominique 1973, *Une crise et son enjeu (Essai sur la position de Lénine en philosophie)*, Paris: Maspero.
Lefebvre, Henri 1947, *Logique formelle et logique dialectique*, Paris: Editions Sociales.
—— 1986, *Le retour de la dialectique*, Paris: Editions Sociales.
—— 2002, *Méthodologie des sciences*, Paris: Economica.
Lenin Vladimir I. 1976 [1909/1920], *Materialism and Empirio-Criticism*, Peking: Foreign Languages Press.
Levins, Richard and Richard Lewontin 1985, *The Dialectical Biologist*, Cambridge, MA.: Harvard University Press.
Macherey, Pierre 1999, *Histoires de dinosaures: Faire de la philosophie, 1965–1997*, Paris: PUF.

Ollman, Bertell 2003, *Dance of the Dialectic: Steps in Marx's Method*, Champaign: University of Illinois Press.
Petry, Michael John (ed.) 1993, *Hegel and Newtonianism*, Dordrecht: Kluwer.
Quiniou, Yvon 1987, *Problèmes du matérialisme*, Paris: Méridiens Klincksieck.
Sartre, Jean-Paul 2004 [1960], *Critique of Dialectical Reason* Volume 1, translated by Alan Sheridan-Smith, London: Verso.
Sève, Lucien 1974, 'Pré-rapport sur la dialectique', in CERM (ed.) 1974.
—— 1980, *Une introduction à la philosophie marxiste*, Paris: Editions Sociales.
—— 1984, *Structuralisme et dialectique*, Paris: Editions Sociales.
—— 1989, '"La pensée" et le mouvant... Sciences de la nature, matérialisme et dialectique en 1939 et 1989', *La Pensée*, 270/271: 75–87.
—— (ed.) 1998, *Sciences et dialectiques de la nature*, Paris: La Dispute.
Sève, Lucien and Janine Guespin-Michel (eds.) 2005, *Emergence, complexité, dialectique*, Paris: Odile Jacob.
Tosel, André 1984, *Praxis. Vers une refondation en philosophie marxiste*, Paris: Editions Sociales.
—— 1995, 'Formes de mouvement et dialectique dans la nature selon Engels', *Revue philosophique*, 4: 433–62.
—— 2001, 'Matérialisme, dialectique et "rationalisme moderne". La philosophie des sciences à la française et le marxisme (1931–1945)', in *Philosopher en français*, edited by Jean-François Mattei, Paris: PUF.
Verret, Michel 1967, *Théorie et politique*, Paris: Editions Sociales.

William Morris and Edward Burne-Jones: Interlacings, Caroline Arscott, New Haven: Yale University Press, 2008.

The Poetry of Chartism: Aesthetics, Politics, History, Mike Sanders, Cambridge: Cambridge University Press, 2009.

Abstract
New books by Caroline Arscott and Mike Sanders return to the vexed problem of Marxism and aesthetics. For some time, there has been an intense suspicion of aesthetic thought in Marxist circles, where it is perceived as an ideology perpetrating a false resolution of contradictions. Arscott and Sanders understand aesthetics to be at the heart of the communist imagination: Arscott offers a detailed investigation of how the body is inhabited in the art of William Morris and Edward Burne-Jones; Sanders considers the figure of the poet in Chartism as a spur to radicalism. Engaging with these books, this review calls for a Marxist reconsideration of aesthetic thought and artistic practice.

Keywords
Aesthetics and politics, Chartism, William Morris, Edward Burne-Jones

Aesthetics and the Communist Imagination

A penny for each conference session titled 'Aesthetics and Politics' – with or without a hyphenated by-line – would probably fund this journal in perpetuity. At the same time, the Left has lately been remarkably reticent about aesthetics. Much *marxisant* work influenced by new historicism has tended to dissolve the artwork into ideology and treat aesthetics as an intellectual mode requiring debunking. From this perspective, art is to be studied as a historical 'discourse' indissolubly bound up with power – usually with gender or colonial domination. In a strong version of this argument, Martha Woodmansee offers a powerful reading of the emergence of aesthetic theory and art as a reflex of the capitalist market; despite its sophistication (and irony), Terry Eagleton's *Ideology of the Aesthetic* also falls into this camp. Deeply influenced by Paul de Man's suspicion of affect, Eagleton represents aesthetic thought as a species of false sublation, offering consolation centred on a bogus wholeness and immediacy.[1] Woodmansee and Eagleton both represent aesthetic theory as ideologically mystificatory. This view, buttressed by Benjamin's reflections on fascism, Adorno's critique of commodity-aesthetics and Debord's account of spectacular society, has provided a powerful injunction against Marxist considerations of aesthetics.[2] None of this is straightforward: Benjamin called for 'the politicisation of aesthetics' (which may or may not be the same as its abandonment), while Adorno and Debord are both profoundly aesthetic thinkers, but all of this has condensed or coalesced into a form of left common-sense. In its Bourdieu-inspired form, the argument often boils down to the philistine: 'she did it for the money'; 'he visited the museum to feel superior'.[3]

1. Woodmansee 1994; Eagleton 1990. For an important challenge to this line of thinking, see Armstrong 2000.
2. Benjamin 1968; Adorno 1991 and 1997; Debord 1994.
3. Bourdieu 1989; Bourdieu and Darbel 1991; for a critique, see Rancière 1991 and 2003.

 DOI: 10.1163/156920610X512507

Paradoxically, this is a view that tells everyone to remain in their place. At the other end of the intellectual spectrum are to be found the defenders of the high-modernist canon. In the general academic debate, much of this takes the form of a revivified Kantianism in which disinterestedness, purposeful purposelessness and the *sensus communis* bring with them liberalism, but its left variant is associated with the champions of Adorno.[4] *Aesthetic Theory* is unquestionably one of the indispensable contributions to a Marxist account of art under capitalism, but the rigid demarcation between high and low forms and the determination to prevent autonomous art's contamination by politics now acts as a blockage to further critical thought and practice.[5] What is more, Adorno's canon now looks deeply troubled by contemporary artists' fascination with everyday-life, hybrid-forms and the drive to heteronomy.[6] Despite the differences within the current debate, the various positions all radically separate art and aesthetics from socialist politics.

There are signs that this mood is beginning to dissolve: for one thing, contemporary art is undergoing a profoundly activist turn; for another, the fascination with the thought of Jacques Rancière marks a significant shift in the critical agenda. Rancière's account of the division of sensibility, emotion and affect, of forms of making and saying, provides a fruitful way of thinking about autonomy and heteronomy, aesthetics and politics.[7] This is not to say that his work is unproblematic: I am unconvinced by the periodisation at the heart of his aesthetics, and often Rancière's argument consists of little more than philosophically-reheated cultural commonplaces. What is more, his recent work on art seems remarkably coy about any mention of capitalism or class. Nevertheless, when read out of his earlier writing focused on the workers' archives, in which the 'distribution of the sensible' is rooted in a hierarchical division of labour, Rancière's argument offers Marxists a powerful way of rethinking art as a socially-generative form.[8] The separation of art and work, knowing and doing; the utopia of aesthetics and the concomitant refusal to remain in your allotted place, all suggest a rich overlap with the thought of Marx – perhaps this is not surprising, since Schiller's *Aesthetic Education of Man* occupies a pivotal position in both accounts[9] (it is amusing to observe how much energy Rancière has expended trying to escape from the gravitational field of Marxism only to find himself pulled back into its orbit by a younger generation).

Marxism is a profoundly aesthetic philosophy and so is socialist politics. In 1848, Mr Justice Maule addressed a group of English workers charged with riot:

> The best course they could take in this was to be careful, to work hard, spend as little money as they could, and improve their knowledge whenever they had the opportunity. Some people in Yorkshire had acquired a very large property indeed,

4. For a range of debates see Beech and Roberts (eds.) 2002, particularly the essays by the editors, Bernstein, Bowie and Day.
5. Adorno 1997.
6. Day 2009.
7. Rancière 2004 and 2009.
8. Rancière 1989 and 1991.
9. Schiller 1982; Marx 1975.

> who had begun life simply as working men: but he never heard of anyone who had raised his condition by going out drilling and joining a Chartist society.[10]

The little homilies make me cringe, but, in terms of the bare facts, no-one could disagree with Justice Maule: becoming a Chartist was likely to get you victimised at your workplace, imprisoned, transported or even shot. And yet Chartism transformed the lives of many London artisans, Black-Country metal-workers, and Lancashire textile-workers. Like Rancière's cobbler-poets, it allowed men and women to imagine another life: some became itinerant lecturers, journalists and booksellers. In 1839, Christopher Doyle, a Manchester-Irish power-loom weaver used a prison-term awarded for 'conspiracy to raise wages' to read Locke and Bacon; others read Walter Scott or taught themselves mathematics.[11] All of this came courtesy of the state that 'freed' them from their compulsion to labour. The history of Chartism is full of stories like this. As Dorothy Thompson observes:

> In the towns and villages of Britain thousands of anonymous men and women organised the Chartist movement, using traditional forms of processions, carnivals, theatrical performances, camp meetings, sermons and services to put the message across of the six points. Flags, banners, caps of liberty, scarves, sashes and rosettes appeared on public occasions. Slogans from the Bible, from literature and from earlier radical movements decorated the banners and placards they carried. Hymns and songs were written and sung, poems were declaimed. Every aspect of the religious and cultural life of the communities was brought into service to press home the Chartist message.[12]

'Message' is probably the wrong term, but it should be clear that Chartism was deeply engaged with the organisation of the senses and emotions. Historians and theorists have had remarkably little to say about this aspect of the struggle, but it is difficult to imagine how any serious communist politics can do without such an account, and even more how it could sidestep a practice of this order.

New books by Caroline Arscott and Mike Sanders make valuable contributions to this project of reinscribing aesthetic affect in socialism. In an unsystematic fashion, both books engage with the English romantic-anticapitalist trend that fed into Marxism. Fredric Jameson has argued that one significant version of Marxism inherited 'the right-wing disdain for business and middle-class culture' from 'the first anti-capitalist critiques of the Romantic period'. This position, he suggests, was rendered 'ambiguous' or 'ambivalent' by the more complex relationship of the working-class movement to industrial development'.[13] In one sense, this is a simplification: the romantic tradition – and this includes belated forms and not just the products from the high period of romanticism – provided a central component of the working-class critique of capitalism; Ruskin was read avidly by English industrial workers and Chartism has significant romantic roots. The destruction of beauty,

10. Quoted in Saville 1997, p. 177.
11. For examples, see Thompson 1986.
12. Thompson 1986, pp. 118–19.
13. Jameson 1998, p. 148.

the despoliation of nature and the displacement of a supposedly 'organic' social order all provided powerful arguments against the squalor of industrial cities, 'sham' commodities and social alienation. Marx grasped that a romantic yearning for a full past and a sense of present emptiness formed an antinomy: 'The bourgeois viewpoint has never advanced beyond this antithesis between itself and the romantic viewpoint and therefore the latter will accompany it as its legitimate antithesis until its blessed end'.[14] Perhaps the most productive development of this line of thought is to be found in those running spats within English Marxism conducted between E.P. Thompson and Perry Anderson.[15] In 'Components of the National Culture' (1968), Anderson argued there had been an almost complete absence of Marxism in English culture, thus passing over both Morris and the historians. Thompson, for his part, insisted Anderson was looking in the wrong places and that Morris – drawing on the romantic criticism of capitalism – had fundamentally transformed Marxism with a moral vision, which it lacked. Anderson, employing his method of double-entry book-keeping (here a plus, there a minus), subsequently acknowledged that he had overlooked the contribution of Morris, but worried about the irrationalism of a politics of desire (in the wake of so-much subsequent Deleuzianism, he had a point). This was a rich, if sometimes intemperate, debate: what now seems certain is that the romantic aesthetic offers Marxism a key affective resource, especially valuable in an era of ecodisaster-capitalism. One further point should be added here: *pace* Jameson, Morris transformed the Tory anticapitalism of Carlyle and Ruskin in a socialist direction through an immanent dialectic (a related pattern might be traced through Lukács, Bloch and Marcuse). I would like to have seen this debate addressed by Saunders and Arscott, but though they do not appraise the existing Marxist literature, both authors make a substantive contribution to thinking about these questions.[16]

Verse and class

Sanders's *The Poetry of Chartism: Aesthetics, Politics, History* examines the role of verse in Chartism, but moves beyond the obvious examples of Ernest Jones or Thomas Cooper's *The Purgatory of Suicides*. Instead, he focuses on the poems published in the Chartist press, particularly the *Northern Star*. There was a surprising amount of them: between 1838 and 1852, 1,500 poems or excerpts appeared in the paper's poetry-column, the work of at least 390 Chartist poets, many of them working men like the poet-shoemaker Jem Blackaby; there were also poems by Shelley, Byron and Shakespeare as well as contemporary poets who were not associated with Chartism (p. 70). Sanders demonstrates that 'Chartist poetic production' played a key role in the *Northern Star* and the politics it fostered. The poetry-column appeared with increased regularity over the period 1838–41, and it migrated from the back of the paper to a central, symbolic position on page three (p. 73). In fact, the *Northern Star* was receiving so much poetry that, at various points, the editor issued mass-rejections rather than write to the individual contributors. In 1838, he noted: 'We get Rhymes of a most rubbishy description by the score. We cannot pretend to enumerate

14. Marx 1973, p. 162.
15. Thompson 1978; Anderson 1980; Anderson 1992.
16. As we will see below, Arscott does engage with Thompson's biography of Morris.

them. We shall select, from time to time, such as we think worth publishing, and burn the rest'. Now that is what you call an editorial rejection! Two years later, he said that the paper 'was glutted with poetry' (p. 72). During 1841, a staggering 146 poems were printed and 127 rejected; Sanders estimates this was the output of between 55 and 74 Chartist poets who provided 92 per cent of the output that year. From 1847 or 1848, there is a marked falling-off of this poetic production, so that, by 1852, only 35 poems appeared, of which 60 per cent were by non-Chartists (p. 71). The figures themselves are remarkable and point to the extraordinary vitality unleashed by the mass-movement, just as they attest to its decline.

In his attempt to think with this material, Sanders draws on a range of theoretical sources: the aesthetic thought of Christopher Caudwell; Rancière and Isobel Armstrong; Cornelius Castoriadis's 'imaginary institution of society'; Raymond Williams's 'structure of feeling'; and Fredric Jameson's notion of the 'political unconscious'. I am not convinced that this material is adequately synthesised and there is something of the 'toolkit'-approach, but Sanders uses this range of ideas to ask intelligent questions. What I take to be his critique of Bourdieu can also be read as enacting a distance from Rancière's writing. These arguments are embedded in the account and need to be drawn out; perhaps I am over-elaborating them. Rancière casts his worker-poets against Marxist politics; for them, art was enough and Marxism involved its own injunction for the worker to remain at his bench.[17] But, in Sanders's version of this argument, the dislocation of art and society enacts a democratic claim to social transformation in which no-one would remain in their socially-allocated role.

Centrally, Sanders wants to know what poetry did for the Chartists and why the rank and file were so committed to poetic production. Sanders suggests that Chartist poetry should be grasped 'as both enabled by its own imaginary, and as one of the means by which the movement sought to articulate (express and join together, hence totalise) its own understanding' of the changes wrought by capitalism (p. 17). *The Poetry of Chartism* pursues this double-address, examining the way that poetry reveals the values and ambiguities of Chartism, and the manner in which it was a socially-generative practice at the heart of the project. Looking back from 1880, Thomas Frost recalled spending time with Blackaby 'in the shoemaker's garret, talking by turns of politics and poetry' (p. 6) For these two Croydon worker-activists, there was no hierarchy between these terms: politics and poetry made them who they were, enacting a double dislocation from the worker's world that was simultaneously a claim to social transformation. An array of the movement's leaders all published poetry, including George Julian Harney, Ernest Jones, Samuel Kydd, James Bronterre O'Brien, Fergus O'Conner and Peter Murray McDouall. It is part of Sanders's argument that the connection between poetry and the prominence or public esteem in which these figures were held is not coincidental. For the Chartists, poetry represented cultural authority, but not in the dismal sense that we encounter it in Bourdieu and his collaborators. Here, 'distinction' was offered as a model for radical emulation. The leadership's cultural authority, proclaimed through poetic taste and sensibility, marked them out as models of transformation for their worker-followers. This was a process of identification in which cultural distance could generate a radical desire to be other than oneself, transforming the subject and society. Poetry marked a radical gap in

17. Rancière 1989.

the subject akin to the 'something more' of later Chartist politics. Interestingly, Sanders cites Anne Janowitz's suggestive argument that, despite Thomas Cooper's growing distance from Chartism, O'Conner could not move against him until he secured an ally of equal poetic status in Ernest Jones (p. 60).

Sanders's central argument in *The Poetry of Chartism* is the claim 'that the capacity of the working classes both to recognise and produce good poetry demonstrated their fitness for the franchise' (p. 77). What we might call the radical poetics of distinction countered the middle-class assertion that they were low, mean, uncultured and suited only to exercise their muscles. Sanders argues that this is why the *Northern Star* insisted on good poetry. The editor's mass-rejections of submitted poems and the presence of exemplary poetic models like Harney's regular column 'Beauties of Byron' played an important part in this project. Raising the tone, increasing the standard of poetry and 'transforming quantity into quality' was central to a politics of aspiration that would produce a democratic transformation of both society and the working class. Similarly, Sanders suggests, 'it was the "combination of literary and intellectual ambition" that made Cooper's *The Purgatory of Suicides* a model of emulation for other Chartist poets' (p. 79). In this sense, the transformative role of Chartist mass-poetry should be viewed as the inverse of the 'gentleman radical' leader, who through his commitment to the cause proclaimed its self-evident rationality and anti-class character.[18]

Sanders suggests that Chartist poetry represented 'the last gasp of an exhausted romanticism' (p. 29). This is an important point, because the radical agenda here does not turn on avant-garde form, but on a gap between, on the one hand, cultural authority and evidently marked affect and, on the other, the dull compulsion of labour. It may well be, as E.P. Thompson thought, that there is some powerful connection between romanticism and communism, but it is also worth noting that utopia can be made from even bad art. Whatever the other strengths of the historical avant-garde, worker-militants were attached to older forms and to the model of cultural authority that these suggested. In many ways, they still are and the rise of modernism stripped them of a powerful affective resource.

The Poetry of Chartism pulls in different directions and, in significant ways, pulls it apart. The second chapter, 'Chartist Poetry and Literary History', is a literature-review, which makes some significant points, but feels like the remnants of an earlier project (a PhD?). In a very different register, the final chapter reads Gerald Massey through Benjamin's concept of messianic time. At this point, the approach and material seem to be going somewhere else, and I cannot help feeling that, while Benjamin might have provided the impetus for this consideration, it would have been more advisable to develop the argument through an engagement with the English antinomian tradition. But perhaps the real issue is that the book drifts into exploring the Chartist 'imaginary' through a reading of the poems. The professional force of literary studies takes over from the desire to think the mass-experience of the poetic. Having said that, Sanders is a good reader and we learn a lot from his accounts. For instance, his treatment of the poetry produced in response to the Newport rising of 1839 shows just how ambivalent the Chartists were about endorsing the use of violence. The Chartist poets refigure the Newport-events as a response to state-violence rather than as an offensive action, and thus locate them in a narrative that fits

18. Belchem and Epstein 1997; Chase 2007.

with what the author calls the myth of Peterloo.[19] John Watkins's verse-drama 'John Frost, or the Insurrection at Newport' came, Sanders suggests, as close to openly endorsing violence as anything produced at the time and this may be why it was not performed and was declined by major radical publishers (p. 124). While this does not set aside the debate on physical and moral force, this reading does reveal how carefully the argument for the use of force was framed and the need to attend to the presentation of arguments. Sanders's readings of the poems also consider the relation between Chartism and Irish nationalism. He finds a growing alignment between Chartist workers and Irish confederates; indeed, he argues that the poetry-column was one of the key sites in which this coalition came into being. He challenges the postmodern 'nostalgia thesis' (p. 165) and draws out the class-values of these writers in a way that allows him to bang together a few (unnamed) revisionist heads. All of this is valuable work and shows how much a project on culture can add to a Marxist understanding of political radicalism; it also reveals that attention to cultural history need not become 'cultural history'. Nevertheless, the move into detailed reading does lose the focus on the politics and poetics of self-transformation with which the book opens. Sanders has written a good book, and if he could have found a way of weaving the warp of the Chartist imaginary with the weft of the Chartist worker-poets' desire to leave their assigned place in the hierarchy of sensibility it would have been an even better one.

Art, the body and socialist biopolitics

Caroline Arscott's *William Morris and Edward Burne-Jones: Interlacings* is a marvellous work. Yale has produced a very attractive book with high-quality illustrations, and Arscott's prose contains some of the very best descriptions of artworks that I have ever read. However, this is not the Morris of pastoral nostalgia: beards, hiking boots and real ale in its socialist version, chintz and carrier-bags in the National-Trust incarnation. Arscott is one of the most-inventive art-historians around. Her work combines dazzling accounts of pictures with a rare methodological adventurousness and political intransigence. For an author largely focused on nineteenth-century British genre-painting, this is a significant achievement. Here, it is only possible to touch on a few of the arguments raised in this important book. The writing on Morris is now extensive; there is even a *Journal of William Morris Studies*, but it is fair to say that the overwhelming focus of serious study has fallen on the poetic work, rather than his designs. Where the visual work has been tackled, the approach has been a sort of source-spotting. In his great biography, Thompson represents Morris's design-work as a retreat from the moral and political engagement evident in the poems of the 1860s and 1870s, leading to a hiatus in his work that lasted until the socialist poems and essays of the 1880s.[20] Thompson's argument is here symptomatic of an English-radical suspicion of all things visual. In contrast, Arscott reveals the same energies and sense of conflict in the design-work

19. The argument is not that the Peterloo-massacre was a myth, but that it set a mythic pattern for radical thinking about violence: an innocent and unarmed people slaughtered by vicious aristocrats and their lackeys.

20. Thompson 1976.

throughout Morris's *œuvre*. Burne-Jones, a sort of late pre-Raphaelite history-painter *manqué*, has received less critical attention, certainly nothing like this. It is one of the great achievements of *Interlacings* to make decoration – textile-fabrics and wallpapers as well as Burne-Jones's decorative painted surfaces – a site of epochal historical and political figuration: 'Burne-Jones was producing work that stood as a melancholy meditation on the dying of history-painting, which he figured as succumbing to the strongly desired forces of decoration, whereas Morris was attempting to encompass the cosmos and remake history in the form of ornament' (p. 27).

The principle of the 'duograph' is at the heart of *Interlacings*. The monograph – the study of a single artist's output – has been central to art-history and drew extensive flak during the period of radical challenge to the discipline in the 1970s and 1980s. The monograph was charged during this period with homogenising contradictions, excluding history and politics and serving the auction-houses. It is a small sign of the times that the monograph is making a forceful comeback. Arscott explores the structure of two related artists' work in an entirely different fashion. Burne-Jones and Morris were life-long friends who met at Oxford and remained close until Morris's death in 1896. Arscott plays off their art, entwining or interlacing their works, so that this is not so much a study of late nineteenth-century art as a detailed reflection upon the body and the aesthetic in relation to two different principles of life. Biography here gives way to the politics of *bios*. Burne-Jones was lethargic, sickly, masochistic, gawky and genteel; in contrast, Morris was corpulent, healthy, strong, full of energy and 'plebeian'. Arscott tracks these different principles through their visual work, linking the former to the armoured body (though, as we will see, she insists that Burne-Jones compromises fascist masculinity) and the latter to socialism. The respective attitude to the Crimea on the part of these artists is revealing: Morris engaged in exercise and drilled with the volunteer-movement out of a desire to fight, whereas Burne-Jones imagined going to the Crimean in order to be shot (p. 20).

Arscott is a Lacanian-inclined Marxist, who also draws heavily on Benjamin (and Ruskin). Here, the contrast between Burne-Jones and Morris is itself a kind of macro-dialectical image, whereas the individual chapters of her study offer micro-Benjaminian constellations: Burne-Jones's armoured figures are played off against modern armaments; Morris's designs are juxtaposed with tattoos or the manuals and techniques of fly-fishing (there is also a brilliant account of Morris's fascination with 'primitive' ornament and his deep hostility to Max Nordau and the anthropology of 'degeneracy'-current at the time). This is an allegorical project of reading: Arscott suggests that Burne-Jones's *Perseus* paintings do 'not punch straight through to the past but nor does he maintain it at due distance, the distance required by consecutive development. Each small perforation in Perseus's armour, joining plate to plate, allows him to move (approximately like an antique hero) but also allows the molten or corrosive substance of time to leak forward and backward. Burne-Jones allows the past to lodge in the flesh of the present'; 'He "laminates" the past and the present' (p. 84). The same might be said about Arscott's historical method. This approach can generate startling insights, but, like the Benjaminian constellation, it can also become random or arbitrary. While Arscott probably would not welcome the comparison, there is also a kind of perverse-Panofskian method at work here – she picks up on iconographic details and pursues them thoroughly, resulting in what can at times seem like wild readings. It has to be said that, sometimes, the effect is unhinged.

However, the payoff is an extraordinary account of Morris's design-work as an allegorical form of utopian modelling in which pattern suggests an analogy for a 'properly functioning human community', where the elements of geometry and naturalism 'correspond to the practical political aims of equality and variety'. Arscott suggests that: 'If an analogy is posited between a harmoniously functioning society and beautiful ornament in applied art, the totality will be marked by symmetry and the repeat, while single elements will show up in their idiosyncratic lively participation' (p. 168). She is not so much interested in what Morris depicts as his dynamic patterning: his process of ordering and organising his material and the way this captures a form of communist imagination. This suggests a dialectic of the one and the many: it is a grand 'utopian vision of totality' that does not edit out 'the dystopian accents of pain and fear of the individual' (p. 201). Morris's designs are wild, dynamic and polymorphously perverse; they imagine the sublation of social contradictions in an allegory performed 'through the twists and turns of plants' (p. 43). Her account is not only the richest exploration of Morris's visual imagination, it also adds enormously to our understanding of his socialist vision.

Arscott is not interested in the representation of the body, or, if she is, it is a mediated and transmogrified body. Rather, her account of sensation and aesthetic sensibility focuses on what it is like to be embodied and how artists might phenomenologically experience and represent their own bodies as if from the inside, giving us an image of materialised sensation. Centrally, her argument turns around the surface of the body and its interior: skin and subcutaneous matter. In this sense, Arscott argues that Morris's designs offer an idea of substantiality that she connects with the subcutaneous body: 'For Morris depth is always softness and surface hardness' (p. 50). The seriality of the commodity-form here meets the substantiality of the body. Morris's patterns dive down beneath the skin into blood, muscle and pulsating matter, giving us a vision of 'living thickness' (p. 27). Surface and depth are always provisional in his work, so that the patterns appear 'full of life' (p. 35). Morris unsettles bourgeois aestheticism, putting together high-flown ideals with 'lewd flesh' (there is an interesting analogy with Adorno here, for whom the 'subcutaneous' was also an aesthetic ideal).[21] This, then, is the body from inside – like Jonah's view of the whale – conjoining pleasure and pain, civility and wildness, utopia and primitivism. In this sense, it should be apparent how Morris is the missing figure from accounts of the historical avant-garde (his incorporation into a theory of the avant-garde would, however, ruin Peter Bürger's schema, where the historical avant-garde necessarily emerges *after* symbolism).[22]

It should be clear that this materialist poetics differs substantially from the way that aesthetics has traditionally been depicted in Marxist thought, as a 'reflection' or 'reflex' of underlying social processes, whether 'the economic' or the struggle of classes. To this effect, Arscott contrasts Morris's vision to Plekhanov's contemporaneous account, which rejected the claim that aesthetic sensation had any ontological primacy: for Plekhanov, aesthetic pleasure was a secondary phenomenon deriving from labour. For Morris, labour was a source of pleasure and no separation could be enforced between work and aesthetic experience. The contrast draws out how innovative Morris was and just what he took from

21. Adorno 2006, p. 91.
22. Bürger 1984.

romanticism. In this sense, the aesthetic that Arscott elaborates is a socially-generative force: Morris was a producer, who created a new vision of socialism with the body, pleasure and pain at its heart (p. 149). This account of Morris suggests that we need to think of aesthetic work as a directly political form that makes its own contribution to socialist politics. It would have been enlightening to see Arscott engage in this vein with Marx's *Economic and Philosophical Manuscripts*.

Whereas Morris is depicted as bodily substantiality, Arscott's Burne-Jones appears as an artist of surface or epidermis. In Burne-Jones's troubled history-painting, the armoured body is far from the impregnable fetish associated with Ernst Jünger and the fascist response to fear.[23] Burne-Jones's figures are 'frail, vulnerable and incomplete' and 'quite unlike the stern and complete image central to fascism and apparently quite widely dispersed in nineteenth- and twentieth-century European and American culture' (p. 74). Burne-Jones gives us a 'fragile' hero and makes it plain to the viewer that the body-armour contains a weak and leaky body associated in fascism with the feminine and the *Untermensch*. This double-representation blocks the fetishistic defence-mechanism of the phallic body evident in fascist ideology. In his final cycle of stained-glass windows for St. Philips Cathedral, Birmingham, which Arscott sees as an attempt to come to terms with Morris's death, Burne-Jones finally found a way to integrate decoration and history in a manner that displaced his sickly vision.

There are risks associated with Arscott's allegorical contrasts. I have already indicated the possibility of the arbitrary conjuncture in the Benjaminian constellation; in addition, the body described is a socially-mediated individual body, but it would have been fascinating to see Arscott pursue the dialectic of the one and the many through the bodily immersion in the crowd – of Morris at Trafalgar Square. Morris's energetic imagery is always likely to displace Burne-Jones and, despite the author's intention, render him a mere counter-point to the key figure. In some ways, this cannot be helped, as Morris is such a dynamic individual, but the account brings with it the danger of importing Nietzschean vitalism into Marxism (these days, some would see this as a real advantage, but Anderson was right on this point, spontaneism and irrationalism have serious costs). It would also have been interesting to see how much Morris drew from the socialist movement; in Arscott's account, he figures as the point of origin. Nevertheless, *Interlacings* is not only the most important work of art-history to appear in many years, it is also is an incredibly creative contribution to Marxist thinking across a range of important topics.

The books by Sanders and Arscott show just how vitally important aesthetic thought is to Marxism and how much there is still to think about. The traditional arguments concerned with alienation and aesthetic prefiguration of hand and mind remain significant, but new forms of art and changed theoretical conjunctures bring other questions to the fore. These two books, which are both, in their distinct ways, concerned with the 'arse-end' of romanticism, make incredibly valuable contributions to revitalising Marxist aesthetics, a subject that appears not as a passive, secondary form – some mere decorative elaboration on the movement – but as an active force in shaping the socialist imagination. Sanders's account of the self-transformation of worker-poets through the politics of distinction and

23. Theweleit 1987.

Arscott's characterisation of the healthy, aesthetic body beyond capital add significantly to our understanding of socialist history and to our sense of what a fully Marxist cultural politics would entail.

Reviewed by Steve Edwards
Open University
s.j.edwards@open.ac.uk

References

Anderson, Perry 1980, *Arguments within English Marxism*, London: Verso.
—— 1992, 'Components of the National Culture', in *English Questions*, London: Verso.
Adorno, Theodor W. 1991, *The Culture Industry: Selected Essays on Mass Culture*, London: Routledge.
—— 1997 [1970], *Aesthetic Theory*, translated by Robert Hullot-Kentor, London: Athlone Press.
—— 2006, *Towards a Theory of Musical Reproduction*, translated by Caroline Beattie and Nick Merriman, Cambridge: Polity Press.
Armstrong, Isobel 2000, *The Radical Aesthetic*, Oxford: Blackwell.
Beech, Dave and John Roberts 2002 (eds.), *The Philistine Controversy*, London: Verso.
Belchem, John and James Epstein 1997, 'The Nineteenth-Century Gentleman Leader Revisited', *Social History*, 22, 2: 174–93.
Benjamin, Walter 1968 [1935], 'The Work of Art in the Age of Mechanical Reproduction', in *Illuminations*, translated by Harry Zohn, London: Fontana.
Bourdieu, Pierre 1989 [1979], *Distinction: A Social Critique of the Judgement of Taste*, translated by Richard Nice, London: Routledge.
—— and Alain Darbel 1991 [1969], *The Love of Art: European Art Museums and their Public*, Cambridge: Polity Press.
Bürger, Peter 1984 [1974], *Theory of the Avant-Garde*, translated by Michael Shaw, Minneapolis: University of Minnesota Press.
Chase, Malcolm 2007, *Chartism: A New History*, Manchester: Manchester University Press.
Day, Gail 2009, 'The Fear of Heteronomy', *Third Text*, 23, 4: 393–406.
Debord, Guy 1994 [1967], *The Society of the Spectacle*, translated by Donald Nicholson-Smith, New York: Zone Books.
Eagleton, Terry 1990, *The Ideology of the Aesthetic*, Oxford: Blackwell.
Jameson, Fredric 1998, *Brecht and Method*, London: Verso.
Marx, Karl 1973 [1857–8], *Grundrisse*, translated by Martin Nicolaus, Harmondsworth: Penguin.
—— 1975 [1844], 'Economic and Philosophical Manuscripts', in *Early Writings*, translated by Rodney Livingstone and Gregor Benton, Harmondsworth: Penguin.
Rancière, Jacques 1989 [1981], *The Nights of Labor: The Workers' Dream in Nineteenth-Century France*, translated by John Drury, Philadelphia: Temple University Press.
—— 1991 [1987], *The Ignorant Schoolmaster: Five Lessons in Intellectual Emancipation*, translated by Kristin Ross, Stanford: Stanford University Press.
—— 2003 [1983], *The Philosopher and His Poor*, edited by Andrew Parker and translated by Corinne Oster, John Drury and Andrew Parker, Durham, NC.: Duke University Press.
—— 2004 [2000], *The Politics of Aesthetics*, translated by Gabriel Rockhill, London: Continuum.

—— 2009 [2003], *The Future of the Image*, translated by Gregory Elliott, London: Verso.
Saville, John 1997, *1848: The British State and the Chartist Movement*, Cambridge: Cambridge University Press.
Schiller, Friedrich 1982 [1794], *On the Aesthetic Education of Man: In a Series of Letters*, edited and translated by E.M. Wilkinson and L.A. Willoughby, Oxford: Clarendon Press.
Theweleit, Klaus 1987 [1977/8], *Male Fantasies*, two volumes, translated by Chris Turner, Erica Carter and Stephen Conway, Cambridge: Polity Press.
Thompson, Dorothy 1986, *The Chartists: Popular Politics in the Industrial Revolution*, Aldershot: Wildwood House.
Thompson, Edward P. 1976, *William Morris: Romantic to Revolutionary*, New York: Pantheon Books.
—— 1978, *The Poverty of Theory and Other Essays*, London: Merlin Press.
Woodmansee, Martha 1994, *The Author, Art, and the Market: Rereading the History of Aesthetics*, New York: Columbia University Press.

Topographies of Class: Modern Architecture and Mass Society in Weimar Berlin, Sabine Hake, Ann Arbor: University of Michigan Press, 2008

Abstract

The Weimar-Republic, and the modernist architecture and planning that was born there, is still a contested place, from whence liberals, reactionaries and Marxists can all trace their lineage. Sabine Hake's *Topographies of Class* attempts to clarify this contestation, through an interdisciplinary study of the modernist geography of the interwar-capital, Berlin. The book offers many new insights into the Weimar-era city, countering a tendency on the Left to reject the twentieth-century city in favour of the romanticised 'capitals of the nineteenth century', with their insurgent proletariat and their lushly ornamented boulevards. *Topographies of Class* is a reminder that, irrespective of the era's rejection of ornament and romanticism, it was a site of class-struggle as intense as that of the Paris of the 1870s. However, Hake's study is dominated by a conception of class as an 'identity', akin to the identity-politics of race or gender, leading to an argument centred on the suppression or expression of 'class-difference' rather than class-struggle. In the process, her reading of the city's modernism becomes overly one-sided, as a period of tension between labour and capital is read, under the influence of Manfredo Tafuri and Italian post-Marxist architectural theory, as being governed almost solely by the logic of Fordist capital.

Keywords

Class, urbanism, metropolis, modernism, architecture, film, press, photography, Fordism, Taylorism, planning, KPD, SPD

The Weimar-Republic, either as cliché of decadence or object for serious scholarship, never seems to go out of fashion. Indeed, its stock rises in times of crisis, as we recall the eventual fate of this particularly fragile liberal democracy when faced with a massive financial crisis. Weimar can largely mean whatever one wants it to mean, alternately a synonym for hedonism or militancy, for revolution or gradualist Social Democracy, for irrationalist expressionism or scientifically-precise Bauhaus-modernism. Nonetheless, the association with crisis, struggle and an especially fertile and dynamic mass-culture is common to all of these stereotyped Weimars. Sabine Hake's *Topographies of Class* presents itself as a corrective to certain Weimar-clichés, through an analysis of the classed nature of urban space in the Republic's capital, attempting to uncover some of the topographic and political-aesthetic nuances usually obscured by the story the unified German capital tells about itself. That is, those images which, post-reunification, feature on tourist-postcards on Unter den Linden. As Hale writes, 'the traffic tower on Potsdamer Platz, the new storefronts on the Kurfürstendamm, the construction site on Alexanderplatz – we have seen it all before' (p. 171). Indeed we have, which makes it rather a shame that it is exactly to these spaces that this book so often returns. Nonetheless, we are in a place rich with conjunctural resonances. Hake presents the Weimar-capital as a collection of lost, foreclosed possibilities from which we could still learn. She lists 'its progressive mass culture, its alternative public sphere, its emancipatory movements, and its revolutionary working class', and claims that here, 'nostalgia does not just mean sentimental attitudes or retrograde tastes; nostalgia attests to the power of the past to remind us of the unredeemed possibilities in the present' (pp. 272–3). Meanwhile, the political relevance of a city which had an amorphous,

 DOI: 10.1163/156920610X512516

apolitical yet proletarianised class of white-collar office-workers (the 'Angestellten') at its heart should be clear for current debates over immaterial labour and the insecure, non-unionised, tedious yet non-manual work that dominates post-industrial European cities.

Metropolis-nostalgia

The familiarity of many of its references is unfortunate, as *Topographies of Class* is an impressive work of original scholarship and historical detail, which nonetheless never manages to go as far in its break with orthodoxies on its subject as it promises. Hake initially presents it as a frankly polemical retort to the dominant trends in urban theory, and their uncritical fixation with the 'unplanned' nineteenth-century city and reduction of modernist architecture and planning to a mere bogeyman, a 'totalitarian' caricature which has skewed the perception of the period, missing the very particular class-relations embodied in the romanticised-Victorian or Wilhelmine city. 'There is no doubt', she writes, that the 'postmodern rejection of modernism [has] contributed to the current romance with the nineteenth century metropolis: a preference for works and texts that locate the attractions of the metropolis in the nineteenth century, a concomitant affinity for urban structures, forms and styles criticised by modernists as products of an architecture of class domination and capitalist exploitation, and an ongoing proliferation of palimpsestic readings, archaeological approaches, and retrospective sensibilities' (p. 14). This fixation with the utterly-ubiquitous 'palimpsest' arises from a certain misunderstanding of Weimar-culture itself, a misapplication of Walter Benjamin's historical-materialist reading of Paris as 'capital of the nineteenth century' to the spaces of heritage and tourism, leading to a concomitant romanticisation and mythologisation of poverty and squalor – the 'psychogeography'-industry in the UK is a particularly remarkable example of this misunderstanding.

In response to this, Hake emphases the complexities of modernism at the very point where it was being formed as a coherent aesthetic position, in the cities of the Weimar-Republic in the decade between 1923 and 1933.

> Denounced as cold, inhospitable, and alienating, modern architecture and urban planning have come to represent the absolute other to the dream world of classical urbanity conjured up by modern and postmodern flâneurs and evoked with nostalgic yearning and sentimental attachment by many scholars working on urban culture. Not surprisingly, memories of the nineteenth century continue to dominate contemporary efforts at urban renewal, from the appropriation of the arcade as a postmodern simulation of urbanity to the preference for historicist forms and styles in the movement of New Urbanism. (p. 14.)

The latter reference, to the planning school which has created deliberately retrograde new towns such as Celebration and Sunshine in the US and Poundbury in the UK, reveals the polemical value of Hake's rereading of modernism, which stresses throughout the 'inherent tension... between the perfect order of the plan and the fragmentation of modern life', which 'can only be resolved in the concrete terms of urban architecture as social practice and political intervention'. Rather than being a mere obliteration of the picturesquely grand and/or dilapidated spaces beloved of the neoliberal *flâneur*, 'modern architecture represents the most important historical attempt to formulate alternatives to the foundation of the metropolis in the spatial politics of class' (p. 15). Indeed, the close links between modern architecture and the very particular political project of Weimar Social Democracy and its attempt to 'level' class-differences are stressed in this study, although to ultimately unsatisfying effect.

Where the problems begin is in Hake's conception of class, which becomes the central preoccupation of this study, although in a rather peculiar form. She correctly notes that, since the work of Manfredo Tafuri and the Venice-school of quasi-Marxist architectural historians,[1] class has been practically ignored in treatments of the period. However, her analysis specifically disowns the Marxist conception of class as economic relation and political consciousness, in favour of class read through the then-contemporary fixation upon the 'masses'.[2] As so often, this begins by disparaging a caricature-Marxism, which – after brief citations of David Harvey and Henri Lefebvre in the Introduction – is generally represented by small walk-on parts for the Kommunistische Partei Deutschlands (KPD), the most popular and powerful Communist Party in the world (outside of the USSR) at that point. 'As should be evident by now, little is to be gained from using class to revive the kind of Marxist orthodoxies that have been rightly criticised for their economic determinism, universalism and unyielding belief in class as the dominant category of identity'. She is keen to impress upon us that there will be no 'rediscovery of working class culture in the capitalist metropolis' (p. 16), though it is unclear why this project should be of such minimal interest. Instead, she tries to steer a third-way between Marxism and a postmodernist interest in 'difference', by defining class not as 'the dominant category of identity, but the dominant identity in crisis', a shifting, warping category, and more generally through discussion of 'the masses'. Given how deeply class-conscious a country the Weimar-Republic was – with a sophisticated Communist counter-culture centred around Willi Münzenberg's media-empire and the high-circulation weekly *Arbeiter Illustrierte Zeitung* (*A-I-Z*) – Hake's approach actually occludes significant class-based and class-conscious topography in favour of a more familiar preoccupation with the apolitical consumerist mass. Such a perspective does have certain uses, however. Hake draws attention to the way in which the modernists of the period attempted to gloss over class-difference through a kind of social-democratic 'levelling' – although it is unclear whether this offends her because of its occlusion of class-conflict at the point of production or because it obscures the 'radical alterity' of class as difference. More interestingly, she sees the (cultural, if not numerical) preponderance of the new white-collar class as an

1. In English, see Tafuri 1976 and Tafuri and Dal Co 1986.

2. In this, *Topographies of Class* is similar to two more directly architectural studies of Weimar-culture, Janet Ward's *Weimar Surfaces* and Kathleen James-Chakraborty's *German Architecture for a Mass Audience*, which emerge from a similar American academic milieu. Both concentrate on urban visual culture and 'the masses', through a similar attempt to undermine the orthodox version of Weimar-modernism encapsulated – through the baleful influence of Philip Johnson and Henry Russell-Hitchcock's exemplary work of depoliticisation at New York's Museum of Modern Art – as 'The International Style'. Neither book makes as grandiose claims as Hake's, however.

indication that Weimar-Berlin was a kind of proto-postindustrial city, where office-work was becoming as central as factory-production, and the mass-media became ever more dominant: 'the electrified, illuminated city announces the dissolution of the time-space continuum by new mass media and anticipates the rise of the virtual city and the postmodern simulacrum'. That, in the form of *A-I-Z*, this mass-media was itself a potential bastion of class-consciousness appears as a mere aside in the discussion of class as mass. This proceeds through an analysis of architecture, journalistic accounts of the city, architectural photography, the novel and, finally, film. Hake moves between these disciplines with an unassuming ease, using Edward Soja's notion of a 'sociospatial dialectic' to shift from one to the other.

Planning and class-power

The book's initial chapters remind us that Berlin was, throughout the 1920s and early 1930s, essentially a Wilhelmine city, defined by a grandiose neoclassical centre, the working-class tenement and courtyard complexes known pejoratively as *Mietskaserne* ('rental barracks') and a general militarisation of space inherited from its original incarnation as a Prussian garrison-town. This meant that Berlin was initially rather uncomfortable as a centre for urban hedonism, due to the channelled nature of its streets – Hake quotes Stephen Spender on the way its occasional tree-lined squares appeared as a mere space to breathe before 'resuming the logic of the street' (p. 23). Coursing through this were the industrial structures of the late-nineteenth and early-twentieth century, whether the electrical industries in Wedding, such as the AEG's architecturally-remarkable Turbine Factory, several large railway-termini and, more pointedly, the areas where the industrial broke into the residential. One could think of the elevated railway that rises out of the ground on Schönhauser Allee, or the Gleisdreieck, a chaotic railway-junction praised with a feverish intensity by the *feuilleton*-writer Joseph Roth. She quotes his 'Affirmation of the Gleisdreieck' as 'a highly critical approach to the "iron landscape" of expanded traffic networks', an 'apocalyptic vision' (p. 24) – but here, her rejection of postmodernism also entails a neglect of irony and dialectics. Roth's essay is not nearly so simple as a hand-wringing protest against this industrial landscape; instead, it offers an ambiguous portrait of its thrilling mechanised power, with a drama that necessarily sits oddly amidst Hake's terse academic prose.[3] Alongside this landscape, there are the areas inhabited by the industrial working class, which, as she herself points out, was always the largest class in Weimar-Berlin, even given the rise of the white-collar *Angestellten*. Hake points out quite rightly that the understandable fascination with 'Red Berlin' has led to a romanticising of the inhuman conditions where it was incubated. 'The areas with highest population density were the centres of the infamous Red Berlin, reason for some architectural historians during the 1970s to romanticise the tenement as the founding site of an authentic working class culture' (p. 30), in a move which would eventually lead to the gentrification of districts like Prenzlauer Berg in the 1990s. The *Mietskaserne* were never

3. 'The world to come will be like this triangular railroad junction, raised to some unknown power. . . . [R]egret for the passing of the old forms is like the grief of some antediluvian creature for the disappearance of a prehistoric habitat'. Roth is not quite joking. Roth 2004, pp. 105–8.

cherished by those who lived in them, even in the militant district of Wedding – but whether their inhabitants were so keen to be moved to the decentralised modernist-suburban colonies planned by the Social Democrats is another matter.

Hake's study of the 'New Berlin', the project of the Social-Democratic Party (SPD) which dominated Berlin during these years, is central to *Topographies of Class*, which stresses the sophistication and complexity of the work of Martin Wagner, the engineer, architect and SPD-member who had ultimate responsibility for city-planning from 1924 onwards. As one of the architects of the New Berlin, Erwin Gutkind (designer of several *Siedlungen* – estates – in some of Berlin's more affluent areas), this entailed an 'extreme decentralisation of the parts, but greatest concentration of the whole' (p. 38) in what has been too-often taken as an imposition of rationalisation upon a largely-mute mass, a view that Hake unsettles but does not entirely break with. Nonetheless, she makes adroit use of the phone-book, to discover where the urban intellectuals of the period actually lived. Unsurprisingly, most of them, with the equally unsurprising exception of *Berlin Alexanderplatz*'s author Alfred Döblin, resided in the comfortable west of the capital. The exceptions, where modernist artists actually lived in the new space of New Berlin, are rather intriguing – the Communist theatre-producer Erwin Piscator lived in Weisse Stadt, one of Martin Wagner's clean-lined modernist *Siedlungen*,[4] while Fritz Lang lived for a time 'in the Luckhart brothers' constructivist row houses on Schorlemer Allee' (p. 106). Sadly, Hake does not ask what the political connotations of these choices may have been for either Piscator or Lang.

Throughout, Hake uses the term New Building – *Neues Bauen* – to describe the architectural idiom of the time, rather than the supposedly-neutral terms 'modernism' or 'International Style' – advisedly, as the term itself is a class-conscious one, a deliberate attempt to use the neutral word *Bauen* rather than the 'artistic' and bourgeois 'architecture' or 'style'. This was best embodied in Berlin by the *Siedlungen* designed, under Wagner, by architects such as Bruno Taut and Otto Rudolf Salvisberg, and in commercial architecture by Erich Mendelsohn.

This attempt to remove the class-connotations of architecture is read in deeply-political terms, in a manner heavily indebted to the analyses of Tafuri. Hake notes the contradictions of Martin Wagner, where the SPD's derivation from Marx and Engels became ever more opaque – 'the original dream of socialism now translated into reformist strategies and administrative solutions.... More a social engineer than a traditional city builder, Wagner was heavily influenced by the ideas of Taylorism and Fordism, which he studied during an exploratory visit to the United States in 1927'. The particular politics of this New Building with reference to the building industry itself are briefly noted – 'the same reasoning that made him support the use of prefabricated elements in construction also informed his ambitious plans for a fully rationalised metropolis. While devoting much of his energies to the question of dwelling, Wagner believed strongly in the primacy of dynamic over static relations, and focused his critical attention on traffic – that is, on the laws of circulation – as the driving force behind all urban development' (p. 40). This

4. It is thought that Piscator's apartment here was the inspiration for Brecht's deeply class-conscious attack on 'the modern Bauhaus dwelling' in the short story 'North Sea Shrimps', where old comrades meet in an example of the New Building, only for it to be deliberately destroyed and desecrated as a reminder of these unsolved conflicts. Brecht 1999, p. 77.

attention to Wagner's technocratic side misses both the political-economic limitations and successes of the New Berlin he planned. We do not learn what the working-class builders of the new city thought of the introduction of the Taylor-system, although it was the case that the contemporary experiments in New Building in 1920s 'Red Vienna' eschewed rationalisation as a deliberate move to reduce unemployment in the building trade.[5] While the building workers do not have a voice here, neither do the skilled workers who had the chance to move from the *Mietskaserne* into some of the most remarkable and spatially-imaginative public housing ever built, something acknowledged when Wagner's *Siedlungen* became UNESCO World-Heritage Sites in 2007.[6] Rather more than a Fordist demiurge ploughing highways through Potsdamer Platz, Wagner was also the planner of some of the urban world's most remarkable public spaces, whether the modernist baths in Wannsee or the landscaped parks and gardens of his 'Horseshoe Estate' in Britz. The attention to traffic seems more an inadvertent premonition of the motorised planning of Le Corbusier and the postwar-period; for all of Wagner's fixation on traffic-circulation, the photos here, and contemporary footage of the city's most congested areas, look positively mild and pedestrian-friendly to the early twenty-first century eye inured to a landscape which genuinely does oppress the non-motorised urbanite.

The contradictions of socialists attempting to administer such a centre of accumulation are brought out well in Hake's study of Martin Wagner. She notes his 'acute awareness of the globalisation of capital'; he would attempt to bring in the American Chapman Investment Group or Paris's Galleries Lafayette to sponsor his schemes at Alexanderplatz and Potsdamer Platz – although both efforts would prove unsuccessful. Wagner's approach is seen as an exemplar of Americanism, the attempt to adapt Fordist methods to a reformist context, in keeping with what was called *weisser Sozialismus*, defined as 'the overcoming of class conflict through technical innovation, increased productivity and the rationalisation of labour and leisure' (p. 96). Hake quotes here a particularly-scathing passage from Tafuri on what this entailed:

> the virtuous linkage of mass production techniques, mass consumption and advertising based on the nuclear family household, Taylorist work organisation, collective wage bargaining, the hegemony of the large corporation, Keynesian demand management, the welfare state and the mass production of standardised housing. (p. 41.)

Yet there is much missing in Tafuri's list, which appears – as in much of his work – to be more an analysis of the European 1960s than the German 1920s. For instance, where in this analysis are the co-operatives – such as the GEHAG, the trade-union building society founded by Wagner in 1924 as an instrument for creating the *Siedlung*? Few have ever seriously analysed GEHAG's allocation-policies, or the demographics of the tenants and purchasers of its subsidised housing, and Hake's account does not alter this. Moreover,

5. See Blau 1999.

6. In chronological order, the building projects given UNESCO-protection are: Gartenstadt Falkenberg, Treptow (1914), Siedlung Schillerpark, Wedding (1924), Hufeisensiedlung, Britz (1926), Wohnstadt Carl Legien, Prenzlauer Berg (1928), Weisse Stadt, Reinickendorf (1929) and Gross-Siedlung Siemensstadt, Spandau (1929).

whatever the aims of Wagner and his stable of architects, 'standardisation' was seldom achieved – and is certainly not the impression given by the richly and artificially-coloured, sinuously-planned rows of housing built under his administration. Not for the first time, only one side of what Tafuri called 'a system of compromises' is emphasised, at the expense of the left side of the brief compact between capital and labour.

There was a complex dialectic of formal and political radicalism in the New Berlin, something that Hake refers to at various points, via the 'flat roof' debate that separated traditionalist and modernist members of the once-unified Deutsche Werkbund. So, at Wagner's settlements in Britz or Zehlendorf, Bruno Taut's flat-roofed blocks were faced by Völkisch pitched-roof blocks by architectural opponents such as Heinrich Tessenow, while traditionalists presented the battle in terms of the tension between rationalist *Gesellschaft* and organic *Gemeinschaft*. Oddly, considering how useful this would appear to be for her purposes, Hake does not mention that this was also a class-fight, not merely between differing styles, but also between white- and blue-collar unions, where the 'blue-collar' GEHAG sponsored modernism and the 'white-collar' GAGFAH Building Society favoured Biedermeier.[7] Bruno Taut certainly regarded this as a directly political issue, and Hake notes that he 'described formal relationships as an expression of social relationships'. She quotes Taut on the Horseshoe Estate in Britz: 'we conceive... the collective mass of similar members as a living being that does not automatically obey the language of power but that, in every single member, carries a collective consciousness'. No KPD member could have said it better. Meanwhile, Hake notes that 'a short documentary, *Sozialistisches Bauen – neuzeitliches Wohnen* (1929), which covered the Horseshoe Estate, expressed it even more succinctly: "Modern architecture means socialist architecture"'. 'Not surprisingly', she continues, 'during the 1929 elections, the SPD used an aerial shot of the Horseshoe Estate to emphasise the close affinities between New Building and social democracy' (p. 47). There is no further discussion of this intriguing documentary or poster. This frustrating tendency to concentrate on the familiar while citing much more unusual research is repeated throughout *Topographies of Class*.

Hake attempts to 'class' the *Siedlungen*, dividing Wagner's efforts between middle- and working-class areas. Sometimes this is a little dubious. She considers, as did Bertolt Brecht, the 'Weisse Stadt' in Reinickendorf to be fundamentally middle-class, and though it would appear the plans and external treatments were basically similar to those of Bruno Taut's Wohnstadt Carl Legien in working-class Prenzlauer Berg, it was certainly in a more bourgeois area. However, Hake contrasts it with the Gross-Siedlung Siemensstadt, which she describes as 'a typical company development', where the architecture consists of 'rather inconspicuous rationalist and functionalist designs'. Hake here manages to conflate the earlier Siemensstadt of the company-architect Hans Hertlein with Martin Wagner's very different Gross-Siedlung Siemenstadt, which had no direct sponsorship from the company itself, being an independent initiative of the SPD-administration. Her unimpressed remarks on the architecture are, of course, subjective, but it should be noted that Hans Scharoun and Hugo Häring's dynamic functionalism and anti-rationalist planning here

7. These conflicts are brought out in Roland V. Wiedenhoeft's tellingly-named *Berlin's Housing Revolution*, which notes that the conflict between pitched and flat roofs in Zehlendorf was also one of 'middle-income versus low-income' (Wiedenhieft 1985, p. 117). My use of 'blue-collar' and 'white-collar' here is taken from Wiedenhoeft.

led Tafuri to consider this as a break with all previous versions of German modernism.[8] Meanwhile, the illustration provided in the book is inaccurate, featuring Hertlein's earlier development and not Scharoun and Wagner's modernist *Siedlung* (pp. 48–9). Hake also fails to mention that Scharoun, the Gross-Siedlung's main architect, lived in one of these blocks for decades.[9] These are not minor mistakes, but oversights that allow the author to present a skewed version of the New Building that is decidedly more Fordist and socially *du haut en bas* than the reality.

Little men, what now?

The second chapter, 'Mapping Weimar Society', discusses the *Angestellten*, the white-collar workers or 'salaried masses' which were so unprecedented and such an object of fascinated study for Weimar-sociologists, who noted that these were essentially proletarians without class-consciousness or solidarity, leaving them 'homeless', as Siegfried Kracauer put it in his book-length study of this new class. As the father-in-law in Hans Fallada's *Little Man, What Now?* sneers at its poor, white-collar hero: 'you white-collar workers think you're a cut above us working men... and why? Because you give your boss not just a week but a whole month's grace before he has to pay you. Because you do unpaid overtime, because you take less than the agreed wage, because you never strike, because you're always the blacklegs'.[10] These are the prototypes of the proletarianised but apathetic office-workers of neoliberalism. Sadly, the analysis of the white-collar workers does not do much more than note their existence and list some contemporary reactions, subsuming them into a wider discussion of the class make-up of the city as understood through the slippery notion of the 'mass'. Citing Ferdinand Leyden's 1933 'geographical monograph' *Gross-Berlin. Geographie der Weltstadt*, we find 'the Wilhelmine spirit still dominating the spatial organisation of class relations, despite the new public housing estates built in the suburbs' (p. 66), and, while the *Angestellten* were constantly increasing, it remained an overwhelmingly working-class city – and a multi-ethnic one. The Jewish population was itself divided along class-terms, with a proletarian east around Alexanderplatz, and an affluent west near the Kurfürstendamm, both conflated by Nazi-propaganda into the bizarre mélange where Judaism stands in both for big capital and for Bolshevism. 'Right-wing polemics frequently used the postal code "Berlin W" and the image of "Kurfürstendamm" as shorthand for racial degeneracy and foreign infiltration' (p. 69), and

8. Tafuri writes of the Gross-Siedlung Siemenstadt as the place where 'the crisis exploded', appropriately enough during the Republic's early-1930s death-agonies – 'the work in which one of the most serious ruptures within the "modern movement" became evident', through a return to a non-Taylorist approach to form. 'If the ideology of the Siedlung consummated, to use Benjamin's phrase, the destruction of the "aura" traditionally connected with the "piece" of architecture, Scharoun's and Häring's "objects" tended instead to recover an "aura", even if it was one conditioned by new production methods and new formal structures' (Tafuri 1976, p. 117).

9. 'Scharoun himself moved with his wife into one of the C-type small flats he designed, where he lived until 1960' (Syring and Kirschenmann 2004, p. 42).

10. Fallada 2009, p. 17.

Berlin's cosmopolitanism made *völkisch* critics proclaim a 'revolt of the country against Berlin' (p. 77). Indeed, the supposed 'classlessness' of the idea of *Volk* is a racialised kin to the déclassé spaces of the Neues Bauen, and the term was occasionally used by the Left, mainly in its more reformist moments, appealing to a transcendence of class in times of crisis.

> The notion of Volk organised a number of highly contradictory meanings. All revealed their origins in conditions of lack and experiences of crisis – the failure of community and solidarity during periods of need, the collapse of class identity and civil society under conditions of struggle, and the dissolution of all stable categories of explanation in the historical encounter with modernity. Providing the missing link between an idyllic past and a heroic future, Volk conjured up visions of unity, harmony, beauty and justice – reason enough for architects from Taut to Tessenow to make it a key category in their otherwise very different urban utopias. (p. 83.)

Hake even finds Siegfried Kracauer using the term as an organic opposition to the 'mass' in his famous essay on the Tiller Girls, 'The Mass Ornament' – although she does not fully note just how much Kracauer favours the uprooted mass in that juxtaposition. The masses are politicised more fully by other writers, but, again, Hake does not consider them worthy of our attention – 'the rare positive attributions that imbued the masses with creative agency were primarily found in socialist or communist writings' (p. 88). Yet we learn little about these writings.

The allusions to a mostly-obscured topography of class-militancy are tantalising indeed. As a preface to her discussion of the New Building she quotes the architectural writer Heinrich de Vries:

> It has only been a few weeks since the most radical group among you decided to distribute 50,000 fliers on Potsdamer Platz, advertisements for a new journal intended to convey your ideas to the working population and gain support for your work. I assume that the thousandth part of these fliers brought 50 workers to you who now urgently wish to see a part of this promised paradise. What would you have to offer these people? Where is the design, the model... tailored to the specific psychological condition of the proletariat? 'Nowhere' is my answer.

This is almost certainly in reference to the Arbeitsrat für Kunst and the Novembergruppe, the two artistic associations that sprang up in response to and support for the November Revolution in 1918, with the close involvement of architects such as Mies van der Rohe, Erich Mendelsohn and, especially, Bruno Taut, who attempted to bring art to the insurgent proletariat. This passage, for Hake, 'suggests two things about the young generation of architects rising to prominence after the war: that they saw the masses as the subject and object of modern architecture, and that they developed formal solutions to the decline of traditional class society and the rise of white-collar society' (p. 98). Yet it suggests so much else! Not only does this passage allude to the very serious attempts to involve the proletariat (not 'the masses') in the New Building, as participants rather than spectators, it also evokes Proletkult-arguments that feature nowhere in *Topographies of Class* – what is this 'specific psychological condition of the proletariat' that de Vries talks about exactly? And what might have happened to these '50 workers'? Were they party-members?

This heady but under-analysed passage leads us into an overview of the New Building, charting its development out of late, utopian expressionism, and its gradual favouring of 'architecture over revolution', while making clear its revolutionary roots. Hake quotes Arthur Holitscher, the contemporary reviewer of Taut's *Die Stadtkrone*, who talks of 'a new, extraordinarily beautiful world that cannot develop out of the old in an evolutionary process but has as its precondition the destruction of all existing conditions' (p. 101). Indeed, 'the trope of revolution continued to dominate architectural debates and haunt the urban imagination throughout the 1920s' (p. 101). Hake is on strong ground here in her critique of the reductiveness of many previous analyses, which saw New Building either as the embodiment of Weimar-democracy, or as an incipient 'International Style' – these two perspectives 'limit their discussion of the German contribution to famous architects like Gropius, Mies and Mendelsohn, and foreground their international achievements at the expense of their collaborative efforts and local initiatives. Both approaches downplay the stylistic range of New Building' (p. 102), as well as ignoring the (very real) overlap with 'moderate modernism' of figures such as Emil Fahrkamp, designer of some striking office-blocks in the New Berlin, and – more disputably – with the 'fascist functionalism' that would be developed by architects such as Herbert Rimpl in industrial building under the Third Reich (although Rimpl's workers' housing was determinedly traditionalist).

Hake finds that class is persistently 'levelled' in the New Building, but claims that 'we receive little guidance from the advocates of proletarian culture and the proponents of socialist building; they either remained silent on the question of modernism, or in the case of communist critics, took dogmatically anti-modernist positions' (p. 103). She then goes on to undermine this statement with her own evidence. Certainly, she notes that the conservative wing of the architectural profession regarded New Building as straightforward *Kulturbolschewismus*. One of her more inspired choices of illustration, a cartoon from the 'conservative professional journal' *Deutsche Bauhütte*, depicting 'the triumphant dream of the modern architect', shows a communist parade of bespectacled Le Corbusier look-alikes, flanked by the hammer and sickle and the cracked concrete of a Fritz Lang cityscape. All Hake can say about this is that it; 'shows that this ideologisation of architecture was not welcomed by everyone' (p. 105). Surely, it shows something weirder and more politically interesting: that, regardless of the architects' protestations that this was a non-communist movement, it was regarded by its critics as being irredeemably Bolshevik. There is not much insight offered by Hake into why this might be the case.

We are then presented with a Communist critic taking a far from dogmatically anti-modernist position. 'In *Das Buch vom Bauen*, Marxist critic Alexander Schwab (under the pseudonym Albert Sigrist) became the first to address openly the underlying political issues and controversies' of the New Building. This study of modernist architecture from a socialist perspective, part of a Jan Tschichold-designed left-wing 'Book Circle' series, gets barely half a paragraph, despite appearing to be the very class-conscious analysis of the New Building that is otherwise missing: it discusses 'the different functions of architecture in the lives of the proletariat and the *haute bourgeoisie* and draws attention to the antagonistic class structure hidden behind the spatial organisation of the capitalist metropolis'. And yet, 'Schwab was fully convinced of the democratising effect of modern architecture and hailed the post-World War I metropolis as an expression both of late capitalism and coming socialism' (p. 106). This sort of sophisticated Marxist perspective on New Building surely needs more treatment than it gets here. Elsewhere, we are with Social Democrats such as the architecture-critic Adolf Behne, whose well-known work is discussed far more extensively than that of Schwab. The project to 'support the emergence of a collective consciousness until "the masses are no longer treated as an object"' is clearly central to the New Building for Behne, who nevertheless finds himself torn between 'acknowledg[ing] class difference as a historical reality [and] absorb[ing] all differences into the utopian dream of a peaceful humanity' (p. 115). Note again the use of 'class difference', not class-conflict, to define this historical reality.

Hollow spaces

Adolf Behne's 1923 work *Der Moderne Zweckbau* (translated into English as *The Modern Functional Dwelling*) made an unusual distinction between rationalism and functionalism, which is elaborated upon here to interesting effect. Behne's usage was not that as currently understood. Functionalism, for him, was something 'biological', where the building was dynamically geared towards a particular use and technical process, in an emulation of the processes of an organic body – so Hugo Häring and Hans Scharoun, or the glossy, advertising-laden commercial architecture of Erich Mendelsohn, were far more functionalist for Behne than the severe style that the term usually denotes. This he defined as 'rationalism'.[11] Hake, like Tafuri before her, sees this rationalism as an immanent critique. 'Unlike the streamlined "advertising architecture" that aestheticised the rule of the commodity, the homogeneous urban structures proposed by rationalists had the advantage of revealing the underlying principles of domination and exploitation' (p. 117). Behne's coinage of *Reklamarchitektur* ('advertising-architecture') to describe Erich Mendelsohn would support this contention. Certainly, this sense of critique seems present for Hannes Meyer and Ludwig Hilberseimer, and it is to the latter that Hake turns, as all architectural historians must, as the incarnation of modernism at its most bleakly, sublimely rationalised.

Hilberseimer's utopian plans and critical works, such as the Simmel- and Nietzsche-quoting *Grosstadtarchitektur* (1926) were so stripped-down, so relentlessly-channelled and rectilinear, so depopulated and unnerving, that they seemed designed to support the critics of New Building, such as Ernst Bloch, in their blasts against this aesthetic. Bloch's text 'Berlin: Functions in Hollow Space'[12] is a critique of modernism for its coldness, technological rationality and disdain for ornament, and echoes the anti-modern broadsides of the traditionalists. But there is also a dialectic in this 'negative utopia' – Hake quotes Bloch's observation that while 'other cities are often mere ghosts of a better past, the

11. See Behne 1996. I attempt to connect this notion of 'energetic functionalism' with the biological-sexual theories of Sergei Eisenstein and Wilhelm Reich in Hatherley 2009.

12. Bloch 1991, pp. 195–208. See also the discussion of Bloch's anti-modernism in Schwartz 2005.

hollow Berlin is possibly – there is no other choice – the ghost of a better future' (p. 122). So, 'by uncovering the ideological project of New Building, Bloch also outlines the possibility of a more critical position, taken by many of the architects mentioned here, that hinges on its ability to externalise the effects of alienation and fragmentation' (p. 123). Accordingly, Hilberseimer's 'City Without Qualities' (the line is Tafuri and Dal Co's) is taken as a deliberately provocative extreme. As the organic functionalist Hugo Häring put it, 'to the extent that human beings are still human, they had better live somewhere else' (p. 124) than in this city. Hake notes what sets Hilberseimer apart from his contemporaries through a comparison between his photo-collages and those of Mies van der Rohe, both depicting prospective schemes in central Berlin. The Hilberseimer scheme merely erases space, replacing it with a becalmed grid in the midst of the surrounding Wilhelmine chaos. The Mies photomontage seems to invigorate the historic city through its use of the pedestrian-perspective rather than the bird's eye. 'Mies at least acknowledges the contingencies and discontinuities of modern urban life. In so doing, he also affirms the power of architecture to articulate the underlying sense of shock and disorientation; the transcendent beauty of his design arises precisely from this complex aesthetic negotiation', as well as from the expressionistic forward-thrust of his building.

Hilberseimer, meanwhile, 'refuses any form of engagement with urban reality and instead offers a perfect demonstration of the traumatic effect of massification, its translation into modernism as a defensive reaction, and what Walter Benjamin diagnoses as "the poverty of experience"' (p. 127). Hake analyses this as the architectural embodiment of neuroses both social and sexual, what she later goes on to call 'a projection of specific bourgeois anxieties about the feared tyranny of the masses' (p. 129). Hilberseimer's massive replanning schemes are seen to be deliberately politically impossible, no doubt fully aware of how impractical it would be to purchase and organise through a 'political process' this vastness of space (at least without the clout and money of a Rockefeller). By deliberately trying to limit any contact between the inhabitants of the city, a Hilberseimer-plan 'reenacts the traumatic experience of massification and ultimately aims at the annihilation of the creative potential of chaos, coincidence and diversity embodied in the modern metropolis' (p. 129). Hilberseimer regarded himself as a socialist, and had a candid political honesty – for him, the metropolis is 'a creation of all-powerful big capital, as an expression of its anonymity... the greatest isolation and closest association of its inhabitants'. Later, the architect himself called his city-plans 'inhuman in every respect', as if to step out of character from the perverse over-identification of the earlier work. By associating Hilberseimer with Walter Benjamin's sketch of the ultra-modernist 'destructive character', Hake builds on Tafuri's account of this enduringly disquieting architect to often brilliant effect.

There is a vast aesthetic gulf between Hilberseimer's 'Big City Architecture', with its (politically prophetic) limits placed upon pedestrian-contact, and the idea of the *flâneur* drifting noncommittally through the different affects and spaces of the metropolis. Weimar Berlin's enduring significance derives from its ability to contain both possibilities. Continuing her critique of the new urbanism and nineteenth-century nostalgia from the Introduction, Hake notes how the *flâneur* later becomes 'a figure of narcissistic self-realisation in the New Subjectivity of the 1970s' (p. 149) and charts two examples of *flânerie* in the Weimar-metropolis. The first is a disdainful account of the work of Berlin-*flâneur* Franz Hessel, which often reads as a disguised attack on today's apolitical urban drifting. Hessel appears to like everything in Berlin, as an exemplar of the blankness of the 'New Objectivity', where all that appears is good and all that is good appears, papering listlessly over the real conflicts in the classed spaces he wanders through. Hessel exhibits 'a tacit acceptance of the status quo, or, even worse [a] sensualist indulgence without any consideration of the social realities bracketed by these playful exercises. Not surprisingly, from the perspective of the native as tourist, inarticulate wonderment is bound to be the standard response to New Building'. Thus, taken by the architect Jean Krämer through Erich Mendelsohn's new buildings on the Kurfürstendamm all the way to his own Mullerstrasse housing scheme in Wedding, Hessel reflects on writing itself as architecture: 'around us grows an entire city out of the architect's words' (p. 154), with the inhabitants of this linguistic city accorded a decidedly econdary role. Hessel becomes (possibly unfairly) the exemplar of the uncritical observer of the shiny surfaces of modern architecture, incapable of seeing the determination of space by class. 'I am still incapable of describing this new Berlin. I can only praise it', he writes. The other, more sophisticated side of Berlin-*flânerie* is exemplified by Siegfried Kracauer, who Hake follows to an exhibition on 'The Dwelling' by Lily Reich and Mies van der Rohe, which Kracauer treats with as critical an eye as he does the Wilhelmine city. At 'The Dwelling', Kracauer sees architecture as 'a steel bath... didactic displays on public health and physical fitness appear to offer nothing but an argument for more rationalisation'. Kracauer concludes that 'it is fitting that of all things, the purely functional buildings are the only true monuments of our times' (p. 165); from here, one can perhaps trace a line to Paul Virilio's attempt to sacralise the Nazi-functionalism of the Atlantic Wall in *Bunker Archaeology*, with the utopian-yet-rational promise of New Building consigned to a romantic past.

Geographies of the press

These accounts of physical space are followed by a study of the affinities and collaborations between the New Berlin and the 'New Vision' in photography, pointedly beginning with a citation of Brecht and Benjamin on the inadequacies of industrial photography in giving a critical picture of industrial relations. This develops through a profile of the newspaper-industry of the time, with at least some attention to the role of *A-I-Z* and John Heartfield's photomontage-work for that magazine. As with Brecht's 'Handbook for City Dwellers', the Berlin-press is seen as a kind of pocket-guide to urban space. 'The majority of illustrated magazines aimed to educate their readers in the appropriate ways of living in the modern metropolis. This meant showing them how to make their way through subway stations and big city traffic, and how to be simultaneously member of the crowd and outside observer, and how to enjoy the various attractions without being overwhelmed by any of them' (p. 176) – as with the popular day-in-the-life photo-story genre. In contrast to this, *A-I-Z*'s use of photographers intended, as Edwin Hoerle put it, to help the readers 'to see with the eyes of our class' (p. 178). There are mentions of *A-I-Z*'s extensive use of untrained 'worker-photographers' and its commemoration of rallies at Mies's Memorial to Rosa Luxemburg and Karl Liebknecht. But this exemplary case of New Building in the service of class-consciousness – whose rough brick was intended to evoke the walls against which the revolutionaries were shot – is discussed no further. 'The photographers of *A-I-Z* and [the affiliated magazine] *Artbeiter-Fotograf* relied primarily on montage techniques to achieve the politicisation of architecture and urban space' (p. 179), accompanying the reportage of writers like Egon Erwin Kisch, particularly in the documentation of the appalling conditions of the *Mietskaserne*. Hake's main example, however, is more mainstream – Alfred Eisenstadt's photo-story of upstairs and downstairs, 'Januskopf Berlin' in Rudolf Mosse's liberal *Weltspeigel*.

The most important part of this section, and the most surprising and original element of *Topographies of Class* for anyone interested in the politics of the period, is an analysis of Mosse's offices, the Mossehaus, (re)designed by Erich Mendelsohn in the early 1920s. This is a fascinating building, about as close as anything came to embodying the contradictions of the Weimar-Republic in one structure. Mosse's offices were designed in a sandstone, *jugendstil*-neoclassical style in 1903. During the 'Spartacus' fighting in January 1919, when the nascent KPD was lured into a military confrontation by the SPD-government, the fighting centred on the capital's newspaper-district, and Spartacists built barricades of newspapers in the lobby of the Mosse-offices. The massive military response led to the front of the building being utterly devastated. This frontage was filled in, and two more storeys added by Mendelsohn, in a particularly-ferocious example of what Tafuri and Dal Co call his 'inebriating'[13] style – thrusting forward, dressed with streamlines, in an experimental concrete construction that managed to kill fourteen workers during its addition to the building. After lying derelict for decades, due to its position adjacent to the Berlin-Wall, it was restored in 1993 – one part of the classical structure was redesigned in the stolid, stone-modern idiom of post-Wall Berlin-architecture, adding an extra layer of determinate meaning to the already-complex structure.

Mosse's press was a supporter of the Weimar-Republic, but the building attests to the suppression of the socialist republic proclaimed by Karl Liebknecht in 1918. Hake shows two deeply-conflicting images of the fate of the original building – the cover of *Weltspeigel* has it smashed up, representing 'Berlin under the rule of terror' (presumably the 'terror' of the Spartacists rather than that of the genuinely terroristic Freikorps); while Willy Romer's photograph, taken during the rising, shows the Spartacists barricaded in by piles of newspaper, in the very entrance that was shot away and then replaced by Mendelsohn's new outgrowth. By the time of the Republic's brief stabilisation, Mosse used a schematised image of the building's corner as a logo, showing how successful Mendelsohn had been in creating an 'advertising-architecture'. This is already politically resonant, but Hake adds an extra layer of complexity by examining the political aesthetics in terms of which this building was represented, alternately by showing its corner as an abstract object, showing one wing as a symmetrical urban intervention, or as a murky big-city object, or as an icon of urban modernism – depending on who was photographing it. The building itself was invested with agency by its critics, in a manner that was profoundly politically revealing. Quoting Hajos and Zahn's 1928 book *Berlin Architecture of the Postwar Period*, 'the building is no longer a passive observer of cars driving by, of the ebb and flow of traffic; it has become a receiving, participating element of movement'. Thus, according to Hake, 'where agency was once the prerogative of social classes, the modernist building now assumes their place as the instrument for a more democratic, egalitarian society'. Other critics found that, 'where revolutionary masses once fought the forces of reaction… Mossehaus remains the vessel that preserves their subversive energy in the formal registers

13. Tafuri and Dal Co 1986, p. 229.

of functionalism' (p. 190). So, if New Building was at worst a form of political substitutionism, putting technical progress in the place of the proletariat, here we have a single building as just such a substitution, a building whose very existence attests to the failure of revolution managing to become its alleged continuation. 'The displacement of social activism onto the dynamism of architectural form', Hake correctly notes, 'once again seems to confirm Tafuri's earlier diagnosis of "architecture instead of revolution"' (p. 196). This fascinating section could easily provide the basis for an entire book, and it shows how intriguing *Topographies of Class* can become when it strays from the familiar.

Yet the book concludes with discussions of two artworks that are well-trodden ground for any scholar or enthusiast for the period – Alfred Döblin's modernist novel *Berlin Alexanderplatz* and Walter Ruttmann's filmic exemplar of the 'New Objectivity', *Berlin: Symphony of a Great City*, which (respectively) 'deconstruct' and 'reconstruct' the subjectivity of the metropolis. There is some interest in the retread of this familiar ground. We are reminded that Alexanderplatz spent much of the Republic as a giant construction-site, first for a new U-Bahn station, then for a total reconstruction of the area under Martin Wagner – first via a prize-winning, architecturally remarkable dynamic-functionalist scheme by the Luckhart brothers, then, when that proved too expensive, through Peter Behrens's more stolid effort. Hake selects a Willy-Romer photograph that shows this centre of proletarian Berlin during a general strike, contrasted with construction-photographs and works by Walter Benjamin's collaborator Sasha Stone, who renders it alternately as a remnant of old Berlin, or as a bristling photomontage of struts, scaffolding and boards. This continues into the analysis of Döblin and his hero Franz Biberkopf, rapist, murderer and representative of the 'upper lumpenproletariat'. The sheer noise of the pile-drivers constructing the new, 'gentrified' Alexanderplatz is constantly disturbing Biberkopf, whose 'relationship to Berlin becomes an ongoing negotiation between identification with its physical structures and projection of his anxieties onto its spatial features' (p. 222). This anxiety provides a bitter contrast with the cleaned-up, technocratic topographies of the prospective new Alexanderplatz. Yet, in a review of contemporary reactions to the novel, Hake's arguments against Communist criticisms sits uneasily with her neglect of class-consciousness – which remains a momentary contrast and dressing on the side of her account of class as 'identity in crisis'. So, we have more brief, frustrating mentions of militant topographies. For instance. 'Klaus Neukrantz in *Barricades in Wedding* (1931) approaches the construction site on Alexanderplatz from the perspective of class struggle but also with a keen appreciation for the spectacle of labour. The communist writer, who earlier denounced *Berlin Alexanderplatz* as "a reactionary and counter-revolutionary attack on the program of organised class struggle" uses the movement of workers, machines and materials in his novel to conjure up a thrilling scene of capitalist productivity'. This dialectical approach to Alexanderplatz's reconstruction is apparently shared by Communist writer Karl Schroeder in the novel *Klasse im Kampf* (1932), yet these are mere asides to the main event.

The reviewer in the KPD daily *Die Rote Fahne* noted how this Alexanderplatz was devoid of the working-class militancy that defined the area as much as Biberkopf's lumpen milieu: 'Berlin-workers, is that your Alex? Without the Party, without politics, without Zorgiebel?' (the controversial SPD chief of police). This seems a rather sharper critique than the proto-Stalinist attacks on Döblin's 'cultural nihilism' from other KPD-critics. Yet the liberal press 'immediately recognised the enormous provocation and literary innovation of *Berlin Alexanderplatz*'. We are left in no doubt which response is the correct one. Hake manages to associate Döblin as novelist with his subjects, irrespective of their very different class-position –

> like his main protagonist, Döblin lacks the sensualism and hedonism available to the bourgeois flâneur in the tradition of Hessel and others. The author's ability to empathise with the suffering of the urban *underclass* [my italics – note this phrase, one that would have rightly outraged any KPD-writer – O.H.] and to speak out for those left out of the program of the New Berlin opens him up to a critical discourse that moves beyond the reductivism of Communist approaches, without abandoning the categories of collectivity and solidarity. (p. 234.)

It seems that the 'underclass' needs its suffering to be articulated by a middle-class writer.

Class-identity politics

The discussion of Alexanderplatz is linked back to the New Building through Döblin's imagery of the city as, alternately, organism and gigantic machine. Hake claims that 'throughout the 1920s, the iconography of the city as machine served to articulate the kind of radical social changes envisioned during the revolutionary days of 1918–19. The idea of revolution survived in the modernist obsession with planning, while the social utopias found a compromise solution in the rationalist or functionalist organisation of quantifiable differences' (p. 237). This is rightly treated with some ambivalence, but its contrast with the tortured figure of Biberkopf seems rather too pat – finally, the part of the working class not included in the SPD's plans has a major part to play in this analysis, but only as suffering, politically-powerless subjects. 'In the futile efforts of Franz Biberkopf to conquer Berlin, Döblin deconstructs not only the disparate elements that constitute the modern metropolis but also the urban discourses that promoted modern architecture as an instrument of social engineering' (p. 241). Biberkopf is the part that does not fit, that cannot be rationalised. This is both convincing and unsatisfying, given the persistent lack of interest in a proletariat that is not helpless, but which is conscious of its class and its collective politics.

We end with the new class, the white-collar protagonists of Walter Ruttmann's 'symphonic' treatment of Berlin. The critique of the flattening-out of class and the lack of dialectics in this city-film is familiar from the work of Siegfried Kracauer, but without his contrast with the more politically-pointed city-films of Dziga Vertov – and, indeed, the Soviets who provided constant interlocutors throughout the period are conspicuous by their absence in this book. Nonetheless, Hake sees the film's attempt at flattening-out class-conflict as 'reenacting a deep ambivalence about mass culture and modernity that, in terms not yet fully acknowledged in the existing scholarship, can only be overcome through its fantasy of a homogeneous mass society' (p. 246). Once again, we have a brief contrast with Communist artworks, specifically 'the KPD's May Day films, which relied on the same candid camera and tracking shots as Ruttmann, but this time to uncover the deep class divisions in the metropolis and to effect a very different kind of mobilisation of the masses'. So, in films like *Red Whitsunday* (1928), *May Day: International Workers' Day*

Celebration (1929) and *Mayday in Berlin* (1930), 'the camera no longer has any interest in the commodities displayed in the shop windows. Instead the cameraman's assertive movements announce the conquest of the street by the revolutionary working class; a short-lived filmic dream, to be sure' (p. 259). One longs for the same depth of analysis she devotes to *Berlin: Symphony of a Great City* to be applied to these films. Finally, we are left with Ruttmann and his *Angestellten*, who 'go about their daily business almost automatically, like cogs in a giant machine' (p. 261). Ruttmann would continue to work under the Nazi-régime, and Hake sees his Third-Reich films as a continuation of the *Berlin* symphony.

So what we are left with is a work of decent analysis and rather impressive research, which promises something far more significant, an analysis of the space of this most-mythologised of capitals through class, media and architecture. The political limitations of the work are frequently apparent. Nothing much appears to be at stake, eventually, despite all of the polemical promise of Hake's attacks on nostalgic *flânerie*, new urbanism and twenty-first century anti-modernism, aside from some nuancing of the existing scholarship. What *Topographies of Class* proves pretty conclusively is that there is still an enormous amount of work to be done on this period. What can our privatised cities learn from the failures and successes of the New Berlin's public-housing programme? Can the mass-press of the KPD provide any kind of a model for a politicised harnessing of new media? And what can we take from the cautionary tale of the *Angestellten*, the 'homeless' office-workers who eventually chose the mythological *Volk* over the realities of their proletarianised class-position, in a context where today they make up such a huge proportion of the working class? *Topographies of Class* is incapable of answering any of these questions, but that it poses them at all, even unintentionally, makes it valuable.

Reviewed by Owen Hatherley
Birkbeck College, London
owenhatherley@googlemail.com

References

Behne, Adolf 1996 [1923], *The Modern Functional Dwelling*, Santa Monica: Getty Texts and Documents [translation of *Der Moderne Zweckbau*].

Blau, Eve 1999, *The Architecture of Red Vienna*, Cambridge, MA.: MIT Press.

Bloch, Ernst 1991 [1935], *Heritage of Our Times*, translated by Neville Plaice and Stephen Plaice, Cambridge: Polity Press.

Brecht, Bertolt 1999, *Collected Short Stories*, London: Methuen.

Fallada, Hans 2009 [1932], *Little Man, What Now?*, translated by Susan Bennett, New York: Melville House.

Hatherley, Owen 2009, *Militant Modernism*, Winchester: Zero Books.

James-Chakraborty, Kathleen 2000, *German Architecture for a Mass Audience*, London: Routledge.

Kracauer, Siegfried 1995 [1963], *The Mass Ornament*, edited and translated by Thomas Y. Levin, Cambridge, MA.: Harvard University Press.

—— 1998 [1930], *The Salaried Masses*, translated by Quintin Hoare, London: Verso [translation of *Die Angestellten*].

Roth, Joseph 2004 [1924], 'Affirmation of the Triangular Railway Junction', in *What I Saw: Reports from Berlin 1920–33*, London: Granta.

Schwartz, Frederick J. 2005, *Blind Spots: Critical Theory and the History of Art in Twentieth Century Germany*, New Haven: Yale University Press.
Syring, Eberhard and Jorg C. Kirschenmann 2004, *Hans Scharoun: Outsider of Modernism*, Cologne: Taschen.
Tafuri, Manfredo 1976, *Architecture and Utopia: Design and Capitalist Development*, Cambridge, MA.: MIT Press.
Tafuri, Manfredo and Francesco Dal Co 1986, *Modern Architecture*, London: Faber and Faber.
Virilio, Paul 2009 [1975], *Bunker Archaeology*, translated by George Collins, New York: Princeton Architectural Press.
Ward, Janet 2001, *Weimar Surfaces: Urban Visual Culture in 1920s Germany*, Berkeley: University of California Press.
Wiedenhoeft, Roland V. 1985, *Berlin's Housing Revolution*, Ann Arbor: UMI Research Press.

New Waves in Philosophy of Technology, edited by Jan Kyrre Berg Olsen, Evan Selinger, and Søren Riis, London: Palgrave Macmillan, 2009.

Abstract

This review-essay examines the multi-author collection *New Waves in Philosophy of Technology*. Particular attention is given to the difference between Marx's and Heidegger's philosophies of technology. The differential impact of Marx and Heidegger on the essays in the collection is assessed, with some implications drawn about the theoretical background of the philosophy of technology as a whole.

Keywords

technology, philosophy of technology, Marx, Heidegger, media- and communications-studies, phenomenology, humanism, posthumanity, Marxist feminism, automation, class-struggle, alienation, Marcuse, Habermas, globalisation.

Don Ihde, in the foreword to this volume, writes that Heidegger, albeit 'a highly revisionist Heidegger', is 'the remaining spectre' in the new waves of philosophy of technology (p. xii). When we turn to the essays themselves, we find that only five of the fifteen essays, in which count we have included the Foreword and the Introduction, do not mention Heidegger explicitly. Even this count could be challenged: two of the five essays that are free of this veritable Heideggerian enframing cite the work of Don Ihde, who draws heavily on the Heideggerian conceptual apparatus in his own work.

Given this, the intellectual historian and the historian of philosophy, to say nothing of the historical materialist, must ask: why does it continue to be Heidegger, and not Marx, who haunts philosophy of technology? What impact have the syntheses of Marx and Heidegger's thought on technology, most notably Marcuse and the early Habermas, had on thought about technology? And is the Heideggerian techno-hauntology true of all fields in which the impact of technology on social relations is a defining element, such as media- and communication-studies, or is the preference for Heidegger over Marx most prominent in the discipline of philosophy?

Marx is certainly present within the analysis of media-technology. Media-Marxists, such as Robert W. McChesney and Todd Gitlin, claim that the mass-media of a capitalist society is manipulated by dominant classes, producing and distributing hegemonic values conducive to capitalist interests. Alongside this, alternative media such as the internet have both hegemonic and counter-hegemonic, participatory dimensions that can be deployed as revolutionary tools. Jinsun Lee's citation of McChesney and Gitlin's work indicates that it is possible 'to liberate communication technology for popular use'.[1] In communications-studies, Heidegger has begun to have a presence, particularly via the hermeneutic tradition of examining rhetoric, but has had little direct influence on empirically-based studies of communication-technologies. Marx remains a much more prominent figure in the field. Why then, when Marx had an impact upon discussions of media-technologies so directly, has he not also haunted the philosophy of technology, in general?

We will return to these questions at some length at the close of this essay, after a more careful sketch of the contents of the *New Waves in Philosophy of Technology*.

1. Lee 2007, p. 6.

DOI: 10.1163/156920610X512525

Let us begin with those essays from the volume influenced, in some way, by Heidegger. To be sure, the essays in the collection do not draw on Heidegger uniformly, uncritically, or in the same way. Due to this, Ihde is right to claim that the Heidegger who emerges as the spectre of the collection is a highly revisionist Heidegger.

Ihde could have gone still further with this claim, since the Heidegger of *New Waves in Philosophy of Technology* is not only a revisionist Heidegger, but also an excellent, sophisticated and meticulously-researched Heidegger. More than one of the essays drawing heavily on Heidegger, and those of Søren Riis and Iain Thomson in particular, link the Heideggerian meditation on technology in the famous 'The Question Concerning Technology' to all of Heidegger's later work, contextualising this meditation in light of works such as the 'Origin of the Work of Art' and the 'Beiträge zur Philosophie (Vom Ereignis)'.

Furthermore, in the essays from the volume that do draw on Heidegger, Heidegger's thought about technology is not limited to what he says in 'The Question Concerning Technology' and the later works, but draws upon he says in his earlier work, including *Being and Time*. There, Heidegger offers a materialist inversion that relates the movements in scientific thought to changed technological possibilities. As Heidegger writes in *Being and Time*, in a passage that has been far less examined than his more summary treatment of technology in 'The Question Concerning Technology',

> reading off the measurements that result from an experiment often requires a complicated 'technological' set-up for the experimental arrangement. Observing with the microscope is dependent upon the production of 'prepared slides'. Archaeological excavation that precedes any interpretation of the 'findings' demands the most massive manual labour. But even the most 'abstract' working out of problems and refining what has been gained, uses, for example, writing materials. As 'uninteresting' and 'obvious' as these components of scientific investigation may be, they are by no means ontologically indifferent. The explicit reference to the fact that scientific behaviour as a way of being-in-the-world is not only a 'purely intellectual activity' might seem unnecessarily complicated and superfluous. If only it did not become clear from this triviality that it is by no means obvious where the ontological boundary between 'theoretical' and 'atheoretical' behaviour really lies.[2]

Efforts to contextualise Heidegger by linking his earlier and later thought on technology to his more summary work in 'The Question Concerning Technology' not only allows us to understand Heidegger and his thought about technology better. It also allows us to understand why the philosophy of science cannot operate in a pristine vacuum that excludes insights from the philosophy of technology.

Nearly every thinker in the volume is committed to the intimacies of science and technology, if not the stronger point of a causal relationship that looks at technological change as the more fundamental phenomenon and scientific theorising as a kind of epiphenomenon. This is an important point for historical materialism, whose tendency,

---

2. Heidegger 1996, p. 328.

following both Marx and Heidegger, should be to regard technology as the materialist element of science and to regard science itself as an historical and material practice.

In *New Waves in Philosophy of Technology*, alongside celebratory treatments of Heidegger's thought, there are also essays that treat Heidegger or his insights at some length as a vehicle for setting to the side this figure and the norms he has imposed on the philosophy of technology. While the essays of Riis and Thomson deepen our understanding of Heidegger and his thought, the essays of Graham Harman and Evan Selinger attempt an exorcism. Harman writes that Heidegger's account of technology is 'sadly monotonous' and that he is 'horribly overrated as a philosopher of technology' (p. 112), while Selinger extends this point to claim that in important instances, evocations of Heidegger in the philosophy of technology 'diminish, rather than enhance, analysis' (p. 273).

We will try to deepen this line of argument at the end of this review-essay, when we return to Marx's distinctive contributions to the philosophy of technology and show the influence of these contributions on the two final essays of the volume: Selinger's discussion of microcredit and Casper Bruun Jensen and Christopher Gad's discussion of the different historical eras of navigational technologies that are present aboard a single ship. Marx's echoes can also be seen in Peter-Paul Verbeek's essay, though here these insights are filtered through the figures of Bruno Latour[3] and Michel Foucault,[4] rather than directly attributed to Marx. Finally, Marx's insight that technology is political is heartily endorsed and deepened in the work of David M. Kaplan.

To be sure, there are other intellectual affinities in the volume besides Heidegger and Marx, though nearly all of these remain influenced by phenomenology – or, in the words of contributor Robert Rosenberger, post-phenomenology – broadly construed. Lest they receive short shrift, this review will also mention those essays that draw on Heidegger not positively or negatively, but only incidentally.

Among the essays influenced by extra-Heideggerian phenomenology or post-phenomenology are the contributions of Jan Kyle Berg Olsen, Benjamin Hale, Peter-Paul Verbeek, Philip Brey and Nick Bostrom. Olsen's historical meditation on entropy and temporality draws on Edmund Husserl in order to sketch the relationships that develop between internal time-consciousness and more objective, natural, or technological measures of time. Hale's argument that technological artefacts are not ethically considerable draws on the later Jürgen Habermas's interesting blend of phenomenology with Anglo-American philosophy of language. Verbeek offers a direct and convincing counter-argument to Hale's position, asking readers to consider that technological objects might be ethically considerable. This argument is imbedded in Verbeek's critique of Enlightenment-humanism, a humanism that posits a very particular and strong but ultimately ideological split between subject and object. The status of humanism is also a flash-point in the comparison of Marx and Heidegger's philosophies, a theme to which we will return.

Verbeek's position is ultimately stronger than Hale's, since Hale relies on the notion that human intentionality is imbedded in technological objects. Hale claims that technological objects are used for the same purposes and in the same ways as their original designer intentionally projects. On the contrary, histories of technologies often reveal that

3. Latour 1993.
4. Foucault 1990/2.

technological artefacts are an amalgamation of accident, cross-fertilisation, considerations of materials and nature, and reapplication beyond the intents of the creator. To use a simple example, and one that Marx meditates on in the *Grundrisse* and again in *Capital*: the Jacquard loom, a French technology designed for weaving patterns into rugs, was later transformed by Charles Babbage into a machine for calculation.

While Hale does consider the objection that technological objects exceed the intentionality of their creators (pp. 228–9), his answer is not satisfactory, since he argues that re-application beyond these intents reverts the object in question to the domain of nature. Hale also mobilises somewhat naïve notions of intentionality and nature. He does not consider that the intentionality that creates the technological artefact may be multiple or that it may go on 'behind the backs' of the human creator or creators, channelling implicit and explicit social, political, and economic norms into the lived realities of objects.

Andrew Feenberg's work offers a very powerful example of this phenomenon. Some machines from the Industrial Revolution were designed to accommodate only the bodies of children.[5] Subsequently, arguments were made that only children could work on the machines thus designed, since only their bodies were on the level the machines required. In a sense, this shows that the machines had reverted, in Hale's terms, to become part of nature in the sense of a built and fixed world that offers itself as an unquestioned ground. But, here, the notion of 'nature' must be placed in brackets, because it too becomes shot through with social and political relations, as Marx argued. Once this consideration is added, one is pushed not towards Hale's conclusion but towards Verbeek's: technological artefacts do in fact themselves embody dimensions that ethical theory ought to address.

Brey and Bostrom pick up on a theme that Verbeek also turns to late in his essay: the idea of posthumanity. Brey draws on Habermas's later work, Francis Fukuyama, and Donna Haraway in order to argue about some potential ethical pitfalls that may plague the condition of posthumanity.[6] Most important for thinkers in the Marxian and Marxist traditions may be the prospect of a new class-system that springs up between humans who receive certain enhancements and alterations and those who do not. Bostrom's more abstract consideration of the future of humanity posits posthumanity as a possible future alongside other possible patterns for the human species, patterns such as extinction, cyclical recurrent collapse, and plateau-states.

Among the contributions in which Heidegger is incidental rather than central are the essays of Keekok Lee, Robert Rosenberger, David M. Kaplan and Graham Harman. Lee's philosophically dense article argues forcefully for the theme we have already seen in both Heidegger and Marx: a synchronicity between the history of technology and the history of scientific theory. According to Lee, this synchronicity has intensified in the post-1850 period, and technology, rather than scientific theory, has taken the lead.

Rosenberger's essay, which deals with the hermeneutics of imaging technologies in neurobiology, also draws on the Heideggerian and Marxist notion of a materialist inversion. However, beyond this theoretical framing, Rosenberger's essay exhibits the kind of empirical consideration of an actual technology that will be so powerful in the Marx-influenced essays that we will discuss towards the end of this review. Rosenberger shows

5. Feenberg 1999, pp. 86–7.
6. Habermas 2003, Fukuyama 2002, and Haraway 1991.

how images produced by technologies are multivalent and subject to multiple stable theoretical interpretations. In order to be encapsulated in an image, an ongoing process must be frozen at a particular instant. This can become the source of debate about what the thus-frozen image actually shows, as it is in the neurobiological case Rosenberger describes. However, the parameters of the imaging technologies themselves tightly circumscribe the domain of possible hermeneutic variations in interpreting the resulting frozen images. Because of this, the images and the ways of interpreting them are, in Rosenberger's words, 'deeply imbedded within the nuances of the specific technologies that make the visualisation of the phenomena at issue possible' (p. 75). Such considerations include the fact that certain phenomena are visualised at all rather than retaining a non-visual status, an issue that has become prominent for feminists and others over the last fifty years in the context of the abortion debate.

Kaplan's essay offers some very effective summary-lists that simplify the terrain of the philosophy of technology. For this reason, it would be an excellent essay for the beginner in the field to read first. Kaplan's lists include a map of how prominent philosophers of technology frame the relationship between the social and the technical (pp. 84–5); a list of culturally dominant technological narratives (p. 89); a list of conventional readings of technology (p. 91); a list of strategies for enabling more critical readings of technology (p. 92); and a list of contemporary films and books that have effectively deployed these strategies, including *Who Killed the Electric Car,*[7] *Fast Food Nation,*[8] and *The Travels of a T-Shirt in the Global Economy.*[9]

Among the critical strategies Kaplan suggests are many already dear to historical materialists, including 'uncovering overlooked or forgotten victims' (p. 92); 'showing how seeming universals are in fact historical' (ibid.); and, in general, showing how technologies are not natural and universal artefacts but political and social ones. Since conventional views of technology-development exclude political considerations by definition and by long habit, Kaplan correctly observes that '[a]nyone who engages in the politics of technology has already stepped out of the conventional view, regardless of one's political convictions' (p. 91).

Harman's contribution is unique to the volume and perhaps to the field of philosophy because it takes a serious look at the famous work of Marshall McLuhan and his son Eric, figures whose texts have rarely been investigated carefully in this way within the discipline of philosophy, even as these theories have been examined and used to a much greater degree in media- and communications-studies and related fields. In particular, Harman looks at four concepts outlined by the McLuhans: enhancement, which 'extends or amplifies some organ or capacity of the user' (p. 109); obsolescence, in which various media are retired; retrieval, in which 'every medium has an older medium [or aspects of an older medium] as its content' (p. 112); and reversal, in which particular media are used in new ways that exceed or even reverse expected uses. Harman argues that the four concepts of enhancement, obsolescence, retrieval and reversal apply not only to technological artefacts but can serve as guides for a metaphysics of nearly all objects.

7. Sony Pictures Classics 2006.
8. Schlosser 2001.
9. Rivoli 2006.

To summarise, the volume *New Waves in Philosophy of Technology* is notable for this set of remarkably diverse contributions. To the editors' credit, the authors' diversity of theme is reflected in the diversity of their training, institutional affiliation, and national location.

Parts I and II of the book are dedicated, respectively, to historical and epistemic/metaphysical treatments of technology. Part III of the book is dedicated to ethical and political issues. The posthumanist discussions and the Hale/Verbeek debate that we sketched above are in Part III, and this sub-section is the freest from the Heideggerian spectre. Part IV of the book, dedicated to comparative treatments of technology, is easily the most critical of Heidegger, favouring empirical examples and some tools garnered from Marx and Marxist feminism, including actor-network theory. This is unsurprising given Heidegger's own allergy to the ethical, political, and empirical in favour of the ontological, metaphysical, and speculative.

With this, let us return to the theme with which we opened the essay: namely, the relative prominence of Heidegger and Marx within the philosophy of technology. To be sure, Heidegger lingers as the more prominent figure in part because of the tradition that has grown up around him. But is that not simply to beg the question: why has that tradition grown up around this figure? And why has it not grown up around Marx's very rich thinking about technology? Particularly, why has it not grown up around a Marx who, in his thinking about technology, has all of the analytical tools offered by Heidegger, plus an explanation for Heidegger's own thought? Let us substantiate these claims.

As is well known, Heidegger's central most parsed and most celebrated insight about technology derives from his short essay 'The Question Concerning Technology'. He argues there that technology's essence is to turn everything into a resource for something else. This essence enables us to see the world as having no solid, primary, substantive goods of value apart from how they can be deployed. Heidegger calls this the tendency of technology to 'enframe' resources. He claims that modernity turns everything into a 'standing reserve' with only instrumental value: as technology gains hold, this instrumentalisation escalates. Heidegger then charts a 'saving power' of technology that occurs through the realisation that this system is unsustainable.

But has Marx not already offered us this critique in his sweeping indictment of the subjugation of use-value to exchange-value, and in the increasing tendency of the capitalist mode of production to effect this subjugation, since as capitalism develops, so does the tyranny of exchange-value? Has Marx not already offered us a vision of the 'saving power' in the form of his discussion of alienated life forms that, driven to the breaking point, spill over into revolution? Prior to Heidegger, Marx put forward the materialist idea that the scientific possibilities of a culture would be reliant on technological infrastructure rather than vice versa.

Marx was led to these ideas by his consideration of class-struggle and, in particular, by his discovery that technology is a site where class-struggle can become particularly fraught. For this reason, Marx – and, following him, theorists of automation such as Georges Friedmann and Raniero Panzieri[10] – begin to pay particular attention to the political dimensions and implications of technological infrastructures. Friedmann, for example, develops Marx's critique of the alienating aspects of nineteenth-century factory-labour into a detailed history of twentieth-century automation. Freidmann offers the insight that

10. Friedmann 1955 and Panzieri 1980.

capitalism does not always develop technology, as is sometimes presupposed by philosophers of technology, but also hinders its development in sites where changes might improve conditions of comfort or safety for workers. This fettering of development – Friedmann calls it the 'hidebound' aspect of certain industries – occurs even when instituting conditions of greater comfort and safety would ultimately also increase profit margins.[11]

Also developing Marx's theory of technology using the lens of class-struggle, Panzieri argues that technologies developed under capitalism embody not the abstract rationality of rendering a system of production more efficient, as is often presupposed, but direct political mechanisms for the consolidation and control of capitalist power. Panzieri thus gestures both to a notion of rationality that is not co-extensive with capitalism and to a different, socialist use of machines.

Marx's theories and the theories of those who follow him are both historically prior to Heidegger's and offer many similar powerful critiques, as the early Herbert Marcuse noted best. However, Marx's thought about technology is superior to Heidegger's because it offers us one additional crucial theoretical tool. Marx does not consider technology as having an essence. Using the lens of class-struggle, Marx explains how the instrumental essence of technology is brought about by its immersion in the capitalist mode of production. In the *Grundrisse*, Marx imagines a use of technology outside of the instrumentalist capitalist confines in which the constant increase of exchange-value is the bottom-line. However negative about technology Marx's account from *Capital* may seem, readers must understand that this account is itself bracketed by the understanding that Marx is talking about technology as it is deployed not in any possible mode of production, but the capitalist mode of production specifically.[12]

Technology does not enframe resources and turn everything into a standing-reserve because of its essence, but because of an historical and political process. We can thus understand Heidegger to have documented not the essence of technology as such, but rather, the essence of capitalist technology.

Marx also shows that it is in the interests of capital for us to understand historical and political processes as natural and inevitable. So long as we understand enframing to be the essence of technology, rather than the essence of technology as it occurs in the capitalist mode of production, we collude with this mode of production by making its historicity disappear. This collusion is the mark of Heidegger's inattention to social and political philosophy, dialectical thought, and politicised epistemologies in favour of ontology, metaphysics, and more traditional epistemological strategies.

Just as technology does not have an essence for Marx, so the human being does not have an essence either, at least in the traditional sense in which the term 'essence' is understood by philosophers. In his account of human beings, Marx is much closer to Aristotle's notion of a 'second nature' that is developed in historical circumstances than he is to the philosophical notion of a human essence, a notion that, by definition, excludes the accidents of history and circumstance. This is why, for Marx, the lives of working-class humans can be alienated and stunted by abhorrent labour-conditions.

11. Friedmann 1955, pp. 173–90.
12. Wendling 2009, pp. 1–11.

In his 'Letter on Humanism', Heidegger famously accuses Marx – along with everyone else except himself and perhaps certain Greek thinkers – of being bound to a traditional humanism shared with Christianity and all of Western philosophy. Heidegger then claims that all such humanism carries metaphysical assumptions along with it, either explicitly or implicitly. Not only is this sweeping set of accusations a flattening out of the many important differences among modern thinkers, it is also wrong in a more specific way in Marx's case. Let us grant, for argument's sake, Heidegger's accusation that Marx is a humanist. Even still, Heidegger would be wrong to suggest that Marx's humanism was grounded in a traditional metaphysics or a non-historical determination of the essence of man.[13]

One additional way to understand the margins of similarity and difference between Marx's and Heidegger's thought about technology comes when we consider the Heidegger-Marx syntheses that we find in Marcuse and the early Habermas. These syntheses are revealing, particularly because both Marcuse and the early Habermas, having worked through both Marx's and Heidegger's theories carefully, ultimately indicate a preference for Marx over against Heidegger. Unsurprisingly, this preference emerges from already-familiar theoretical considerations.

Some of Marcuse's thought on technology, especially *One Dimensional Man*, first published in 1964, seems to remains closer to Heidegger's sense of the technological enframing, and has certainly been read as such. But even in *One Dimensional Man*, Marcuse is never without a sense that this enframing is due to capitalism, a Marxian insight that he acknowledges explicitly. When we look beyond *One Dimensional Man* into both Marcuse's earlier and later work, this becomes clearer.

Ten years earlier, in 1955's *Eros and Civilization*, Marcuse retains Marx's utopian view that technology could produce the material wealth needed to found a liberated society. Marcuse claims there that 'the excuse of scarcity, which has justified institutionalized repression since its inception, weakens as man's knowledge and control over nature enhances the means for fulfilling human needs with a minimum of toil'.[14]

Marcuse also explicitly recognises the political dangers of technophobic primitivism, and here it is not difficult to detect the criticism of the figure he had stopped mentioning: Martin Heidegger. In a recently translated text from his collected papers called 'Some Social Implications of Modern Technology', Marcuse writes:

> Technics hampers individual development only insofar as they are tied to a social apparatus that perpetuates scarcity, and this same apparatus has realized forces that may shatter the specialized historical form in which technics is utilized. For this reason, all programs of an anti-technological character, all propaganda for an anti-industrial revolution, serve only those who regard human needs as a by-product of the [current] utilization of technics. The energies of technics readily join forces with a terroristic technocracy [and, here, Marcuse footnotes the Nazi 'ideology of blood and soil and the glorification of the peasant [as] an integral part of the imperialistic mobilization of industry and labor']. [...] The philosophy of the simple life, the struggle against big cities and their culture

13. Heidegger 1977, pp. 225–6.
14. Marcuse 1966, p. 92.

> frequently serves to teach men distrust of the potential instruments that could liberate them.[15]

Marcuse is very close, in this passage, to the Marx who criticises Luddite workers who are smashing machinery, targeting the Luddite inability to distinguish between the means of production, machines, and the mode in which these machines are being deployed. He is much closer to Marx here than he is to Heidegger's sweeping indictment of technology as a whole: in fact, he implicitly accuses Heidegger of taking the essence of technology as it is developed under capitalism for the essence of technology as such. He then shows how this elision enables an anti-modern ideology.

Ultimately, the Luddites and Heidegger suffer from the same inability to distinguish between the production of material wealth by machines and the system of value in which this use of machines is currently imprisoned: they lack of a concept of material wealth separate from value. Opposition to machinery is therefore a tempting but insidious form of false consciousness, a form of false consciousness that philosophies like Heidegger's can be used to abet and to extend. According to Marcuse, following Marx, when we smash machines, we go to work against material wealth, and thus against our own freedom from labour.

According to Ben Agger, Marcusian thought about technology thus includes the concept of 'a new science and technology' liberated from capitalist confines.[16] Marcuse develops this concept most fully in *An Essay on Liberation* (1969). In Marcuse's vision, new, socialist technologies not delimited to capitalist shaping would be accompanied by a new science and new forms of cognition. According to Agger, these new forms of cognition would be 'freed from positivist fact-fetishism and a dualist theory of knowledge'.[17] We might also add that these new forms of cognition would be freed from the split between speculative/theoretical and empirical/practical knowledge, a split that has plagued not only the philosophy of technology and Marxian thought, but Western epistemology as a whole.

Marcuse's notion of a new science and technology is helpful because it drew direct criticism, in 1968, from Habermas. It thus allows us to understand what the two thinkers share in addition to that which divides them, as direct points of contention nearly always describe an area where two thinkers share enough conceptual terrain to formulate an explicit dispute.

When Habermas criticises Marcuse, in 1968, for the idea of a new science and technology, it is on the grounds that this new science and technology is not possible. As Agger puts it, for Habermas, and particularly for the early Habermas of *Knowledge and Human Interests*, 'cognition is in principle oriented to the mastery of nature (society and the environment)'.[18] Agger thinks he detects a conservatism in Habermas here, a conservatism that ultimately points to 'un-Marxian' political reformism.[19]

---

15. Marcuse 1998, p. 63.
16. Agger 1976.
17. Agger 1976, p. 161.
18. Ibid.
19. Agger 1976, pp. 174–81.

This supposed Habermasian conservatism with regard to Marcuse's notion of a new science and technology takes us deep into the debates within critical theory about the nature of instrumental reason as a whole. These complex debates bear on the issue of the operation of reason in modernity, and they make up a terrain in which the question of technology is only a small part. We will only gesture to them here.

Whatever conservatism we may detect, however, in the early Habermas, is certainly not conservatism of the Heideggerian strain. In early encounters with both Heidegger and Marx, whatever his subsequent and numerous criticisms of Marx have been, Habermas indicated a clear propensity for Marx's thought. This is most evident in the early Habermas's choices of guiding figures to criticise and develop, since Marx is especially prominent. Moreover, in an interview, Habermas claims that his encounter with Marxist thought '[was the point that] philosophical and political things began to come together for the first time'.[20]

Conversely, Habermas's 1959 essay 'Martin Heidegger: The Great Influence', even as it acknowledges Heidegger's importance to systematic philosophical thought 'in the framework of the university'[21] remains a sweeping criticism of some of the mystification of the Heideggerian language, influence, philosophical abstraction, and, in Habermas's own words, 'mode of contact with reality'.[22] Interestingly, Habermas's 1959 essay also highlights Marcuse's early work comparing the insights of *Being and Time* to those found in Marx's thought.[23]

Habermas's early work on the issue of technology and, more broadly, on the interaction between Heidegger and Marx is both more voluminous and more ambiguous than we have been able to sketch here. We hope only to have given enough of a sampling that the interested reader will be able to follow out these threads on his or her own. We can, nonetheless, note a pronounced preference for Marx over Heidegger in both Marcuse and the early Habermas.

Let us use these insights to return to the essays that make up the *New Waves of Philosophy of Technology*. When we do so, we observe that those essays that draw on Marx instead of Heidegger tend to have absorbed the critical point, drawn from the history of class-struggles around technology, that technology does not have a singular essence. For this reason, these essays are especially strong. There is a practical outcome of this orientation. The essays take what Don Ihde, in the Foreword, calls an 'empirical turn' (p. x). Because of this turn, the essays do not speak of technology monolithically or as having a singular essence. Rather, they look at very particular technological objects, networks, systems, practices, or constellations in order to discover and uncover the epistemological, moral, and political complexities of how they operate.

Though Marx appears already in Ihde's Foreword, his ideas appear in Verbeek and Kaplan as discussed above, and the empirical turn can be observed in many of the volume's essays, Marx has the most direct influence on the collaborative essay by Casper Bruun Jensen and Christopher Gad and the single-author treatment of globalisation by Evan

20. Habermas 1986, p. 77.
21. Habermas 1983, p. 53.
22. Habermas 1983, p. 54.
23. Ibid.

Selinger. Together, the two essays make up Part IV of *New Waves in Philosophy of Technology*.

Early in the Jensen/Gad treatment of technology, they note their commitment to the empirical turn, writing that 'we do not know a priori what technologies must be like or what they can do' (p. 293). Jensen and Gad proceed from this fundamental methodological orientation, an approach that they call 'the radically de-essentialising approach to the question of what technology is and does' (p. 300). Jensen and Gad look at two specific technologies: the Zimbabwe bush-water pump and a fishery inspection-vessel. Jensen and Gad use these examples to show how technologies entering new environments are adapted for contextual use in a complex web of actors and agents that include both humans and non-humans. For example, the bacterium e coli is an agent in the complex network that develops around the water-pump in Zimbabwe. The differences in social class and nationality between pump-designers and pump-users are also part of this network. Jensen and Gad show that technologies thus considered in context exceed many of the philosophical categories ascribed to them from a more abstract perspective: they 'are neither autonomous nor fully determined by their users' (p. 298). Citing the work of feminist philosopher of actor-network theory Marilyn Strathern,[24] Jensen and Gad show that technologies 'create simultaneously more and less of both modernity and tradition' (p. 301).

Jensen and Gad thereby offer not only a criticism of some essential strains of the philosophy of technology, especially those we find in Heidegger, but a critique of the discipline of philosophy itself. Jensen and Gad explicitly target philosophy's 'craving for generality' (p. 299) and its hesitance to deal with 'the philosophically relevant concerns [that are] dealt with outside of university departments' (p. 297). As an example of the latter, Jensen and Gad suggest that the multiple navigational technologies from different generations that are aboard a single fishing vessel present a real, practical epistemological problem. It is not hard to recognise in the Jensen-Gad critique of philosophy an echo of the critique of philosophy mobilised so famously, and so many years before, by Marx.

Indeed, perhaps the *New Waves in Philosophy of Technology*'s location in the discipline of philosophy partly contributes to Heidegger's prominence in the essays over against Marx, who remains a figure that philosophy as a discipline has never fully embraced. When philosophy has embraced Marx, it has been in its more marginal historical and continental schools, and there only with hesitation. Sometimes Marx's philosophical value is attributed only to his early works, thereby eliminating the continuing philosophical content of his later works along with all of his substantive philosophy of technology.

Beginning with a deconstructive reading of how canonical databases such as the Philosopher's Index prioritise abstract topics such as 'ethics', 'metaphysics' and 'aesthetics' over more concrete issues such as 'globalisation', 'development ethics' and 'technology transfer', Selinger's essay also worries over whether philosophy as a discipline works 'to perpetuate the long-standing and unfortunate stereotype that philosophy is an esoteric and other-worldly enterprise' (p. 268). In his argument, Selinger acknowledges the influence of Marx directly (p. 281). He asks the properly Marxist question of whether what we perceive as moral values are not implicitly capitalist values (p. 285). Selinger applies this question, explicitly mobilising the method of analysing class-struggle around

24. Strathern 1996, pp. 37–52.

technology to describe the forms of subjectivity experienced by women who rent out time on mobile phones in Bangladesh. Selinger then uses his finding to criticise development-narratives that identify the time-renting practice as a straightforward way for Bangladeshi women to access economic and social power.

As a whole, the *New Waves in Philosophy of Technology* will be useful to the historical materialist who wishes to orient herself to the norms and fractures of the philosophy of technology, a discipline which has grown up enough to begin to have its own history.

Amy E. Wendling
Creighton University, Omaha, Nebraska
wendling@creighton.edu
Elizabeth M. Sokolowski
Creighton University, Omaha, Nebraska
elizabethsokolowski@creighton.edu

References

Agger, Ben 1976, 'Marcuse and Habermas on New Science,' *Polity*, 9, 2: 158–81.

Feenberg, Andrew 1999, *Questioning Technology*, London: Routledge.

Foucault, Michel 1990/2 [1984], *The History of Sexuality*, Vols. 1–3, London: Penguin.

Friedmann, Georges 1955, *Industrial Society: The Emergence of the Human Problems of Automation*, Toronto: Collier-Macmillan.

Fukuyama, Francis 2002, *Our Posthuman Future: Consequences of the Biotechnology Revolution*, Farrar: Strauss and Giroux.

Gitlin, Todd 1972, 'Sixteen Notes on Television and the Movement', in *Literature in Revolution*, edited by George White and Charles Neuman, New York: Holt, Rinehart & Winston.

Habermas, Jürgen 1971, *Knowledge and Human Interests*, Boston: Beacon.

—— 1983, *Philosophical-Political Profiles*, translated by Frederick G. Laurence, Cambridge, MA.: MIT.

—— 1986, *Autonomy & Solidarity: Interviews*, edited by Peter Dews, London: Verso.

—— 1991, 'Discourse Ethics', in *Moral Consciousness and Communicative Action*, Cambridge, MA.: MIT Press.

—— 2003, *The Future of Human Nature*, London: Polity.

Haraway, Donna 1991, *Simians, Cyborgs, and Women: The Reinvention of Nature*, London: Routledge.

Heidegger, Martin 1977, 'The Question Concerning Technology', 'The Origin of the Work of Art', and 'The Letter on Humanism', in *Basic Writings*, edited by David Krell, New York: Harper & Row.

—— 1989, 'Beiträge zur Philosophie (Vom Ereignis)', in *Gesamtausgabe*, edited by Friedrich-Wilhelm von Herrmann, Vol. 65, Frankfurt: V. Klostermann.

—— 1996, *Being and Time: A Translation of Sein und Zeit*, translated by Joan Stambaugh, Albany: State University of New York Press.

Husserl, Edmund 1970, *The Crisis of European Sciences*, Evanston: Northwestern University Press.

Latour, Bruno 1993, *We Have Never Been Modern*, Cambridge, MA.: Harvard.

Lee, Jinsun 2007, 'How Alternative, and For What?: Reconceptualizing Alternative Media in the Global Age', conference paper from the International Communication Association annual meeting, 6, available at: <http://web.ebscohost.com/ehost/pdf?vid=8&hid=108&sid=8f9ff2a9-4c4b-4898-ad17-07f60c11dc6c%40sessionmgr4> (accessed August 23, 2009).

Marcuse, Herbert 1966, *Eros and Civilization: A philosophical inquiry into Freud*, Boston: Beacon.
—— 1969, *An Essay on Liberation*, Boston: Beacon.
—— 1991, *One Dimensional Man: Studies in the Ideology of Advanced Industrial Society*, Boston: Beacon.
—— 1998, 'Technology, War and Fascism', in *Collected Papers of Herbert Marcuse*, Volume 1, edited by Douglas Kellner, New York: Routledge.
Marx, Karl 1973, *Grundrisse: Foundations of the Critique of Political Economy (Rough Draft)*, translated by Martin Nicolaus, London: Penguin.
—— 1990, *Capital: A Critical Analysis of Capitalist Production*, London 1887.
—— *Marx-Engels Gesamtausgabe* (MEGA), 2nd Edition, Vol. 9, Berlin: Dietz.
McChesney, Robert 1999, *Rich Media, Poor Democracy: Communication Politics in Dubious Times*, New York: The New Press.
McLuhan, Marshall and Eric McLuhan 1988, *Understanding Media: the Extensions of Man*, Cambridge, MA.: MIT Press.
Paine, Chris 2006, 'Who Killed the Electric Car?', *Sony Pictures Classics.*
Panzieri, Raniero 1980, 'The Capitalist Use of Machinery: Marx versus the Objectivists', translated by Quintin Hoare, in *Outlines of a Critique of Technology*, edited by P. Slater, London: Pluto.
Rivoli, Pietra 2006, *The Travels of a T-Shirt in the Global Economy: an Economist Examines the Market, Power, and Politics of World Trade*, New York: Wiley Press.
Schlosser, Eric 2001, *Fast Food Nation: the Dark Side of the All-American Meal*, New York: Harper Perennial.
Strathern, Marilyn 1996, 'Enabling Identity? Biology, Choice and the New Reproductive Technologies', in *Questions of Cultural Identity*, edited by S. Hall and P. du Gay, London: Sage.
Wendling, Amy 2009, *Karl Marx on Technology and Alienation*, London: Palgrave Macmillan.

BRILL

Historical Materialism 18 (2010) 209–216

historical materialism
research in critical marxist theory

brill.nl/hima

Historical-Critical Dictionary of Marxism

General Intellect

A: d̲akā' 'ām. E: general intellect. F: intellect général. R: obščaja intelligencija. S: inteligencia general. C: putong de zhiliɛ́ 普通的 智力.

Marx uses the expression 'general intellect' (in English) only once, but in a context that can be understood as offering a perspective on the high-tech mode of production and the crisis-ridden form that it assumes in capitalism. 'General intellect' stands for tendentially generally accessible knowledge that has become the decisive foundation of social production and that affects increased productivity such that it drives the capitalist market-economy, regulated through the value of labour, towards its historical limit. – The expression 'general intellect' has become a sloganistic term for political mobilisation above all in Italian post-workerism – at the cost of theoretical arbitrariness.

1. **Marx** speaks of the 'general intellect' in the *Grundrisse* (706) – in the manuscript, the passage is double-lined in the margin (*MEGA* II.1.1, 582 et sq.) – in order to grasp the tendency that enables science [*Wissenschaft*] to become the main force of production. The context is the section on fixed capital and the development of the forces of production (690–709). In post-workerism, this section, following **Panzieri** (1961), is referred to in a one-dimensionally abbreviated manner as the 'fragment on machines' (e.g., **Virno** 1996a, 9) or the 'chapter on machines [*capitolo sulle machine*]' (**Negri** 1998c, 169). **Marx**'s analysis, however, unfolds in the strategic triangle formed of the relations between the producers, the accumulated cultural-cognitive-technical potential ('general intellect') and capital, in order to uncover the emancipatory and historical-theoretical dimensions of the development of the forces of production.

In **Marx**, the discussion of 'general intellect' stands in substantive-theoretical proximity to the concept of *general or universal labour*. A prognostic social fantasy has been ignited on the displacements and contradictions that **Marx** anticipates in this relationship, ascribing an extraordinary significance to this small section of the *Grundrisse*.

The discussion of 'general intellect' concerns the entirety of the products and functions of 'general social labour' (694) or 'general scientific labour' (700): 'Accumulation of knowledge and of skill, the general productive forces of the human brain' (694), 'general progress' (694), 'development of the general powers of the human head' (705), 'general social knowledge' (706). The interest here is in the 'transformation of the production-process [...] into a scientific process' (700) through the conquest 'of the forces of nature by the social intellect' (709). On the one hand, the productivity of labour depends increasingly on 'the general state of science and the progress of technology, or the application of this science to production' (705); on the other hand, the development of the sciences is selectively 'forced' (699) by the capitalist valorisation-process in that 'invention' is transformed into a 'business' (702).

1.1 **Marx** analyses the capitalist form-determination of these processes and their potential, but also, and conversely, the repercussion of the scientific rendering of production on the capital-relation, on the regulation of social production through exchange-value, and not least on the relation of the working subjects to the general powers of science. He

DOI: 10.1163/156920610X512534

anticipates that the 'great foundation-stone of production and wealth' will no longer be the time-measured 'immediate labour that human beings themselves perform', but, instead, that the key issue will be their 'appropriation of their own general productive power, their understanding and control of nature through their existence as social bodies' (705; trans. modified). A further perspective is connected here, that of the 'social individual' whose individuation unfolds in a medium of accumulated potencies more unlimited than under previous forms of articulation. The idea in the sixth of the *Theses on Feuerbach* indicates that the human essence has its reality in the historical '*ensemble* of social relations' (cf. *MECW* 5, 4). This includes the complex 'social inheritance' – language and culture, but also the 'technical environment [*Geräteumwelt*]' and practical technical know-how – that functions as a medium of humanisation. Insofar as science becomes the main productive force, the traditional class-based limitations on chances of accessibility and of appropriation tend to become permeable.

The capitalist form-determination causes the enormously increasing scientific-technical potential initially to confront workers as fixed capital and posits 'the increased productive-power of labour [...] as its debilitation' (702). 'Science [...] does not exist in the worker's consciousness, but rather acts upon him through the machine as an alien power, as the power of the machine itself' (693). Social knowledge and the general intellect thus function 'as an attribute [...] of fixed capital' (694); and it is 'not in the worker, but in capital, that general social labour manifests itself' (694; trans. modified), the fruits of which are reaped gratis by the latter.

'Direct labour' becomes reduced 'qualitatively to an indeed indispensable, but nevertheless subaltern, moment vis-à-vis general scientific labour and the technological application of the natural sciences'; as 'individual', it [direct labour] remains productive only 'in the common labours that subordinate the forces of nature' so that its 'elevation to social [labour] appears as a reduction of individual labour to helplessness vis-à-vis the concentrated commonality represented in capital' (700; trans. modified).

What has been frequently overlooked in the interpretive literature is that, up to this point, **Marx**'s analysis is based on developments that, by the middle of the nineteenth century, were so far developed in England that they had found their classical description already before **Marx**. The relevant section of the *Grundrisse* begins with a citation from the French translation (1836) of a work by Andrew **Ure**, which **Marx** had excerpted in 1845 in Brussels. But **Marx** then let himself be borne along by the theoretical analysis beyond the existing relations in order to uncover anticipatorily the emancipatory potential of general social knowledge and intellect.

Thereby, the historical limit of capitalism comes into view simultaneously with the necessary (not sufficient) prerequisite for the emancipation of labour from wage-labour. Capital functions as a 'processual contradiction' in that 'it strives to reduce labour-time to a minimum' (706; trans. modified) – not the labour-time of the workers, rather the 'quantum required to produce a specific object'; 'while on the other hand it posits labour-time as the only measure and source of wealth' or, succinctly stated, as the 'exchange-value of the use-value' (705). It 'works toward dissolving itself as the form dominating production' (700). The regulation founded on exchange-value 'breaks down' when the purely quantitatively-measured labour and therewith the surplus-labour of wage-workers has become marginal to the production of social wealth (705).

Note. – Obviously unable to imagine anything about the meaning of **Marx**'s actually abbreviated formulation that grasps labour-time as the 'exchange-value of use-value', the Moscow editors of the 1930s supplemented the passage with: 'exchange-value [the measure] of use-value' (cf. *Grundrisse* 1953, 593). But abstract labour measured in time actually forms the 'substance' of the exchange-value of a product ('use-value'), while exchange-value can never be the measure of use-value. – The editors of the second *MEGA* and, following them, those of the *MEW* (Vol. 42) have retained the insertion – the *MEGA* (II.1.2, 581), curiously, even in an artificially antiquated writing-style as 'das

Maaß' [Tr. note: instead of the contemporary 'das Maß'], which has encouraged the most remarkable theories among the post-workerists.

1.2 In addition to the internal-economic argument for the break-down theorem, **Marx** pursues two further lines of argumentation that more readily point to the conditions of emancipatory political activity. The first points to the quantitative side of the contraction of labour-time, the second to the qualitative side of the strategic repositioning of workers in their relation to social knowledge-potentials and to the control of the production-process.

Quantitatively. – Capital's minimisation of 'human labour [as] expenditure of energy' in relation to the individual product 'will redound to the benefit of emancipated labour, and is the condition of its emancipation' (701); the 'degradation' of the individual 'to mere worker', the individual's 'subsumption under labour', is now potentially reaching its end (708).

Qualitatively. – 'Labour no longer appears so much to be included within the production process; rather, the human being comes to relate more as watchman and regulator to the production process itself. [...] He inserts the process of nature, transformed into an industrial process, as a means between himself and inorganic nature, mastering it. He steps to the side of the production process instead of being its chief actor' (705). – Although **Marx** only has mechanisation in mind, in a decisive point his description outpaces the existing facts, for the worker's stepping-out of the immediate production-process and into the position of 'watchman and regulator' presupposes the development of a complex steering technology with feedback-mechanisms.

Marx had no conception of computerisation as the concrete form which has made it possible to transform technology, whether in the form of process-technological equipment or machine-tools, into closed 'physical systems' by attaching them to measuring and regulation techniques and 'chaining' them to other machine-complexes in which no living labour at all is included anymore. On this basis, **Marx**'s analysis – whose formulation ('no longer [appears] so much') points toward the limited removal [*gebremste Abheben*] of the given situation in his time – has retrospectively acquired a prognostic-descriptive content.

1.3 The immediate issue is the technology of the first phase of industrialisation in the nineteenth century that was characterised by the steam-engine. **Marx** cites an 1840 text of the reformist entrepreneur Robert **Owen**, in which **Owen** criticises his capitalist colleagues because they treat people as 'secondary and subordinate machines' and because they invest only in 'soulless mechanisms' rather than in their workers. But, as **Marx** recognises, the process of rendering production scientific requires the same of the individual – and even further, the 'full development of the individual [...] as the greatest productive power', which the increasing socially-available time actually makes possible. If 'real economy consists of saving labour-time', this however 'in no way' means 'the *renunciation of pleasure*, rather the development of power [Tr. note: English in original], of productive capacities and therewith both the capacities and means of pleasure' (711; trans. modified). Referring to **Owen**'s train of thought, **Marx** reflects on the immanently capitalist categorisation of such human development – a century later, it is called 'human capital': 'From the standpoint of the direct production process it can be regarded as the production of *fixed capital*, this fixed capital being man himself' (711–12).

From the standpoint of the critique of political economy, mechanical systems are '*organs of the human brain, created by the human hand*; objectified knowledge-power' (706; trans. modified). Though fixed capital necessarily manifests itself in technical systems, 'knowledge-power' is however not necessarily fixed capital. People, moreover, are never capital even if capital can incorporate their labour-power. – Referring to **Fourier**, whose notion of work becoming play he rejects, **Marx** sketches the dialectic of free-time and labour-time and emphasises the transformation of the working subject: 'Free-time – which is both idle time and time for higher activity – has naturally transformed its possessor into a different subject, and he then enters into the direct production process as this different subject. This process is then both discipline, as regards the human being in the process of becoming; and, at the same time, practice [*Ausübung*], experimental science, materially creative and objectifying science, as regards the human being who has become, in whose head exists the accumulated knowledge of society' (712).

1.4 This provides the context in which the expression 'general intellect' appears: 'The development of fixed capital indicates to what degree general social knowledge has become a direct force of production, and to what degree, hence, the conditions of the process of social life itself have come under the control of the general intellect and been transformed in accordance with it' (706).

A secular tension is concentrated in this sentence: the statement that the social conditions of life 'have come under the control of the general intellect and been transformed in accordance with it' is ambiguous because it can refer equally to the natural as well as the social conditions of life. It could seem that **Marx** means only the practical, technical 'conditions of the process of social life', the social machinery. But such an interpretation misunderstands the dialectical-experimental mode of thinking that was deposited in the manuscript of 1857–8.

The **Marx** of the *Grundrisse* pays attention to tendencies and inquires into empirical signs on which latent possibilities can be read. Even if he sees that the scientific-technical deployment of natural processes remains blocked by class-antagonistic strategies and by private strategies that compete against one another in the marketplace, which create a régime of secrecy concerning technical knowledge, and which exclude others from its use, he also sees therein the objective possibility of a control in the sense of the 'general intellect'. The 'degree' that can be read from fixed capital and that indicates how far the creation of forces of production as 'immediate organs of social praxis' (ibid.) has progressed is what is meant by latency. The latently developing possibility remains, of course, sidetracked into a self-referential valorisation-process that ever faster undermines the life-conditions – both natural and social – of the species.

2. The microelectronic revolution in the last third of the twentieth century seems at least partially to have confirmed **Marx**'s 'general intellect' prognosis of the increasing scientific constitution of capitalist production through the erosion of its capitalist forms. Paolo **Virno**, who sees it in this way, considers **Marx**'s thesis 'hardly "Marxist"', because according to it 'abstract knowledge, precisely on the basis of its autonomy from production, would be nothing less than the main force of production' (1990, 10; also 1996a, 22). However, knowledge that is applied to production is not 'autonomous from production', and **Virno**'s own thesis of the 'self-driven growth of knowledge separate from work' (1996a, 21) overlooks the increasing subsumption of knowledge-production to the capital-process. Also off the mark is **Virno**'s view that **Marx** 'fully identified "general intellect" (or knowledge as the main force of production) with fixed capital' and overlooked the fact that it simultaneously 'manifests itself as living labour, scientific-technical intelligentsia, mass intellectuality [*Massenintellektualität*]' (1990, 12). This last point describes an important moment, but absolutises it and overlooks the fact that the 'general intellect', as Rossana **Rossanda** noted, 'quickly lets itself be transformed into "dead labour"' (1991/96, 71).

2.1 At the same time as the 'Wall' fell and European state-socialism of the Soviet kind collapsed, masses of students in Italy occupied the universities. This was the hour of the birth of post-workerism. After the mass Fordist working class, the subject of monotonous, repetitive assembly-line work (cf. **Wright** 2000) and the class-basis of Italian workerism, of Autonomia operaia, was forced out of the factories and dissolved, the remaining intellectuals in the movement, witnessing the protest-movement in the universities, identified students as part of the new revolutionary subject, which they named, as successor to the 'mass-worker', the 'mass-intellectuality'. 'Anything but marginal', it was stated in an appeal of February 1990 (**Bascetta** et al.), this mass-intellectuality is 'at the centre of capitalist accumulation and the exposed nerve of a mode of production of which knowledge is the main component'. Marco **Melotti** and others (1996) questioned the postulation of such a 'universal class'.

The first issue of *Luogo Commune*, a periodical newly founded during this 'conjuncture' in November 1990, reprinted large sections of the erroneously called 'Machine Fragment' from the *Grundrisse*, in which Marx speculatively uncovers the potentialities of the development of the productive forces for the working subjects. The reprint is interrupted with citations from student-resolutions. Two articles are devoted to the 'general intellect' (**Virno** 1990, **Giannoli** 1990). Since then, the expression 'general intellect' has functioned as one of the main identifying terms of post-workerism – connected above all with the problematic concept of 'immaterial labour' (referring to all labour that is not predominantly corporeal or 'manual' labour producing immediately material goods).

While the post-workerists are convinced that we live in the 'epoch of the general intellect' (**Giannnoli** 1990, 19) – that is, 'that a world of production dominated by the "general intellect", as **Marx** proposed in the *Grundrisse*, has become daily reality and the nerve-center of the accumulation of wealth' (**Moulier Boutang** 1998, 7), that moreover 'the realm of the general intellect is the globalisation of the economy' (**Castellano** 1994, 53) and that all labour is tending toward becoming 'immaterial' – for **Modugno** these developments indicate that the social power of the 'general intellect' 'has already gone over directly into the hands of post-Fordist capital' and seals the new mode of production, 'the definitive separation of the human brain from the "general intellect"' (1994, 14, 16; likewise **Pala** 1997, 66). This critique, however, must itself be confronted with the fact that 'high technology' has in fact displaced knowledge and competence at the individual site of labour – even if in a contradictory form (cf. PAQ 1987). 'Automation leads to higher qualifications' – this battle-cry issued against the current in 1975 (Frigga **Haug** et al.) has essentially been confirmed (which, of course, is accompanied by the fragmentation of the working class, increasing mass-unemployment and the increase of precarious kinds of employment). **Virno** calls the result of this process a 'redistribution' of the 'general intellect' 'in the interior of living labour' (1990, 13).

2.2 The determinations that are attributed to the 'general intellect' vary with the various calls of social groups to join with the plural autonomous-communist subject (the 'multitude' in post-workerist jargon). 'The "general intellect" encompasses artificial languages, informations- and systems-theories, even the most informal "language games".' (**Virno** 1990, 13) The specialisation of language-games notwithstanding, 'general intellect' should literally be understood as 'intellect in general', just as in speaking a momentary and unrepeatable expression is actualised out of the inexhaustible potential of a language (**Virno** 1996b, 194f). In this view, 'general intellect' is a 'real abstraction equipped with material operability' because it consists of 'objective concretisations of knowledge' (**Virno** 1996a, 23). – The unity of the expression only superficially holds the diversity of the intended meanings together. 'Diffused intellectuality' and 'general intellect' 'name the multitude, which inheres in the power of knowledge as such', 'the unitary power that constitutes the many and varied life-forms as forms-of-life'; they are supposed 'to form the guiding concept and unitary center of a future politics' (**Agamben** 1996, 156).

Jean-Marie **Vincent** gives to the Marxian term 'general intellect' the meaning of 'a plural, multi-formed intelligence conceived in continuous transformation', of an 'intelligence évolutive des situations', which really has become such a decisive resource for the 'post-Fordist' economy that production would collapse if the scientific-technical intellectuals were to refuse to serve it (1993, 122). **Vincent** describes the logic of the new intellectual labour as dialogical, communicative and reflexive, non-linear, oriented toward complementarity and playfully accompanying changing situations. On the other hand, he accords to the valorisation-logic the opposite of all this which (with the exception of the repression of reflexivity in relation to the maximisation of profit) is not overly convincing, for even advanced entrepreneurial leadership orients itself according to these parameters. However, he describes society's 'general intellect' as multiply blocked by reductions in accessibility, exclusions, property-rights, and so on, which derive from the form-determination of capital or the commodity. On the other hand, in turn, it would shrink the characteristic forces of production of the high-tech intellectual labourers and cripple their development if they were cut off from general intellectual circulation. Thus capital's blockades, for their part, are trapped in a contradiction; and hence the attempt selectively to open the borders. The neoliberal tactic, with which the field of the 'general intellect' is to be divided and domesticated, is its polarisation into winners and losers (1993, 123).

Antonio **Negri** categorises post-Fordism 'as the regime of the "general intellect"', or as 'the mode of production based on the "general intellect"' to which the socialisation of services is adequate 'as a tendency, the central element' (1998b, 173, 1177, 174). Maurizio **Lazzarato** explains this as the most modern sector of the economy, as the 'heart of the new capitalist production'; everything else he declares to be unproductive (1996, 12).

2.3 Here, the discussion of the epoch of the 'general intellect' seems to lead to the conclusion that high-tech forces of production with intellectualised and flexible-work requirements (cf. PAQ 1987) have become the standard. But, if we get stuck at this point, then the main idea that **Marx** originally bound to the expression would disappear and the theorem of the 'general intellect' would be stripped of its critical power. **Negri** attempts to reckon with this insofar as he treats the 'general intellect' as 'the ramifications of the expenditures of the human brain in the interior of capital' and insists that this process has already 'reached the point where the social intellectuality of labour can reappropriate fixed capital, that unparalleled materiality of socialisation' (1998b, 175).

Actually, however, it can only be in the narrowed capitalist-technologised sense that one maintains that, in **Marx**'s words, 'the conditions of the process of social life itself have come under the control of the general intellect and been transformed in accordance with it' (706). It would be a similar 'Lorianism' (**Gramsci**) to insist that this condition predominates, as does Negri's statement that he 'has been thinking constantly since the seventies': 'We already live in communism' (1996b, 106) even if it is only the 'communism of capital' – which **Moulier Boutang** (1998, 8) calls the 'growing socialisation of the inseparable network of science and production'. But it is precisely the character of this 'socialisation', which is multiply antagonistic precisely because it is determined by particularistic profit-strategies, that needs to be analysed. As fruitful as it is to pay attention to the 'increasingly comprehensive reappropriation of techno-scientific knowledge by the proletariat' (**Negri** 1998a, 78), it is to the same degree senseless to announce the 'end of each and every difference between production and life' (79) and on this illusionary basis to suggest to the socially diffused existing intellectuals of all kinds, above all to the individualised and often isolated participants or graduates of some 'higher' education, that they are the new 'social/societal workers' *par excellence* (**Negri** 1996a, 88) 'without the passage through wage-labour being necessary' (**Lazzarato/Negri** 1992, 34). With an exaggeration that drives its kernel of truth to absurdity, **Negri** (1996a) announces that 'in the center of society and the order of power' now stands 'a kind of production that consists of linguistic activities'.

3. If **Marx** speaks of 'general intellect [*allgemeiner Verstand*]' in an attempt historical-materialistically to concretise Hegel's 'universal spirit [*allgemeiner Geist*]' (**Hegel** 1977, 16), then this is metaphorical, a speculative compression – strictly speaking, an inadmissible personification. **Marx**'s 'general intellect' exists as little as an empirical subject as does **Rousseau**'s *volonté générale*; there is only a certain level of scientifically-based cultural techniques, and also a crowd of intellects that develop themselves individually in its medium, and whose development presupposes – regardless of how they are gained, distributed, and made accessible – the socially-accumulated masses of knowledge that are used in a spe-

cific manner, as well as the transmission of skills for their appropriation and use. With an eye toward socio-political praxis, **Marx** in *Capital* Volume III speaks 'more concretely [*diesseitiger*]' of the 'associated intellect [*assoziierter Verstand*]' (*MECW* 37, 256; trans. modified). This corresponds to the political goal of 'associations of free and equal producers consciously acting according to a common and rational plan' (*MECW* 23, 136).

The category of 'general intellect' is not only meaningful in the prospective sense of transcending capital. As already efficacious, the 'general intellect' is blocked, and precisely in this state of being blocked it is negatively present in that its blockage produces crises. The capitalist thwarting of the 'allgemeiner Verstand', that is, the fact that all social processes are carried out 'brainlessly' as market-processes with a partial and abstract rationality, puts the existential conditions of the species at risk. An economic order established according to social potential for rationality would orient itself toward goals like ecological sustainability and social justice.

Vincent indicates, implicitly, that the category of the 'general intellect' in its Marxian sense requires a critical distance from existing relations. 'Because of its plural character and the manifold exchange-acts in which it develops, which make up its strength' (1993, 126f), he sees the 'general intellect' as limited in its 'generality', 'that is, in its ability to influence that which it helps to set in motion (production, consumption)' (129). It would promote the multi-dimensionality of individuals and would frame a mode of life whose tendency would be to transform labour into 'free activity' (ibid.). The 'collective intellectual and social power that the "general intellect" unfolds' is however being diverted by capital and used for purposes of its valorisation to the same degree to which political intervention is directed away from the structuring and distribution of the powers of society' (ibid.).

In analogy with the discussion of the class-in-itself that must become a class-for-itself, one could say: the epoch of transnational high-tech capitalism is, by virtue of its scientifically constituted [*verwissenschaftlichten*] mode of production, the epoch of the 'general intellect'-in-itself; it falters on the threshold of the task of establishing the efficacy of a plural-universal reason. The fact that capitalism has become global does not mean that it has become more rational in general. What has become global is its systemic irrationality that results from the bustle of myriads of antagonistically operating 'particular intellects'. Its 'intellectuality', however, is developed in a medium whose expanded reproduction nourishes itself globally. In terms of its possibility, this 'intellectual medium' has, for the first time, become general. The contradictions between the general intellect [*allgemeiner Verstand*] and the capitalist exclusion of 'universality [*Allgemeinheit*]' from its realisation mark the struggles of the internet-age.

Bibliography: G. Agamben 1996, 'Form-of-Life', trans. by C. Casarino, in Virno and Hardt 1996, 151–6; A Bascetta, P. Bernocchi, E. Modugno 1990, 'Il bandolo della matassa all'incrocio tra sapere e vita', in *il manifesto*, 27 Feb., 1990; M.L. Castellano 1993, 'General Intellect e spazio del politico', in *Derive Approdi* 5/6, 43–8; M.L. Castellano 1994, 'L'Organizzazione del General Intellect', in *Derive Approdi* 5/6, 50–3; G.I. Giannoli 1990, 'Il gi timbra il cartellino', in *Luogo Comune* 1, 16–19; A. Gorz 1997, *Misères du présent, richesse du possible*, Paris; F. Haug et al. 1975, 'Automation führt zu Höherqualifikation – Thesen über Hand- und Kopfarbeit', in *Demokratische Erziehung* 1. Jg., H. 4, 90–6; W.F. Haug 2000, '"General intellect" und Massenintellektualität', in *Argument* 235, 42. Jg., 183–203; G.W.F. Hegel 1977, *Phenomenology of Spirit*, trans. by A.V. Miller, Oxford; M. Lazzarato 1998, 'Immaterielle Arbeit. Gesellschaftliche Tätigkeit unter den Bedingungen des Post-fordismus', in Negri, Lazzarato, Virno 1998, 53–65 (Italian: 'General intellect – verso l'inchiesta sul lavoro immateriale', in *Riff Raff. Attraverso la produzione sociale*, April 1993, 65–71); M. Lazzarato 1996, 'Klassenkampf in der Postmoderne', in *Die Beute*, 3. Jg., Nr. 10, 8–17; M. Lazzarato and A. Negri 1992, 'Lavoro immateriale e soggettività', in *Derive Approdi* 0, 31–7; K. Marx 1973, *Grundrisse*, Harmondsworth; K. Marx 1983 [1953], *Grundrisse der Kritik der politischen Ökonomie (Rohentwurf)*, *MEW* 42/*MEGA* II.1.1–2, Berlin/GDR; K. Marx and F. Engels 1975–2005, *Marx Engels Collected Works*

(*MECW*), London; M. Melotti, R. Sbardella, M. Antignani 1996, 'Ma quale classe generale?!', in *il manifesto*, 12 April, 14; E. Modugno 1994, 'Grundrisse Postfordisti', in *Klinamen. Derive APPRODI*, Naples, 13–19; Y. Moulier Boutang 1998, 'Vorwort' in Negri/Lazzarato/Virno, 5–22; A. Negri 1996a, 'Die Wiederaneignung des öffentlichen Raumes', trans. by A. Löhrer, in *Die Beute* 12, 80–90; (abbreviated version of 'Réappropriations de l'éspace public', in *Futur Antérieur* 33/34, 1996; A. Negri 1996b, 'Verlangt das Unmögliche, mit weniger geben wir uns nicht zurfrieden', interview by P. Buzari and T. Atzert, in *Die Beute*, H. 4, 92–108; A. Negri 1998a [1993], '*Repubblica costituente.* Umrisse einer konstituierenden Macht', in Negri et al. 1998, 67–82; A. Negri 1998b, 'Elend der Gegenwart – Reichtum des Möglichen' (Review of Gorz 1997), trans. by. T. Atzert and H.-P. Krebs, in *Die Beute*, Nr. 2, 170–80 (French: in *Futur Antérieur*, Nr. 43); A. Negri 1998c [1978], *Marx oltre Marx*, Rome; A. Negri, M. Lazzarato, P. Virno 1998, *Umherschweifende Produzenten. Immaterielle Arbeit und Subversion*, ed. by T. Atzert, Berlin; G. Pala 1996, 'La muta intelligenza. Il *general intellect* e l'egemonia del capitale: una premessa' in *la Contradizione – bimestrale di marxismo* 57, 58–70; G. Pala 1997, 'CO/no/SC(I)ENZA – note critiche su intelletto generale e capitale fisso', in *la Contraddizione – bimestrale di marxismo* 61, 59–70; R. Panzieri 1961, 'Sull'uso capitalistico delle macchine nel neocapitalismo', in *Quaderni Rossi* 1, 53–72; PAQ (Projektgruppe Automation und Qualifikation) 1987, *Widersprüche der Automationsarbeit. Ein Handbuch*, Berlin/W; R. Rossanda 1996 [1991], 'Two Hundred Questions for Anyone Who Wants to Be Communist in the 1990s', trans. by M. Boscagli, in Virno and Hardt 1996, 61–78; J.-M. Vincent 1993, 'Les automatismes sociaux et le "general intellect"', in *Futur antérieur* 16, 121–30; P. Virno 1996a [1990], 'The Ambivalence of Disenchantment' in Virno and Hardt (eds.) 1996, 12–34; (Italian: 'Citazioni di fronte al pericolo', in *Luogo Commune* 1, 9–13); P. Virno 1996b, 'Virtuosity and Revolution: The Political Theory of Exodus', trans. by E. Emory, in Virno and Hardt 1996, 189–210; P. Virno and M. Hardt (eds.) 1996, *Radical Thought in Italy – A Potential Politics*, Minneapolis-London; S. Wright 2000, 'Negris Klassenanalyse. Die autonomistische italienische Theorie der siebziger Jahren', in *Argument* 235, 42. Jg., 161–81.

Wolfgang Fritz Haug
Translated by Joseph Fracchia

Association, automation, development of the productive forces, disposable time, division of labour, *ensemble* of social relations, formal abstraction/real abstraction, high-tech mode of production, immaterial labour, information-society, internet, labour in general, labour-organisation, labour-time, Lorianism, mass-intellectuality, mass-worker, matter, mental/manual labour, post-Fordism, post-workerism, science, scientific-technological revolution, self-valorisation, value, workerism.

Allgemeine Arbeit, Arbeitsorganisation, Arbeitsteilung, Arbeitszeit, Assoziation, Automation, disponible Zeit, Ensemble der gesellschaftlichen Verhältnisse, Formalabstraktion/Realabstraktion, geistige/körperliche Arbeit, hochtechnologische Produktionsweise, immaterielle Arbeit, Informationsgesellschaft, Internet, Lorianismus, Massenarbeiter, Massenintellektualität, Materie, Operaismus, Postfordismus, Postoperaismus, Produktivkraftentwicklung, Selbstverwertung, Wert, Wissenschaft, wissenschaftlich-technische Revolution.

BRILL

Historical Materialism 18 (2010) 217–219

historical materialism
research in critical marxist theory
brill.nl/hima

Notes on Contributors

Emmanuel Barot is a lecturer at the University of Toulouse II – Le Mirail (France), and is a member of the Centre de Recherche d'Histoire des Idées (Nice Sophia-Antipolis). He is a member of the organising committee of the 'Marx au XXIe siècle: l'esprit et la lettre' (Université Paris I – Sorbonne, France) seminar. His research is in comparative epistemology and political theory. He has published the following books: *Lautman* (Paris, Belles-Lettres, 2009), *Camera Politica. Dialectique du réalisme dans le cinéma politique et militant* (Paris, Vrin, 2009), and *Révolution dans l'Université. Quelques leçons théoriques et lignes tactiques tirées de l'échec du printemps 2009* (Paris, La Ville Brûle, 2010).

emmanuel-barot@orange.fr

William Beik is Professor of History Emeritus at Emory University. His books and articles offer a critical analysis of seventeenth century French social relations and popular protest. His latest study is *A Social and Cultural History of Early Modern France* (Cambridge University Press, 2009).

wbeik@comcast.net

Ben Fine is Professor of Economics at the School of Oriental and African Studies, University of London. His recent books include *From Political Economy to Economics: Method, the Social and the Historical in the Evolution of Economic Theory*, awarded the 2009 Gunnar Myrdal Prize and *From Economics Imperialism to Freakonomics: The Shifting Boundaries Between Economics and Other Social Sciences*, awarded the 2009 Deutscher Prize, both with Dimitris Milonakis, 2009, Routledge; and *Theories of Social Capital: Researchers Behaving Badly*, Pluto 2010.

bf@soas.ac.uk

Steve Edwards teaches art-history at the Open University. He is an editor of the *Oxford Art Journal* and of *Historical Materialism*. Author of *The Making of English Photography: Allegories* (Pennsylvania State University Press, 2006), his latest book *Martha Rosler, The Bowery in Two Inadequate Descriptive Systems* will be published by Afterall Books in 2011. He is a convenor of the London based seminar Marxism in Culture <http://www.marxisminculture.org>.

S.J.Edwards@open.ac.uk

Adam Hanieh is a Lecturer in the Development Studies Department, School of Oriental and African Studies, University of London.

ahanieh@gmail.com

Owen Hatherley is a journalist and researcher on political aesthetics, based at Birkbeck College, London. He has contributed to *Frieze*, the *Guardian* and the *New Left Review*,

DOI: 10.1163/156920610X512543

among others. He is the author of *Militant Modernism* (Winchester: Zero, 2009) and the forthcoming *A Guide to the New Ruins of Great Britain* (London: Verso, 2010).
owenhatherley@yahoo.co.uk

Wolfgang Fritz Haug was formerly Professor at the Freie Universität Berlin. He is the founder (1959) and co-editor of the journal *Das Argument*, co-editor of the complete critical edition of Antonio Gramsci's *Prison Notebooks* in German and editor of *Das historisch-kritische Wörterbuch des Marxismus*. Among his numerous books are *Kritik der Warenästhetik* (1971), *Vorlesungen zur Einführung ins 'Kapital'* (1974), *Elemente einer Theorie des Ideologischen* (1993) and *High-Tech-Kapitalismus* (2003). In English translation: *Critique of Commodity Aesthetics* (1986), and *Commodity Aesthetics, Ideology & Culture* (1987). A translation of *Philosophieren mit Brecht und Gramsci* (1996) will be published in the *Historical Materialism* Book Series in 2011.
wfh@inkrit.org

Henry Heller teaches history at the University of Manitoba, Winnipeg, Canada. His most recent books are *The Bourgeois Revolution in France: 1789–1815* (New York: Berghahn Books, 2006) and *The Cold War and the New Imperialism 1945–2006* (New York, Monthly Review Press, 2006).
heller@cc.umanitoba.ca

David Parker is Emeritus Professor of History at the University of Leeds. His studies of early-modern France include *Class and State in Ancien Regime France: The Road to Modernity?* (London: Routledge, 1996); his most recent book is *Ideology, Absolutism and the English Revolution. Debates of the British Communist Historians 1940–1956* (London, Lawrence and Wishart, 2008).
D.Parker@Leeds.ac.uk

John Roberts is Professor of Art & Aesthetics, University of Wolverhampton, and author of *The Intangibilities of Form: Skill and Deskilling in Art After the Readymade* (Verso 2007).
jorob128@aol.com

Elizabeth M. Sokolowski is a senior History of Philosophy Major at Creighton University in Omaha, Nebraska. She is currently researching Marx, feminist philosophy, and technology. She is a member of the Creighton University Honors Program and Phi Sigma Tau, the International Honor Society for Philosophy.
ElizabethSokolowski@creighton.edu

Kees van der Pijl teaches international relations and global political economy at the University of Sussex. His work deals with the history of international thought and transnational class-formation in the global political economy, most recently *Global Rivalries from the Cold War to Iraq* (Pluto/Sage, 2006). He is currently completing a trilogy on modes of foreign relations of which two volumes have appeared. His web textbook, *A Survey of Global Political Economy*, is accessible at <www.sussex.ac.uk/ir/1-4-7-1.html>.
K.Van-Der-Pijl@sussex.ac.uk

Amy E. Wendling is Assistant Professor of Philosophy at Creighton University in Omaha, Nebraska. Her first book, *Karl Marx on Technology and Alienation*, was published by Palgrave Macmillan in 2009. She is also the author of numerous articles on subjects such as political theory, feminist theory, philosophy of technology, and Georges Bataille. Her new work is on Marx's crisis-theory, Adam Smith, the history of political economy, and the concept of labour. Amy Wendling's archival research on Marx was funded by grants from both the J. William Fulbright Foundation and the Social Science Research Council. She is a member of the interdisciplinary CAQTUS collaborative for research into the future of culture, business, marketing, and globalisation.

wendling@creighton.edu

BRILL

Historical Materialism 18 (2010) 221–233

historical materialism
research in critical marxist theory
brill.nl/hima

Back Issues

HISTORICAL MATERIALISM 1

Ellen Meiksins Wood on the non-history of capitalism • **Colin Barker** on Ellen Wood • **Esther Leslie** on Benjamin's Arcades Project • **John Weeks** on underdevelopment • **Tony Smith** on theories of technology • **Michael Lebowitz** on the silences of *Capital* • **John Holloway** on alienation • **Peter Burnham** on globalisation and the state • **Fred Moseley** on the US rate of profit • *reviews* by **Matthew Beaumont** on Bloch • **Benno Teschke** on Guy Bois • **Peter Linebaugh** on Robin Blackburn

HISTORICAL MATERIALISM 2

China Miéville on architecture • **Gregory Elliott** on Perry Anderson • **Andrew Chitty** on recognition • **Michael Neary & Graham Taylor** on alchemy • **Paul Burkett** on neo-Malthusian Marxism • **Slavoj Zizek** on risk society • *reviews* by **Geoff Kay** on Freeman & Carchedi • **Ben Watson** on Adorno and music • **Mike Haynes** on the Russian Revolution • **Elmar Altvater** on David Harvey • **Martin Jenkins** on Althusser and psychoanalysis • **Esther Leslie** on Benjamin

HISTORICAL MATERIALISM 3

Symposium on Leninism and political organisation: **Simon Clarke** • **Howard Chodos & Colin Hay** • **John Molyneux** • **Alan Shandro** • **Jonathan Joseph** • **Peter Hudis** • **John Ehrenberg** • *Plus* **Paul Burkett** on Ted Benton • **Werner Bonefeld** on novelty • *reviews* by **Michael Lebowitz** on Felton Shortall • **Gareth Dale** on East Germany • **Adrian Budd** on Kim Moody • **Giles Peaker** on John Roberts • **Chris Bertram** on analytical Marxism • **Ken Hammond** on Vietnam

HISTORICAL MATERIALISM 4

Symposium on Brenner and the world crisis, Part 1: **Alex Callinicos** • **Guglielmo Carchedi** • **Simon Clarke** • **Gerard Duménil & Dominique Lévy** • **Chris Harman** • **David Laibman** • **Michael Lebowitz** • **Fred Moseley** • **Murray Smith** • **Ellen Meiksins Wood** • *Plus* **Hal Draper** on Lenin • **Tony Smith** on John Rosenthal • *reviews* by **Rick Kuhn** on Australian trade unionism • **Charles Post** on Terence Byres • **Edwin Roberts** on pragmatism and American Marxism • **Alan Wald** on Michael Löwy • **Matt Worley** on British Communism

HISTORICAL MATERIALISM 5

Symposium on Brenner and the world crisis, Part 2: **Werner Bonefeld** • **Alan Freeman** • **Michel Husson** • **Anwar Shaikh** • **Tony Smith** • **Richard Walker** • **John Weeks** • *Plus* **Geoff Kay** on abstract labour and capital • **Craig Brandist** on ethics, politics and dialogism' • *reviews* by **John Gubbay** on Erik Olin Wright • **Alan Johnson** on the Third Camp • **Sean Sayers** on Marx on Russia • **Adrian Haddock** on Andrew Collier • **Gregor Gall** on organised labour • **Greg Dawes** on postcolonial theory

DOI: 10.1163/156920610X524900

HISTORICAL MATERIALISM 6

Alan Shandro on Marx as a conservative thinker • **Patrick Murray** on abstract labour • **Deborah Cook** on Adorno and Habermas • **Andrew Kliman** on intrinsic value • **Felton Shortall** vs. **Mike Lebowitz** on the limits of *Capital* • **Fine, Lapavitsas & Milonakis** vs **Tony Smith** on Brenner • *reviews by* **Mike Cowen** on James C. Scott • **Alan Carling & Paul Nolan** on Jared Diamond • **Jonathan Joseph** on Derrida • **Ian Birchall** on Romain Rolland

HISTORICAL MATERIALISM 7

Tony Burns on ancient Greek materialism • **Chik Collins** on Vygotsky and Voloshinov • **Paul Wetherly** on Giddens • **Patrick Murray** on abstract labour, part II • **Geert Reuten** on Patrick Murray • **John Kelly** vs. **Gregor Gall** on class mobilisation • *reviews* by **Noel Castree** on Manuel Castells • **Paul Blackledge** on Perry Anderson • **Paul Jaskot** on art history • **John Roberts** on Adorniana • **Andrew Hemingway & Paul Jaskot** on T.J. Clark • **Larry Wilde** on human nature • **Paul Jaskot** on Marxism and art history • an interview with Slavoj Zizek

HISTORICAL MATERIALISM 8

Focus on East Asia: Paul Burkett & Martin Hart-Landsberg on East Asia since the financial crisis • **Michael Burke** on the changing nature of capitalism • **Giles Ungpakorn** on Thailand • **Vedi Hadiz** on Indonesia • **Dae-oup Chang** on South Korea • **Raymond Lau & Dic Lo** on China • **Jim Kincaid** on Marxist explanations of the crisis • **Joseph T. Miller** in Peng Shuzhi • **Paul Zarembka** & **Sean Sayers** debate Marx and romanticism • **Ted Benton & Paul Burkett** debate Marx and ecology • *reviews* by **Walden Bello, Alex Callinicos, Paul Burkett, Brett Clark** and **John Bellamy Foster**

HISTORICAL MATERIALISM 9

Peter Gowan, Leo Panitch & Martin Shaw on the state and globalisation: a roundtable discussion • **Andrew Smith** on occult capitalism • **Susanne Soederberg** on capital accumulation in Mexico • **David Laibman** on the contours of the maturing socialistic economy • **John Rosenthal** on Hegel Decoder: A Reply to Smith's 'Reply' • **Jonathan Hughes** on analytical Marxism and ecology • *reviews* by **Alex Callinicos, Warren Montag, Kevin Anderson** and **Tony Smith**

HISTORICAL MATERIALISM 10:1

Ellen Meiksins Wood on infinite war • **Peter Green** on "the passage from imperialism to empire": a commentary on *Empire* by Michael Hardt and Antonio Negri • **John Holloway**: Going in the wrong direction: or, Mephistopheles: not Saint Francis of Assisi • **Ray Kiely** on actually existing globalisation, deglobalisation, and the political economy of anticapitalist protest • **Enzo Traverso** on Bohemia, exile and revolution • *interventions* by **Patrick Murray**: reply to Geert Reuten, and **Paul Burkett**: analytical Marxism and ecology • *reviews* by **Erik Olin Wright** and **Harry Brighouse, Paresh Chattopadhyay, Chris Arthur, John Foster, Alex Law, Thomas M. Jeannot** and **Richard Saull**

HISTORICAL MATERIALISM 10:2

Paris Yeros on Zimbabwe and the dilemmas of the Left • **Sam Gindin** and **Leo Panitch** on gems and baubles in *Empire* • **Marcus Taylor** on neoliberalism in Chile • **Sean Creaven** on Bhaskar's *Dialectic* and Marxism • **Paul Nolan** on Darwinian aspects of historical materialism • *interventions* by **Jason C. Myers** on ideology after the welfare state, **Tony Smith** on Hegel, and **Robert Albritton** with a response to Chris Arthur • *film review* by **Mike Wayne** on Robert Guédiguian's *La ville est tranquille* • *reviews* by **Milton Fisk, Ian Birchall, Dave Beech**, and **Gregor Gall**

HISTORICAL MATERIALISM 10:3

Giovanni Arrighi on lineages of empire • **Ellen Meiksins Wood** on landlords and peasants, masters and slaves: class relations in Greek and Roman antiquity • **Peter Thomas** on philosophical strategies: Althusser and Spinoza • *archive*: **Richard B. Day** on Pavel V. Maksakovsky's Marxist theory of the cycle and **Pavel V. Maksakovsky** on the general theory of the cycle • *intervention* by **Neil Davidson**: Stalinism, 'nation theory' and Scottish history: a reply to John Foster • *reviews* by **Ian Birchall, Ian Buchanan** and **Simon Bromley**

HISTORICAL MATERIALISM 10:4

Symposium on Marxism and fantasy: **China Miéville** • **Mark Bould** on the dreadful credibility of absurd things • **Stuart Elden** on Lefebvre, Rabelais and intellectual history • **Ishay Landa** on Tolkein's political unconscious • **Mike Wayne** on utopianism and film • **Anna Kornbluh** on for the love of money • **Alex Law** and **Jan Law** on magical urbanism • **Ben Watson** on Adorno, Tolkein, Burroughs • *commentary* by **Ana Dinerstein** on the battle of Buenos Aires: crisis, insurrection, and the reinvention of politics in Argentina • *archive*: **Jurriaan Bendien** • **Ernest Mandel**: anticipation and hope as categories of historical materialism • *interventions*: **Carl Freedman** with a note on Marxism and fantasy • **Fredric Jameson** on radical fantasy • **Steve Shaviro** on capitalist monsters. *reviews* by **Neil Maycroft, Mark Bould, Andrew M. Butler, Mike Haynes**, and **Tony Smith**

HISTORICAL MATERIALISM 11:1

Alfredo Saad-Filho on the political economy of Lula's election • **Maria Turchetto** on Hardt and Negri • **George Liodakis** on the role of biotechnology in the agro-food system • **Paul Paolucci** on the scientific and the dialectical method • **Sean Sayers** on creative activity and alienation in Hegel and Marx • **Martin Hart-Landsberg and Paul Burkett** on development, crisis and class struggle in East Asia • **Dan Bousfield** on export-led development and imperialism • **Jim Kincaid** on underconsumption versus the rate of profit • **Christopher J. Arthur** on the Hegel-Marx connection • **Tony Smith** on the homology thesis • **Christopher J. Arthur** once more on the homology thesis • *reviews* by **Scott MacWilliam, Ian Birchall** and **Pete Glatter**

HISTORICAL MATERIALISM 11:2

Tony Smith on globalisation and capitalist property relations: a critical assessment of David Held's cosmopolitan theory • **Paul Cammack** on the governance of global capitalism: a new materialist perspective • **William Brown** on the World Bank, Africa and politics: a comment on Paul Cammack's analysis • **Simon Pirani** on class clashes with party: politics in Moscow between the civil war and the New Economic Policy • **Glenn Rikowski** on alien life: Marx and the future of the human • *Interventions*: **James Gordon Finlayson** on the theory of ideology and the ideology of theory: Habermas contra Adorno • **Deborah Cook** with a response to Finlayson • **Alex Callinicos** on egalitarianism and anticapitalism: a reply to Harry Brighouse and Erik Olin Wright • *reviews by* **Enzo Traverso, Chik Collins, Craig Brandist, Christopher Arthur**, and **Bob Jessup**

HISTORICAL MATERIALISM 11:3

Simon Bromley with reflections on *Empire*, imperialism and United States hegemony • **Jairus Banaji** on the fictions of free labour: contract, coercion, and so-called unfree labour • **Alan Milchman** on Marxism and the Holocaust • **Alfredo Saad-Filho** and **Marta Harnecker** with commentaries on understanding the past to make the future • an *interview* with Michael Hardt • *Interventions by* **Angela Dimitrakaki** on art and politics continued: avant-garde, resistance and the multitude in Documenta 11 • *by* **Andrew Levine & Elliott Sober** with a reply to

Paul Nolan's 'What's Darwinian About Historical Materialism?' • **Paul Nolan** on Levine and Sober: a rejoinder • *reviews* by **Kees van der Pijl, Colin Mooers, Ray Kiely, Ian Birchall, Alan Shandro, Pranav Jani**, and **Neil Larsen**

HISTORICAL MATERIALISM 11:4

Symposium: *The American Worker* – **Alan Johnson** on 'The American Worker' and the absurd-truth about Marxism • **Daniel Gaido** on 'The American Worker' and the theory of permanent revolution • **Karl Kautsky** on Werner Sombart's *Why Is There No Socialism in the United States?* • **Paul Le Blanc** on the absence of socialism in the United States: contextualising Kautsky's 'The American Worker' • **Loren Goldner** on the non-formation of a working-class political party in the United States, 1900–45 • **Stephen Resnick** and **Richard Wolff** on exploitation, consumption, and the uniqueness of US capitalism • **Noel Ignatiev** on whiteness and class struggle • **Alan Johnson** on equalibertarian Marxism and the politics of social movements • **Peter Hudis** on workers as reason: the development of a new relation of worker and intellectual in American Marxist humanism • *Archive* by **Franz Mehring** with a literary review of Hermann Schlüter's *Die Anfänge der deutschen Arbeiterbewegung in Amerika* and with an obituary of Friedrich Sorge • *Intervention* by **Christopher Phelps** with "Why Wouldn't Sidney Hook Permit the Republication of His Best Book?" • *film review* by **Bryan D. Palmer** on Martin Scorsese's *The Gangs of New York* • *reviews* by **Kim Moody, Mary McGuire, Bryan D. Palmer, Alan Wald, Gerald Friedman, Graham Barnfield, Robbie Lieberman, Sharon Smith** and a *rejoinder* by **Nelson Lichtenstein**

HISTORICAL MATERIALISM 12:1

Wal Suchting on Althusser's late thinking about materialism • **Alan Carling** on The Darwinian Weberian: W.G. Runciman and the microfoundations of historical materialism • **Peter E. Jones** on discourse and the materialist conception of history: critical comments on critical discourse analysis • *interventions* by **John McIlroy** with critical reflections on recent British Communist Party history • by **John Foster** on Marxists, Weberians and nationality: a response to Neil Davidson • *review articles* by **Paul Wetherly, Paul Blackledge, Paul Burkett, Jan Dumolyn, Steve Wright** • *a conference report* by **Enda Brophy** on the *Operaismo a Convegno* conference

HISTORICAL MATERIALISM 12:2

Brian Kelly on materialism and the persistence of race in the Jim Crow South • **Domenico Losurdo** on towards a critique of the category of totalitarianism • **Massimo De Angelis** on separating the doing and the deed: capitalism and the continuous character of enclosures • **James Furner** on Marx's critique of Samuel Bailey • *interventions* by **Paresh Chattopadhyay** replying to Mike Haynes • **Mike Haynes** responding to Chattopadhyay • **David McNally** responding to Chik Collins • **Chik Collins** responding to McNally • *review articles* by **Vasant Kaiwar, Pete Green, Samuel Friedman** and **Matthew Caygill**

HISTORICAL MATERIALISM 12:3

Dimitri Dimoulis and **John Milios** on Commodity Fetishism vs. Capital Fetishism: Marxist Interpretations vis-à-vis Marx's Analyses in *Capital* • *Symposium on Moishe Postone's 'Time, Labor and Social Domination'* • **Guido Starosta's** Editorial Introduction • **Moishe Postone** on Critique and Historical Transformation • **Robert Albritton** on Theorising Capital's Deep Structure and the Transformation of Capitalism • **Christopher J. Arthur** on Subject and Counter-Subject • **Werner Bonefeld** on Postone's Courageous but Unsuccessful Attempt to Banish the Class Antagonism from the Critique of Political Economy • **Joseph Fracchia** on Transhistorical Abstractions and the Intersection of Historical Theory and Social Critique • **Peter Hudis** on The

Death of the Death of the Subject • **Geoffrey Kay** and **James Mott** on Concept and Method in Postone's *Time, Labor and Social Domination* • **David McNally** on The Dual Form of Labour in Capitalist Society and the Struggle over Meaning: Comments on Postone • **Karen Miller** on The Question of Time in Postone's *Time, Labor and Social Domination* • **Michael Neary** on Travels in Moishe Postone's Social Universe: A Contribution to a Critique of Political Cosmology • **Marcel Stoetzler** on Postone's Marx: A Theorist of Modern Society, Its Social Movements and Its Imprisonment by Abstract Labour • *Reviews* • **Sumit Sarkar** on the Return of Labour to South Asian History: Raj Chandavarkar's *The Origins of Industrial Capitalism in India: Business Strategies and the Working Classes in Bombay, 1900–1940* and *Imperial Power and Popular Politics: Class, Resistance and the State in India, c. 1850–1950*, Ian Kerr's *Building the Railways of the Raj*, Dilip Simeon's *The Politics of Labour under Late Colonialism: Workers, Unions and the State in Chota Nagpur, 1928–1939*, Janaki Nair's *Miners and Millhands: Work, Culture and Politics in Princely Mysore* and Chitra Joshi's *Lost Worlds: Indian Labour and its Forgotten Histories* • Chris Harman on William Smaldone's *Rudolf Hilferding: The Tragedy of a German Social Democrat* and F. Peter Wagner's *Rudolf Hilferding: The Theory and Politics of Democratic Socialism* • **Loren Goldner** on Joao Bernardo's *Poder e Dinheiro. Do Poder Pessoal ao Estado Impessoal no Regime Senhorial, Séculos V–XV* • **Branwen Gruffyd-Jones** on Sean Creaven's *Marxism and Realism: A Materialistic Application of Realism in the Social Sciences*

HISTORICAL MATERIALISM 12:4

Nick Dyer-Witheford on 1844/2004/2044: the return of species-being • **Marcel Van Der Linden** on council communism • *Symposium: Marxism and African Realities* • **Liam Campling**'s editorial introduction • **Pablo L.E. Idahosa and Bob Shenton** the africanist's 'new' clothes • **Henry Bernstein** on considering Africa's agrarian questions • **Patrick Bond** on bankrupt Africa: imperialism, subimperialism and the politics of finance • **Ray Bush** on undermining Africa • **Alex Nunn and Sophia Price** on managing development: EU and African relations through the evolution of the Lomé and Cotonou Agreements • **Alejandro Colas** on the re-invention of populism: Islamist responses to capitalist development in the contemporary Maghreb • **Christopher Wise** on geo-thematics, and orality-literacy studies in the Sahel • **Carlos Oya** on the empirical investigation of rural class formation: methodological issues in a study of large and mid-scale farmers in Senegal • **Franco Barchiesi** on the ambiguities of 'liberation' in left analyses of the South-African democratic transition • **Brian Raftopoulos and Ian Phimister** on Zimbabwe now: the political economy of crisis and coercion • *Interventions* • **David Moore** on Marxism and Marxist intellectuals in schizophrenic Zimbabwe: how many rights for Zimbabwe's Left? A comment • **Ashwin Desai** on magic, realism and the state in post-apartheid South Africa • *Review Articles* • **Paresh Chattopadhyay** on 'Karl Marx – Exzerpte und Notizen: Sommer 1844 bis Anfang 1847', in *Gesamtausgabe (MEGA) vierte Abteilung. Band 3* • **Nigel Harris** on *Trade in Early India: Themes in Indian History*, edited by Ranabir Chakravarti, and Michael McCormack's *Origins of the European Economy: Communications and Commerce, AD 300–900* • **Surinder S. Jodhka** on Tom Brass's *Towards a Political Economy of Unfree Labour* and *Peasants, Populism and Postmodernism* • **Henry Vandenburgh** on *Habermas, Critical Theory, and Health*, edited by Graham Scrambler

HISTORICAL MATERIALISM 13:1

Commentary • **Lecio Morais and Alfredo Saad-Filho** on Lula and the Continuity of Neoliberalism in Brazil: Strategic Choice, Economic Imperative or Political Schizophrenia? • *Articles* • **Joseph Fracchia** on Beyond the Human-Nature Debate: Human Corporeal Organisation as the 'First Fact' of Historical Materialism • **Craig Brandist** on Marxism and the Philosophy of Language in Russia in the 1920s and 1930s • **Sean Homer** on Cinema and Fetishism: The Disavowal of a Concept • **Paul Burkett** on Entropy in Ecological Economics: A

Marxist Intervention • *Intervention* • **Marcus Taylor** on Opening the World Bank: International Organisations and the Contradictions of Capitalism • *Reviews* • **Anastasia Nesvetailova** on Robert J. Shiller's *Irrational Exuberance*, Kavaljit Singh's *Taming Global Financial Flows: Challenges* and *Alternatives in the Era of Globalization. A Citizen's Guide* and Walden Bello, Nicola Bullard and Kamal Malhotra's Global Finance: New Thinking on Regulating Speculative Capital Flows • **Michael Calderbank** on Jean-Michel Mension's *The Tribe*, Ralph Rumney's *The Consul* and Elizabeth Wilson's *Bohemians: The Glamorous Outcasts* • Greg Tuck on Esther Leslie's *Hollywood Flatlands: Animation, Critical Theory and the Avant-Garde* • **Peter Sarris** on Jairus Banaji's *Agrarian Change in Late Antiquity – Gold, Labour and Aristocratic Dominance* • **Yumiko Iida** on Harry Harootunian's *Overcome by Modernity: History, Culture, and Community in Interwar Japan* • *Historical-Critical Dictionary of Marxism* • **Wolfgang Fritz Haug** (introduced and translated by Peter Thomas) on Dialectics

HISTORICAL MATERIALISM 13:2

The Isaac and Tamara Deutscher Memorial Prize Lecture (Part I) • **Benno Teschke** on Bourgeois Revolution, State Formation and the Absence of the International • *Debating the Hegel-Marx Connection: A Symposium on Christopher J. Arthur's 'The New Dialectic and Marx's "Capital"'* • **Jim Kincaid**'s editorial introduction • **Alex Callinicos** on Against the New Dialectics • **Patrick Murray** on The New Giant's Staircase • **Jim Kincaid** on A Critique of Value-Form Marxism • **Jacques Bidet** on The Dialectician's Interpretation of *Capital* • **Ian Hunt** on The Economic Cell-Form • **Robert Albritton** on How Dialectics Runs Aground: The Antinomes of Arthur's Dialectic of Capital • **Christopher J. Arthur**'s Reply to Critics • *Intervention* • **Sean Creaven** on *Marxism and Realism*: A Reply to Branwen Gruffyd Jones • *Review articles* • **Bob Jessop** on Antoine Artous's *Marx, L'Etat et la politique* • **Alan Milchman** on Domenico Losurdo's *Heidegger and the Ideology of War: Community, Death, and the West* • **Daniel Lazare** on *51 Documents: Zionist Collaboration With the Nazis*, edited by Lenni Brenner • **James Devine** on Michael Perelman's *Transcending the Economy: On the Potential of Passionate Labor and the Wastes of the Market* • German Books for Review • *The Historical-Critical Dictionary of Marxism* • **Frigga Haug** (translated by Peter Thomas) on Gender Relations

HISTORICAL MATERIALISM 13:3

The Isaac and Tamara Deutscher Memorial Prize Lecture (Part II) • **Neil Davidson** on How Revolutionary Were the Bourgeois Revolutions? • *Articles* • **Jean-Jacques Lecercle** on Deleuze, Guattari and Marxism • **Rick Kuhn** on Henryk Grossman and the Recovery of Marxism • **Thomas Marois** on From Economic Crisis to a 'State' of Crisis: The Emergence of Neoliberalism in Costa Rica • **Bob Cannon** on Retrieving the Normative Content of Marxism: From a Subject-Centred to an Intersubjective Critique of Capitalism • *Interventions* • **Karl Beitel** on The US, Iraq, and the Future of Empire • **Mike Wayne** on Fetishism and Ideology: A Reply to Dimoulis and Milios • *Review Articles* • **Paul Blackledge** on Brian Manning, 21 May 1927–24 April 2004: Historian of the People and the English Revolution • **Brian Manning** on *Winstanley and the Diggers, 1649–1999*, edited by Andrew Bradstock • **Andrew Hemingway** on *The Philistine Controversy*, edited by Dave Beech and John Roberts • **Michael Keaney** on Bastiaan van Apeldoorn's *Transnational Capitalism and the Struggle over European Integration* • **Paul Dillon** on *Evald Ilyenkov's Philosophy Revisited*, edited by Vesa Oittinen • **Eric Piper** on Raya Dunayevskaya's *Power of Negativity: Selected Writings on the Dialectic in Hegel and Marx* • *Conference Report* • **Peter Hudis** on Rosa Luxemburg in China: The 'Rosa Luxemburg' Conference 21–2 November 2004 – South China Agricultural University, Guangzhou, China • *The Historical-Critical Dictionary of Marxism* • **Bastiaan Wielenga, Hermann Klenner and Susanne Lettow** on Justice

HISTORICAL MATERIALISM 13:4

The Isaac and Tamara Deutscher Memorial Prize Lecture (Part II) • **Neil Davidson** on How Revolutionary Were the Bourgeois Revolutions? (contd.) • *Articles* • **Deborah Cook** on The Sundered Totality of System and Lifeworld • **Fotini Vaki** on Adorno Contra Habermas and the Claims of Critical Theory as Immanent Critique • **Gary Farnell** on Benjamin as Producer in *The Arcades Project* • *Commodity Fetishism and Revolutionary Subjectivity: A Symposium on John Holloway's* 'Change the World without Taking Power' • **Guido Starosta's** Editorial Introduction • **Daniel Bensaïd** on a Recent Book by John Holloway • **Marcel Stoetzler** on How to Make Adorno Scream, Some Notes on John Holloway's *'Change the World without Taking Power'* • **Michael A. Lebowitz** on Holloway's Scream: Full of Sound and Fury • **Massimo de Angelis** on How?!?! An Essay on John Holloway's *Change the World without Taking Power* • **Leigh Binford** on Holloway's Marxism • **John Holloway:** No • *Interview* • **Max Blechman, Anita Chari, Rafeeq Hasan** on Democracy, Dissensus, and the Aesthetics of Class Struggle: An Exchange with **Jacques Rancière** • *Review Articles* • **Ian Birchall** on Robert Barcia's *La véritable histoire de Lutte Ouvrière*, Daniel Bensaïd's *Les trotskysmes* and *Une lente impatience*, Christophe Bourseiller's *Histoire générale de l'ultra-gauche*, Philippe Campinchi's *Les lambertistes*, Frédéric Charpier's *Histoire de l'extrême gauche trotskiste*, André Fichaut's *Sur le pont*, Daniel Gluckstein's & Pierre Lambert's *Itinéraires*, Michel Lequenne's *Le trotskysme: une histoire sans fard*, Jean-Jacques Marie's *Le trotskysme et les trotskystes*, Christophe Nick's *Les trotskistes*, and Benjamin Stora's *La dernière génération d'octobre* • **Simon Kennedy** on G.A. Cohen's *Karl Marx's Theory of History: A Defence* • **Maria Elisa Cevasco** on Fredric Jameson's *A Singular Modernity: Essay on the Ontology of the Present* • **Tony Smith** on *Phases of Capitalist Development: Booms, Crises and Globalizations*, edited by Robert Albritton, Makoto Itoh, Richard Westra and Alan Zuege • **John Michael Roberts** on *Masses, Classes and the Public Sphere*, edited by Mike Hill and Warren Montag • German Books for review • *Historical-Critical Dictionary of Marxism* • **Peter Ives** on Grammar

HISTORICAL MATERIALISM 14:1

Article • **Andrew Burke** on Nation, Landscape, and Nostalgia in Patrick Keiller's *Robinson in Space* • *Symposium: On Costas Lapavitsas's 'Social Foundations of Markets, Money and Credit'* • **Jim Kincaid** on Finance, Trust and the Power of Capital • **Gary Dymski** on Money and Credit in Heterodox Theory: Reflections on Lapavitsas • **Dick Bryan and Michael Rafferty** on Money in Capitalism or Capitalist Money? • **Makoto Itoh** on Political Economy of Money, Credit and Finance in Contemporary Capitalism – Remarks on Lapavitsas and Dymski • **Kazutoshi Miyazawa** on the Anarchical Nature of the Market and the Emergence of Money • **Costas Lapavitsas** on Power and Trust as Constituents of Money and Credit • *Interventions: Replies to Ana Dinerstein on the Argentine Crisis* • **Guido Starosta** Editorial Introduction • **Alberto Bonnet** on *¡Que se vayan todos!* Discussing the Argentine crisis and insurrection • **Juan Iñigo Carrera** on Argentina: The Reproduction of Capital Accumulation Through Political Crisis • **Juan Grigera** on Argentina: On Crisis and a Measure for Class Struggle • *Review Articles* • **Paresh Chattopadhyay & Martin Thomas** on Stephen A. Resnick and Richard D. Wolff's *Class Theory and History: Capitalism and Communism in the USSR* • **Alan Freeman** on Guglielmo Carchedi's *For Another Europe: a Class Analysis of European Economic Integration* • **Loren Goldner** on Christophe Bourseiller's *Histoire générale de l'ultra-gauche* • **Christopher May** on Mark Poster's *What's the Matter with the Internet?*

HISTORICAL MATERIALISM 14:2

Article • **Robert Bond** on Speculating Histories: Walter Benjamin, Iain Sinclair • *The Isaac and Tamara Deutscher Memorial Prize Lecture* • **Michael A. Lebowitz** on The Politics of Assumption, the Assumption of Politics • *Symposium: The Dark side of Marx's 'Capital': On Michael Lebowitz's*

'Beyond Capital' • **Pablo Ghigliani's** Editorial Introduction • **Colin Barker** on Capital and Revolutionary Practice • **Werner Bonefeld** on Marx's Critique of Economics. On Lebowitz • **Al Campbell and Mehmet Ufuk Tutan** on Beyond Capital: A Necessary Corrective and Four Issues for Further Discussion • **Leo Panitch and Sam Gindin** on Bringing the Working Class In: Mike Lebowitz's *Beyond Capital* • Interventions • **John Milios and Dimitri Dimoulis** on Louis Althusser and the Forms of Concealment of Capitalist Exploitation. A Rejoinder to Mike Wayne • **Patrick Murray** on In Defence of the 'Third Thing Argument': A Reply to James Furner's 'Marx's Critique of Samuel Bailey' • Review Articles • **John Haldon** on Igor M. Diakonoff's *The Paths of History* • **Jeff Noonan** on Kojin Karatani's *Transcritique: On Kant and Marx* • **Lee Salter** on Mike Wayne's *Marxism and Media Studies: Key Concepts and Contemporary Trends* • **Mark O'Brien** on *Global Unions? Theory and Strategies of Organised Labour in the Global Political Economy*, edited by Jeffrey Harrod and Robert O'Brien • **Chris Wright** on *What Is to Be Done? Leninism, Anti-Leninist Marxism and the Question of Revolution Today*, edited by Werner Bonefeld and Sergio Tischler • *The Historical-Critical Dictionary of Marxism* • **Wolfgang Fritz Haug** on Historical-Critical

HISTORICAL MATERIALISM 14:3

Articles • **Martin Hart-Landsberg & Paul Burkett** on China and the Dynamics of Transnational Accumulation: Causes and Consequences of Global Restructuring • **Paresh Chattopadhyay** on Passage to Socialism: The Dialectic of Progress in Marx • **Christopher J. Arthur** on The Inner Totality of Capitalism • **Geoff Kennedy** on Digger Radicalism and Agrarian Capitalism • **Andrew Robinson & Simon Tormey** on Žižek's Marx: 'Sublime Object' or a 'Plague of Fantasies'? • *Interventions* • **John Eric Marot** on Trotsky, the Left Opposition and the Rise of the Stalinism: Theory and Practice • **Martin Thomas** on Three Traditions? Marxism and the USSR • *Review Articles* • **Carl Freedman** on Christopher Hitchens's *Why Orwell Matters*, Jeffrey Meyers's *Orwell: Wintry Conscience of a Generation* and John Newsinger's *Orwell's Politics* • **Ian Birchall** on Jean-François Fayet's *Karl Radek (1885–1939)* • **Charles Post** on Robert J. Steinfeld, *Coercion, Contract, and Free Labor in the Nineteenth Century* • **Charles Post** on Roger L. Ransom's and Richard Sutch's *One Kind of Freedom: The Economic Consequences of Emancipation* • **Marcel Stoetzler** on Michael Forman's *Nationalism and the International Labor Movement, The Idea of the Nation in Socialist and Anarchist Theory* • **Geoff Kennedy** on Neal Wood's *Reflections on Political Theory: A Voice of Reason From the Past* • *The Historical-Critical Dictionary of Marxism* • **Wal Suchting** on Epistemology

HISTORICAL MATERIALISM 14:4

Symposium: On David Harvey's 'The New Imperialism' • **Sam Ashman**'s Editorial Introduction • **Ellen Meiksins Wood** on Logics of Power: A Conversation with David Harvey • **Noel Castree** on David Harvey's Symptomatic Silence • **Bob Sutcliffe** on Imperialism Old and New: A Comment on David Harvey's The *New Imperialism* and Ellen Meiksins Wood's *Empire of Capital* • **Robert Brenner** on What Is and What Is Not Imperialism? • **Sam Ashman** and **Alex Callinicos** on Capital Accumulation and the State System: Assessing David Harvey's *The New Imperialism* • **Ben Fine** on Debating the 'New' Imperialism • **David Harvey**'s Comment on Commentaries • *Intervention* • **Mike Lebowitz** on The Politics of *Beyond Capital* • *Literature Review* • **Stuart Elden** on Some Are Born Posthumously: The French Afterlife of Henri Lefebvre • *Review Articles* • **Peter Green & Martin Thomas** on Nigel Harris's *The Return of Cosmopolitan Capital* • **Mark Bould** on Carl Freedman's *The Incomplete Projects: Marxism, Modernity and the Politics of Culture* • **Neil Lazarus** on David Macey's *Frantz Fanon: A Life* • **Loren Goldner** on Franklin Rosemont's *Joe Hill: the IWW and the Making of a Revolutionary Working Class Counter Culture* • **Vincent Présumey** on *Revolutionary History: From Syndicalism to Trotskyism – Writings of Alfred and*

Marguerite Rosmer • **Elena Isayev** on Guy Bradley's *Ancient Umbria* • *The Historical-Critical Dictionary of Marxism* • **Karen Ruoff Kramer** on Jeans

HISTORICAL MATERIALISM 15:1

Articles • **Alberto Toscano** on From Pin Factories to Gold Farmers: Editorial Introduction to a Research Stream on Cognitive Capitalism, Immaterial Labour, and the General Intellect • **Carlo Vercellone** on From Formal Subsumption to General Intellect: Elements for a Marxist Reading of the Thesis of Cognitive Capitalism • *Symposium: Ernest Mandel and the Historical Theory of Global Capitalism* • **Marcel van der Linden**'s *and* **Jan Willem Stutje**'s Editorial Introduction • **Jairus Banaji** on Islam, the Mediterranean and the Rise of Capitalism • **Patrick Karl O'Brien** on Global Economic History as the Accumulation of Capital through a Process of Combined and Uneven Development. An Appreciation and Critique of Ernest Mandel • **Michael R. Krätke** on The History and Logic of Modern Capitalism. The Legacy of Ernest Mandel • **Marcel van der Linden** on The 'Law' of Uneven and Combined Development: Some Underdeveloped Thoughts • **Jan-Willem Stutje** on Concerning *Der Spätkapitalismus*: Mandel's Quest for a Synthesis of Late Capitalism • *Review Articles* • **Spencer Dimmock** on Jane Whittle's The Development of Agrarian Capitalism: *Land and Labour in Norfolk, 1440–1580* • **João Bernardo** on Alessandro Orsini's *L'Eretico della sinistra. Bruno Rizzi élitista democratico* • **Anthony Chase** on the *Leiden Journal of International Law's* 'International Symposium on Marxism and International Law' • **Alan Thornett** on Ralph Darlington's and Dave Lyddon's *Glorious Summer: Class Struggle in Britain in 1972* • *The Historical-Critical Dictionary of Marxism* • **Peter Thomas** on Absolute Historicism

HISTORICAL MATERIALISM 15:2

Isaac and Tamara Deutscher Memorial Prize Lecture • **Kevin Murphy** on Can We Write the History of the Russian Revolution? A Belated Response to Eric Hobsbawm • *Articles* • **David Camfield** on The Multitude and the Kangaroo: A Critique of Hardt and Negri's Theory of Immaterial Labour • **Peter Thomas**' Editorial Introduction • **Roberto Finelli** on Abstraction versus contradiction: Observations on Chris Arthur's *The New Dialectic and Marx's 'Capital'* • **Samuel Knafo** on Political Marxism and Value Theory: Bridging the Gap between Theory and History • **Jan Dumolyn** on The Political and Symbolic Economy of State Feudalism. The Case of Late Medieval Flanders • *Archive* • **William S. Lewis**' Editorial Introduction • **Louis Althusser**'s Letter to Comrades on the PCF Central Committee • *Review Articles* • **Jan Rehmann** on Domenico Losurdo's *Nietzsche, il ribelle aristocratico. Biografia intellettuale e bilancio critico* • **Ian Birchall** on Michel Surya's *La Révolution rêvée: Pour une histoire des intellectuels et des œuvres révolutionnaires 1944–1956* • **Markar Melkonian** on Richard Rorty's *Achieving Our Country: Leftist Thought in Twentieth-Century America, Philosophy and Social Hope, and Against Bosses, Against Oligarchies* • **Pat Devine** on Michael Albert's *Parecon: Life After Capitalism* • **Paulo L. dos Santos** on Alfredo Saad-Filho's *The Value of Marx* and Ben Fine's and Alfredo Saad-Filho's *Marx's 'Capital'* • *The Historical-Critical Dictionary of Marxism* • **Bob Jessop** on Statism

HISTORICAL MATERIALISM 15:3

Articles • **Paolo Virno** on General Intellect • **Axel Kicillof** and **Guido Starosta** on Materiality and Social Form: A Political Critique of Rubin's Value-Form Theory • *Symposium: Ellen Meiksins Wood and* Empire of Capital • **Paul Blackledge**'s Editorial Introduction • **David Harvey** on In What Ways Is the 'New Imperialism' Really New? • **William I. Robinson** on The Pitfalls of Realist Analysis of Global Capitalism: A Critique of Ellen Meiksins Wood's *Empire of Capital* • **Prasenjit Bose** on 'New' Imperialism? On Globalisation and Nation-States • **François Chesnais** on The Economic Foundations and Needs of Contemporary Imperialism • **Ellen Meiksins**

Wood's Reply to Critics • *Intervention* • **Sam Moyo** and **Paris Yeros** on The Zimbabwe Question and the Two Lefts • *Review Articles* • **Wolfgang-Fritz Haug** on Jan Rehmann's Postmoderner Links-Nietzscheanismus. Deleuze & Foucault. Eine Dekonstruktion • **Richie Nimmo** on *Marx and Wittgenstein: Knowledge, Morality and Politics*, edited by Gavin Kitching and Nigel Pleasants • **Alexander Gallas** on *Entfesselter Kapitalismus: Transformation des europäischen Sozialmodells and Klassen und soziale Bewegungen: Strukturen im Kapitalismus*, edited by Joachim Bischoff, Paul Boccara, Robert Castel and Klaus Dörre • **Daniel Gaido** on Oliver Nachtwey's *Weltmarkt und Imperialismus: Zur Entstehungsgeschichte der klassischen marxistischen Imperialismustheorie* • *The Historical-Critical Dictionary of Marxism* • **John Bellamy Foster** on Earth

HISTORICAL MATERIALISM 15:4

Articles • **Helmut Reichelt** on Marx's Critique of Economic Categories: Reflections on the Problem of Validity in the Dialectical Method of Presentation in *Capital* • **Roland Boer** on The Perpetual Allure of the Bible for Marxism • **Gavin Fridell** on Fair-Trade Coffee and Commodity Fetishism: The Limits of Market-Driven Social Justice • **Viren Swami** on Evolutionary Psychology: 'New Science of the Mind' or 'Darwinian Fundamentalism'? • **Jim Kincaid** on Production vs. Realisation: A Critique of Fine and Saad-Filho on Value Theory • *Review Articles* • **Steve A. Smith** on Kevin Murphy's *Revolution and Counterrevolution: Class Struggle in a Moscow Metal Factory* • **Samuel Knafo** on Gérard Duménil's and Dominique Lévy's *Capital Resurgent: Roots of the Neoliberal Revolution* • **Michael Heinrich** on Karl Marx's *Das Kapital. Kritik der politischen Ökonomie, Dritter Band in Gesamtausgabe* (MEGA) • *The Historical-Critical Dictionary of Marxism* • **Jan Rehmann** on Earth

HISTORICAL MATERIALISM 16:1

Articles • **Giuseppe Tassone**'s and **Peter Thomas**'s Editorial Introduction to Vittorio Morfino • **Vittorio Morfino** on *Causa sui* or *Wechselwirkung*: Engels between Spinoza and Hegel • **Oliver Nachtwey & Tobias Ten Brink** on Lost in Transition: the German World-Market Debate in the 1970s • **Rakesh Bhandari** on The Disguises of Wage-Labour: Juridical Illusions, Unfree Conditions and Novel Extensions • *Intervention* • **Ana C. Dinerstein** on Here Is the Rose, Dance Here! A Riposte to the Debate on the Argentinean Crisis • *Archive* • **Paul Burkett & John Bellamy Foster** on The Podolinsky Myth: An Obituary. Introduction to 'Human Labour and Unity of Force', by Sergei Podolinsky • **Sergei Podolinsky**'s Human Labour and Unity of Force • *Review Articles* • **Chris Harman** on Christopher Dyer's *An Age of Transition? Economy and Society in England in the Later Middle Ages* and John Landers's *The Field and the Forge: Population, Production and Power in the Pre-Industrial West* • **Matthew G. Hannah** on Peter Brückner's *Ulrike Meinhof und die deutsche Verhältnisse* • **Wolfgang Wicht** on Bernd Blaschke's *Der 'homo oeconomicus' und sein Kredit bei Musil, Joyce, Svevo, Unamuno und Céline* • **Zoë Marriage** on Georges Nzongola-Ntalaja's *The Congo from Leopold to Kabila: A People's History, Reinventing Order in the Congo: How People Respond to State Failure in Kinshasa*, edited by Theodore Trefon and *The African Stakes of the Congo War* edited by John F. Clark • *The Historical-Critical Dictionary of Marxism* • **Peter Thomas** on Immanence

HISTORICAL MATERIALISM 16:2

Isaac and Tamara Deutscher Memorial Prize Lecture • **Chris Wickham** on Productive Forces and the Economic Logic of the Feudal Mode of Production • *Articles* • **Jefferey R. Webber** on Rebellion to Reform in Bolivia. Part I: Domestic Class Structure, Latin-American Trends, and Capitalist Imperialism • **John Roberts** on The 'Returns to Religion': Messianism, Christianity and the Revolutionary Tradition. Part I: 'Wakefulness to the Future' • **David Kristjanson** on Gural Postmodern Contributions to Marxian Economics: Theoretical Innovations and their Implications for Class Politics • *Interventions* • **Greig Charnock** on Competitiveness and

Critique: The Value of a New-Materialist Research Project • **Alex Callinicos** on Marxists, Muslims and Religion: Anglo-French Attitudes • *Review Articles* • **Sharad Chari** on Patrick Bond's *Elite Transition, Against Global Apartheid, Talk Left, Walk Right,* and *Unsustainable South Africa* and Ashwin Desai's *Arise Ye Coolies, We Are the Poors* and, with Vishnu Padayachee, Krish Reddy and Goolam Vahed, *Blacks in Whites* • **Alexander Anievas** on Martin Shaw's *Theory of the Global State: Globality as an Unfinished Revolution,* and William I. Robinson's *A Theory of Global Capitalism: Production, Class, and the State in a Transnational World* • **Peter Green** on Rick Kuhn's *Henryk Grossman and the Recovery of Marxism* • **Loren Glass** on Jean Baudrillard's *The Spirit of Terrorism,* Paul Virilio's *Ground Zero,* Slavoj Žižek's *Welcome to the Desert of the Real,* Jeffory A. Clymer's *in a New Age of War,* and Susan Willis's *Portents of the Real: A Primer for Post-9/11 America* • **Owen Hatherley** on Ilya Ilf 's and Evgeny Petrov's *Ilf and Petrov's American Road Trip* • *The Historical-Critical Dictionary of Marxism* • **Lise Vogel** on Domestic-Labour Debate

HISTORICAL MATERIALISM 16:3

Articles • **Jim Holstun** on Utopia Pre-Empted: Kett's Rebellion, Commoning, and the Hysterical Sublime • **Jefferey R. Webber** on Rebellion to Reform in Bolivia. Part II: Revolutionary Epoch, Combined Liberation and the December 2005 Elections • **John Roberts** on The 'Returns to Religion': Messianism, Christianity and the Revolutionary Tradition. Part II: The Pauline Tradition • *Intervention* • **Ben Fine** on Debating Lebowitz: Is Class Conflict the Moral and Historical Element in the Value of Labour-Power? • *Archive* • **Daniel Gaido** on Marxism and the Union Bureaucracy: Karl Kautsky on Samuel Gompers and the German Free Trade Unions • **Karl Kautsky** on Samuel Gompers • *Review Articles* • **Panagiotis Sotiris** on Louis Althusser's *Philosophy of the Encounter: Later Writings, 1978–1987* • **Andrew Robinson** on Antonio Negri's *Books for Burning: Between Civil War and Democracy in 1970s Italy* • **Christoph Herrman** on Pietro Basso's *Modern Times, Ancient Hours: Working Lives in the Twenty-First Century* • **Yaşar Aydin** on *Komplexität und Emanzipation,* edited by Alex Demirovic • **Samuel R. Friedman** on Alexander Saxton's *Religion and the Human Prospect* • *Historical-Critical Dictionary of Marxism* • **Victor Wallis** on Innovation

HISTORICAL MATERIALISM 16:4

Articles • **Martijn Konings and Leo Panitch** on US Financial Power in Crisis • **Joseph Fracchia** on The Capitalist Labour-Process and the Body in Pain: The Corporeal Depths of Marx's Concept of Immiseration • **Jefferey R. Webber** on Rebellion to Reform in Bolivia. Part III: Neoliberal Continuities, the Autonomist Right, and the Political Economy of Indigenous Struggle • **Steve Wright** on Mapping Pathways Within Italian Autonomist Marxism: A Preliminary Survey • **Roland Boer** on A Titanic Phenomenon: Marxism, History and Biblical Society • *Interventions* • **Ben Fine and Alfredo Saad-Filho** on Production vs. Realisation in Marx's Theory of Value: A Reply to Kincaid • **Jim Kincaid** on Production versus Capital in Motion: A Reply to Fine and Saad-Filho • *Review Articles* • **Enzo Traverso** on Arno Mayer's *The Furies: Violence and Terror in the French and Russian Revolutions* • **Paul Mattick** on David Harvey's *Limits to Capital* • **Owen Hatherley** on Judd Stitziel's *Fashioning Socialism – Clothing, Politics and Consumer Culture in East Germany* • *Historical-Critical Dictionary of Marxism* • **Georges Van Den Abbeele** on Fable

HISTORICAL MATERIALISM 17:1

Articles • **Marcus E. Green and Peter Ives** on Subalternity and Language: Overcoming the Fragmentation of Common Sense • **Henry Heller** on The *Longue Durée* of the French Bourgeoisie • **Michael Löwy** on Capitalism as Religion: Walter Benjamin and Max Weber • **Daniel Cho** on Adorno on Education, or, Can Critical Self-Reflection Prevent the Next Auschwitz? • *Reflections on 'Gewalt'* • **Étienne Balibar** on Violence • **Massimilano Tomba** on Another Type of *Gewalt*: Beyond Law. Re-Reading Benjamin • *Interventions* • **Guglielmo Carchedi** on The Fallacies of 'New Dialectics' and Value-Form Theory • **Christopher J. Arthur** on Contradiction and Abstraction: A Reply to Finelli • *Review Articles* • **Benjamin Noys** on Ian Parker's *Revolution in Psychology: Alienation to Emancipation* and Yannis Stavrakakis's *The Lacanian Left: Psychoanalysis, Theory, and Politics* • **Marcel Bois** on Christian Gotthardt's *Die radikale Linke als Massenbewegung. Kommunisten in Harburg-Wilhelmsburg 1918–1933* • **Tyson E. Lewis** on Peter McLaren's *Capitalists and Conquerors* and McLaren and Ramin Farahmandpur's *Teaching Against Global Capitalism and the New Imperialism*

HISTORICAL MATERIALISM 17:2

Isaac and Tamara Deutscher Memorial Prize Lecture • **Rick Kuhn** on Economic Crisis, Henryk Grossman and the Responsibility of Socialists • *Articles* • **David McNally** on From Financial Crisis to World-Slump: Accumulation, Financialisation, and the Global Slowdown • **Steve Edwards** on Apocalyptic Sublime: On the Third Brighton Photo Biennial • *Symposium on the Global Financial Crisis* • **Samantha Ashman**'s Editorial Introduction • Glossary of Technical Terms • **Costas Lapavitsas** on Financialised Capitalism: Crisis and Financial Expropriation • **Gary A. Dymski** on Racial Exclusion and the Political Economy of the Subprime Crisis • **Paulo L. Dos Santos** on On the Content of Banking in Contemporary Capitalism • *Reflections on 'Gewalt' (contd.)* • **Luca Basso** on The Ambivalence of *Gewalt* in Marx and Engels: On the Interpretation of Balibar • *Review Articles* • **Ian Hudson & Mark Hudson** on Gavin Fridell's *Fair Trade Coffee: The Prospects and Pitfalls of Market Driven Social Justice*, Daniel Jaffee's *Brewing Justice: Fair Trade Coffee, Sustainability, and Survival*, and Laura Raynolds's, Douglas Murray's & John Wilkinson's *Fair Trade: The Challenges of Transforming Globalization* • **Richard Westra** on Pierre Bourdieu's *Firing Back: Against the Tyranny of the Market 2*, *Global Turbulence: Social Activists' and State Responses to Globalization*, edited by Marjorie Griffin Cohen and Stephen McBride, John Rapley's *Globalization and Inequality: Neoliberalism's Downward Spiral* and *Anti-Capitalism: A Marxist Introduction*, edited by Alfredo Saad-Filho • **Michele Filippini** on Alberto Burgio's *Gramsci storico* • **Richard Seymour** on Markku Ruotsila's *John Spargo and American Socialism* • **Robert Knox** on Alain Supiot's *Homo Juridicus* • *Historical-Critical Dictionary of Marxism* • **Stefan Bollinger & Juha Koivisto** on Hegemonic Apparatus

HISTORICAL MATERIALISM 17:3

Articles • **Massimo de Angelis** and **David Harvie** on 'Cognitive Capitalism' and the Rat-Race: How Capital Measures Immaterial Labour in British Universities • **Iain Pirie** on The Political Economy of Academic Publishing • **Maria Turchetto** on Althusser and Monod: A 'New Alliance'? • *Reflections on 'Gewalt' (contd.)* • **Vittorio Morfino** on The Syntax of Violence. Between Hegel and Marx • *Archive* • **David Fernbach**'s Editorial Introduction to Paul Levi's *Our Path: Against Putschism* and *What Is the Crime: The March Action or Criticising It?* • **Paul Levi** on *Our Path: Against Putschism* • **Paul Levi** on *What Is the Crime: The March Action or Criticising It?* • *Interventions* • **Alberto Toscano** on Partisan Thought • **Ben Fine** and **Alfredo Saad-Filho** on Twixt Ricardo and Rubin: Debating Kincaid Once More • **Jim Kincaid** on The Logical Construction of Value Theory: More on Fine and Saad-Filho • *Review Articles* • **Christian Høgsbjerg** on Frank Rosengarten's *Urbane Revolutionary: C.L.R. James and the Struggle for a New Society* and Brett St Louis's *Rethinking Race, Politics, and Poetics: C.L.R. James' Critique of Modernity* • **Robert T. Tally Jr** on Loren Goldner's *Herman Melville: Between Charlemagne and the Antemosaic Cosmic Man: Race, Class, and the Crisis of Bourgeois Ideology in the American Renaissance Writer* • **Seongjin Jeong** on Iain Pirie's *The Korean Developmental State: From Dirigisme to Neo-Liberalism* • *Historical-Critical Dictionary of Marxism* • **Peter Thomas** on Catharsis

HISTORICAL MATERIALISM 17:4

Articles • **Elizabeth Esch and David Roediger** on One Symptom of Originality: Race and the Management of Labour in the History of the United States • **Massimiliano Tomba** on Historical Temporalities of Capital: An Anti-Historicist Perspective • **Karl Beitel** on The Rate of Profit and the Problem of Stagnant Investment: A Structural Analysis of Barriers to Accumulation and the Spectre of Protracted Crisis • *Intervention* • **Andrew Milner** on *Archaeologies of the Future*: Jameson's Utopia or Orwell's Dystopia? • *Review Articles* • **Panagiotis Sotiris** on Warren Montag's *Louis Althusser*, William S. Lewis's *Louis Althusser and the Traditions of French Marxism*, and Gregory Elliott's *Althusser: The Detour of Theory* • **Julian Müller** on *Poulantzas lesen. Zur Aktualität marxistischer Staatstheorie*, edited by Lars Bretthauer, Alexander Gallas, John Kannankulam and Ingo Stützle • **Benjamin Noys** on Gregory Elliott's *Ends in Sight: Marx/Fukuyama/Hobsbawm/Anderson* • **Ian Birchall** on Reiner Tosstorff 's *Profintern: Die Rote Gewerkschaftsinternationale 1920–1937* • *Historical-Critical Dictionary of Marxism* • **Wolfgang Fritz Haug** on Immaterial Labour

HISTORICAL MATERIALISM 18:1

Articles • **Alberto Toscano** on Beyond Abstraction: Marx and the Critique of the Critique of Religion • *Symposium on Giovanni Arrighi's 'Adam Smith in Beijing: Lineages of the Twenty-First Century'* • **Liam Campling**'s Editorial Introduction • **Christopher Chase-Dunn** on *Adam Smith in Beijing*: A World-Systems Perspective • **Richard Walker** on Karl Marx between Two Worlds: The Antinomies of Giovanni Arrighi's *Adam Smith in Beijing* • **Leo Panitch** on Giovanni Arrighi in Beijing: An Alternative to Capitalism? • **Lucia Pradella** on Beijing between Smith and Marx • **Flemming Christiansen** on Arrighi's *Adam Smith in Beijing*: Engaging China • *Intervention* • **Michael A. Lebowitz** on Trapped inside the Box? Five Questions for Ben Fine • *Review Articles* • **Donald V. Kingsbury** on Steve Ellner's *Rethinking Venezuelan Politics: Class, Conflict and the Chávez Phenomenon*, Eva Golinger's *Bush vs. Chávez: Washington's War on Venezuela*, and Gregory Wilpert's *Changing Venezuela by Taking Power: The History and Policies of the Chávez Government* • **Jeff Kinkle** on Guy Debord's *Correspondence: The Foundation of the Situationist International (June 1957–August 1960)*, Michèle Bernstein's *All the King's Horses, and* McKenzie Wark's *50 Years of Recuperation of the Situationist International* • **Frédérick Guillaume Dufour** on Pierre Bourdieu's *The Social Structures of the Economy* • **Robert J. Knox** on Bill Bowring's *The Degradation of the International Legal Order? The Rehabilitation of Law and the Possibility of Politics* • *Historical-Critical Dictionary of Marxism* • **Christopher J. Arthur** on Capital in General

ORDER FORM

❑ Yes, I would like to subscribe to **Historical Materialism**, *Research in Critical Marxist Theory*, ISSN 1465-4466, starting with **Volume 18 (2010)**

I take out an:

- ❑ Institutional subscription (print + E) EUR 342.-/US$ 466.-
- ❑ Individual subscription (print only) EUR 65.-/US$ 88.-
- ❑ Institutional subscription (e-only) EUR 285.-/US$ 388.-

❑ Please, send me back issues of **Historical Materialism** at EUR 25.-/US$ 37.- each.

Issue Number: 1 ❑ 2 ❑ 3 ❑ 4 ❑ 5 ❑ 6 ❑ 7 ❑ 8 ❑ 9 ❑ 10:2 ❑ 10:3 ❑ 10:4 ❑
11:1 ❑ 11:2 ❑ 11:4 ❑ 12:1 ❑ 12:2 ❑ 12:3 ❑ 12:4 ❑ 13:1 ❑ 13:2 ❑
13:3 ❑ 13:4 ❑ 14:1 ❑ 14:2 ❑ 14:3 ❑ 14:4 ❑ 15:1 ❑ 15:2 ❑ 15:3 ❑
15:4 ❑ 16:1 ❑ 16:2 ❑ 16:3 ❑ 16:4 ❑ 17:1 ❑ 17:2 ❑ 17:3 ❑ 17:4 ❑
18:1 ❑

FOR THE QUICKEST AND MOST ACCURATE SERVICE, PLEASE INCLUDE YOUR CLIENT NUMBER (IF ORDERED AT BRILL BEFORE)

FIRST NAME	CLIENT NO.
LAST NAME	M/F
JOB TITLE	
ORGANISATION	
ADDRESS HOME/WORK	
POSTAL CODE/CITY	
COUNTRY	
TELEPHONE	TELEFAX
E-MAIL	DATE
SIGNATURE	YOUR REF.

❑ I enclose a cheque ❑ Send me a pro forma invoice ❑ Charge my credit card:

Card no. ____________________ Signature ____________________

Exp. Date ____________________ CVC Code* ____________________

*last 3 digits on signature strip on back of card

VAT no.

Residents of the Netherlands and residents of other EU countries without a VAT number are liable for value added tax on all given prices

Please send or fax this form to:

Brill, c/o Turpin Distribution
Stratton Business Park, Pegasus Drive, Biggleswade,
Bedfordshire, SG18 8QB, United Kingdom
Tel: +44 (0) 1767 604954 • Fax: +44 (0) 1767 601640
E-mail: brill@turpin-distribution.com

ALL PRICES ARE VALID UNTIL 31 DECEMBER 2010. THEREAFTER PRICES MAYBE SUBJECT TO CHANGE WITHOUT PRIOR NOTICE. PRICES DO NOT INCLUDE VAT (APPLICABLE ONLY TO RESIDENTS OF THE NETHERLANDS AND RESIDENTS OF OTHER EU MEMBER STATES WITHOUT A VAT REGISTRATION NUMBER). PRICES DO NOT INCLUDE SHIPPING & HANDLING EXCEPT FOR JOURNALS WHERE SHIPPING & HANDLING IS INCLUDED IN THE PRICE (APPLICABLE TO ALL CUSTOMERS WORLDWIDE). US DOLLAR PRICES ARE VALID ONLY FOR CUSTOMERS IN CANADA, USA AND MEXICO. PLEASE NOTE THAT DUE TO FLUCTUATIONS IN THE EXCHANGE RATE, THE US DOLLAR AMOUNTS CHARGED TO CREDIT CARD HOLDERS MAY VARY SLIGHTLY FROM THE PRICES ADVERTISED.